THE RIGHT TO FREEDOM OF ASSEMBLY

In legal decisions and commentary, freedom of assembly is widely cherished as a precious human right and as indispensable for the preservation of democratic governance. But despite this rhetoric assemblies are subject to extensive regulation, such as prior restraints, and restrictions on the time, place and manner of assemblies.

This comparative study examines five influential jurisdictions and reveals similarities and inconsistencies between them. It finds that freedom of assembly is often subjugated to freedom of expression in a way that disregards the expressive potential of assemblies. The shortcomings include the misconstrued content neutrality and public forum doctrines in the US, blanket bans and other restrictions based on intangible and distant harm in the UK, preventative restrictions and viewpoint discrimination in Germany, and the uncertain status of freedom of assembly and opaque judicial reasoning in France. Such inconsistencies also present challenges for the European Court of Human Rights in developing a coherent assembly doctrine. The book argues that it is time for jurisprudence to move away from a narrowly focused concept of expression, and recognise the creative and expressive value of freedom of assembly.

Volume 6 in the series Hart Studies in Comparative Public Law

Hart Studies in Comparative Public Law
Recent titles in this series:

Parliaments and Human Rights
Redressing the Democratic Deficit
Edited by Murray Hunt, Hayley Hooper and Paul Yowell

The Right to Freedom of Assembly
A Comparative Study
Orsolya Salát

An Inquiry into the Existence of Global Values
Through the Lens of Comparative Constitutional Law
Edited by Dennis Davis, Alan Richter and Cheryl Saunders

The Scope and Intensity of Substantive Review
Traversing Taggart's Rainbow
Edited by Hanna Wilberg and Mark Elliott

Entick v Carrington
250 Years of the Rule of Law
Edited by Adam Tomkins and Paul Scott

Administrative Law and Judicial Deference
Matthew Lewans

Soft Law and Public Authorities
Remedies and Reform
Greg Weeks

Legitimate Expectations in the Common Law World
Edited by Matthew Groves and Greg Weeks

The Dynamics of Exclusionary Constitutionalism
Mazen Masri

Constitutional Courts, Gay Rights and Sexual Orientation Equality
Angioletta Sperti

Principled Reasoning in Human Rights Adjudication
Se-Shauna Wheatle

Human Rights and Judicial Review in Australia and Canada
Janina Boughey

The Foundations and Traditions of Constitutional Amendment
Edited by Richard Albert, Xenophon Contiades and Alkmene Fotiadou

The Right to Freedom of Assembly

A Comparative Study

Orsolya Salát

·HART·
PUBLISHING
OXFORD AND PORTLAND, OREGON
2017

Hart Publishing
An imprint of Bloomsbury Publishing Plc

Hart Publishing Ltd
Kemp House
Chawley Park
Cumnor Hill
Oxford OX2 9PH
UK

Bloomsbury Publishing Plc
50 Bedford Square
London
WC1B 3DP
UK

www.hartpub.co.uk
www.bloomsbury.com

Published in North America (US and Canada) by
Hart Publishing
c/o International Specialized Book Services
920 NE 58th Avenue, Suite 300
Portland, OR 97213-3786
USA

www.isbs.com

First published in hardback, 2015
Paperback edition, 2017

British Library Cataloguing-in-Publication Data
A catalogue record for this book is available from the British Library.

ISBN: PB: 978-1-50991-601-6
HB: 978-1-84946-721-6

Typeset by Compuscript Ltd, Shannon
Printed and bound in Great Britain by
Lightning Source UK Ltd

To find out more about our authors and books visit www.hartpublishing.co.uk. Here you will find extracts, author information, details of forthcoming events and the option to sign up for our newsletters.

Acknowledgements

This project benefited from the support of many persons: it is clearly impossible to list them all.

First of all, many thanks to my doctoral supervisor, András Sajó, for his ever open-minded advice, his tolerance, and his ironic wit during these years. Michael Hamilton, one of the finest experts in the field, gave invaluable comments on a very early draft, and wrote a very useful evaluation of the final version of the dissertation. In this revised version, I have sought to take all his suggestions into account, as well as the observations of Vladimiro Zagrebelsky, the second reader.

I am grateful for research opportunities at Yale, Sorbonne and Heidelberg, made possible by grants from the Central European University and the German Academic Exchange Service. I spent a truly essential period of research in Zurich, for which I remain immensely indebted to Matthias Mahlmann and the University of Zurich. I also have to thank my colleagues at ELTE University Budapest, Faculty of Social Sciences—Balázs Majtényi in particular—for releasing me from some of my university duties in the final phase of the writing. Many thanks to an anonymous reviewer and Bill Asquith from Hart Publishing for thought-provoking criticism and suggestions. I would like to thank the copy editor, Anne Atkinson, for her careful and thorough work on the manuscript as well as the Hart Publishing Production team of Mel Hamill, Tom Adams and Charlotte Austin, and the proofreader, Ceri Warner.

Finally, thanks to my friends: Joseph Windsor for linguistic, Nóra Szabó for logistic, and Zita Veronika Tóth and Javid Gadirov for conceptual help, and my parents, brother and Bogyó for their support and patience.

This book was initially meant to be dedicated to all of these people. But in an extraordinary twist of life, personal and political, it is now dedicated to two persons who have not played any part in its writing. The first one is Milán Rózsa, human rights activist, who died recently at the age of 26. He will be dearly missed in future protests and the public life of my country, even by those, who like me, did not know him personally. The other one is Ede Csürös, and he is not yet one year old. I can only hope that he will not be forced to participate in as many protests as his mother has. He, too, was born a Hungarian.

Contents

Introduction

Was das freie Versammlungs- und Vereinigungsrecht zu bedeuten hat und wie wichtig es für die Freiheit ist, weiß ja jedes Kind und ist nicht nötig, viel davon zu sagen.[1] (Theodor Mommsen)

I. THE CHALLENGE OF FREEDOM OF ASSEMBLY

IN LEGAL DECISIONS and commentary, freedom of assembly is widely cherished as a precious human right, indispensable for the individual person, for groups within society, and for the whole society, including for the preservation of democratic governance. However, even at a superficial glance it becomes apparent that constitutional law and human rights law allow so many and such serious limits on freedom of assembly that is more constrained than perhaps any other right, especially free speech. Prior restraints such as permits, bans and conditions, and restrictions on the time, place and manner of the assemblies abound in every jurisdiction, de facto *in addition* to general restrictions allowed on speech or expression, as courts reconfigure the activities at assemblies within the framework of freedom of speech or opinion.

Other disciplines, namely, psychology and sociology, which engage with assemblies on a more empirical basis, echo a similar ambivalence. Mass psychology finds 'masses' dangerous, emotionalised and prone to evil manipulation,[2] where group membership contributes to hostility, reduces rationality, and so on.[3] Social movement studies—in apparent contradiction—claim to

[1] [What the right to free assembly and association has to mean, and how important it is for freedom, every child knows, and there is no need to say much about that.] Theodor Mommsen, *Die Grundrechte des deutschen Volkes. Mit Belehrungen und Erläuterungen* (Frankfurt, Klostermann, 1969) 52.

[2] Gustave Le Bon, *The Crowd. A Study of the Popular Mind* (New York, MacMillan, 1896); William McDougall, *The Group Mind* (Cambridge, Cambridge University Press, 1920); Sigmund Freud, *Massenpsychologie und Ich-Analyse* (Leipzig, Wien, Zürich, Internationaler Psychoanalytischer Verlag, 1921).

[3] Eg Henri Tajfel, 'Experiments in Intergroup Discrimination' in Michael A Hogg and Dominic Abrams (eds), *Intergroup Relations. Essential Readings* (Philadelpia, Psychology Press, 2001) 178; Marylinn B Brewer, 'Ingroup Bias in the Minimal Intergroup Situation. A Cognitive-Motivational Analysis' (1979) 98 *Psychological Bulletin* 307; Marylinn B Brewer and Roderick M Kramer, 'The Psychology of Intergroup Attitudes and Behaviour' (1985) 36 *Annual Review of Psychology* 219; Leon Festinger, A Pepitone, T Newcomb, 'Some Consequences of De-individuation in a Group' (1952) 47 *Journal of Abnormal and Social Psychology* 382.

document a rational and rationalisable panoply of motivations,[4] grievances, structures,[5] organisations[6] and events of contestation;[7] pointing out incentives for moderation,[8] and describing the creation and transfer of meaning which is incommunicable by other means and ways.

More philosophical approaches either ignore freedom of assembly[9] or oscillate between Schmittian acclamation and fear of subversion,[10] even going as far as questioning whether there is any basis for freedom of assembly in a democracy which guarantees freedom of speech.[11]

Gatherings of people in public clearly have a potential to transcend or transgress normalcy, be it the psychological, moral, or religious status quo, the political mainstream, the ordinary rules of the game of democracy (or any other form of government), or even social peace. Revolutions and pogroms start with assemblies, and end—or so we hope—with the establishment of other assemblies, allegedly deliberative and representative ones. What remains in between is freedom of assembly. The object protected by freedom of assembly is fundamentally in-between, mirroring and realigning the line between our fears and hopes, between past and future, reason and emotion, people and government, minority and majority. The object protected by freedom of assembly is also in-between in another regard,

[4] Eg Ted Robert Gurr, *Why Men Rebel* (Princeton, Princeton University Press, 1970); Thomas Crawford and Murray Naditch, 'Relative Deprivation, Powerlessness, and Militancy: The Psychology of Social Protest' (1970) 33 *Psychiatry* 208; Clark McPhail, 'Civil Disorder Participation. A Critical Examination of Recent Research' (1971) 36 *American Sociological Review* 1058.

[5] Eg David S Meyer and Debra C Minkoff, 'Conceptualizing Political Opportunity' (2004) 82 *Social Forces* 1457.

[6] Eg Elisabeth S Clemens, 'Organizational Repertoires' in Jeff Goodwin and James M Jasper (eds), *The Social Movement Reader. Cases and Concepts* (Chichester, Blackwell, 2003) 187; John D McCarthy and Mayer N Zald, *The Trend of Social Movements in America: Professionalization and Resource Mobilization* (Morristown, NJ, General Learning Press, 1973); John D McCarthy and Mayer N Zald, 'Resource Mobilization and Social Movements. A Partial Theory' (1977) 82 *American Journal of Sociology* 1212; Mayer N Zald and John D McCarthy (eds), *Social Movements in an Organizational Society* (New Brunswick, Transaction Books, 1987).

[7] Eg Charles Tilly, *Contentious Performances* (Cambridge, Cambridge University Press, 2008).

[8] Eg Marisa Chappell, Jenny Hutchinson and Brian Ward, '"Dress modestly, neatly ... as if you were going to church": Respectability, Class and Gender in the Montgomery Bus Boycott and the Early Civil Rights Movement' in Peter Ling and Sharon Monteith (eds), *Gender in the Civil Rights Movement* (New York, Routledge, 2013) 69.

[9] It is telling how Mill does not have a single word about freedom of assembly in his chapter on freedom of speech in *Liberty*. John Stuart Mill, *On Liberty* (1859, David Spitz ed, 1975) ch II, 17–53. Note also that Benjamin Constant did not include freedom of assembly in his constitutional draft.

[10] John D Inazu elaborated in detail how Rawlsian liberalism does not provide a sufficient basis for the freedom inherent in assemblies either. John D Inazu, *Liberty's Refuge. The Forgotten Freedom of Assembly* (New Haven, Yale University Press, 2012) especially ch 4.

[11] Tamás Gyorfi, 'The Importance of Freedom of Assembly: Three Models of Justification' in András Sajó (ed), *Free to Protest: Constituent Power and Street Demonstration,* Issues in Constitutional Law, vol 5 (Utrecht, Eleven International Publishing, 2008) 1.

between the solitude of the writer or the vulnerability of the speaker and the discipline and strength of the police and army. For some, it might seem to be something between the individual and the people. It is also something in-between the argumentation of the press and the decision-making of the voting booth, referenda or legislation. It speaks as much as it acts. It asserts, shouts and wills, but it has no power to impose. It is a performance, a creation—but only of meaning. It is theatre, but not art. It threatens, but does not kill. It is disobedience, protest or conspiracy but not revolution.

It is a challenge to all of us, and certainly a challenge to the well-educated, literate judges and scholars whose natural form of communication is the argumentative essay. Assemblies are sometimes too messy and disorderly for a learned mind, sometimes too organised and disciplined for a free one. Still, sometimes even judges take to the streets. How do they draw the limits on this activity when pursued by others—often by radical others?

Before answering this question, the object of the enquiry needs to be defined more precisely.

II. A CONCEPT OF ASSEMBLY

There is no universally accepted definition of assembly in either jurisprudence or scholarship. The—often implicit—notions of assembly are framed by historical experience, the political and legal–doctrinal context. These will be discussed in chapter one.

However, as every investigation necessarily proceeds from some preliminary assumption about the object to be examined, it is useful to make that assumption explicit. In comparative law, the awareness of this preliminary assumption is particularly important, because a biased assumption about the object of enquiry simply derails the whole investigation from the outset. There is less space for error if this preliminary notion is too broad rather than too narrow.

In this widest possible sense, one could define assembly as the common presence of at least two persons in a common space at the same time.

In order to be meaningful, however, a concept, broad as it is, needs to be distinguished from other concepts. In human rights law, this means delineation from activities not protected by human rights, and a delineation from activities protected by human rights other than the subject of enquiry, in our case, freedom of assembly.

Some instances of people being together at the same time in the same place evidently fall outside of legal protection. This includes group violence, just as individual violence is not protected by human rights. Legal documents specifically require that the activity of assembly be *peaceful* (or peaceable), testifying to a general aversion of law to assemblies, not present with regard to other, typically individually exercised rights. More intriguing is the question of whether any peaceful types of group behaviour, such as, for instance, standing in a queue, ought also not to be protected by freedom of assembly. *Common* presence has to imply that the persons have some *link* with each other beyond the mere coincidence of being at the same place at the same time. Thus, the link might be some *shared* activity, emotion, opinion or the like. An important question is how law defines that link, or, more precisely, how it selects what sort of link it accepts and what sort it does not. As will be seen below, different courts do not define this link in the same way, and this question is hotly contested in some countries. As to the above example, in my view, standing in a queue as such is not an assembly, but it can easily turn into one, for instance, if people outraged by the waiting time start discussing how to handle it or start protesting against it.

In contrast, it appears less problematic—and has not given rise to significant controversy in practice either—to distinguish the scope of assembly from that of the private and family life or privacy. It is assumed that some sense of privateness or intimacy brings a grouping of people within the scope of privacy rights, and freedom of assembly is reserved for more social (including political) gatherings. A family dinner or excursion, in general, falls within the right to private life, and not within freedom of assembly. Therefore, I will not deal with these instances of 'assembly' in this book any further. This does not mean, however, that limitation of the scope of assembly by some courts to political gatherings will not be discussed and criticised as overly restrictive.

As to the spatial element of the concept, physical assemblies differ in significant respects from 'virtual assemblies'. Though it is conceivable that the 'digital commons' shares enough characteristics with the physical commons to make them a sufficiently unified object of discussion, this book only deals with offline, real-life, or physical assemblies that take up a segment of real space. In fact, this book adheres to the view that an important characteristic of assembly, from a legal point of view, is its *taking place and taking a stance*, also in the strict senses of the words.

The temporal element in the above preliminary definition is relevant because it distinguishes—at least for my purposes—assembly from association. Exercising the right to association does not cease if the assembly of the association has ended. Restrictions related to the membership in a group affect the right to association, while restrictions related to the meeting of the group affect the right to assembly. Furthermore, not only associations (or members of associations) can hold assemblies—anyone can. Thus a temporary bond between participants already establishes a claim to freedom of assembly, but not to freedom of association. This might be commonsense for a European audience, but it is not in the United States. For instance, John D Inazu has written a book about freedom of assembly according to its title, but often discusses issues pertaining to freedom of association in the European and international understanding.[12] Inazu is justified in applying 'assembly' in this broader sense because that offers the most effective way for criticising the 'expressive association' doctrine of the Supreme Court, and because association is not mentioned in the First Amendment. However, as both assembly and association do appear in most European and international human rights documents, this (comparative) book will follow this more widespread use of the concepts, although without claiming that the two rights are not closely related, or that their relationship is fully clarified.

While for most audiences, the distinction between association and assembly is fairly clear, it is much more difficult to differentiate assembly from *expression*. Later on, this confusion will play a central role in my argument. Here it suffices to explore only how the collective, spatial, and temporary nature of assembly contributes to the *specificities of expression* on such occasions. For that, it is useful to differentiate between types of assemblies, although the categories are not exact and most assemblies are a mix of these types.

First, collective expression at *demonstrations* is generally of the sort which is proclamative rather than argumentative, and aims first of all at exerting *pressure* by the sheer significance of the *number* of people present. Assembly is essentially about quantity, and particularly so in a democracy. Furthermore, demonstration-type assemblies not incidentally make use of material objects and symbols of all kinds: material and symbolic aspects are an essential component of generating and conveying expression via the specific form of assembly. Symbols at an assembly are not only *rhetorical* (which is regularly the case with most types of expression), but importantly are also *material* (such as flags, placards, uniforms, effigies, fire, etc) and *bodily, including visual and aural* (such as marching in formation, specific hand gestures, chaining yourself to a fence, dancing, shouting and chanting loud slogans and songs, etc). Assemblies also often make use of the symbolic potential of specific places or dates: the spatiality[13] and temporality of an assembly might be expressive.

The message at demonstrations largely falls within a few recognisable categories: protest, dissent, outrage, grievance, joy, threat, hate, empathy, commemoration and other *emotionally laden and moral* content. Most demonstrations have a central purpose of addressing the rest of society and government, because participants feel their cause is *particularly important*

[12] John D Inazu, *Liberty's Refuge. The Forgotten Freedom of Assembly* (New Haven, Yale University Press, 2012), for instance, discusses state interference within the membership of a group, especially ch 4.

[13] Timothy Zick, *Speech Out of Doors, Preserving First Amendment Liberties in Public Places* (Cambridge, Cambridge University Press, 2009).

and worthy of public attention.[14] Such expression is naturally *committed, animated, agitated, often disruptive,* and so on, perhaps best contrasted with the scholarly expression of a mathematician or the disengaged scientist in the positivist fashion.

It is these characteristics that have led many commentators, as mentioned, especially in the tradition of crowd psychology, to see protesting 'masses' as *by nature* irrational, dangerous, and prone to violence, as a place where the individual loses his capacity to reason.[15] It remains certainly—and relevantly—true that more people can generally cause more destruction than a single individual, and in that sense, assemblies are potentially more dangerous than individuals. Still, most of these early assumptions were later shaken by research in social psychology. The 'deindividuation' hypothesis[16] collapsed when tested empirically:[17] there is no mass mind, neither is there any automatic irrationality or anti-normativity in 'crowds'. Mainstream social psychology—in particular, social identity theory—shows that persons in a 'mass' (in fact, a group) follow group norms which make group identity salient in the particular situation. Participating in a group enables a switch from norms related to personal identity to situational norms related to group or social identity.[18] Thus, crowd behaviour—though different from individual behaviour—is still rational in that it follows a norm (although of course the norm might be murderous, destructive, invidious or simply mistaken).

The second type of assembly with regard to expression is a 'meeting'. Meetings, as opposed to demonstrations, are occasions for collective expression in the sense of *deliberation and discussion.* These assemblies have—compared with demonstrations—an inward tendency: the participants are engaging first of all each other, not the outside world. Meeting-type or deliberative assemblies might make less use of symbols, be less emotionalised (though not necessarily), and are thus often seen as less

[14] Charles Tilly describes social movements by characteristics of 'WUNC' symbols, ie showing worth, unity, number, and commitment. Charles Tilly, *Social Movements, 1768–2004* (Boulder, Paradigm Publishers, 2004).

[15] With different overtones, see the works of Le Bon, McDougall or Freud, above n 2.

[16] Eg Leon Festinger, A Pepitone and T Newcomb, 'Some Consequences of De-individuation in a Group' (1952) 47 *Journal of Abnormal and Social Psychology* 382; PG Zimbardo, 'The Human Choice: Individuation, Reason, and Order vs Deindividuation, Impulse and Chaos' in WJ Arnold and D Levine (eds), *Nebraska Symposium on Motivation,* vol 17 (Lincoln, NE, University of Nebraska Press, 1969) 237; E Diener, 'Deindividuation: The Absence of Self-Awareness and Self-Regulation in Group Members' in Paul B Paulus (ed), *Psychology of Group Influence* (Hillsdale, Erlbaum, 1980); S Prentice-Dunn and RW Rogers, 'Effects of Public and Private Self-awareness on Deindividuation and Aggression' (1982) 43 *Journal of Personality and Social Psychology* 503.

[17] Tom Postmes and Russell Spears, 'Deindividuation and Antinormative Behavior: A Meta-Analysis' (1998) 123 *Psychological Bulletin* 238.

[18] Steven Reicher, Russell Spears and Tom Postmes, 'A Social Identity Model of Deindividuation Phenomena' in Wolfgang Stroebe and Miles Hewstone (eds), *European Review of Social Psychology,* vol 6 (Chichester, Wiley, 1995) 161.

dangerous by law (this is, eg the case in France and Germany). Note however that conspiracy needs exactly this kind of assemblies, and that social psychology shows that intra-group discussion enhances hostility towards other groups.[19]

Often, meetings do not primarily *aim* at expression, but have a different focus (most importantly, religion, but also other activities such as artistic, sport, recreational, or any other activity). However, when the state intervenes into their business, it will generally be related in one way or another to expression: if nothing else, then state intervention will relate at least to *potential expression of group identity through shared activity*.[20]

A final type of collective expression in an assembly, in my view, is the interaction between a lone demonstrator or performer and her audience. Here the observable expression *stricto sensu* is not necessarily collective (though the audience might react to the performer); still, the event as such is fundamentally collective and expressive at the same time.

These three types of collective expression—demonstration, meeting and performance—are easily mixed with each other in many ways. Meetings and demonstrations might come about at the initiation of a speaker or performer. Meetings (of the organisers or the core) might precede or follow demonstrations (of the larger public). An assembly might have deliberative (introverted) and demonstrating (extroverted) parts as well (such as an open-air film screening and discussion within the context of a Pride Parade). Or it might even not be possible to distinguish these aspects from each other (such as the Occupy movement's many assemblies, in fact demonstrating deliberation). That is one of the reasons why the different jurisdictions examined below apply diverging categorisations of assemblies.

In sum, I consider the contemporaneous common presence of at least two persons in a common space to be an assembly. From among these assemblies, the book—in line with jurisprudence—will not deal with those which are so intimate that they are better protected by the right to private and family life.

Furthermore, this book takes the stance that the so-conceived ('public') assembly is always at least potentially expressive, either in the sense of creating or in the sense of conveying a socially comprehensible meaning, something all of us easily understand and potentially internalise. Sometimes, for that creation or conveyance to come about, an assembly looks essentially like a theatre, a symbolic re-enactment, carefully set in place and time.[21] In

[19] Laura GE Smith and Tom Postmes, 'Intra-Group Interaction and the Development of Norms which Promote Inter-Group Hostility' (2009) 39 *European Journal of Social Psychology* 130.

[20] This is very aptly shown by Inazu, *Liberty's Refuge*, above n 12.

[21] Eg Matthias Reiss (ed), *The Street as Stage: Protest Marches and Public Rallies Since the Nineteenth Century* (Oxford, Oxford University Press, 2007); Baz Kershaw, 'Fighting in the Streets: Dramaturgies of Popular Protest, 1968–89' (1997) 13 *New Theatre Quarterly* 255.

this regard, an assembly is certainly strategic,[22] but not more than a theatrical play, an opera, Hundertwasser or Dalí. Or, for that matter, the rhetoric of a politician, the most sacred object of freedom of speech. Some prefer to read Shakespeare, but most prefer to see it—partly because that is also re-enactment. As the circle of creation and conveyance is complete, there is no way to claim that what has acquired a meaning in social interaction somehow does not convey it. Still, as I will try to show below, courts often exactly claim that.

That means that this book contends that freedom of expression doctrines are framed in a way that leaves out an important bulk of actual expression, and denies it the protection of rights without justification. This is especially true about the United States, which comparative lawyers traditionally cherish as the world champion of freedom of expression. But it is also true, to a large extent and for different reasons, of Germany, France and the United Kingdom. The European Court of Human Rights—after an initial period of almost complete disregard for the value of freedom of assembly—has recently strengthened protection of assemblies as much as perhaps an international court can.

III. STRUCTURE

In order to reveal general problems in the nature of freedom of assembly, a sufficiently wide pool of comparative material is necessary. It still has to remain reasonably narrow in order to be manageable, and to avoid falsely attributing problems to assembly which arise from systematic deficiencies elsewhere in a legal order. Therefore, this book deals with generally well-functioning, human rights respecting democracies, and maps even among them only the representatives of influential constitutional traditions. It will analyse in detail the assembly-related jurisprudence of constitutional and supreme courts and quasi-judicial bodies of the United Kingdom, France, the United States and Germany. The jurisprudence of the European Court of Human Rights adds an international dimension. Especially in cases where the European Court proves either especially cautious, or especially rights-protective, it is reasonable to suspect a general problem or pattern less visible from within the legal order of the nation state.

In discussing the particular issues in each of the jurisdictions, hard choices had to be made as to the order of discussion, that is which court to consider first and which next. Mostly, I sought to start with the court where the particular issue has been especially controversial or where the court

[22] Maybe even in the—negative—sense associated with strategic as opposed to communicative action by Habermas. Jürgen Habermas, *The Theory of Communicative Action* (Thomas A McCarthy tr, vol 1 1984, vol 2 1987, Boston, Beacon Press).

had created a model or determined the conceptual frame in an influential way. Often, but by far not always, I begin with the US Supreme Court, and rarely if ever with the French Constitutional Council or the Conseil d'État. The German Federal Constitutional Court and courts in the United Kingdom are mostly in the middle, and sometimes are the starters, while the European Court of Human Rights is always the last for reasons of its internationality. I also do not insist on finding, or inventing, answers to each question, to each issue examined in every jurisdiction; rather, I have sought to find the answers only where they exist. This method is justified in a project aspiring to form a general view of the nature of freedom of assembly by examining arguments that judges actually employ and weigh in their reasoning.

A caveat: the many important questions of practical policing of—especially unpeaceful—assemblies are largely left out of the scope of this study, not least because these are traditionally seen as issues pertaining not to the right of assembly, but to right to life, bodily integrity, right to liberty, and so on. This omission is not meant to imply that some of these aspects could not be conceptualised as interferences with freedom of assembly as well, or that they could not rightly be the object of another enquiry.

Chapter one discusses origins, forms and values of assembly in order to provide a general framework for discussion. The remaining chapters deal with the limits of the right to freedom of assembly, which often coincide with the limits of freedom of expression. Chapter two discusses prior restraints on assemblies and shows that, tellingly, this is an area where assembly is not reconfigured as speech by courts. Chapters three to five analyse 'substantive limits', that is those values which are considered so important that they prevail over assembly. Substantive limits include the prevention of violence, disorder or crime (chapter three); prevention of coercion, direct action and disruption (chapter four); and the protection of dignity (chapter five). There is no separate chapter examining the protection of property as a limit on freedom of assembly because issues pertaining to it are either covered in chapters three and four or are conceptualised as restrictions on the place of an assembly. The remaining chapters discuss restrictions related to the time (chapter six), manner (chapter seven) and place (chapter eight) of assembly, and claim that those issues (sometimes seen as secondary, as 'modality', 'speech plus', or 'conduct') belong equally to the core of freedom of assembly as the 'substantive' issues. The Conclusion provides an assessment of the comparative findings, an evaluation and critique, and suggests a path forward for jurisprudence in this unduly neglected area of law.

1

Origins, Forms and Values

I. HISTORICAL ORIGINS OF THE RIGHT TO FREEDOM OF ASSEMBLY

PEOPLE HAVE, OF course, always assembled in some of the senses discussed above, though some forms of assembly came into being only later. For instance, social movement literature shows there was no practice of demonstration before the nineteenth century.[1] There is no specific treatise on the history of assemblies as such. Social movement studies, for example the works of Charles Tilly, show a complex development of a whole repertoire of movements, an element of which is assembly.[2] Tilly also demonstrates that democracy, especially high capacity democracy, contains violent protest.[3] Thus it is likely that before the modern democracies, assemblies tended to turn violent more easily than today. Also, in earlier eras, much more prone to open and legitimate violence in interpersonal relations, assemblies such as festivities or popular protests were more likely to also be occasions of mob violence. Ruff, for instance, tells the story of how in the early modern times, local 'youth abbeys' exercised half-legitimate, often violent control over marriages throughout Europe, manifested clearly in assemblies.[4] Regularised and ritualised group violence was also part of social life because of the lack of a state monopoly on violence. In addition, the function of popular protest from early on has been essentially conservative, or reactionary to innovation by central authorities, and such violent conservative riots were often led by local elites.[5] In general, regimes which are by nature less responsive to popular will logically oppress social movements more, and drive them into violence.

These appear to be the factors why freedom of assembly has not been legally recognised before the middle of the nineteenth century, except in the United States. As with many other rights, assemblies were not the object of

[1] Charles Tilly, *Social Movements, 1768–2004* (Boulder, Paradigm Publishers, 2004) 33.

[2] Ibid.

[3] See especially Charles Tilly, *Contentious Performances* (Cambridge, Cambridge University Press, 2008), and Charles Tilly, *Democracy* (Cambridge, Cambridge University Press, 2007).

[4] Julius R Ruff, *Violence in Early Modern Europe* (Cambridge, Cambridge University Press, 2001) ch 5 on ritual group violence, especially 160–63.

[5] Ibid, 184–88.

legal protection, but legal persecution or at least official suspicion, control and aversion. Tellingly, 'tumultuous petitioning' (above 10 petitioners) was made illegal in England in 1649, reaffirmed in a 1661 Act, which was repealed only in 1986.[6]

Both the literature and the case law often view freedom of assembly as related to the right to petition. However, I only found a clear legal–historical connection between petition and assembly in the United States. There, assembly, as will be shown, is indeed historically related to the right to petition, understood to be a right of the Englishmen, and in this sense claimed by American settlers against the Crown and the English Parliament.

The right to petition itself has a long and dynamic history. One author traces its first appearance back to as early as somewhere between 959 and 963, that is to the so-called Andover Code.[7] In the relevant part of the Andover Code, Edgar the Peaceful stated:[8]

> 2. And no one is to apply to the king in any suit, unless he may not be entitled to right or cannot obtain justice at home. 2.1. If that law is too severe, he is then to apply to the king for alleviation.

This or similar versions of a right of petitioning for redress reoccured in several Royal Charters, and then was famously reinforced in the 1215 Magna Carta. The difference between the early Charters and the Magna Carta is significant. The early Charters are all written by the monarch, and it seems, they were adhered to only as long as it was convenient for the monarch. Smith cites the prologue to the Laws of Canute which also entailed a guarantee of petition as typical for the early understanding: 'This is the ordinance in which King Canute determined with the advice of his councilors, for the praise of God and for his own royal dignity and benefit'.[9] Thus at this time the aim of granting some sort of a right to petition was not in the interest of the petitioner, but for the praise of God, and for the dignity and benefit of the King. These aims might be intended to mean something such as objective truth of justice, which in the medieval understanding would necessarily overlap with the 'interests' of the people: still, a petition 'right' based on these criteria could be easily turned into a clause of discretion.

[6] Sch 3 of the Public Order Act 1986, repealing the Tumultuous Petitioning Act 1661, www.legislation.gov.uk/ukpga/1986/64/schedule/3/enacted.

[7] Don L Smith, 'The Right to Petition for Redress of Grievances: Constitutional Development and Interpretations' (PhD, Texas Tech University, 1971). University Microfilms, A XEROX Co, Ann Arbor, Michigan, 12.

[8] Dorothy Whitelock (ed), *English Historical Documents*, Vol I (New York, Oxford University Press, 1948) 396 as cited by Smith, 'Petition', ibid, 112.

[9] Ibid, 419 as cited by Smith, 'Petition', above n 7, 14.

Later on, the Magna Carta used somewhat stronger language,[10] and, with time, and through various detours,[11] the right to petition developed into a proper common law right. At the same time, petitions became the most important form of broadening parliament's power vis-à-vis the monarch. This is a significant change not only in the history of 'democracy', but because it shows again a potential inherent in the right to petition. In a certain sense, and incrementally over the centuries, the petition as a form has turned into substance: the right to complain has transformed into power to change the law.[12] This process was then completed—at least from hindsight it appears as a logical subsequence—by the widening of franchise and the elaboration of the idea and practice of a representative government.

An analogous pattern appears to have worked in the colonial context: the renunciation of representation undermined English sovereignty in the colonies, and the result here was also the overcoming of a previous regime, and the creation of new rights. In the English case, the right to petition significantly contributed to the development of representative government. In the American case, later, the perceived violation of the right to petition supported the legitimacy of the revolution, and, as a by-product, freedom of assembly started to regularly appear in post-revolution state constitutions.

During colonial times, the Molasses Act of 1733 provoked the first petition coming from the American colonies. Sir John Barnard, speaking on behalf of Rhode Island, the petitioning colony, made a claim that the new inhabitants of the colonies have claim to an *even stronger* right to petitioning:[13]

> [T]he people of every part of Great Britain have a representative in the House who is to take care of their particular interests as well as of the general interest of the nation ... but the people who are the petitioners ... have no particular representatives in this House, therefore, they have no other way of apply or of offering their reasons to this, but in the way of being heard at the bar of the House by their agent here in England.

[10] Paragraph 61 Magna Carta, available, eg www.fordham.edu/halsall/source/mcarta.asp.

[11] *Cf* Smith's analysis of the history of petition after the Magna Carta. At times, Kings would deny any obligation on their part not to ignore or at least not to punish petitioners, while at other times, petitioners, in or through Parliament would claim 'ancient liberties' while indeed creating new ones. Smith, 'Petition', above n 7, 17–30.

[12] By 1414, the Commons successfully secured that the petitions of people which are transmitted in the form of bills by the Commons to the House of Lords and the monarch cannot be modified by the latter ones without the assent of the Commons. See, eg www.parliament.uk/about/living-heritage/evolutionofparliament/originsofparliament/birthofparliament/overview/lawmakers.

[13] George Elliot Howard, *Preliminaries of the Revolution 1763–1775*, Vol XIII in AB Hart (ed), *The American Nation: A History* (New York, Harper and Brothers, 1905) as cited in Smith, 'Petition', above n 7, 56.

Settlers regularly claimed the right of petition as a right of British subjects.[14] Some petitions, such as that against the Stamp Act,[15] were finally successful, while others, notably against the Townshend Act,[16] invoked repression. Repression went so far that several colonial legislatures, which supported Massachusetts' initial protest against the Townshend Act, were dissolved by the Governors.[17] The situation radicalised further in that the Virginia House of Burgesses proclaimed that, solely, it had the right to impose taxes in Virginia. Along with that proclamation, however, the House felt it necessary once again to confirm the right to petition:

> [I]t is the undoubted privilege of the inhabitants of this colony, to petition their sovereign for redress of grievances; and that it is lawful and expedient to procure the concurrence of his majesty's other colonies in dutiful addresses, praying royal interposition in favour of the violated rights of America.[18]

Importantly, at the First Continental Congress 'the good people of the several colonies' declared[19]

> [t]hat the inhabitants of the English colonies in North-America, by the immutable laws of nature, the principles of the English constitution, and the several charters or compacts, have the following RIGHTS:
>
> ... Resolved, N.C.D. 8. That they have a *right peaceably to assemble*, consider of their grievances, and petition the king; and that all prosecutions, prohibitory proclamations, and commitments for the same, are illegal. (emphasis added)

Here the right to assembly appears already as a natural precondition of the right to petition, a development clearly missing from English law.

[14] See, eg the Stamp Act Congress's resolution to the Declaration of Rights and Grievances of 19 October 1765: 'That it is the right of the British subjects in these colonies, to petition the king or either house of parliament'. Zachariah Chafee (ed), *Documents on Fundamental Human Rights*, Preliminary edn (Cambridge, Harvard University Press, 1951–52) 149 as cited in Smith, 'Petition', above n 7, 64.

[15] 1765 (5 George III, c 12). Full title: An act for granting and applying certain stamp duties, and other duties, in the British colonies and plantations in America, towards further defraying the expences of defending, protecting, and securing the same; and for amending such parts of the several acts of parliament relating to the trade and revenues of the said colonies and plantations, as direct the manner of determining and recovering the penalties and forfeitures therein mentioned, available at America's Homepage, Historic Documents of the United States, ahp.gatech.edu/stamp_act_bp_1765.html. The Act evoked strong resistance, including the Stamp Act Congress, on which the representatives of the colonies adopted a petition against a British measure for the first time. See the documents in Lewis Cruger (ed), *Journal of the first Congress of the American Colonies, in opposition to the Tyrannic Acts of the British Parliament, Held at New York, 7 October 1765* (New York, Winchester, 1846), text available at archive.org/details/journaloffirstco00stam. The Stamp Act was repealed by the Act Repealing the Stamp Act 1766, available at avalon.law.yale.edu/18th_century/repeal_stamp_act_1766.asp.

[16] The Townshend Act, November 20, 1767 available at avalon.law.yale.edu/18th_century/townsend_act_1767.asp.

[17] Smith, 'Petition', above n 7, 63.

[18] Chafee, *Documents*, above n 14, 150 as cited in Smith, 'Petition', above n 7, 64.

[19] Declaration and Resolves of the First Continental Congress, 14 October 1774, available at the Avalon Project avalon.law.yale.edu/18th_century/resolves.asp.

Afterwards, similarly worded guarantees were enshrined in several state constitutions. In each of those cases there was a conjunction of assembly and petition. For example, the Pennsylvania Constitution of 1776 and the Vermont Constitutions of both 1777 and 1786 all proclaimed 'That the people have a right to assemble together, to consult for their common good, to instruct their Representatives, and to apply to the Legislature, for redress of grievances, by address, petition, or remonstrance'. Interestingly, the 1776 North Carolina Constitution omitted exactly the reference to address, petition or remonstrance, that is the oldest right.[20]

As to the federal constitution, during the debate representative Mr Sedgwick opposed the inclusion of freedom of assembly as being superfluous next to freedom of speech.[21] This was because freedom of speech self-evidently includes freedom of assembly. After a very short debate at which Congressman Page recalled the famous 1670 *Penn* trial over a 'tumultuous assembly',[22] this motion was rejected, and the assembly clause was included in the federal constitution. There was basically no debate on it because the debate was dominated by a serious motion to include a right of the people to instruct their representatives. Importantly, James Madison, who was keen on determining the proper number of *legislative* assemblies,[23] did not raise any objection in relation to the right of the *people* peaceably to assemble.

In any case, by the time of the revolution, and especially the drafting of the constitution, petition and assembly had become intertwined in the minds of the colonial people. Remarkably, the right to peaceably assemble was a new right, not one of the rights of the Englishmen, and it was never included in any sense in the English constitution. The colonists thereby claimed a right which the English in England never had as a right. What happened was an incremental change in meaning, whereby petition started to include assembly, in some state constitutions with the addition 'to consult for the common good'. Note that the state level texts are often unclear about whether the people are entitled to assemble in order to consult for the common good and to petition or whether these are separate rights. The federal constitution forbids Congress to make any law abridging 'the right

[20] A very similar provision became part of the Alabama Constitution of 1819, available at the Avalon Project avalon.law.yale.edu/19th_century/ala1819.asp.

[21] *Annals of Debates of Congress*, 14 August 1789, 759 ff, available at memory.loc.gov/cgi-bin/ampage?collId=llac&fileName=001/llac001.db&recNum=381.

[22] See in more detail, John D Inazu, 'The Forgotten Freedom of Assembly' (2010) 84 *Tulane Law Review* 565, 575–76.

[23] See, eg 'In all very numerous assemblies, of whatever character composed, passion never fails to wrest the sceptre from reason. Had every Athenian citizen been a Socrates, every Athenian assembly would still have been a mob'. James Madison, 'The Total Number of the House of Representatives', No 55 in John Jay, Alexander Hamilton and James Madison, *The Federalist on the New Constitution, Written in 1788* (Hallowell, Masters, Smith & Co, 1852) 256.

of the people peaceably to assemble, and to petition the Government for a redress of grievances', which does not suggest that assembly is dependent on either petition or on requesting redress of grievances.

In social practice, assembly life has been quite intensive since the early days of the new republic. John D Inazu tells the story of a politically active citizenry claiming and practicing a broadly understood freedom of assembly including political discussions, pamphleteering, memorials, but also festivities, parades and the like around the Democratic–Republican Societies, which though short-lived, and easily suppressed, certainly influenced the outcome of the next election when Jefferson became President.[24]

In the early jurisprudence of the Supreme Court freedom of assembly did not play an important role, but neither did free speech. In the first half of the twentieth century some important cases mentioned right to free assembly, mostly together with the right to free speech.[25]

In England, the right to petition has clearly not implied a right to assembly in either of the above senses—that is, neither in the sense of presenting or consulting on a petition in assembly—nor as logically following from the right to petition as a separate right to assembly. The mentioned ban on tumultuous petitioning remained in force from 1649 until 1986, in itself disproof of recognition of a right to assembly at least in the sense of a right continuously flowing from a right to petition. Furthermore, the common law breach of the peace has traditionally been 'breathtakingly broad, bewilderly imprecise in scope',[26] providing police with such powers related to assemblies which also defeated any claim as to the existence of a 'right'.

Dicey also famously proclaimed that 'it can hardly be said that our constitution knows of such a thing as any specific right of public meeting' and 'The right of assembling is nothing more than a result of the view taken by the Courts as to individual liberty of person and individual liberty of speech'.[27]

Interestingly, in UK legal history, recent decades have seen an extraordinary mushrooming of legislative restrictions on freedom of assembly from public order laws to terrorism and antisocial behaviour legislation; even harassment provisions are applied to restrict protest—while this is the first time that arguably something of a *right* to freedom of assembly in the United Kingdom is emerging due to the ECHR (European Convention on Human Rights) and section 6 of the Human Rights Act 1998. The UK history also shows that having

[24] Inazu, 'The Forgotten Freedom of Assembly', above n 22, 575–81.

[25] Eg, *De Jonge v State of Oregon*, 299 US 353 (1937), *Hague v Committee For Industrial Organization*, 307 US 496 (1939), *Herndon v Lowry*, 301 US 242 (1937), *Whitney v People of State of California*, 274 US 357 (1927).

[26] Helen Fenwick, *Civil Liberties and Human Rights*, 4th edn (Abindgon, New York, Routledge, 2007) 660.

[27] Albert Venn Dicey, *Introduction to the Study of the Law of the Constitution* (Indianapolis, Liberty Fund, 1982) 170.

a right does not necessarily imply less restriction on its exercise than during the times when it was only a liberty.

In Germany and France, there was not any proper right to petition, let alone assemble, until well into the nineteenth or even twentieth century constitutions. Neither does a historical connection seem to have existed between petition and assembly, unlike in the United States. Some authors in Germany mention the so-called aristocratic privilege of self-assembly of the estates in the medieval Holy German Empire as a particular appearance of freedom of assembly, without 'the moment of generalisation', that is a privilege which was to be later extended to the whole society.[28] Others mention the right to petition, but without further concretisation, so it most probably refers to the right to petition as it evolved in England.

Freedom of assembly itself started to emerge in the early nineteenth century in Germany, after the feudal regime of capriciously revocable permits had faded away.[29] An 1802 treatise reports that an assembly can be banned for reasons of public safety and order, but the ban cannot be imposed arbitrarily or at the whim of the police. What is more, already at this time the author emphasises that only prior notice can be required, not request for permission.[30]

Later on, however, German states which adopted a constitution in the early constitutionalist era between 1814 and 1824 did not include freedom of assembly in their basic document. They thought freedom of assembly was necessary in a state where there was no representation of the citizens, but it did not fit a representative state structure.[31] As we see this is quite the opposite of what underlies English, and especially American, constitutional history: there it is exactly the representative government which has to guarantee freedom of assembly, as an independent right or in conjunction with the right to petition. This opposition mirrors the partly still existing tension between German and US courts with regard to the value protected by freedom of assembly, to be discussed below under democracy-related values.

Soon after 1815, the rest of the German states that kept the feudal constitution (re)turned to authoritarian government, which was repressive

[28] Eg Otto Depenheuer, 'Art 8' ann 10 in Roman Herzog, Rupert Scholz, Matthias Herdegen and Hans H Klein (eds), *Maunz/Dürig Grundgesetz,* Loseblatt-Kommentar 62nd Ergänzungslieferung (München, Beck, 2011).

[29] *Cf* 'Versammlungen und Vereine sind an eine jederzeit widerrufliche landesherrliche Genehmigung gebunden, politische Vereinigungen aber und alle geheimen Gesellschaften sind unter allen Umständen strafbare Vergehen'. (Assemblies and unions are bound to a permit which the feudal landlord can revoke at any time, while political associations and every secret society are under any circumstances criminalised.) Otto von Gierke, *Das deutsche Genossenschaftsrecht*, Vol 1 (1868) 873 as cited by Depenheuer, above n 28, ann 16.

[30] Günther Heinrich von Berg, *Handbuch des teutschen Policeyrechts*, 2nd edn (Erster Theil, 1802) 244 as cited by Depenheuer, above n 28, ann 18.

[31] Roellecke, 'Versammlungsfreiheit' in *Görres-Staatslexikon* as cited by Depenheuer, above n 28, ann 19.

of freedom of assembly (and association). The German Confederation (Deutscher Bund, 1815–66) adopted in 1819 the Karlsbader Resolutions, which targeted—among other liberties—secret or not authorised alliances, especially fraternities which were traditionally politically active at German universities.[32]

Still, the repressive legal environment could not prevent 30,000 people from gathering at Hambach between 27 and 30 May 1832—under the guise of a popular feast, but in reality to discuss political reforms and the state of liberties.[33] It provoked a reaction from the German Confederation, which not only banned any political unions, but introduced permit requirements for every such festivity which is 'as to the time and place neither usual nor allowed'. Even on permitted popular assemblies, 'addresses or suggestions for resolutions should incur an enhanced penalty'.[34]

The 1849 Paulskirche Constitution did protect freedom of peaceful and unarmed assemblies in its article 8, but it has never entered into force.[35] The Weimar Constitution of 1919, similarly to the Grundgesetz, guarantees freedom of assembly without permit or prior notice in general, but it allows for prior notice in cases of open air assemblies, and also for prior ban in case of immediate danger to public safety.

In France, significantly, the Declaration of 1789 does not include freedom of assembly at all. The Constitution of 1791 guaranteed 'as natural and civil rights ... the liberty of the citizens to assemble peacefully and without arms, in accordance with the laws of police'.[36] Article 7 of the Declaration of Rights included in the Montagnard Constitution of June 24, 1793 (which was never applied) repeated this same formulation.[37]

Most of the revolutionaries, so explains Duguit, were suspicious of any collective right or any right of a group because of the dangers partial loyalties represent for national unity and the general will, the latter being derivable only from individual wills.[38] The few proclamations of freedom of

[32] § 3 des Bundes-Universitätsgesetzes vom 20 September 1819, cited after Depenheuer, above n 28, ann 19.

[33] For an analysis, see Pia Nordblom, 'Resistance, Protest, and Demonstrations in Early Nineteenth-Century Europe: The Hambach Festival of 1832' in Matthias Reiss (ed), *The Street as Stage: Protest Marches and Public Rallies Since the Nineteenth Century* (Oxford, Oxford University Press, 2007) 61–83.

[34] § 3 des Bundes-Universitätsgesetzes vom 20 September 1819, cited after Depenheuer, above n 28, ann 19.

[35] Verfassung des Deutschen Reichs vom 28 März 1849, available at verfassungen.de/de/de06-66/verfassung48-i.htm.

[36] Title Premier, § 2, Consitution de 1791, available at mjp.univ-perp.fr/france/co1791.htm.

[37] See www.conseil-constitutionnel.fr/conseil-constitutionnel/francais/la-constitution/les-constitutions-de-la-france/constitution-du-24-juin-1793.5084.html.

[38] Duguit as cited by Pierre-Henri Prélot, *Droit des libertés fondamentales*, 2nd edn (Paris, Hachette, 2010) 289.

assembly in the mentioned documents during the Revolution are considered not more than 'paying lip service' by a French law professor today.[39]

Later French history illustrates the ambivalence of classic liberalism and freedom of assembly, too, in that Benjamin Constant did not include it in the 1815 Additional Act to the Constitutions of the Empire,[40] which he drafted for Napoleon and which was approved in a plebiscite,[41] but was never really applied due to the defeat of Napoleon.

Freedom of assembly was not mentioned in constitutional documents until the Second Republican Constitution of 1848 which in article 8 guaranteed freedom of peaceful assembly within the limits of rights of others and public safety.[42] Unusually, this article protects first freedom of association, then freedom of peaceful and unarmed assembly, then petition and then freedom of *manifestation* of thoughts by press or in other ways, and then prohibits censorship of the press. This order of guarantees is actually the opposite of what is in general the standard order in human rights documents (opinion, press, petition, assembly, association).

In any case, all these documents were rebutted later, and none of them serves as point of reference in contemporary constitutional discourse either. Freedom of *manifestation* (more or less, freedom of demonstration) has since 1995 been interpreted as part of freedom of expression of opinions and ideas as granted in the 1789 Declaration,[43] while freedom of meeting (*réunion*) is a legislatively granted right from 1881,[44] but it has not been elevated to constitutional status.

What is the overall picture that emerges from this short look at legal historical predecessors of the right to assembly? Much remains uncertain, as if to confirm the claim about the neglected nature of freedom of assembly not only by courts and comparative lawyers, but by legal historians alike. I have not been able to verify exactly why the American colonists started to think that petition is intertwined with assembly as a right, while clearly their English peers did not, apart from the fact that the Crown had repressed violently the assemblies of the settlers many times. It seems most likely that this very fact, this experience, and not a legally perceived relationship, preceded the inclusion of an assembly right before the right to petition in the many documents of the evolving American system. It also remains unexplained

[39] Ibid.

[40] Acte additonnel aux constitutions de l'empire du-22-avril-1815, available at www.conseil-constitutionnel.fr/conseil-constitutionnel/francais/la-constitution/les-constitutions-de-la-france/acte-additonnel-aux-constitutions-de-l-empire-du-22-avril-1815.5103.html.

[41] András Sajó, *Constitutional Sentiments* (New Haven, Yale University Press, 2011) 249, fn 10, 359.

[42] Art 8 www.conseil-constitutionnel.fr/conseil-constitutionnel/francais/la-constitution/les-constitutions-de-la-france/constitution-de-1848-iie-republique.5106.html.

[43] Decision no 94-352 DC, 18 January 1995 (Loi d'orientation et de programmation relative à la sécurité).

[44] Law of 30 June 1881 on the freedom of meeting (Loi sur la liberté de réunion).

in any serious detail why Madison actually did not give a single word of caution with regard to assemblies of people as compared to assemblies of representatives, if not simply because he was preoccupied with preventing the introduction of bound mandates for representatives—certainly a vital question.

France's very inconsistent history testifies to great aversion on the part of both Rousseauists and later liberals to a right of assembly. A right to assembly allegedly both prevents the realisation of the general will because it fragments it, and poses a danger to individual liberty, a strange coincidence.[45] According to some early German views, there is no need for freedom of assembly if there is a representative government. This link might have been seen similarly by those during the debate on the First Amendment, who would have struck out the reference to the right of assembly, but would have included a right of the people to instruct their representatives. Thus, freedom of assembly might appear superfluous also in a system of 'bound mandate', which, as mentioned, Madison in turn might have feared significantly more than the right to peaceful assembly. All these contingencies and inconsistencies of the legal history of freedom of assembly left their mark on the forms of assembly recognised by the right, which will be discussed next.

II. MEETING, MARCHING OR SPEAKING: FORMS OF ASSEMBLY

A. United Kingdom: Stationary and Moving Assemblies

In the United Kingdom, the law traditionally has not granted a right to freedom of assembly; therefore, the conceptions as to the forms of assembly are to be understood from the laws regulating public order. The act which currently controls a large segment of freedom of assembly in the United Kingdom is the Public Order Act 1986 (POA). The POA was born out of a perceived need to provide stronger power to the police in cases of assembly in reaction to the 1984–85 miners' strike, one of the country's most serious events of public disorder in the twentieth century. The 1986 act still governs the law of freedom of assembly in England, although quite a few additional laws have been adopted specially targeting terrorism and 'anti-social behaviour'. The Criminal Justice and Police Order Act 1994 (CJPOA) inserted the notion of trespassory assembly as sections 14A–14C in the 1986 Act. One of the most important recent modifications has been section 57 of the Anti-social Behaviour Act of 2003, which reduced the number of participants

[45] A similar suspicion was manifest in early French and German liberalism with regard to freedom of association. See Gábor Halmai, *Az egyesülés szabadsága. Az egyesülési jog története* (Freedom of Association. The History of the Right to Association) (Budapest, Atlantisz, 1990) 28–31.

required in an assembly before the police may impose conditions from 20 to 2. Thus, for purposes of restriction, one can safely assume that an assembly of two is an assembly in English law. Note however that this is not a guarantee of heightened legal protection, but quite to the contrary, an authorisation for interference.

Otherwise, the public order law of the United Kingdom with regard to assemblies has not been monolithic. Historically, the so-called right to passage divided the law related to assemblies into two identifiable classes: processions and stationary meetings. Throughout the nineteenth century the right to passage preferred processions to meetings, according to one commentator because of sympathy towards the Salvation Army which marched, and because of hostility towards the socialist movement which regularly held mass street meetings.[46] Nevertheless, the law was considerably changed when confronting the Fascist marches in the first half of the twentieth century. The 1936 POA, largely targeting the Mosleyan movement, authorised the police to ban processions in a given area if an officer was of the opinion that imposing conditions was not sufficient to prevent serious public disorder. This, however, did not mean that the legal schemes for dealing with processions and meetings were integrated.

The possible theoretical unlawfulness of any kind of stationary meeting has endured well into the 1980s. A 1987 case, *Hirst and Agu*[47] first recognised that a non-moving demonstration is not necessarily an unlawful use of the street (though this interpretation is still quite far from acknowledging a fundamental right of assembly). Yet even recent amendments to the 1986 POA preserved the traditional duality of processions and stationary meetings, not only in a formal sense, but also in the sense of some substantive differences, which will be discussed later.

B. France: *Réunion* and *Manifestation*

In France, two, or, rather, three kinds of assemblies (*rassemblements*) are differentiated. An assembly might be a *manifestation*, a *réunion*, or an *attroupement*. One element of the definition of these concepts seems to be the place where people assemble; others are the aim, the organisation and the modality. None of these elements is completely clear.

As to the place, one thing is clear: a *manifestation*, which is closest in meaning to demonstration in English, is an assembly on the public route (*voie publique*). The concept of public route, however, is also slightly

[46] Rachel Vorspan, '"Freedom of Assembly" and the Right to Passage in Modern English Legal History' (1997) 34 *San Diego Law Review* 935–90.

[47] *Hirst and Agu v Chief Constable of West Yorkshire* [1987] *Crim LR* 330, 85 Crim App R 143 (QB).

unclear, *voie* normally meaning road, and not necessarily including, for example, square. It is not included in the definition if *manifestation* means only moving or also stationary assemblies. Certainly, in contrast, a *réunion* is a stationary assembly, thus it is likely that under *manifestation* a procession or march is understood.

An assembly might be a *réunion* which means meeting, more in the static than in the active sense, somewhat like reunion in English (if the French mean the act of gathering or coming together, they use *rencontre*).

The usual translation of assembly into French as *réunion* causes some confusion. Some would allege that the ECtHR (European Court of Human Rights)[48] and the American jurisprudence place *manifestation* in the category of *réunion*, clearly misunderstanding that 'assembly' as a matter of linguistic convention can both be a meeting and a demonstration (let alone the text of the First Amendment which actually speaks about 'the right of the people peaceably to *assemble*'). Others, however, albeit a minority, use the word *réunion* so that it presumably includes[49] both meeting and demonstration.

According to the classic definition of the Commissaire du Gouvernement Michel in his conclusions[50] to the famous *Benjamin* judgment[51] of the Conseil d'État of 1933: 'a réunion constitutes a momentary grouping of persons formed in order to listen to exposition of ideas or opinions, in order to consult for the protection of interests'.[52] The comma in the original implies that the two aims are disjunctive, alternative.

Bernard Stirn would understand *réunion* to be 'un groupement de caractère momentané, organisé en vue d'un objet déterminé'.[53] That means that he does not find it necessary to specify the aims of listening to an exposition of ideas or opinions or consulting for the protection of interests as stated in the conclusions of Michel to the *Benjamin* judgment.

According to the Court of Cassation, a passing meeting (*rencontre*) of persons who do not have between themselves any relationship (*engagement*)

[48] Eg Alain Boyer argues that 'the silence of the European convention of human rights did not prevent the European Court of Human Rights to consecrate, on the basis of Article 11, ie freedom of assembly (réunion), the freedom of demonstration (manifestation)'. Alain Boyer, 'La liberté de manifestation en droit constitutionnel français' (2001) 44 *Revue française de droit constitutionnel* 675, 684.

[49] This seems to be the stance taken by Duguit: Léon Duguit, *Traité de droit constitutionnel, Vol 5, Les libertés publiques,* 2nd edn (Paris, Fontemoing-Boccard, 1925) § 29. *La liberté de réunion.*

[50] Reproduced in Marceau Long, Prosper Weil, Guy Braibant, Pierre Delvolvé and Bruno Genevois, *Les grands arrêts de la jurisprudence administrative*, 15th edn (Paris, Dalloz, 2005) 290.

[51] CÉ, 19 May 1933, *Benjamin,* Recueil Lebon, 541.

[52] 'La réunion constitue un groupement momentané de personnes formé en vue d'entendre l'exposé d'idées ou d'opinions, en vue de se concerter pour la défense d'intérêts'.

[53] Bernard Stirn, *Les libertés en Question*, 6th edn (Paris, Montchrestien, 2006) § 36 (no page number).

is not a *réunion*. That is why it denied the quality of *réunion* to the faithfuls' gathering, who, leaving the mass, stayed to listen to an improvised speech of a delegate.[54] Also, the Conseil d'État affirmed that the meeting (*rencontre*—ie in the active and not planned sense) of consumers in a café is not a *réunion*. The Commissaire du Gouvernement Corneille defined *réunion* in his conclusions to this case as an assembly concerted or organised for the defence of common ideas or interests.[55] This early formulation of the *Delmotte* case was extended in the *Benjamin* case also to include listening to exposition of ideas or opinions, with the apparent implication that a literary lecture would fall within the scope of *réunion*. The Commissaire du Gouvernement argued that since there was a chance that someone from the audience would react to what the speaker was saying, a discussion might develop, and that is why the lecture is closer to a *réunion* than to a mere spectacle.[56]

Still, although both are different from a spectacle, there should be some difference between *réunion* and *manifestation*. Again, more according to common sense than to any specific legal or judicial definition, a *réunion* is convened in order to listen to a speaker, who might be the only person expressing his opinion, without the others necessarily sharing it, while on the other hand, *manifestation* is about conveying a message to the outside world, that is all the demonstrators' opinions are expressed by participating physically at the *manifestation*.[57] In the words of Bernard Stirn, *manifestation* presents a dual quality by being organised on the public route and by having an aim of expressing a collective *sentiment*.[58] The line is in my view blurred, since there can be—and usually is—one or more speakers at the *manifestation*, who might react to each other, with different views, and, also, demonstrators might express differing views, or it might not be possible to differentiate between demonstrators and audience. In the same vein, it is possible that at a *réunion* more people express opinions, same or different, or discuss some proposition. While Alain Boyer would paint a picture of the participants of the *réunions* as passive,[59] Colliard and Letteron would differentiate *réunions* and *manifestations* from the *spectacle*, where the spectators are passively observing the 'actors'.[60] Thus, they would claim that the underlying criterion of *réunion* is that it is about expressing and *exchanging* views.

It is hard to deny that the novelty of the *Benjamin* judgment was that the mere possibility of exchange of ideas, or communication between

[54] Cass, 14 March 1903, *du Halgouët*.
[55] CÉ, 6 August 1915, *Delmotte*.
[56] Conclusions Michel (1933) *Dalloz Périodique* 3, 54, *Benjamin*.
[57] Boyer, *La liberté de manifestation*, above n 48, 685.
[58] Stirn, *Les libertés*, above n 53, § 37.
[59] Boyer, *La liberté de manifestation*, above n 48.
[60] Claude-Albert Colliard and Roseline Letteron, *Libertés publiques*, 8th edn (Paris, Dalloz, 2005) 493.

speaker and listener, changes a spectacle into a *réunion*. The difference between *réunion* and *manifestation* lies therefore not so much in the fact that the people at the *réunion* are not necessarily expressing or exchanging their views. At least linguistic convention rather imposes delineation from membership: the dividing line is who is considered to be part of a *réunion* or a *manifestation*. *Réunion* is conceptualised as a gathering of those who speak and those who listen, meaning that both the speaker and the audience belong to the *réunion*. A *manifestation*, to the contrary, is conceptualised to include only those who demonstrate, and not their audience or spectators. That leads one to the affirmation of a common goal or issue which ties the group together. At the *réunion*, the non-speakers are listening and might speak, there is no non-interested person affected. At the *manifestation*, in contrast, the common goal will include addressing outsiders who might be interested, disinterested, disturbed, or delighted by the *manifestation*. There is no outsider at the *réunion*, while the whole point of the *manifestation* is to interpellate others who do not participate at the demonstration itself, but possibly might join it.

The relevance of the distinction is that *réunions* on public roads are flatly prohibited in French law,[61] even though it seems that the authority remains free to authorise the usage of the public route for a *réunion*.[62] This led some commentators to define *réunion* as not taking place on the public route, a move which shows very clearly the *loi*-directed thinking of French jurists. Jean Morange would, for example, distinguish *réunion* and *manifestation* by the sole criterion that *manifestation* takes place on the public route.[63] However, to my mind, it is rather a decision of the legislator which precludes *réunions* on public roads, and not a question of linguistic convention, let alone essential difference. Otherwise, it would have been neither necessary, nor sensible, for the legislator to prohibit *réunions* on public roads.

Furthermore, French law is definitely not elaborate enough to clarify whether for the purposes of constitutional protection, the scope of freedom of assembly includes '*réunions sur la voie publique*' or not. If so, the legislative prohibition of *réunions* on the public route could theoretically be examined for conformity with the constitution. If not, *réunion* in the sense of the constitution would be limited to *réunions* not on the public route. However, the question itself is moot, so far at least, since neither the Conseil Constitutionnel nor the Conseil d'État has granted in any sense

[61] Art 6 of the Law of 30 June 1881, reaffirmed by the Decree-Law of 23 October 1935, and art L 211-1 Code de la Sécurité Intérieure, replacing the Decree-Law by Ordinance no 2012-351 of 12 March 2012.

[62] CÉ, 3 May 1974, *Mutuelle Nationale des étudiants de France*, no 83702, Recueil Lebon.

[63] Jean Morange, *Manuel des droits de l'homme et libertés publiques* (Paris, Presses Universitaires de France, 2007) 196, before § 140.

fundamental rights protection, or analogous protection, to the *liberté de la réunion*. The legal sources of *liberté de réunion* are the same as the legal sources of prohibiting *réunions* on the public route.

On the other hand, *réunions* enjoy definitely more protection than *manifestations*, for example, there is no notification requirement in the case of *réunions*. Furthermore, French law differentiates private from public *réunions*. Public *réunions* are those which are open to the public in the sense that participants are not invited by name. Private *réunions* are not regulated at all.[64] *Manifestations* on the public route are perceived to be more dangerous to public order than *réunions*.[65] Nonetheless, as *réunions* are prohibited on the public route, it seems that the legislator deems *réunions on the public route* (i) the most dangerous or obstructive, followed by *manifestations* (ii), then *public réunions not on public route* (iii)—which are then *réunions* taking place in closed areas or in buildings, owned by the state or by private entities to which people are not invited by name, but everybody is free to join—and, lastly, *private réunions* (iv), to which people are invited by name, are perceived to be the least dangerous or otherwise in need of regulation.

However, as the line between *manifestation* and *réunion* is extremely blurred if not non-existent, it is highly unlikely that the categorisation, together with the ban of *réunions* on public route, is really enforced. Suppose an announcement has been posted on a billboard on the street about an upcoming *réunion* of the teachers of lycée X to discuss the new educational reform plans. As the public *réunion* is by definition something to which everybody can come, it is within the concept of the (public) *réunion* that the organisers advertise it in order to inform strangers about the event. According to French law, this event cannot happen on public roads, unless it can be perceived as a *manifestation*. As probably there would be some audience, outsiders, etc who would come out of curiosity to observe the discussion, this might turn it into a *manifestation* according to the approaches sketched above. What renders a public *réunion* into a *manifestation*, ultimately is the presence and reaction of outsiders. For example: probably, public gardens which are fenced and have opening hours, such as that of the Jardin des Tuileries, are not a public route, thus, public *réunion* can be held there, what is more, without prior notice.[66] However, depending on who comes, the gathering may easily become a *manifestation* in the sense that it is about addressing outsiders and not 'discussing an issue among us'. What is more, who is supposed to bear responsibility if the *réunion* 'transgresses'

[64] Colliard and Letteron, *Libertés publiques*, above n 60, 498.

[65] Ibid, 499.

[66] It is possible that lower level park regulations actually preclude *réunions* without prior notice, or else, etc, but my point is to show the logic of the legislative framework.

and becomes a *manifestation* in the sense that people leave the garden, and, let us say, start blocking the traffic on the Concorde square?

Most probably, whenever one wants to organise any sort of gathering on the public route, one will qualify it as *manifestation* and then one will notify the police (or préfet) about the event. Presumably, however, if someone wishes to avoid the duty of notification, he or she will claim that the event is a *réunion* and the place is not a public route. A route—*voie*—would conceivably be a way on which there is traffic, that is streets in any case, but also squares insofar as there are crossroads or crossing traffic. As I can see it, exclusively pedestrian places would not necessarily qualify as *voie publique*, therefore, a square might be either a *voie publique* or not, or even some parts of a square might be *voie publique* while other parts are not.

In effect, it is likely that the difference between '*réunion*' and '*manifestation*' cannot be maintained solely with reference to the modality of the assembly, that is, its dialogical as opposed to monolithically expressive nature, but also relates to the destination of the place used. This is similar to the German approach discussed below.[67]

Finally, French law has traditionally distinguished the concept of '*attroupements*'. *Attroupements*, in the formulation of the criminal law, are assemblies which are capable (susceptible) of disturbing public order. It is, therefore, again an improper concept in the sense that it is just spelling out the limits of legal assemblies. Stirn would claim that *attroupements* are—apart from the tendency to disturb public order—unorganised as well.[68] Intuitively, one might think that disorderly assemblies are unorganised, since disorderly and unorganised seem close in meaning. However, in this case, law is counterintuitive: there is nothing about organisation in the legal definition of *attroupement* in article 431-1 Code Penal, and from experience in other jurisdictions it is clear that spontaneous demonstrations can easily be orderly and peaceful.

That a demonstration or *réunion* should be driven by a common goal is self-evident and not expressed explicitly anywhere in decisions. That is why, as mentioned above,[69] a passing meeting ('*rencontre*') of persons who do not have among themselves any relationship ('*engagement*') is not a *réunion*. Accordingly, the Court of Cassation denied the quality of *réunion* to the faithfuls' gathering, who, leaving the mass, stayed to listen to an improvised speech of a delegate. What is more, the common goal is not simply a common goal of the theatre-goers to enjoy the performance, but implies some sort of active interest.[70] As we have seen in the *Benjamin* judgment,[71] the possibility of a dialogue between speaker and listener

[67] Below text accompanying nn 102–30.
[68] Stirn, *Les libertés*, above n 53, 168, § 37.
[69] Judgment in *du Halgouët*, above n 54 and accompanying text.
[70] Colliard and Letteron, *Libertés publiques*, above n 60, 493.
[71] Judgment in *Benjamin*, see above n 51 and accompanying text.

renders a mere spectacle into a *réunion*. One could then argue, as for example, Colliard and Letteron do, that the common goal present both at any *manifestation* and *réunion* is to exchange ideas or defend interests, in other words the *Benjamin* conclusions are extended to *manifestations* as well.[72]

However, Alain Boyer points out a difference between *réunions* and *manifestations* with regard to the common goal. He thinks that the people at the *réunion* come together in order to listen to a message, while people in the *manifestation* are expressing a message by their presence. Therefore, he is only willing to accept that there might be in both cases expression of opinion, though in the *réunion* the only necessary element of freedom of expression the participants are exercising is 'freedom to be informed', and the speaker exercises freedom of speech. In contrast, at the *manifestation*, the demonstrators (all in one, and one-by-one) express an opinion. Therefore, he thinks it is justified and necessary to attach freedom of demonstration to freedom of expression, and not to freedom of reunion.[73] To express *an* opinion is a necessary common goal of the demonstrators; and Boyer would specify the goal as being addressing the government, or public opinion.[74]

Léon Duguit derives freedom of *réunion* from freedom of opinion in a way that gives a possibility to define *réunion* from its function. Freedom of opinion in Duguit's view implies the freedom to manifest, to communicate one's thoughts to others, and, consequently, 'the liberty to convene réunions of men where these thoughts will be exposed publicly'.[75] Therefore, freedom of opinion implies freedom of *réunion* (which, in my reading, by Duguit covers both meetings and demonstrations). Further on, he makes clear that this approach to *réunion* neither excludes, nor necessitates the possibility of debate or contradictory statements on the *réunion*, the point is to present an opinion or a 'report'.

C. United States: Expressivity Discounted by 'Forum' and 'Action'

In the United States, contrary to the approach taken in the United Kingdom or France, little attention is paid to the possible different forms a gathering might take as long as they are expressive. That is, for the purposes of First Amendment protection, currently there is no initial difference between an indoor or outdoor meeting, just as between a stationary or moving assembly (procession). There used to be a difference until about the end of the nineteenth century between assemblies on parks and streets, and moving

[72] Colliard and Letteron, *Libertés publiques*, above n 60, 493.
[73] Boyer, 'La liberté de manifestation', above n 48, 685.
[74] Ibid.
[75] Duguit, *Traité*, above n 49, 339.

assemblies. Indoor meetings (the clear case of *réunion* in the French understanding) are also covered by the First Amendment.

Whether out- or indoor, however, the extent and the manner of the protection will depend on the kind of 'forum' to which access is sought. Government property and private property naturally enjoy different status, but more interestingly, within government property there has evolved a complicated classification in the 'public forum' jurisprudence. After a long history of twists and changing emphasis on which Robert Post's 1987 article[76] is the seminal analysis, the public forum doctrine classifies government-owned places in three categories.

First, most highly protected is the public forum, that is streets and parks which were 'time out of mind, immemorially held in public trust for purposes of assembly, communicating thoughts between citizens, and discussing public questions'.[77] On such 'quintessential public forums'[78] as they are called in the *Perry* decision, general First Amendment standards apply; a compelling state interest needs to be shown for content-based restrictions (see chapters three to five), and some legitimate interest for content-neutral restrictions (see chapters six to eight), the required link between the two is strongly varying.

Secondly, there is the limited public forum, government property which was opened up for communication by the government. Here it is quite unclear what sort of standard applies. Robert Post actually already thought in 1987 that the limited public forum is dead. *Perry* claims that as long as the state keeps the forum generally open, the same standards apply as on the traditional public forum. Decisions discussed in more detail under place restrictions[79] below will prove Post's point, for example a publicly accessible military base can discriminate on the basis of content, that is it belongs to the third, rather than to the second category.

The third category consists of 'Public property which is not, by tradition or designation, a forum for public communication'.[80] On such non-public forums the state, in addition to time, manner, and place (TMP) restrictions, 'may reserve the forum for its intended purposes, communicative or otherwise, as long as the regulation on speech is reasonable and not an effort to suppress expression merely because public officials oppose the speaker's view'.[81]

[76] Robert Post, 'Between Governance and Management: The History and Theory of the Public Forum' (1987) 34 *University of California at Los Angeles Law Review* 1713.

[77] First mention *Hague v CIO*, 307 US 515, 516 (1939).

[78] *Perry Education Association v Perry Local Educators' Association*, 460 US 37, 45 (1983).

[79] See Ch 8.

[80] 460 US 46.

[81] Ibid.

How these three—or, in effect—two standards operate in practice will also be made clear in this book, even though it is structured not along the lines of the US public forum doctrine, but along the line of prior restraint–substance–modality restrictions, more common to the other jurisdictions.

What sort of 'assemblies'—though again, the expression 'assembly' is basically never used—are worthy of First Amendment protection is also delineated by the *speech plus* theory, that is expressivity does not matter if it is done by 'action'. Speech plus is not a fully-fledged doctrine, but the Supreme Court, especially Justice Hugo Black, found it often useful to differentiate elements of assembly into 'speech' and 'conduct' or 'action', and to accord lesser protection to the latter ones. Justice Black's view regarding conduct being unprotected perhaps expresses most clearly the judicial aversion and/or ignorance as to how meaning is generated on assemblies. Justice Black is still considered a champion of free speech, precisely because he meant anything that is speech should be protected absolutely. As early commentators put it: '*peaceful, orderly* and almost *academic discussion* is the only mode of communication which Black would absolutely protect'.[82]

In a classic *speech plus* reasoning, in *Cox v New Hampshire*[83] from 1941 the Supreme Court has accepted the fact-finding of the state court according to which the gathering

> was a march in formation, and its advertising and informatory purpose did not make it otherwise ... It is immaterial that its tactics were few and simple. It is enough that it proceeded in an ordered and close file as a collective body of persons on the city streets.[84]

That it was a march in formation, resulted in the applicability of a statute requiring special permit for parades even on sidewalks, and, thus, in conviction of otherwise peaceful Jehovah's Witnesses who were moving in four/five single line groups and holding up signs. Thus, the qualification of their activities as a march actually worsened their legal status, which would have been otherwise just that of the simple passers-by or shopper on the sidewalks. As Edwin Baker pointed out, the only legally relevant difference between the conduct of the 88 Jehovah's Witnesses gathering at the intersections on a street of Manchester, New Hampshire, and the other hourly 26,000 passers-by who crossed the intersection was that the Witnesses engaged in First Amendment activity:[85] they were 'marching in formation'. Certainly, that a group shows its unity by formation (which was in this case

[82] NN, 'Reflections on Justice Black and Freedom of Speech' (1972) 6 *Valpariso University Law Review* 316, 323.

[83] *Cox v New Hampshire*, 312 US 569 (1941).

[84] 312 US 574.

[85] Edwin Baker, *Human Liberty and Freedom of Speech* (Oxford, Oxford University Press, 1992) 138.

a very modest formation, the reader should not have the image of Hitlerian militant marches in her mind) renders the group expressive. The court does not say explicitly that the formation rendered the parade under the protection of the First Amendment, however. The court only stresses that the permit requirement is not aimed at the expressive content. It accepted the State Supreme Court's interpretation that the statute

> prescribed 'no measures for controlling or suppressing the publication on the highways of facts and opinions, either by speech or by writing'; that communication 'by the distribution of literature or by the display of placards and signs' was in no respect regulated by the statute; that the regulation with respect to parades and processions was applicable only 'to organised formations of persons using the highways,' and that 'the defendants, separately, or collectively in groups not constituting a parade or procession', were 'under no contemplation of the Act'

and the act only served to secure public convenience in the use of the streets.[86]

Thus, the court considered the permit (and fee) requirement attached basically to 'formation' as not burdening the expressive aspects of the activity. It remains unclear, and even incomprehensible, why the justices thought the Witnesses were building the formation, if not for expressive purposes. Rather, it would seem that the formation is clearly part of the expression, just as Charles Tilly would state, it is one of the WUNC (worth, unity, numbers and commitment) displays which contributes to the unity of the group.[87]

This limited understanding of expression was reinforced in a 1965 case where it was 'emphatically rejected'[88] that

> the First and Fourteenth Amendments afford the same kind of freedom to those who would communicate ideas by conduct such as patrolling, marching, and picketing on streets and highways, as these amendments afford to those who communicate ideas by pure speech.

It appears, therefore, that the US Supreme Court attempts to make a distinction between what is considered physical, external, or maybe what takes up a space, and what is considered 'the message'.

D. The European Court of Human Rights: Subsidiarity and Functionality

The European Court of Human Rights (ECtHR) has only recently contended that freedom of assembly, in the same way as its twin right of association in

[86] 312 US 575 ff.
[87] Charles Tilly, *Social Movements, 1768–2004* (Boulder, Paradigm Publishers, 2004) 4.
[88] *Cox v Louisiana*, 379 US 536, 555 (1965).

article 11,[89] has an autonomous meaning under the Convention.[90] Already the Commission has noted, and the ECtHR since embraced that 'freedom of assembly covers both private meetings and meetings in public thoroughfares as well as static meetings and public processions';[91] and it can be exercised by individuals and those organising the assembly.[92] Most probably, however, it does not cover *ad hoc*, accidental gatherings of people without a purpose, or for purely social purposes.[93]

Protests and direct actions where only one or few participants appear will be covered by the freedom of expression right in article 10.[94] Article 11 is in general considered *lex specialis* to article 10, thus article 10 doctrines can always apply to assemblies, while the connection is not valid the other way around.

This merging conceptual approach does not have such negative consequences as the supersession of assembly by speech elsewhere for two main reasons. More importantly, the ECtHR does not—at least so far—apply any modality doctrine which would allow for more restriction on the 'form' of expression than on the 'content'. In relation to the press, the ECtHR has already declared in 1991 that 'not only the substance of the ideas and information expressed, but also the form in which they are conveyed' is protected by article 10.[95] In 2009, the ECtHR expressly applied this doctrine to an assembly advocating reproductive rights on a boat off the Portuguese shores which was prevented entering territorial waters by a war vessel. A demonstration *on a boat on the territorial waters of a state* was considered by the ECtHR to be the 'mode of diffusion of information and ideas', restrictions on which, in certain situations, 'can affect in an essential

[89] *Chassagnou v France*, Application nos 25088/94, 28331/95 and 28443/95, Judgment of 29 April 1999, (1999) ECHR 22, § 100.

[90] *Tatár and Fáber v Hungary*, Application nos 26005/08 and 26160/08, Judgment of 12 June 2012.

[91] *Rassemblement jurassien and Unité jurassienne v Switzerland*, Application no 8191/78, Decision on admissibility, 10 October 1979, DR 17, 108, 118 ff, and *Christians Against Racism and Fascism (CARAF) v United Kingdom*, Application no 8440/78, Decision on admissibility, 16 July 1980, DR 21, 138, 148. *Barankevich v Russia*, Application no 10519/03, Judgment of 26 July 2007, 47 *EHRR* 266, § 25.

[92] *Rassemblement jurassien*, ibid and *CARAF*, ibid.

[93] The Commission, eg noted that 'There is … no indication in the … case-law that freedom of assembly is intended to guarantee a right to pass and re-pass in public places, or to assemble for purely social purposes anywhere one wishes. Freedom of association, too, has been described as a right for individuals to associate 'in order to attain various ends'. *Anderson and Nine Others v United Kingdom*, Application no 33689/96, Decision on admissibility, 27 October 1997, 25 EHRR CD 172.

[94] Eg *Hashman and Harrup v United Kingdom*, Application no 25594/94, Judgment of 25 November 1999, 30 EHRR 241.

[95] *Oberschlick v Austria (No 1)*, Application no 11662/85, Judgment of 23 May 1991, 19 EHRR 389, § 57.

manner, the substance of the information and ideas in question'.[96] Thus in these cases the ECtHR appears clear about the meaning generating function of modalities.

However, the ECtHR recently contended that 'even otherwise protected expression is not equally permissible in all places and all times'.[97] From this, one could infer a step in the direction of applying different standards to the modality and to the substance of the expression. Still, in my view, this stance is fundamentally different from the stance taken in the United States, because it does not split the expression into a superior and inferior aspect, but includes in the 'meaning' also time and place: 'interference ... might be legitimate when the particular place and time of the otherwise protected expression unequivocally changes the *meaning* of a certain display' (emphasis added).[98]

Furthermore, and not less importantly, another recent decision implies a clear and empirically tenable distinction between expression and assembly for the purposes of fundamental rights restriction. The case involved a two-person performance next to the Hungarian Parliament consisting of hanging out several items of cloths on the fence, symbolising 'the Nation's dirty laundry' in protest against the political crisis ongoing since 2006. The performance lasted only a few minutes, followed by a dialogue with journalists, and then ended. The performers were later fined for 'abuse of freedom of assembly' as they had not notified their 'demonstration'.

The ECtHR dismissed the government's argument that the performance was to qualify as assembly, which would fall under the assembly law, and can be subjected to prior notice. To the contrary, the ECtHR doubted that such a short two-person 'event could have generated the gathering of a significant crowd warranting specific measure on the side of the authorities'.[99] Had the specific measure been warranted, then freedom of assembly (instead or alongside freedom of expression) would be applicable, which would allow for imposition of the notification requirement.[100] By requiring advance notice for the 13 minute two-person performance, however, 'The national authorities' approach to the concept of assembly does not

[96] *Women on Waves v Portugal*, Application no 31276/05, Judgment of 3 February 2009, §§ 38–39.

[97] *Fáber v Hungary*, Application no 40721/08, Judgment of 24 July 2012, § 58. The case concerned removal, detention and an administrative fine as a result of display of an Arpad-striped flag (which is an old Hungarian flag, but which was used by the Arrow Cross Movement in WWII) at a site where Jews were murdered in great numbers at the Danube in Budapest during WWII. The Court found violation of art 10, therefore, the mentioned text actually only leaves open a possibility, and does not state a doctrine or principle.

[98] Ibid.

[99] *Tatár and Fáber*, above n 90, § 29.

[100] In the case at hand, the fine was imposed with regard to a prior restraint unacceptable on core political speech, thus the right to freedom of expression as guaranteed by art 10 was found violated.

correspond to the rationale of the notification rule'.[101] The rationale of the notification rule is effective coordination and facilitation of the assembly, and prevention of public disorder or protection of the rights of others. The lack of these specific concerns rendered the short two-person performance under article 10 instead of article 11, confirming the fall-back nature of article 10 (or the *lex specialis* status of article 11) as it was developed earlier, and implying that for the assembly law to kick in, some additional, specific concerns are required. In this regard, the freedom of assembly is considered freedom of expression discounted by the mentioned police powers, a kind of 'freedom of expression minus'.

In sum, it appears that the ECtHR: (i) is willing to recognise the expressive potential of the 'modalities' of an assembly, and (ii) still might allow heavier or different restrictions on assemblies than on speech, if those restrictions correspond to the additional externalities of assemblies.

E. Germany: Assembly and Demonstration

i. Narrow, Enlarged or Wide Notion of Assembly

In and about the jurisprudence of the German Federal Constitutional Court (GFCC), there has always been quite an intense debate as to the notion of assembly (*Versammlung*).

The text (article 8 I of the German Basic Law, 'GG' in the following) itself says that 'every German has the right without notice or permission, peacefully and without arms, to assemble'; article 8 II GG: 'For assemblies under the open sky, this right can be restricted by law or on the basis of a law'. Thus, at first sight, it seems that article 8 I protects the act of assembling, just as the text of the First Amendment might suggest, except that it is not the right of the people, but of the individual German citizen. In other respects, however, the German debate employs similar terms to what the French lawyers are arguing. Literature and jurisprudence agree that the accidental, passing gathering of people is not an assembly protected by the constitution, similarly to France and the other countries where the issue is less explicit. Thus, there should be some common goal which connects the participants together, and the goal should also be actively common, not that of the theatre-goers. What that goal might be, however, is heavily debated, and even the GFCC seems to change sides on the issue. According to the 'narrow' notion of assembly, the goal must be about collective formation and expression of opinion in public matters.[102] The 'enlarged' notion

[101] *Tatár and Fáber*, above n 90, § 40.

[102] Eg Wolfgang Hoffmann-Riem, 'Kommentar zu art 8' in Erhard Denninger, Wolfgang Hoffmann-Riem, Hans-Peter Schneider and Ekkehard Stein (eds), *Kommentar*

of assembly includes not only communication about public matters,[103] but private ones as well, while the 'wide' notion[104] dispenses with the goal of collective formation and expression of opinion or will, that is the goal is irrelevant as long as there is an inner connection among the participants who strive to achieve a common goal, be what it is.

The implications of the different notions are significant. In the first case, freedom of assembly only covers political assemblies,[105] in a sense it is reduced to a sort of political right. Proponents of this narrow understanding argue with historical interpretation, which, however, seems to have only rather weak ground. It has been shown that historical documents (notably the 1848 Constitution of Paulskirche, the Prussian Constitution of 31 January 1850, or even the Bavarian Statute of 26 February 1850) have not typically limited freedom of assembly to questions of political or public matters,[106] though later courts started to interpret 'assembly' in a narrow way, including only political assemblies.

In the second case, that is when an assembly has to have a goal of collective formation and expression of opinion or will on public *or* private matters, the value attached to freedom of assembly is the value of communicative freedom as a social value.

It is only in the last case, applying a wide notion of assembly, that individual personality as a value comes to the fore, and where not only expression, but also any kind of (common) activity is protected. Therefore, it is only in this last instance that the assembly is protected because of the potential for 'personality development' of the participants. Here German literature, and, partly, the court stress that at the assembly the person unfolds her personality in the group, the assembly is 'personality unfolding in group form'[107] whereby the element of expression might be incidental, but not the rationale for the constitutional protection.

Recently, a partly similar, but in my view also importantly different, notion of assembly has been put forward in the later editions of the Maunz-Dürig

*zum Grundgesetz für die Bundesrepublik (*AK-GG) (Neuwied, Hermann Luchterhand Verlag, 2001) ann 15 ff.

[103] Philip Kunig, 'Kommentar zu art 8' in Ingo von Münch and Philip Kunig (eds), *Grundgesetz-Kommentar I*, 5th edn (München, Beck, 2000).

[104] Roman Herzog, 'Kommentar zu art 8' in Roman Herzog, Theodor Maunz and Günter Dürig (eds), *Maunz-Dürig Grundgesetz* (München, Beck, 2005); Wolfram Höfling, 'Kommentar zu art 8' in Michael Sachs (ed), *GG–Grundgesetz Kommentar,* 5th edn (München, Beck, 2009); Helmuth Schulze-Fielitz, 'Kommentar zu art 8' in Horst Dreier (ed), *Grundgesetz. Kommentar,* Vol I, 2nd edn (Tübingen, Mohr Siebeck, 2004).

[105] Alfred Dietel, Kurt Gintzel and Michael Kniesel, *Versammlungsgesetz*, 15th edn (Köln, Carl Heymanns, 2008) 35, ann 5.

[106] Ulrich Schwäble, *Das Grundrecht der Versammlungsfreiheit (Art 8 GG*) (Berlin, Duncker & Humblot, 1975) 97 ff, cited also by Anna Deutelmoser, 'Angst vor den Folgen eines weiten Versammlungsbegriffs?' (1999) 3 *Neue Zeitschrift fur Verwaltungsrecht* 240, 241.

[107] Herzog, 'Kommentar zu art 8', above n 104, ann 10–16.

commentary by Depenheuer. He argues that freedom of assembly protects the act of assembling for whatever purpose, but it does not protect anything else, especially it does not protect expression, communication, use of the street, noise, etc.[108] This view has been understood to advocate the wide understanding of assembly by some.[109] I think what is gained in scope by the dispensation with a common goal, is lost by the exclusion of anything else than assembling itself. Thus I do not consider Depenheuer arguing for a wide scope, it is rather a kind of literary interpretation akin to that of Justice Black in the US Supreme Court, except of course that Black applies it to speech, and Depenheuer to assembly.

The Constitutional Court itself has been reluctant to conclusively decide the issue for many years. In the seminal 1985 case (*Brokdorf*), the court could be understood to accept the wide notion.[110] However, in the so-called *Sitting Blockade III* decision from 2001, it describes an assembly as 'a local gathering of several persons for the purpose of common discussion or demonstration which aims at participating in the public formation of opinion'.[111] The German original does not necessarily differentiate between formation of public opinion and public formation of opinion. It remains disputed if the court thereby embraces the enlarged or the narrow understanding of assembly, since public opinion can be formed in private just as public, 'political' matters. I agree with those authors, who emphasise the futility of the distinction of public and private matters in this particular regard,[112] because it necessarily enables the state to become the censor about what belongs to which category. To illustrate the problem Schulze-Fielitz mentions a North-Rhine-Westphalia judgment in which inline-skaters' city run was not considered an assembly even though the inline-skaters wanted to raise the issue of recognising inline-skates as vehicles for the purposes of street traffic,[113] in other words a rather public matter.

Nonetheless, the GFCC appears to side with ordinary courts in denying constitutional protection to 'solely entertaining' street events, such as the Love Parade, though the relevant decision was only a denial of a motion for preliminary injunction, and not a full judgment on the substance of the question.[114] Here we see a drawback of the 'judicial democratisation'

[108] Otto Depenheuer, 'Kommentierung zu Art. 8' in Roman Herzog, Rupert Scholz, Matthias Herdegen and Hans H Klein (eds), *Maunz-Dürig Grundgesetz*, (München, Beck, 2011).

[109] Dietel, Gintzel and Kniesel, *Versammlungsgesetz*, above n 105, 35, fn 11.

[110] Bodo Pieroth and Bernhard Schlink, *Staatsrecht II. Grundrechte*, 27th edn (Heidelberg, CF Müller, 2007) ann 693.

[111] BVerfGE 104, 92, 104 (2001).

[112] Dietel, Gintzel and Kniesel, *Versammlungsgesetz*, above n 105, 37, ann 12.

[113] OVG Nordrhein-Westphalen, NVwZ 2001, 1316 as cited by Schulze-Fielitz, 'Kommentar zu art 8', above n 104, ann 27, 897, n 107.

[114] BVerfG, 1 BvQ 28/01, 12 July 2001.

of freedom of assembly,[115] and the limits of functionalist interpretation of basic rights which easily turns 'values' to be protected into 'limits' to be enforced: if freedom of assembly serves democratic self-governance, then *a contrario* assemblies which do not fulfil this purpose will be denied constitutional protection.

On the other hand, the text (article 8 GG) itself clearly refers to two types of assemblies. In one category belong assemblies which take place *unter freiem Himmel* (under the free sky), which is interpreted to mean assemblies which are not delimited (by wall, fence, etc) from the side. Such open air spaces would be the streets, squares, (unfenced) parks, and many more, most recently also other 'places of communication', such as (open areas at) airports.[116]

In the other category belongs every other assembly, that is which is surrounded by wall or fence. The at least partial overlap with French law is apparent: the first places would be largely *voie publique*, while the latter are not *voie publique* (there cannot be traffic). Nonetheless, what is considered '*unter freiem Himmel*' in German law, might eventually not qualify as *voie publique* in French law, if there is no crossing traffic. As article 8 GG stipulates, in paragraph I, that freedom of assembly cannot be subject to prior notice or authorisation, and paragraph II only allows limits by law for assemblies under the free sky, it might appear that assemblies similar to *réunions* cannot be restricted in any way, and it also might appear that prior notice or authorisation is not meant by the 'limit by law' (*Gesetzesvorbehalt*) in paragraph II.

However, this clear division of the constitutional text has been largely eliminated by systematic interpretation. First, the modalities (*Art und Weise*) of any sort of assembly belong under article 8,[117] while the content of any sort of assembly belongs under article 5 I, right to freedom of opinion.[118] What this means will be discussed in more detail under the next heading on demonstration and the relation between freedom of assembly and freedom of opinion. Secondly, prior notice was found constitutional in cases of assemblies under the free sky, as will be discussed in the next chapter.

ii. Demonstration and the Relation Between Freedom of Assembly and Freedom of Opinion

Another debate, with regard to conceptualities of freedom of assembly, revolves around demonstration, an ever more important and sometimes troublesome phenomenon of civil society in Germany. Demonstration is not

[115] See under 'democracy related' values, below text accompanying nn 155–73.
[116] BVerfGE 128, 266 (2011).
[117] BVerfGE 104, 92, 103 (2001); BVerfGE 111, 147, 154 (2004).
[118] BVerfGE 82, 236 (1990), 258; BVerfGE 90, 241, 246 (1994).

a legal term; it is not mentioned in either the Basic Law or in the Law on Assemblies and Processions.

Thus, whether demonstration is protected by any constitutional right, depends on interpretation of both the particular right and also the nature of demonstration. Candidates from the Basic Law are freedom of opinion, freedom of assembly, freedom of association, and general freedom of action and personality right in article 2 I, and even the principle of democracy as enshrined in article 20 (and entrenched in the eternity clause of article 79 III).

Some would deny any claim to constitutional protection, at least when it comes to 'large demos',[119] saying that the gathering and going to the place of the demonstration itself is protected by article 8, freedom of assembly, but not the actual demonstration. Still, the majority of the authors confirm the constitutional protection of demonstrations, some conceptualising it as an aspect of freedom of assembly, others as a comprehensive category under which falls freedom of assembly, while again others consider it a combination of freedom of opinion and freedom of assembly.

Roman Herzog famously attached freedom of demonstration to article 2 I, that is the general personality right including general freedom of action. In this understanding, the point of demonstration is 'personality unfolding in group form'. Thereby he established a connection to human dignity, de-emphasising (though not downplaying) the political importance of article 8, and highlighting participation at a demonstration as a human need of the individual amongst increasing risks of isolation.[120]

Most authors locate freedom of demonstration partly in article 5 (freedom of opinion), and partly in article 8, freedom of assembly. This is the doctrine of complementary delimitation (*komplementäre Verschränkung*), according to which demonstration as substance, as message is protected by article 5, while the modalities (arriving, gathering, standing, marching, dispersing, but as it will be apparent, many more) fall under the scope of article 8.[121] In this understanding, freedom of demonstration is a medium of freedom of opinion; it is the instrument for collectively expressing opinions. The one single real event 'demonstration' is covered in its partial aspects by two different basic rights.[122]

[119] Hans A Stöcker, 'Das Grundrecht auf Demonstrationsfreiheit—eine ochlokratische Fehlinterpretation' (1983) *Die Öffentliche Verwaltung* (DöV) 993.

[120] Herzog, 'Kommentar zu art 8', above n 104, ann 10–16.

[121] Kunig, 'Kommentar zu art 8', above n 103, ann 37 in art 8, Schwäble, *Das Grundrecht*, above n 106, 59, Konrad Hesse, *Grundzüge des Verfassungsrechts der Bundesrepublik Deutschland*, 20th edn, (Heidelberg, CF Müller, 1995) ann 404, and many more as cited by Dietel, Gintzel and Kniesel, *Versammlungsgesetz*, above n 105, 43, fn 49.

[122] Hofmann, BayVBl, 1987, 131, as cited by Dietel, Gintzel and Kniesel, *Versammlungsgesetz*, above n 105, 43, n 52.

This approach has been almost consistently also employed or at least implied in the jurisprudence of the GFCC,[123] in spite of that it has not remained without strong critique. Critics claim that freedom of demonstration is a distinct (even if not distinctly enumerated) basic right, because the expression of opinion of the collectivity is qualitatively different from either the individual speaker or the discussing group. The bodily, direct presence of several persons at the same time and place makes demonstration specific. Being together, same time, same place, conveys a stance, an expression itself. This is very much an aspect the GFCC itself stresses in the *Brokdorf* decision,[124] but only in par with the modality theory mentioned above.

The debate, theoretical as it might sound, is certainly not without practical implications. If a demonstration falls within article 8, it can be limited differently than if it falls under article 5, freedom of expression of opinions.

Article 8 only allows for limitations with regard to assemblies 'under the free sky', while article 5 naturally does not include such a spatial distinction on the limits of freedom of opinion. Secondly, outdoor assemblies according to article 8 can be restricted in a statute, that is the form of the limitation is prescribed, but not the substance. Article 5 II, however, lists as limits of freedom of opinion general laws, protection of personal honour, and youth protection, and article 5 I prohibits censorship.

The *Holocaust Denial* decision[125] also informs us about the view of the GFCC between articles 5 and 8, more to the point of the relation between expression and assembly, and not the question of demonstration addressed more in *Brokdorf*. The court interpreted a condition of no Holocaust denial imposed on a closed indoor meeting as a restriction to be judged by standards of article 5 II. It explained that as the contested condition itself refers to 'certain expressions, which the organiser is supposed neither to mouth, nor to tolerate',[126] its constitutionality depends on whether the expressions themselves 'are permitted or not'. An expression which cannot be constitutionally prohibited, cannot form the basis for an imposition of condition for the purposes of the assembly law, either, or so the court holds.

It remains unclear why it is not possible that constitutionally proscribable expressions are in fact not proscribed in the law on assembly, or why the right to assembly, as a right 'without limits' in this (indoor meeting) case, cannot prevail over the limits of freedom of opinion.

[123] BVerfGE 69, 315, 343, 345 (*Brokdorf*, 1985); BVerfGE 82, 236, 258; BVerfGE 124, 300 (2009) *Rudolf Heß memorial march*, § 96.

[124] BVerfGE 69, 315, 344, see also below the different meanings of the value of expression. Somewhat surprisingly, Dietel, Gintzel and Kniesel do not appear to be aware of this part of the *Brokdorf* decision, and impute this idea solely to scholars in Dietel, Gintzel and Kniesel, *Versammlungsgesetz,* above n 105, 44.

[125] BVerfGE 90, 241 (1994).

[126] BVerfGE 90, 241, 250.

This situation is known as *Grundrechtkonkurrenz*, competitition of basic rights in German doctrine, and it is not settled which right should be then applicable in general, that is the one with the more, or with the less limits.[127] From the general basic rights friendliness of the Basic Law the less limits alternative would follow, and this view is generally shared by the majority of German scholars.[128] The GFCC has not settled the question in general.

Application of the general scholarly view to the case of competing 'opinion' and 'assembly' rights would result, at least as to indoor meetings, in the prevalence of the right to assembly, as that has less limits.

In contrast, the GFCC interprets the assembly guarantee as being about the modality, while the substantive guarantee is freedom of opinion. In the *Holocaust Denial* case, the court explains that the prohibition on Holocaust denial does not violate article 8 I GG even if the right to assembly in closed places is not subject to limits according to article 8 II. Simply, the court argues that expressions which can be constitutionally prohibited under article 5 II are not protected by article 8 either. [129]

This, in effect, results in the confirmation of the theory, rejected by scholars, that the right with more limits is applicable when two rights are competing, especially if one accepts that the split into content and modality is artificial and false.

On the other hand, when it comes to open air meetings and demonstrations, article 5 II's general law requirement imposes at first sight a higher justificatory burden on the state than the simple 'condition of limit by law' (*einfaches Gesetzesvorbehalt*) in article 8 II. Thus, for demonstrations, the court has chosen the right with the less limit.

The third *Sitting Blockade* decision sheds some light on what the GFCC means by content versus modality. There, the constitutionality of duress (*Nötigung*) as applied to sitting blockades was measured not on article 5, but on article 8, because the conviction has not attached to the 'expression, but to the action of blockade aiming at raising attention',[130] as if to say the restriction was content-neutral. The question has to be put again: how is it that 'an action which aims at raising attention' is not qualified as 'expressive'?

[127] Ingo von Münch, 'Kommentar zu Vorb. art 1–19', ann 43 in Ingo von Münch and Philip Kunig (eds), *Grundgesetz-Kommentar I*, 5th edn (München, Beck, 2000) with further references.

[128] Ibid.

[129] BVerfGE 90, 241, 249 (1994).

[130] BVerfGE 104, 92, 103 (2001).

III. FUNDAMENTAL RIGHT, OR 'MERE' COMMON LAW LIBERTY

Freedom of assembly has different status in the jurisdictions examined, it is not necessarily a constitutional or basic right, but might be a statutory right or just a liberty.

In the United Kingdom, originally, freedom of assembly was not recognised as a fundamental right. It is arguably not truly recognised as such today either, since the Human Rights Act (HRA in the following) does not allow a prevalence of freedom of assembly over explicit, contrary statutory provision which cannot be interpreted in conformity with the European Convention on Human Rights, for such cases only the way of discretionary legislative change initiated by courts via a declaration of incompatibility is foreseen.

It seems that freedom of assembly has been protected only as a liberty, a 'mere negative liberty'. A liberty in this interpretation meant only that individuals are free to do what is not prohibited, insofar and only as long as it is not prohibited.[131] By exercising a liberty, one does not commit an unlawful act. In the terminology of Hohfeld, freedom of assembly was only a privilege.

This has two important consequences. First, liberty can easily be taken away, by legislation or even by common law. Secondly, as liberty does not amount to a claim-right, there is confusion about the positive or negative nature of liberty. Some contemporary legal commentators suggest that liberty is not enforceable as opposed to a *positive right* in the European Convention on Human Rights or even a *fundamental right* in the US Bill of Rights.

It seems to me, however, that liberty differs from those two, otherwise different conceptions of rights, not in its enforceability, but in its rank. This rank, on the other hand, follows not even simply from the nature of liberty, but from the constitutional system of the United Kingdom. Parliamentary sovereignty, to put it simply, easily trumps liberties in England while rights in the ECHR and in the US Constitution are supposed to form limits on governmental (including legislative) powers. Liberties are not 'constitutional' or 'human' rights in England because their nature is determined by their relatively low ranking in the hierarchy of norms. It is especially dangerous—it appears to me—to mistake liberties for negative rights as opposed to positive rights in the Strasbourg jurisprudence.

Negative right means a claim-right for non-interference on the part of the state, such as freedom of speech in the United States. Positive right means a duty of the state to provide protection for the individual against some harm, or, in a loose sense, a duty of service provided by the state to the people.

[131] *Cf* also Richard Stone, *Textbook on Civil Liberties and Human Rights,* 5th edn (Oxford, Oxford University Press, 2004) 343.

Under the ECHR, freedom of assembly is both a negative and a positive right meaning that people have a right to assembly free from undue interference, while the state is obliged to take positive measures to facilitate the exercise of the negative right, for example by protecting the demonstrators from violent attacks, or to investigate cases where a violation of the negative right has apparently occurred.[132]

In any case, in England, freedom of assembly traditionally has been only part of the general liberty of citizens which could be restricted by law. As an important decision has put it, which was later cited by Dicey: 'English law does not recognise any special right of public meeting for political or other purposes. The right of assembly ... is nothing more than a view taken by the Court of the individual liberty of the subject'.[133] The only limit to that power of regulation was some sort of reasonableness.[134]

This approach has had particularly disturbing consequences on freedom of assembly from a constitutional point of view. Freedom of assembly concerns are almost completely substituted by public order concerns. In most of the casebooks on civil liberties, there is a chapter about public order law, and not on freedom of assembly. The textbooks, of course, only reflect the state of the law in the field. In the United Kingdom there are currently in force a number of statutes entitled Public Order Act, Criminal Justice and Public Order Act, Crime and Disorder Act, Anti-social Behaviour Act, and the like, all with a focus on preventing disturbances, and none with a focus on securing a fundamental right. There is, accordingly, no single statute which would even allude to *the right* of assembly. The tendency is also clear: the statutes enacted later in time all enhance the powers of the police, all criminalise some previously lawful behaviour, and in most of the cases widen the scope of police discretion in handling protests.

Freedom of assembly also ranks lower than some other rights or freedoms in UK law. Certainly, the tradition to protect rights in criminal procedure is much more strongly embedded, though this is one area where recent anti-terrorism legislation might render moot even centuries-long legal truisms. Some media freedom cases also suggest a tendency to declare the existence of a common law 'constitutional right'[135] in the realm of freedom of expression. This is certainly not the case with freedom of assembly, not even after the coming into force of the Human Rights Act in 2000.

Unlike in Britain, that freedom of assembly is a fundamental right was never questioned in the United States. In *Hague v Committee for Industrial*

[132] See, eg *Plattform Ärzte für das Leben v Austria*, Application no 10126/82, Judgment of 21 June 1988, 13 EHRR 204.

[133] *Cf Duncan v Jones* [1936] 1 KB 218.

[134] *Cf Nagy v Weston* [1965] 1 WLR 280; [1965] 1 All ER 78.

[135] Helen Fenwick, *Civil Liberties and Human Rights*, 4th edn (Oxford, Routledge, 2007) 470, referring to *Simms* [1999] 3 All ER 400, [1999] TLR, 9 July, and to *Reynolds* [1999] 4 All ER 609, [1999] 3 WLR 1010.

Organisation the Supreme Court summarised earlier statements on the right to free assembly:[136]

> [I]t is clear that the right peaceably to assemble and to discuss these topics, and to communicate respecting them, whether orally or in writing, is a privilege inherent in citizenship of the United States which the [Fourteenth—O.S.] Amendment protects. …
>
> In the Slaughter-House Cases it was said:
>
> 'The right to peaceably assemble and petition for redress of grievances, the privilege of the writ of habeas corpus are rights of the citizen guaranteed by the Federal Constitution.'
>
> In United States v. Cruikshank, the court said:
>
> 'The right of the people peaceably to assemble for the purpose of petitioning Congress for a redress of grievances, or for any thing else connected with the powers or the duties of the national government, is an attribute of national citizenship, and, as such, under the protection of, and guaranteed by, the United States. The very idea of a government, republican in form, implies a right on the part of its citizens to meet peaceably for consultation in respect to public affairs and to petition for a redress of grievances. If it had been alleged in these counts that the object of the defendants was to prevent a meeting for such a purpose, the case would have been within the statute, and within the scope of the sovereignty of the United States.'
>
> *No expression of a contrary view has ever been voiced by this court.* (Emphasis added)

The concurring justices found even broader the constitutional protection accorded to freedom of assembly, as they considered it is made applicable to the states by the Due Process Clause of the Fourteenth Amendment, not the somewhat declined Privileges and Immunities Clause, as the lead opinion of the plurality judgment would claim. The main difference between lead and concurrence is as to the subject of the right, not so much as to the fundamental nature of the right. The Privileges and Immunities Clause only extends to citizens while the Due Process Clause to anybody coming within the jurisdiction of the United States. Nowadays one can safely maintain that in the United States the latter view prevails with regard to the fundamental right to free assembly, even if courts basically never talk of assembly, only about expression.

In Germany, the Basic Law itself only grants freedom of assembly to citizens of the Federal Republic of Germany. This, on the one hand, clearly does not hinder the recognition of freedom of assembly as a fundamental or basic right, which similarly to the United States, enjoys highest rank among

[136] *Hague v Committee for Industrial Organisation*, 307 US 496, 512 ff (1939), internal citations omitted.

the possible rights and entitlements in the German legal order.[137] What is more, freedom of assembly, according to the text of article 8 GG, is unlimited except in cases of assemblies under the open sky. This ostensible illimitability, however, is significantly reduced in the interpretation of the GFCC, as for such rights, the court introduced the concept of inherent limitations, that is limits flowing from other constitutional rights are acceptable even on seemingly unlimited rights.

In an opposite trend, another textual limit is interpreted away, too, which had the effect of broadening basic rights protection. In general, article 2 I of the Basic Law protects general freedom of action as a human right, under which non-citizens' freedom of assembly can be subsumed. Secondly, the federal assembly law—and also Länder legislation adopted after the federalism reform[138]—grants freedom of assembly to everyone, as only this would be in accordance with the ECHR.[139] It is unrealistic that any Land will in the future restrict the right to citizens. In any case, in the German constitutional order, freedom of assembly is safely engrained as a basic human right.

In France, as noted above, the freedom of *manifestation* has been attached to article 11 of the Declaration des droits de l'homme et du citoyen du 1789 (Declaration of the Rights of Man and Citizen 1789 (DDHC)) by the Constitutional Council (CC),[140] and that way it has a constitutional rank. Freedom of *réunion* is 'only' statutorily granted, even if that protection is more extensive as there is no prior restraint, and since the *Benjamin* decision the Administrative Court strictly examines whether the interference was proportionate. It has to be stressed that the statutory nature of the guarantee of freedom of *réunion* does not appear to bother French lawyers. Quite to the contrary, they certainly prefer the legislative guarantee over a 'constitutional' guarantee proclaimed by the Constitutional Council. Jean Morange in comparing countries of common law and countries of 'legislative law' (France) explains that the value of the first is its unity and

[137] This does not mean there might not be differences among basic rights themselves: dignity is considered unlimitable (inviolable is the term in the Basic Law), while freedom of opinion also enjoys a very high status, maybe second to dignity—if such hierarchisations make sense at all in the *ad hoc* balancing of the German Constitutional Court.

[138] A note: the federalism reform (Gesetz zur Änderung des Grundgesetzes vom 28 August 2006 (BGBl I S 2034) has transferred the competence on assemblies to the Länder, but that does not render the Federal Assembly Law in itself moot, because each Land can decide whether to adopt a partially or completely new Assembly Law, or stay partially or completely under the Federal Assembly Law. In any case, the Länder are bound to observe constitutional jurisprudence of the GFCC. As this book deals with the constitutional content of the right to free assembly, I shall not examine separately the various legislative measures which had already been enacted by the various Länder, unless they had already been affected by the GFCC.

[139] Dietel, Gintzel and Kniesel, *Versammlungsgesetz*, above n 105, 47.

[140] Decision no 94-352 DC, 18 January 1995 (Loi d'orientation et de programmation relative à la sécurité).

flexibility, while of the second is predictability and clarity,[141] not considering that laws are also in need of interpretation, let alone that laws themselves might be substantively objectionable, unconstitutional or violating 'human rights'.

Still, historically, freedom of *réunion* is granted in a law from 1881 (which could always become interpreted by the Constitutional Council as belonging to the fundamental principles recognised in the laws of the Republic, and thus get constitutional value), but the freedom of *manifestation* was only regulated in 1935 in a so-called Decree-Law, an Act issued by the executive but having legislative value (in 2012, the regulation was codified into the Code of Internal Security). Finally, again Morange explains that the *liberté de réunion* has been traditionally understood as more precious than freedom of demonstration because it appeared 'more intellectual', and, thus, more worthy of protection in line with the Enlightenment basis of French law.[142] The 'idealist'[143] definition given by the Commissaire du Gouvernement Michel to freedom of *réunion* in *Benjamin* is also a reflection of this approach according to Morange.[144]

Thus, all in all, this shows it is not useful to transpose into French law the categories of ranking in discussing freedom of demonstration and meeting. Despite the fact that hierarchy of norms is in general an integral part of French doctrine (scholarship), it is not really applied to a particular right. The fact that freedom of demonstration was first granted higher status in 1995, testifies at once both to the general later emergence of the form of demonstration (as explained by social movement studies), and to the late constitutionalisation of the French legal system.

A last enigmatic feature of French law is, or used to be, that organisers and participants have a different status. Traditionally, it was understood that organisers did not have a constitutionally protected right to either *réunion* or *manifestation*, while to participate at a demonstration was a fully protected activity.[145] Courts and authorities nowadays, however, do not appear to be concerned about that, and so I will not either.

IV. THE VALUE OF FREEDOM OF ASSEMBLY: CONTEMPORARY JUDICIAL RATIONALES

After having discussed legal antecedents, forms, and status of freedom of assembly, it is now time to attempt some more abstract, but still judicially

[141] Jean Morange, *La liberté d'expression* (Bruxelles, Bruylant, 2009) 74.

[142] Ibid, 63.

[143] Ibid.

[144] Ibid.

[145] Hubert G Hubrecht, 'Le droit français de la manifestation' in Pierre Favre (ed), *La manifestation* (Paris, Presses de Sciences Po, 1990) ch 5.

focused analysis, of what is the sense of protecting assemblies according to the courts.

Courts bring about several, shorter or longer explanations when they decide a case in which a party claims a violation of his or her right to assembly or protest. In the following I will examine those explanations or judicial rationales one by one, since they shed light on a few problems related to the adjudication of assembly claims.

For sake of clarity, rationales are best discussed in three main categories: (i) expression-related, (ii) democracy-related, and (iii) liberty-related values.[146]

A. Expression-related Values

There is an apparently obvious link between freedom of assembly and expression. Still, courts differ in their perception of the more precise relation of the two, as I showed above, in relation to rights.

The French Constitutional Council frames freedom of demonstration as collective expression of ideas and opinions, while freedom of meeting, *réunion,* is more about exchange of ideas and opinions. What ideas and opinions mean in this regard is not further clarified, thus we can assume that it does refer to any kind of message, in any case, the question is not even asked.

The German court also stresses collective expression, however, there the focus is shifted from the message to the person expressing the message. The demonstrator, in the German understanding, 'displays his personality in a direct way'; demonstrators 'take up a position in the real sense of those words (*Stellung nehmen*) and testify to their point of view'.[147] Thereby, the court draws the attention to the physical, bodily nature of assemblies and demonstrations. In that way, the value to be protected is the person's willingness or desire to show support for a point of view by her body. It is not 'speech' coming from the brain and the mouth, neither opinions or ideas, but the human body as it stands in front of the public that is worthy of constitutional protection.

It is impossible not to notice that the German court eventually discards, or at least significantly weakens, the importance of the collective aspects of assembly and demonstration with this focus on each protestor's body taking a stance, filling up a concrete place. On the other hand, the focus on physically taking a stand also values the act of taking a stand more than the individual message, and in this sense it emphasises material, quantitative

[146] Though these categories are somewhat artificial, and in reality, expression, liberty and democracy obviously intermingle, they emphasise the different focus different courts take.

[147] BVerfGE 69, 315, 345, as translated by www.utexas.edu/law/academics/centers/transnational/work_new/german/case.php?Ibid=656.

aspects of demonstrations, and a specific feature compared to an argumentative essay which I think is otherwise the paradigmatic view of the object protected by freedom of expression. The German court in this regard very clearly sees a specificity of public assemblies. Note however that the quantitative or bodily aspects of a demonstration are still integrated into an expression rationale, and not understood as the self-standing characteristic of assemblies. Apparently, the court takes 'expression of personality' as the general category within which fall something like 'intellectual' expression on the one hand, and 'bodily' expression, on the other.

At the Strasbourg level, the relation between expression as value and assembly is rather simple, or certainly not overtheorised: even though assemblies are covered by the autonomous right of article 11, which is *lex specialis* in relation to article 10,[148] cases arising under that article shall also be read in the light of article 10. As the court explains: 'the protection of personal opinions, secured by Article 10, is one of the objectives of freedom of peaceful assembly as enshrined in Article 11'.[149] As one of the functions of article 11 is to safeguard freedom of expression,[150] article 10 doctrines are also applicable. This has—theoretically—a particular relevance in cases of political protest as according to the Strasbourg jurisprudence, political speech, or public debate related to issues of public interest, enjoy a strong protection,[151] the same should apply to political protests.[152] The ECtHR is also aware of the specific characteristics of assemblies in enhancing the expressive potential of the lonely speaker or writer:[153]

> [I]n qualifying a gathering of several people as an assembly, regard must be had to the fact that an assembly constitutes a specific form of communication of ideas, where the gathering of an indeterminate number of persons with the identifiable intention of being part of the communicative process can be in itself an intensive expression of an idea. The support for the idea in question is being expressed through the very presence of a group of people, particularly… at a place accessible to the general public. Furthermore, an assembly may serve the exchange of

[148] *Ezelin v France*, Application no 11800/85, Judgment of 26 April 1991, Series A no 202, § 35.

[149] Ibid, § 37 and *Galstyan v Armenia*, Application no 26986/03, Judgment of 15 November 2007, § 96.

[150] One may wonder what else—besides the protection of expression of personal opinions—might be the objective of art 11. The fact that it is left open by the Court, does not, in itself, lend support to the relation of freedom of assembly and constituent power.

[151] *Oberschlick v Austria (No 1)*, Application no 11662/85, Judgment of 23 May 1991, Series A no 204, § 58: 'freedom of political debate is at the very core of the concept of a democratic society which prevails throughout the Convention'.

[152] *Cf* 'The protection of opinions and the freedom to express them is one of the objectives of freedom of assembly and association enshrined in Article 11 … In this connection it must be borne in mind that there is little scope under Article 10 § 2 for restrictions on political speech or on debate on questions of public interest'. *Öllinger v Austria*, Application no 76900/01, Judgment of 29 June 2006, § 38.

[153] *Tatár and Fáber*, above n 90, § 38.

ideas between the speakers and the participants, intentionally present, even if they disagree with the speakers.

Thus, freedom of assembly according to the ECtHR furthers expressive values in several regards. It can be: (i) about individual expression of the speakers; (ii) collective expression signifying (ii)(a) the quantity of support for an idea, or (ii)(b) support for the idea that the issue is worth discussing; finally, (iii) it enables exchange of ideas between supporters and dissenters.

As mentioned, in the United States, freedom (or the right) of assembly is—but for a very few, mainly early cases—missing from the dictionary of the Supreme Court, which either simply talks about the First Amendment, or freedom of speech, or sometimes freedom of expression in cases related to assemblies. Thus, the value of the demonstrations and protests are in general considered to be the same as that of free speech. One dissent at the Supreme Court argued that speech by conduct can actually convey a message more precisely than if told in words. In the *Sleeping Tent* (demonstration for homeless persons) case Justice Marshall—joined by Justice Brennan—quoted Judge Edwards from the DC circuit:[154]

> By using sleep as an integral part of their mode of protest, respondents 'can express with their bodies the poignancy of their plight. They can physically demonstrate the neglect from which they suffer with an articulateness even Dickens could not match'.

This point of view, rejected by the majority, rightly emphasises an important and valuable feature of protest demonstrations which is lacking in other 'forms of speech': that re-enactment and concrete, even theatrical display are not only more apt to induce empathy and emotions, but also more precisely express, because they more directly represent and demonstrate a particular issue, drawing attention to a situation of crisis in our common life, and thus making it comprehensible. This has always been a characteristic potential of protest and demonstration, and this potential deserves principled recognition in law as well.

However, too often this potential is ignored by law, even constitutional and human rights law, because of a forced doctrinal split into content and modality, and a satisfaction with requiring state neutrality only as to content. Such is the case in the United States and Germany, while in the other countries the argumentation is not even transparent enough to clarify the court's view in this regard.

The ECtHR appears to be the only court which, by attributing expressive values to the mentioned aspects of assemblies, does not lower the standard of review. When the clash in this regard, between the ECtHR and national

[154] *Community for Creative Non-Violence v Watt*, 227 US App DC 19, 34; 703 F 2d 586, 601 (1983) (Edwards J concurring). At 468 US 288, 306, *Clark v Community for Creative Non-Violence*, Marshall and Brennan JJ, dissenting.

jurisdictions, will be openly exposed is hard to tell, but it might transform assembly law fundamentally. So far, however, this clash potential appears to be dormant.

Therefore, strangely, even though freedom of assembly is often protected in the language of freedom of expression in courts, de facto this reference to expression does not necessarily benefit the demonstrator, as it will be visible in the chapters on time, manner, and place restrictions. Non-intellectual, physical, material, including ritualistic or theatrical moments of assemblies, get read out from the enhanced constitutional protection by denying them the quality of 'expression'. This way, the protection accorded to assemblies also mirrors what counts as expression in the eyes of judges. An argumentative essay, with rationally supported facts and conclusions, in other words what a scholarly or judicial piece is supposed to be, is certainly more worthy of protection under this standpoint than a messy protest where people want to sleep in a park. Reading the decisions on assembly by having in mind argumentative essay as the paradigmatic case of expression explains many of the apparent inconsistencies, and deliberately weakened jurisprudential standards, which are then unsurprisingly inadequate to protect the specific potentials of assembly.

B. Democracy-related Values

Most widespread, and most problematic, democracy-related values are even more diverse in the interpretation of different courts than expression-related values, mostly for reasons of the inconsistent use of the concept of democracy or self-government (to which I now temporarily contribute).

i. 'Inherent in the Form of Republican Government'

According to the US Supreme Court, freedom of assembly is inherent in the republican form of government. In *DeJonge v Oregon*, the Court cites an early case, *US v Cruikshank*, saying that 'The very idea of a government, republican in form, implies a right on the part of its citizens to meet peaceably for consultation in respect to public affairs and to petition for a redress of grievances'.[155] Republican form of government, in general US understanding, means representative democracy (ie in the Madisonian sense), where citizens are supposed to be able to freely assemble so they can discuss public issues in the expectation that that discussion will influence governmental decisions. *Cruikshank,* however, also refers to the federal government, and that in turn makes the inherency quote quite

[155] *DeJonge v Oregon*, 299 US 353, 364 (1937) citing *United States v Cruikshank*, 92 US 542, 552 (1875).

ambiguous, at least for the contemporary reader. *Cruikshank* was decided before incorporation, that is before the Bill of Rights came to be applied to the states, and that is the main motivating force behind the argument from inherency. Thus there cannot be too much read into this—though much quoted—early case, if not only by saying that since it is cited later over and over again, it has acquired a new meaning independent of incorporation.

ii. 'A Moment of Original, Untamed, Direct Democracy'

According to the German court's most famous sentence on the nature of the right in question, the exercise of freedom of assembly, especially demonstration, is a 'moment [a piece, literally] of original, untamed, direct democracy'[156] which prevents the operation of politics to 'petrify into the routine' of daily business.

This view, so close to Carl Schmitt's acclamation idea, is false in every, but for the most metaphorical, sense. The exercise of freedom of assembly is neither original, nor untamed, nor direct, nor democracy, at least in nowadays' legal and political systems.

First of all, assemblies are not exercising public power, and rightly so, as they do not possess any legitimacy for it. Assemblies are anything but untamed (*ungebändingt*), as law, German law included, imposes so many limits on the exercise of this right that for some it might appear to be not a right at all. It is not direct, as it is not an exercise of legitimate public power because 'the People' (*das Volk*) is never present at a demonstration, not even the majority, or any significant number compared to the entire polity. Admittedly, the people present in the demonstration might be so numerous that it challenges the authority of the state, and it overwhelms police to incapacitation. In that sense, assemblies are able to gain power, de facto power, to ruin and destroy, but this is hardly what the GFCC (and Konrad Hesse, the originator of the quote) meant. I cannot interpret this—often repeated—reference in *Brokdorf* other than as a romantic metaphor, with close to zero effective meaning.

Similarly, the idea hinted in *Brokdorf* that freedom of demonstration is especially important in the *Bundesrepublik because* representative governments, such as that instituted by the Basic Law, only allow for referenda in limited cases, and *therefore* freedom of assembly plays a more important role, is equally half-baked. Representative systems limit referenda because of (justified or unjustified) fear that people can be manipulated, or they are otherwise less apt than a fewer number of elected representatives within a system of separation or at least division of powers, to decide on questions

[156] BVerfGE 69, 315, 347 (1985), *Brokdorf*, quoting Konrad Hesse, *Grundzüge des Verfassungsrechts der Bundesrepublik Deutschland*, 14th edn (Heidelberg, CF Müller, 1984) 157.

involved in governance. If so, assemblies (especially demonstrations), certainly provide even less of a forum to decide on any of such issues than referenda, certainly can be manipulated to an equal extent if not more, and are prone, equally or more, to irrationality and emotionalisation.

The German experience which mandated the constitutionally entrenched suspicion against referenda is essentially the same with regard to marches during the National Socialist era. Thus it is neither logical in theory, nor historically justified, to consider assemblies (and certainly not demonstrations) as a kind of benign functional substitute for referenda. If referenda are dangerous, assemblies are even more so. The function of referendum and assembly is also quite different, defeating any claims for substitution. People *decide* on a referendum while they do not decide on an assembly.

iii. 'Formation of Political Will and Opinion in a Representative Democracy'—Stabilising Role?

What really makes an assembly important from the viewpoint of democracy is actually the other rationale the German court stresses in this regard: assemblies contribute to the 'formation of political will and opinion in a representative democracy',[157] they provide a channel for expressing discontent with the course the government takes, and thus constitute 'a necessary condition of a political early warning system'.[158]

Formation of political *opinion* refers to public opinion in my view, while contribution to formation of political *will* includes also exerting some pressure on actual decision-making processes, but no decision-making itself. Even if we suppose that the elected government actually realises the political programme for which it was elected, freedom of assembly serves as a tool for any minority in general, for those whose interests are either never, or temporarily not, taken into account by majoritarian mechanisms.

This rationale is actually the opposite of the previous one: assemblies are perceived to be eminently *in*directly related to public power, exerting a mediating function from the people to government. I even think the two rationales are irreconcilable, as this one presupposes, the previous one denies a functioning, legitimate representative system. Thus, the less legitimate and representative a system is, the more the above discussed direct democracy argument gains strength and justification. Countries examined in this book are functioning, legitimate representative systems, a fact which counsels against the judicial construction and legitimisation of parallel centres of power (unless the court wants to go outside the system, eg by adopting a Marxist stance). Naturally, however, the more a system turns

[157] BVerfGE 69, 315, 347.
[158] Ibid.

authoritarian and illegitimate, the more it becomes necessary and legitimate for assemblies of people to take over.

Note how much the German court is aware of the double dual nature of assemblies, expressing *and* forming opinion *and* will, even if the court overall, or at least in rhetoric, fails—see the direct democracy argument just discussed—to keep the conceptualisation of will formation within the bounds of representative government.

That the indirect, mediating rationale is to prevail, despite all the grand rhetoric of 'untamed, direct democracy', is supported by a further assertion in *Brokdorf*: that assemblies play a *stabilising*[159] *role* in a representative democracy by functioning as the above mentioned 'necessary condition of a political early warning system'.[160] However, for assemblies to be considered *stabilising*, a minimally responsive representative government is presupposed, and, also, only those assemblies can be stabilising which do not aim at destabilisation. Unless these conditions are fulfilled, assemblies might just as well be destabilising, for better or worse.

A best light reading of these lines of the *Brokdorf* decision thus, in my view, requires government to consider the opinions (and will) expressed and formed on assemblies, even if government decides not to bow to the pressure exerted. To exert pressure is certainly considered legitimate because of the duality of opinion and will. On the other hand—as will be shown later in the parts related to the scope and limits of the right—the court in final evaluation endorses potentially subversive and/or coercive assemblies to a much lesser extent than it might seem from these general principles spelled out in *Brokdorf*.

iv. 'Essential to the Poorly Financed Causes of Little People'

A slightly different application of the democracy-enhancing rationale is famously formulated by Justice Black, in striking down a ban on door-to-door leafleting, since such means of communication are 'essential to the poorly financed causes of little people'.[161]

In the United States no specific application of the little people argument to freedom of assembly in a strict sense (ie not door-to-door leafleting) can be found in the decisions, but as leafleting is part of the activities typically accompanying assemblies, the decision is highly relevant. The German court in *Brokdorf* also acknowledges, in general terms, that influencing the political process is easier for big associations, financially strong sponsors, or mass media, and that is why freedom of assembly is especially important

[159] BVerfGE 69, 315, 348.

[160] Ibid. The quote as translated by www.utexas.edu/law/academics/centers/transnational/work_new/german/case.php?Ibid=656.

[161] *Martin v City of Struthers*, 319 US 141 (1943) 146.

for ordinary citizens and civil society organisations that otherwise lack access to media or the potential to influence political processes.[162]

v. Self-governance and Democracy Arguments in Free Speech Jurisprudence Applied to Assemblies

A final democracy-related rationale actually emerges from considering the relation between expression and assembly from an angle different from the one applied above as to the relation of assembly and expression.

Famously, the *general free speech doctrine* of especially, but not exclusively, the US Supreme Court, relies strongly on a so-called *self-government or democratic theory rationale* for the protection of speech, which then is *applicable to assemblies* as well if they are considered expressive. It is not possible to discuss various interpretations of the self-governance speech theory of the US Supreme Court here, but interpretations vary strongly from Alexander Meiklejohn[163] to Robert Post[164] to Cass Sunstein[165] and many more,[166] all operating within the assumption that speech, especially on matters political, is essential to foster and maintain a liberal democracy, and thus deserves special, enhanced legal protection. US political speech doctrine is well-known for explicitly furthering a conscious (and 'fearless') citizenry, transplanting Millian and Miltonian truth seeking arguments into constitutional jurisprudence. Justice Holmes' *Gitlow* dissent also clearly underlies the idea that public speech should be able to translate into political action should the 'dominant forces of the country'[167] so decide, as it is 'the only meaning of free speech'.[168]

Indeed, many great free speech decisions based on one or other democratic speech theory actually involved assemblies, even if that does not merit any legal recognition in the judgment itself. Justice Brandeis has written the

[162] BVerfGE 69, 315, 346.

[163] Alexander Meiklejohn, *Political Freedom: The Constitutional Powers of the People* (Westport, CT, Greenwood Press, 1960); Alexander Meiklejohn, 'The First Amendment is an Absolute' (1961) *Supreme Court Review* 245.

[164] Robert Post, 'Community and the First Amendment' (1997) 29 *Arizona State Law Journal* 473; Robert Post, 'Racist Speech, Democracy, and the First Amendment' (1991) 32 *William and Mary Law Review* 267; Robert Post, 'Meiklejohn's Mistake: Individual Autonomy and the Reform of Public Discourse (1993) 64 *University of Colorado Law Review* 1109; Robert Post, 'Recuperating First Amendment Doctrine' (1995) 47 *Stanford Law Review* 1249; Robert Post, 'The Constitutional Status of Commercial Speech' (2000) 48 *University of California at Los Angeles Law Review* 1.

[165] Cass R Sunstein, *Democracy and the Problem of Free Speech*, 2nd edn (New York, Free Press, 1995).

[166] Eg Owen Fiss, *The Irony of Free Speech* (Cambridge, Harvard University Press, 1996). For an overview of US speech theories, see Matthew D Bunker, *Critiquing Free Speech. First Amendment Theory and the Challenge of Interdisciplinarity* (Mahwah, NJ, London, Lawrence Erlbaum Publishers, 2001).

[167] *Gitlow v New York*, 268 US 652, 672 (1925) (Holmes J dissenting).

[168] Ibid.

famous *Whitney* concurrence[169] to an assembly case, and most of the clear and present danger dissents of Holmes are about assemblies, only the regulations discussed were clearly content-based, and often aimed at 'associational speech'. The *Brandenburg* case concerning a Klu-Klux-Klan assembly, decided decades later, solidified the case law relating to incitement.

Justice Brandeis in *Whitney* is exceptional in that he articulates a positive or affirmative principle; the ideal of civil courage which since then underlies much of First Amendment jurisprudence, as Vincent Blasi[170] has shown. But the concurrence is also remarkable as it does refer to assembly next to speech, a rare case. Clearly, Justice Brandeis understood assemblies as deliberative meetings where reasoned argument might prevail, a view somewhat inapplicable to demonstrations which tend to only assert a stance or thematise an issue, and are less dialogical and discussing. On the other hand, mass hysteria according to him originates not from people assembling, but from government, as manifest in the paranoia of the Red Scare.[171] Thus, I still consider Justice Brandeis would apply a very similar reasoning to demonstrations as well, because demonstrations are even more clearly practices of civil courage, and are the essential occasions to prevent falling into public 'inertia'.

As discussed above (the relation between expression and assembly), the ECtHR also strongly endorses a democratic rationale of article 10 which is then applied to assemblies as well.

The Conseil Constitutionnel has not elaborated on this issue, but the collectivisation of articles 10 and 11 of the individualistic DDHC in the decision constitutionalising freedom of demonstration is certainly in line with an (untheorised or unspoken) democracy rationale of the *mediating sort*. Indeed, this would not be surprising as the Conseil Constitutionnel had rejected Le Chapelier traditions in relation to associations much earlier.[172] Thus—as a lesser danger—it is logical to also cease considering assemblies as obstacles to, and confounders of, the full expression of the general will in the *loi*. It might be all the more so as there is no mentioning whatsoever of the sovereign in decisions relating to demonstration or *réunions*. Any parallel to the German idea of similarity with referenda is also excluded because of the jurisprudence of the Council to de Gaulle's constitution amending

[169] *Whitney v California*, 274 US 357 (1927). See also Vincent Blasi, 'The First Amendment and the Ideal of Civic Courage: The Brandeis Opinion in *Whitney v California*' (1987) 29 *William and Mary Law Review* 653.

[170] Ibid.

[171] See Blasi, 'Civic Courage', above n 169, 386, with reference to *Pierce v United States*, 252 US 239, 269 (1920) (Brandeis J, dissenting); *Schaefer v United States*, 251 US 466, 482–83 (1920) (Brandeis J, dissenting).

[172] Decision no 71-44 DC, 16 July 1971 (Loi complétant les dispositions des articles 5 et 7 de la loi du 1er juillet 1901 relative au contrat d'association).

(and violating) referendum which was found to be indeed the original, untamed, direct voice of the sovereign.[173]

To sum up, democracy rationales proposed by the courts differ from each other. A large number of rationales consider assemblies as providing a *mediating* platform between the people (minority, majority, the non-powerful ordinary citizens, etc) and government, or in other words, public opinion and governmental decision-making, including lawmaking. It varies from court to court, or even case to case, if assembly is considered important for self-government, because it provides an expressive means for the poor, those lacking access to media, or more because assemblies are occasions for deliberation, or because they signal discontent to government, etc.

Not exactly in these words, but the formation argument by the German court clearly emphasises the agenda setting function of assemblies, too, and might also refer to the potential of assemblies to provide forum of crystallisation for emerging political forces. The reverse, self-government theory of *speech* actually first characterises something as speech, and then explains its high protection by its instrumentality to further self-governance.

At the other end of the spectrum there is only the idea of the untamed direct democracy mentioned in *Brokdorf*, the opposite of the representative, mediating rationales.

C. The Value of Liberty

Finally, freedom of assembly protects liberty, or furthers liberty again in a few senses.

As explained above, for Dicey and the classic English understanding, freedom of assembly was not a right, only a liberty, meaning it could be restricted by reasonable laws, regulations or common law. The value protected is the unspecified liberty of the subjects, which—as exigencies require—can be limited in rational and formal ways (by law especially).

In the German understanding, freedom of assembly is a *Freiheitsrecht*, naturally securing a state-free zone for private initiatives, but this 'freedom right' is a claim right obliging the state not to interfere with its free exercise. Positive state obligations flowing from freedom of assembly do not contradict the nature of *Freiheitsrecht*. At least in theory, the negative aspect of a freedom right has priority over the positive aspect, as the court regularly stresses that basic rights are first of all *Abwehrrechte*, rights to avert state interference within a sphere of freedom.[174]

[173] Decision no 62-20 DC, 6 November 1962.

[174] See only *Lüth*, BVerfGE 7, 198, 204 (1958): 'With no doubt, basic rights are first of all defined to secure a sphere of freedom of the individual against interferences by the public power, they are rights of the citizen against the state to avert interference.' That is why, eg

Clearly, Roman Herzog's idea about freedom of assembly providing a space for personality unfolding in group form is closely related to both liberty and dignity, as it is the case also with the general personality right in German doctrine.

In French legal scholarship, freedom of assembly is discussed under the heading *liberté publique*, a traditional concept in complete flux since the 1990s. *Liberté publique* is translated as civil liberty and as *bürgerliche Freiheit* in scholarly articles in the field.[175] *Liberté fondamentale*, the newer concept, is translated as fundamental right by some, but it still obviously keeps its liberty-centered function. It seems that with the passage from *liberté publique* to *liberté fondamentale* or *droits de l'homme* in legal teaching, and partially in positive law,[176] the French are moving in the direction of German, American or ECtHR understanding of rights. This evolving question, however, belongs to another discussion.[177]

the idea that demonstrators are obliged to cooperate with police because that is how they can promote their own freedom of assembly earned so much critique.

[175] See, eg the following articles in *Jus Politicum* (*Revue de droit politique*), in French, German, and English versions here www.juspoliticum.com/+-libertes-publiques-+.html?lang=en.

[176] See the *liberté référé* procedure introduced in 2000, art L 521-2 of the Code de Justice Administrative states: 'if the judge of référés receives a request justified by urgency, he can order any measure necessary to protect a fundamental freedom if a public law legal person [ie public authority] has, in exercising its powers, inflicted a grave and manifestly illegal attack on that freedom'.

[177] See, eg Véronique Champeil-Desplats, 'Des "libertés publiques" aux "droits fondamentaux": effets et enjeux d'un changement de denomination' www.juspoliticum.com/IMG/pdf/JP5_Champeil_corr01-2.pdf; Olivier Beaud, 'Remarques introductives sur l'absence d'une théorie des libertés publiques dans la doctrine publiciste. Ouverture d'un colloque de l'Institut Villey', www.juspoliticum.com/Remarques-introductives-sur-l.html, (2010–11) 5 *Revue Internationale de droit politique* entitled 'Mutation ou crépuscule des libertés publiques?', www.juspoliticum.com/-No5-.html.

2

Prior Restraints, Exemptions and Bargain

I. PRIOR RESTRAINT IN GENERAL

FREEDOM OF ASSEMBLY is the right where prior restraints abound. The duty to notify or even apply for a permit is a common feature of national jurisdictions. Advance notice and permit might give occasion even to a prior ban of an assembly, and it is a regular option for the police to impose some conditions on route, date, duration, appearance, or even content of the message. Some legal orders like the German establish a duty to cooperate with police before the assembly takes place, again others might require high permit fees or insurance. These might have an effect of either completely preventing the assembly or changing its message one way or the other.

Traditionally, prior restraint referred to censorship of press products. It is in this area where the special dangers of prior restraint were reflected by philosophers, lawyers and writers. Censorship in England was introduced in a sixteenth-century law requiring royal permission for every press product. John Milton refers to several reasons against a newly reintroduced censorship of press products in his 1644 pamphlet *Areopagitica* in the midst of the revolution. According to Milton, censorship is bad because truth will win in the long run if it can freely encounter with falsehood,[1] and no book should be eliminated in advance because[2]

> as good almost kill a man as kill a good book: who kills a man kills a reasonable creature, God's image; but he who destroys a good book, kills reason itself, kills the image of God, as it were in the eye.

Blackstone writes in his Commentaries:[3]

> The liberty of the press is indeed essential to the nature of a free state; but this consists in laying no previous restraints upon publications, and not in freedom from

[1] '[T]hough all the winds of doctrine were let loose to play on the earth, so Truth be in the field, we do injuriously, by licensing and prohibiting, to misdoubt her strength. Let her and Falsehood grapple; who ever knew Truth put to the worse, in a free and open encounter?' John Milton, *Aeropagitica. A Speech of Mr John Milton for the Liberty of Unlicensed Printing to the Parliament of England* (1644) (Richard C Ebb (ed), Cambridge, Cambridge University Press, 1918) 58.

[2] Ibid, 7.

[3] William Blackstone, *Commentaries on the Laws of England* as cited in *Near v Minnesota*, 283 US 697, 714 (1931).

> censure for criminal matter when published. Every freeman has an undoubted right to lay what sentiments he pleases before the public; to forbid this, is to destroy the freedom of the press; but if he publishes what is improper, mischievous or illegal, he must take the consequence of his own temerity.

Though sometimes similar in argument, another famous proponent of free speech, John Stuart Mill, in the nineteenth century, intended to provide arguments for a much freer press and speech in general than Milton.[4] Milton, just as Blackstone, can be distinguished from John Stuart Mill in that the previous commentators would consider traditional *ex post facto* restrictions acceptable, even desirable, their main concern being the abolition of prior restraint.

Closer to our time, Thomas Emerson reasoned that prior restraint is more inhibiting than subsequent punishment since:[5]

— it is likely to bring under government scrutiny a far wider range of expression;
— it shuts off communication before it takes place;
— suppression by a stroke of a pen is more likely to be applied than suppression through a criminal process;
— the procedures do not require attention to the safeguards of the criminal process;
— the system allows less opportunity for public appraisal and criticism;
— the dynamics of the system drive toward excesses, as the history of all censorship shows.

Martin Redish takes up only some of Emerson's reasons arguing that administrative prior restraints 'authorise abridgment of expression prior to a full and fair determination of the constitutionally protected nature of the expression by an independent judicial forum', but thinks that no other basis 'exists on which to disfavor prior restraints as compared to subsequent punishment schemes'.[6] Redish, therefore, finds that prior restraints imposed by the judiciary, in a procedure accompanied by a fair and full hearing, should be considered less problematic than administrative prior restraints and judicial prior restraint issued in a procedure with lacking guarantees, as the evil of prior restraint lies in the lack of due process. Blackstone also did not mean by 'prior restraint' a restriction on speech which 'a fair and impartial *trial* shall be adjudged of a pernicious tendency'.[7]

[4] John Stuart Mill, *On Liberty*, ch II (1859) (David Spitz (ed), (New York, WW Norton, 1975) 17–53.

[5] Thomas Emerson, *The System of Freedom of Expression* (New York, Vintage Books, 1970) 506.

[6] Martin H Redish, 'The Proper Role of the Prior Restraint Doctrine in First Amendment' (1984) 70 *Virginia Law Review* 53, 57.

[7] St George Tucker, *Blackstone's Commentaries: With Notes of Reference, to the Constitution and Laws, of the Federal Government of the United States; And of the Commonwealth of Virginia* (1803) (Clark, NJ, Lawbook Exchange, 1996) 152.

In my view even judicially supervised prior restraint is more pernicious than judicially supervised posterior restraint, though certainly Blackstone and Redish are right in claiming that administrative restraint is always more pernicious to liberty than restraints found justified in a fair and impartial trial.

In the case of freedom of assembly, both of these distinctions are relevant, because most often prior restraints are of an administrative kind, and often courts are not accorded prompt and substantive review powers, and even if they formally are, they might feel unfit for reviewing questions deemed 'policing'.

An assembly differs significantly from freedom of the press, thus the question arises to what extent the aforementioned dangers of censorship apply to permit and/or advance notice of assemblies, and the resulting possibilities of prior ban and conditions. Censorship of press products, as argued by Milton, hinders the 'discovery of truth', and equals the 'destruction of reason'. This argument clearly applies to freedom of 'assembly as meeting', or what the French call *réunion*, where there is a discussion of ideas. It applies much less to demonstrations and protests where there is no discussion, and the point is to 'take a stance' and show support or exert political pressure. However, as demonstration is also communication, is also a meaning–producing act, thus, it can also contribute to the discovery of truth. Even if some 'truth' is rather 'discovered' alone, its distribution or effective dissemination to a larger audience is necessary in a democracy where 'truth' translates into law only if supported by a certain number of people, or representatives of the people. This is a function fulfilled by assemblies, including demonstrations.

Furthermore, if one accepts that comprehension is not a solely intellectual and sterile undertaking, that is not only argumentative essays but also symbolic appeals or staged performances contribute to it, then assemblies fulfil a function to which prior restraint is harmful even in cases where there is no intention or hope to translate the message into law. It is not that an assembly does not produce and convey meaning (and, in this sense, 'truth') though—at most—it might be that an assembly is potentially more immediately dangerous than a scholarly or newspaper article.

Emerson's concerns are also largely valid in relation to freedom of assembly: the possibility of prior ban administered by an authority within the executive power runs the risk of being overbroad, inflicted without proper investigation and thus either intentionally or accidentally in error, as the protestors did not have the chance to actually behave lawfully. Also, administrative discretion inherent in issuing permits and accepting or denying notifications might be exercised arbitrarily, that is by favouring demonstrators promoting a mainstream or government-endorsed view, while disadvantaging less mainstream views and groups.

Emerson's argument from public appraisal and criticism applies in modified form to freedom of assembly: again, as to meetings, discussion there actually facilitates the very fact of public appraisal and criticism, and secondly, as to demonstrations, they often serve to put an issue to the agenda of public discourse.

On the other hand, it should be conceded, assemblies might be more *immediately* dangerous than argumentative essays, the paradigmatic press product. As John Stuart Mill's example suggests:[8]

> An opinion that corn-dealers are starvers of the poor, or that private property is robbery, ought to be unmolested when simply circulated through the press, but may justly incur punishment when delivered orally to an excited mob assembled before the house of a corn-dealer, or when handed about among the same mob in the form of a placard.

Already the bodily presence of several persons enhances the potential for violence as violence needs bodies (except in the sense used by Catherine MacKinnon), while with a newspaper article one first has to read it, think it over, and go around and 'attack the corn-dealer'. Certainly these barriers are partly not present at all on assemblies in front of the house of the corn-dealer. Thus, Mill is right, even if social movement studies often describe soberness and deliberate moderation in assemblies. However, Mill does not say, quite to the contrary, that assemblies in front of the house of the corn-dealer can be banned in advance. The most he would accept, maybe, is that a condition might be imposed on the organiser not to say that corn-dealers are starvers of the poor, because that would amount to incitement too close to actual harm. Still, the text itself only speaks about punishment, which is inflicted necessarily only after the incriminated sentences had been uttered in a concrete situation.

In the following, jurisprudence on advance notice and permits will be discussed first, followed by the issue of possible prior bans and prior imposition of conditions on assemblies as those presuppose the awareness of authorities about an upcoming event, allegedly secured by the advance notice or permit requirement. Finally, the question of exemptions from prior restraint (in effect notice and permit) will be discussed, to also emphasise a curious similarity of legal treatment of tradition and spontaneity.

II. ADVANCE NOTICE OR PERMIT

A. United States: Proprietary Theory, Fight Against Vagueness and the Turn to Content-neutrality

i. Governmental Property versus Vagueness

'Permit requirements were unheard of through most of the nineteenth century' as an expert of legal history of the right to assembly in the United States testifies.[9] When they were introduced, however, courts largely upheld them.

[8] Mill, *On Liberty*, above n 4, 53.

[9] Tabatha Abu El-Haj, 'The Neglected Right of Assembly' (2009) 56 *University of California at Los Angeles Law Review* 543, 545. She continues: 'As late as 1881, Chicago, Denver, Detroit, St. Paul, and San Francisco had no permit requirements for assemblies in their

The first paradigmatic decision on permit to access public parks and streets comes from Justice Holmes while still sitting at the Supreme Judicial Court of Massachussetts, in the *Davis* case from 1895.[10]

Holmes' argument, upholding the permit, was essentially that the owner of public property (the state or, by delegation, the city) is in a similar situation as a private owner to completely control uses of the property, thus, it can also limit the uses which it allows (the greater power includes the lesser).[11] The Supreme Court of the United States basically approved of this view in the case,[12] which is commonly called 'the proprietary theory' of public forums.

The analogy with private property is fallacious for several reasons. Streets and parks are not owned by private persons (or, if private persons own similarly looking parcels of land, they are not considered to be streets and parks), and their function is public use, for the benefit of the user, and not for the owner.

Also, at the constitutional level, it can be argued that the law cannot confer property rights on the government in the same vein as to private persons, since the rationale of protecting property is the protection against governmental intrusion.[13]

Furthermore, the ordinance in question in the *Davis* case authorised the mayor to deny permit at his discretion. Both Justice Holmes and the US Supreme Court explained this unlimited discretion again with reference to the proprietary theory: as the greater power includes the lesser, the power to absolutely ban public speaking includes the power to allow use of public places under whatever conditions (ie depending on a discretionary decision of the mayor) the legislative finds fit. As Abernathy points out, the simplistic formula of 'the greater power includes the lesser' ignores the dangers inherent in unlimited legislative delegation.[14]

The proprietary theory of public places came under attack only 42 years later at the US Supreme Court, in *Hague v Committee of Industrial*

streets. In fact, it was not until July 7, 1914 that New York City adopted a permit requirement for parades and processions in its streets, and as late as 1931 the city did not require permits for street meetings'.

[10] *Commonwealth v Davis*, 162 Mass 510, 39 NE 113 (1895). An ordinance prohibited different kinds of public addresses in or upon any kinds of public grounds without first acquiring a permit form the mayor.

[11] For the legislature absolutely or conditionally to forbid public speaking in a highway or public park is no more an infringement of the rights of a member of the public than for the owner of a private house to forbid it in his house. When no proprietary rights interfere, the legislature may end the right of the public to enter upon the public place by putting an end to the dedication to public uses. So it may take the less step of limiting the public use to certain purposes. *Commonwealth v Davis*, 162 Mass 510, 511 (1895) per Holmes J.

[12] *Davis v Commonwealth of Massachusetts*, 167 US 43, 17 S Ct 731 (1897).

[13] M Glenn Abernathy, *The Right of Assembly and Association*, 2nd edn (Columbia, SC, University of South Carolina Press, 1981) 111.

[14] Ibid, 110 ff.

Organisation.[15] The lower courts found in favour of the labour demonstrators, and affirmed that their right of passage (not assembly!)[16] upon the streets and access to the parks of the city and other rights (eg to a hearing, etc) were violated. Writing for the Supreme Court, Justice Roberts famously modified the Holmesian proprietary theory, nonetheless without having truly rebutted its fundamental assumptions. He wrote that even though public property, streets and parks have been—from time immemorial—held in trust for the use of the public for purposes of assembly and public discussion.[17]

The *Davis* and *Hague* cases have been subject to considerable scholarly discussion ever since their adoption. I find it is important to point out that Justice Roberts did not reject the basic rationale of the *Davis* judgment: he did not question that as a rule places the title of which belongs to the state or municipality, can be controlled by the government as fully as if it were a private owner. It is just that he replied with his own common law view to the common law view picked by Justice Holmes: 'trust' for the benefit of the public is a catchy analogy, but it clearly stays within the paradigm of common law property rights,[18] or as Harry Kalven points out, it only allows for a kind of First Amendment easement[19] on the otherwise absolutely controlled 'private' property of the state.

[15] *Hague v Committee of Industrial Organisation*, 307 US 496 (1939). A challenge was brought against a Jersey City ordinance which prescribed that no public assembly can be held without the permit of the director of public safety. Respondents wanted to organise meetings and explain to workingmen the purposes of the National Labor Relations Act, and other issues related to the labour activities of the Committee of Industrial Organisation. They were denied a permit and even ousted from the city by force, and they were also subject to searches, seizures, and criminal persecution. There was no allegation of violence, fraud, disorderliness, etc committed by the respondents, neither any danger of it.

[16] This reference clearly shows the inherited conceptual tools of the English law. Interestingly, the historical existence of the right to passage and its obvious influence on early American court cases do not seem to register for nowadays otherwise excellent First Amendment scholars, eg Edwin Baker, speculate pages long on what could be the reason for the early privileging of parades over street and park meetings in 19th century America, and he can only imagine ideological ones. Basically the same is true of the classic writer in the field, Glenn Abernathy. See Baker, *Human Liberty and Freedom of Speech* (Oxford, Oxford University Press 1992) 139–42, and Abernathy, *The Right of Assembly*, above n 13, 94–98, on whom Baker largely seems to rely, Baker, ibid, 318 and 320, fns 3, 9 and 13.

[17] The quote is at 307 US 515, 516: 'Wherever the title of streets and parks may rest, they have immemorially been held in trust for the use of the public and, time out of mind, have been used for purposes of assembly, communicating thoughts between citizens, and discussing public questions. Such use of the streets and public places has, from ancient times, been a part of the privileges, immunities, rights, and liberties of citizens. The privilege of a citizen of the United States to use the streets and parks for communication of views on national questions may be regulated in the interest of all; it is not absolute, but relative, and must be exercised in subordination to the general comfort and convenience, and in consonance with peace and good order; but it must not, in the guise of regulation, be abridged or denied'.

[18] Geoffrey Stone, 'Fora Americana: Speech in Public Places' (1974) *Supreme Court Review* 233, 238. See also Abernathy, *The Right of Assembly*, above n 13, 111, who calls it the 'private ownership theory of public property'.

[19] Harry Kalven Jr, 'The Concept of Public Forum: *Cox v Louisiana*' (1965) *Supreme Court Review* 1, 13.

The easement idea probably stems from Judge Clark sitting on the trial court, who proposed that a distinction should be made between parks and streets, and as to the use of parks, an easement of assemblage should be included.[20] The Supreme Court adopted this idea but without restricting it to parks, thus, it applies to streets as well. Thus, for those (maybe all) parks and streets, which have been for a long time used for purposes of assembly and public discussion, an exception has been carved out. As the argument is supported by tradition, not by a normative idea, its application can be limited.[21]

The *Hague* judgment did not overrule *Davis*, for which one reason might be that at the time *Davis* was decided, First Amendment standards were not incorporated and thus were inapplicable to the states.[22]

Technically, however, the court distinguished *Davis*, even if in a rather unconvincing way. It said that the ordinance in *Davis* was different since it not only regulated the right to assembly, but also various other activities, and, unlike the Jersey City ordinance concerned in *Hague*, it was 'a general measure to promote the public convenience in the use of the streets or parks'.[23]

Significantly, the *Hague* trust argument does not mean that the permit system is impermissible, just that there should not be too much discretion in granting it. The ordinance authorised the Director of Public Safety to refuse a permit only for the 'purpose of preventing riots, disturbances or disorderly assemblage'. The courts did not find any evidence of a danger of riots, disturbances or disorder, and, what is more, found the ordinance, on its face, unconstitutional. In a similar vein to that argued above, concerning the difference between prior restraint for violence prevention and for practical reconciliation of competing uses, Justice Roberts explains:[24]

> [The ordinance] does not make comfort or convenience in the use of streets or parks the standard of official action. It enables the Director of Safety to refuse a permit on his mere opinion that such refusal will prevent 'riots, disturbances or disorderly assemblage'. It can thus, as the record discloses, be made the

[20] 'For some quite, in our opinion, illogical reason the American cases do not seem to stress the obvious difference between a street and a park. We are not willing to eliminate the latter. It seems to us that the purpose of most parks is the recreation of the public ... We include in that word recreation an easement of assemblage ... We hold then that a municipality's proprietary right is subject to an easement of assemblage in such parks as are dedicated to the general recreation of the public'. *CIO v Hague*, 25 F Supp 127, 145 (DCNJ, 1938) as quoted by Abernathy, *The Right of Assembly*, above n 13, 119.

[21] What is more, tradition is not meant to be common law history. It is a metaphoric statement which is supposed to evoke emotional support for the proposition. The high tone of the metaphor, however, does not make up for the lack of a clear constitutional theory.

[22] *Cf* Geoffrey R Stone, Louis M Seidman, Cass R Sunstein, Mark V Tushnet and Pamela S Karlan, *The First Amendment*, 2nd edn (New York, Aspen, 2003) 296.

[23] 307 US 515.

[24] 307 US 516.

> instrument of arbitrary suppression of free expression of views on national affairs, for the prohibition of all speaking will undoubtedly 'prevent' such eventualities. But uncontrolled official suppression of the privilege cannot be made a substitute for the duty to maintain order in connection with the exercise of the right.

Note that the court would consider 'comfort or convenience' a less discretionary standard than prevention of disorder and violence. Thus, I argue, it is to say that comfort or convenience is understood rather narrowly, for example when permits for two demonstrations are requested for the same time and place, but this has never been clarified by the Supreme Court. Clearly, Martin Redish would advocate such an interpretation of the First Amendment which restricts administrative (and non-adversarial judicial) decision-making to the duties of the 'reservationist' who resolves schedule conflicts in favour of the first applicant for a demonstration.[25] That would in effect transform the permit system in a notification system, as it is practiced, or at least theoretically, strived for elsewhere.

Edwin Baker goes even further or, rather, in fundamentally different way. He suggests that the current, mandatory permit systems should be changed to a voluntary one.[26]

However, the US jurisprudence evolved and seems evolving neither in the Redishian nor Bakerian fashion. It quite clearly does not question the acceptability of prior restraint as such, be it judicially or administratively imposed. The question around which the doctrine on prior restraint revolves is not whether and what, but how. Through further cases on prior restraints on freedom of assembly and protest, the court refined the above approach, without clearly rejecting the underlying proprietary theory. There is a strong legal technical jargon which came to be applied in matters of permit system, fees and the like, making the doctrine of prior restraints on assemblies not necessarily clearer or more consistent.[27] The general doctrine of prior restraint was allegedly found applicable to protests and demonstrations, though this does not mean that permit requirements would be per se or even presumptively unconstitutional (unlike in 'general' prior restraint doctrine). In *Cox v New Hampshire*, a case decided just two years

[25] '[T]he clear constitutional preference for a judicial rather than an administrative determination would seem to require the administrators to resort to the judiciary to restrain a proposed demonstration for reasons other than schedule conflicts. Though authorities not given notice of a planned demonstration obviously will have insufficient opportunity to seek a judicial order, most demonstration planners will wish to notify the authorities if only to reserve the exclusive opportunity to parade at their chosen time and place'. Redish, above n 6, 85.

[26] Baker, *Human Liberty*, above n 16, 137.

[27] 'Presently these regulatory devices [ie prior restraints] are subject only to the most amorphous of constitutional controls. Although the Supreme Court has favored street protestors with volumes of rhetoric and numerous after-the fact legal victories, it has contributed virtually nothing in the way of concrete standards and procedures that have any impact when constitution is most needed—before and during the demonstration'. Vincent Blasi, 'Prior Restraints on Demonstrations' (1969–70) 68 *Michigan Law Review* 1482.

after *Hague v CIO*, the court unanimously upheld the conviction of a group of Jehovah's Witnesses who assembled peacefully and non-disruptively on the sidewalks (!) without first having obtained a permit, without much theorising about the point of the permit system. Dicta in *Cox* indicates that the court finds the permit system something which enhances, rather than restricts, the rights of citizens in the use of public streets:[28]

> Civil liberties, as guaranteed by the Constitution, imply the existence of an organised society maintaining public order without which liberty itself would be lost in the excesses of unrestrained abuses. The authority of a municipality to impose regulations in order to assure the safety and convenience of the people in the use of public highways has never been regarded as inconsistent with civil liberties but rather as one of the means of safeguarding the good order upon which they ultimately depend.

In later cases, the court explicitly talks about 'competing uses of public forums'[29] and there is no indication that freedom of assembly would enjoy a privileged status among uses of the street. At least, however, there remains a significant difference between the language of the US and the English courts: the US courts do not think that the primary use of the street is passage or transport, etc.

A further strain in the doctrine of prior restraint evolved in a curious intermingling with the doctrine on vagueness and overbreadth, sometimes found problematic in the literature.[30] Still, the strongest protection against prior restraint of assembly is offered by vagueness (and, to a lesser extent, overbreadth) jurisprudence. Several decisions reiterate that a licensing statute or ordinance granting 'unbridled discretion' to a government official constitutes a prior restraint and 'may result in censorship',[31] and that 'a law subjecting the exercise of First Amendment freedoms to the prior restraint of a license, without narrow, objective, and definite standards to guide the licensing authority, is unconstitutional'.[32]

For example, in *Cantwell v Connecticut*, an important case involving Jehovah's Witnesses, the statute in question prohibited

> solicitation of money, services, subscriptions or any valuable thing for any alleged religious, charitable or philanthropic cause, from other than a member of the organisation for whose benefit such person is soliciting or within the county

[28] *Cox v New Hampshire*, 312 US 569, 574 (1941).

[29] Eg *Forsyth County v Nationalist Movement*, 505 US 123, 129 (1992).

[30] Eg John Calvin Jeffries, 'Rethinking Prior Restraint' (1983) 92 *Yale Law Journal* 409.

[31] *Lakewood v Plain Dealer Publishing Co*, 486 US 750, 757 (1988) cites '*Shuttlesworth, supra*, at 349 US 151; *Cox v Louisiana*, 379 US 536 (1965); *Staub v City of Baxley*, 355 US 313, 355 US 321–22 (1958); *Kunz v New York*, 340 US 290, 340 US 294 (1951); *Niemotko v Maryland*, 340 US 268 (1951); *Saia v New York*, 334 US 558 (1948)' to this effect.

[32] *Shuttlesworth*, 349 US 147, 150, 151 (1969).

> in which such person or organisation is located unless such cause shall have been approved by the secretary of the public welfare council.[33]

The court found the statute unconstitutional, and spelled out two principles with regard to solicitation on public streets. The first one is that only ministerial authority, and not discretion, can be constitutionally vested in administrative city officials, and a decision on the religious nature of the solicitation is a discretionary decision. Furthermore, the court declared applicable a principle established as to prior restraint in general speech and press cases. With reference to *Near v Minnesota*,[34] the court affirmed that a 'statute authorising previous restraint upon the exercise of the guaranteed freedom by judicial decision after trial is as obnoxious to the Constitution as one providing for like restraint by administrative action'.[35]

The Supreme Court thus rejected that the wrong of a discretionarily imposed prior ban on demonstration can be corrected by later judicial action. As the judiciary will also rely on the authorising legal text, it is not possible for them to review whether there was abuse in exercising the discretion. As another US Supreme Court decision in *Lakewood*

[33] *Cantwell v Connecticut*, 310 US 296, 301 ff (1940). The Witnesses went to a Catholic-populated area of New Haven, solicited books, and, if permitted, played phonograph records (critical of Catholicism, but directly advocating the beliefs of Jehovah's Witnesses). The listeners were not Witnesses and the solicitors did not have a permit. Jesse Cantwell played a phonograph record to two Catholic men who, 'incensed by the contents of the record, wanted to strike Cantwell unless he went away, so he rather left indeed. There was no suggestion that he was personally offensive or entered into any argument with anyone'. 310 US 296, 303, Supreme Court summarising the fact finding of the lower court.

[34] *Near v Minnesota*, 283 US 697 (1931), was about a perpetual injunction imposed in an adversarial procedure against a newspaper. The statute applied authorised the court to shut down a newspaper after a malicious, scandalous and defamatory publication unless the statement was either true or published 'with good motives and for justifiable ends'. That the court qualified the injunction as prior restraint, instead of invalidating the law for other (chilling effect, vagueness, etc) reasons, was criticised heavily by some. Eg Jeffries, above n 30, 414 ff. The claim is that the court decided *Near* on wrong procedural grounds instead of substantive ones, while it still reached the correct result. The wrong procedural grounds, ie the qualification of an injunction issued in an adversarial process as impermissible prior restraint, has also put the prior restraint doctrine on the wrong track for the future, which is unfortunate. To be truthful to history, I think one has to add that the reason for the allegedly improper confusion of procedural and substantive concerns might be that the court in *Near* did not necessarily have so many alternatives in 1931, when none of the substantive doctrines of free speech was fully elaborated, let alone supported by a majority of the court. However, the recourse to the evil of prior restraint might have struck a familiar chord and constituted a common denominator among the justices. It is also useful to add that the *Near* claim that 'a statute authorising previous restraint upon the exercise of the guaranteed freedom by judicial decision after trial is as obnoxious to the Constitution as one providing for like restraint by administrative action' takes up a different, far more complex use in later cases. As explained in the main text, in *Cantwell* it is said that the possibility of judicial review of an administrative prior restraint imposed on the basis of a law which grants unbridled discretion does not correct the vice of prior restraint. Thus, though *Near* has been about injunction issued in a 'due process', it also holds for administrative prior restraints, and it does have a relation to vagueness and overbreadth.

[35] *Cantwell*, 310 US 306.

(on prior restraint related to newsracks, but equally applicable) stated, while allowing facial challenge to permit ordinances granting unfettered discretion: 'The absence of express standards makes it difficult to distinguish "as applied" between a licensor's legitimate denial of a permit and its illegitimate abuse of censorial power'.[36]

Apart from this impossibility for the court to review the exercise of discretion, there is another recurring argument against vagueness: the evil of self-censorship or chilling effect. *Lakewood* quotes[37] language from *Thornhill v Alabama*[38] which is worth recalling here:

> Proof of an abuse of power in the particular case has never been deemed a requisite for attack on the constitutionality of a statute purporting to license the dissemination of ideas.... The power of the licensor against which John Milton directed his assault by his 'Appeal for the Liberty of Unlicensed Printing' is pernicious not merely by reason of the censure of particular comments, but by the reason of the threat to censure comments on matters of public concern. It is *not merely the sporadic abuse of power by the censor, but the pervasive threat inherent in its very existence* that constitutes the danger to freedom of discussion. (Emphasis added)

Dissemination of ideas and freedom of discussion are the particular values which are to be protected against fear and against self-imposed restraints which would otherwise chill speech clearly constitutionally protected.

After so many affirmations on narrow and objective standards required for prior restraints on solicitation, canvassing, book selling, labour picketing, solicitation of membership of organisation, and so on, *Shuttlesworth v City of Birmingham*[39] was—apart from invalidating a completely standardless and arbitrary customary permit system in *Niemotko*[40]—the first modern case on permits required specifically for assemblies where the court found

[36] *City of Lakewood*, 486 US 750, 758 (1988).

[37] 486 US 757.

[38] *Thornhill v Alabama*, 310 US 88, 97. Thornhill, on its own, is again a rather easy case, and it is not clearly about prior restraint. The petitioner was saying to one of his co-workers that 'they were on strike, and did not want anybody to go up there to work', in a peaceful manner, without the use of threat or any abuse. He was charged and convicted on the basis of an anti-loitering and anti-picketing statute which flatly prohibited a wide range of communicative acts except if done with a lawful excuse. Its significance lies not so much in the invalidation of the act, but rather in the idea (quoted in the main text) that not only 'the sporadic abuse of power of the censor' but 'the pervasive threat' of its very existence is what really undermines free speech.

[39] 394 US 147 (1969). The decision's role in the civil rights movement is explained in David Benjamin Oppenheimer, 'Kennedy, King, Shuttlesworth and Walker: The Events Leading to the Introduction of the Civil Rights Acts of 1964' (1995) 29 *University of San Francisco Law Review* 645, 650–54.

[40] The 1951 case of *Niemotko v Maryland* was about a park meeting permit system, where there was absolutely no standard, however vague, to be applied, and arguably there was even no legal base (no ordinance or regulation, just a sort of custom required permit for public meetings in parks) for the issuance of permits. *Niemotko v Maryland*, 340 US 268 (1951).

invalidity of standards.[41] *Shuttlesworth* involved a march organised by a black minister, who was earlier 'clearly given to understand'[42] that his march would never be allowed in Birmingham. The ordinance prescribing the permit requirement conferred upon the local administrators an absolute power to refuse a parade permit whenever they thought 'the public welfare, peace, safety, health, decency, good order, morals or convenience require that it be refused'. The State Supreme Court in the appellate procedure four years later construed this language so narrowly, that it would pass constitutional muster. Nonetheless, the US Supreme Court made clear that such 'an extraordinary clairvoyance for anyone to perceive that this language [of the ordinance quoted above] meant what the Supreme Court of Alabama was destined to find that it meant more than four years later',[43] is not expected by the Constitution.

Thus, the Supreme Court clearly rejected the argument that Shuttlesworth should have turned to the courts before he went on with the march. A law subjecting the right of free expression in publicly owned places to the prior restraint of a license, without narrow, objective, and definite standards is unconstitutional, and a person faced with such a law may ignore it and exercise his First Amendment rights.

Note, however, Justice Harlan's concurring opinion, where he would not dispense with the requirement to apply for a permit because a minor official interpreted a law in a way which was contrary to the Constitution. Rather, he finds problematic the lack of an effective and speedy remedy when facing such an official.[44] Thus, one can say, Harlan's view is less radical, and might be closer to the view of the ECtHR (European Court of Human Rights) as put forward in *Baczkowski,* discussed below. At the same time, Harlan has a point, and this point seems to have been painfully ignored by the court not so much in *Shuttlesworth* (the particular facts of which might indeed call for a radical dispensing of the permit application duty), but in later cases.

The obligation to provide an effective and speedy remedy is conspicuously missing from the US jurisprudence on freedom of assembly. The only case Justice Harlan is able to cite in 1969 is *Freedman v Maryland*,[45]

[41] At least I am not aware of any such case decided since *Cox v New Hampshire* gave such a generous approval to permit schemes, and the court in *Shuttlesworth* certainly does not cite any case where the ordinance requires a permit specifically for *assembly*, be it a march, meeting or otherwise. See *Lovell v City of Griffin*, 303 US 452–53, 58 S Ct 669; *Schneider v State*, 308 US 159, 165, 60 S Ct 152; *Largent v Texas*, 318 US 419, 422, 63 S Ct 668, 669; *Jones v City of Opelika*, 316 US 602, 62 S Ct 1241, adopted *per curiam* on rehearing, 319 US 104, 63 S Ct 890; *Staub v City of Baxley*, 355 US 319, 78 S Ct 280; *Freedman v Maryland*, 380 US 51, 56–57, 85 S Ct 734, 737–38, 13 L Ed 2d 649, all as cited in *Shuttlesworth*, 394 US 151.

[42] 394 US 158.

[43] Ibid.

[44] Ibid, 161.

[45] *Freedman v Maryland*, 380 US 51 (1965).

a *movie censorship* decision, which prohibits the state from requiring persons to invoke 'unduly cumbersome and time-consuming procedures before they may exercise their constitutional right of expression'.[46] *Freedman* also takes into account that judicial remedy, even if formally granted, might come too late and be too costly to be meaningful.[47] The Supreme Court, however, which neither before, nor after *Shuttlesworth* has fully accepted that the *Freedman* rationale applies to freedom of assembly, continues to ignore serious procedural inadequacies in the permit system of several states. This, together with the rising hegemony of the single focus on content neutrality, is a development which might threaten freedom of speech and assembly to a far greater extent than it seems at first glance.[48]

Finally, permit fees are the other issue where the US Supreme Court limited the discretion available to administrative officials, but at the same time the Court did not question the basic acceptability of the fee paying duty. That it is normal to pay a fee for the use of a public place for expressive purposes has again a clear connotation of proprietary theory, an author talks in this regard (without mentioning the proprietary theory) of a false assumption of a two-party business relationship between the speaker and government.[49] It remains unclear what exactly is the cost for which the fee can be exacted, and it is hard to resist the connotation of a 'rental fee'. The case of *Cox v New Hampshire* found the fee requirement, as such, acceptable—even adjustable fees were constitutional. A fee, which is 'not a revenue tax, but one to meet the expense incident to the administration of the Act and to the maintenance of public order in the matter licensed',[50] is constitutionally permissible, and the local government should enjoy flexibility in adjusting the fee to the varying circumstances of the particular assembly, as long as it does it in a fair and non-discriminatory way. The court even noted that the flexible adjustment might 'rather conserve than to impair' freedom of assembly.[51]

The case of *Cox* did not specify the limits of the fee exacting authority. In two cases on advance fees on selling literature, rendered shortly after *Cox*, a flat fee not matching the expenses incurred by the government was

[46] Harlan's summary in *Shuttlesworth*, 394 US 162.

[47] *Freedman v Maryland*, 380 US 61.

[48] *Cf* Edward L Carter and Brad Clark, 'Death of Procedural Safeguards: Prior Restraint, Due Process and the Elusive First Amendment Value of Content Neutrality' (2006) 11 *Communication Law & Policy* 225. With similar overtones in the context of 'national security' see Nick Suplina, 'Crowd Control: The Troubling Mix of First Amendment Law, Political Demonstrations, and Terrorism' (2005) 73 *George Washington Law Review* 395.

[49] David Goldberger, 'A Reconsideration of *Cox v New Hampshire*: Can Demonstrators be Required to Pay the Costs of Using America's Public Forums?' (1983) 62 *Texas Law Review* 403, 412.

[50] *Cox v New Hampshire*, 312 US 569, 577 (1941), again quoting the state Supreme Court's decision.

[51] Ibid.

found unconstitutional.[52] Then, in 1992, the Supreme Court in *Forsyth County v Nationalist Movement*,[53] struck down an adjustable permit fee regulation.[54] The ordinance entitled the administrator to adjust the fee so as to meet the cost 'incident to the administration of the ordinance and to the maintenance of public order',[55] identical to the interpretation given by the state court in *Cox v New Hampshire*.[56] The Georgia ordinance in *Forsyth*, however, was further construed to allow the county administrator to charge the maximum fee, or even no fee at all, or, in any case, less than the cost incident to the administration and maintenance of public order.[57] This meant a fatal difference compared with *Cox*, and rendered the ordinance content-based according to the US Supreme Court, since the judgment on how much police force the maintenance of public order would require is necessarily based on the content of the speech.[58] *Forsyth* has not clearly decided whether only nominal fees are permitted, though this was a controversy between the circuits because of a Supreme Court precedent (*Murdock*) invalidating a fee considered a flat tax on door-to-door solicitation of religious literature which can be read as allowing for nominal fees.[59] Instead *Forsyth* said that the respective language in *Murdock* 'does not mean that an invalid fee can be saved if it is nominal, or that only nominal charges

[52] *Murdock v Pennsylvania*, 319 US 105 (1943), *Follett v Town of McCormick*, 321 US 573 (1944). For an analysis of the line of cases from *Cox* till 1983, see Goldberger, 'A Reconsideration of *Cox*', above n 49.

[53] *Forsyth County, Georgia v Nationalist Movement*, 505 US 123 (1992).

[54] The regulation at hand was enacted after civil rights demonstrations had been either seriously attacked or disturbed by counter-demonstrations organised by the Nationalist Movement, causing the police in charge of containing the counter-demonstrators unusually high costs, around $700,000. The ordinance adopted in reaction required every permit applicant to pay in advance a sum not more than $1,000 for each day of an assembly.

[55] *Forsyth*, above n 53, 126–27.

[56] *Cox v New Hampshire*, 312 US 569, 577 (1941).

[57] *Forsyth*, above n 53, 131.

[58] It remains unclear if in considering costs incident to maintaining public order is always content-based, or because anticipation of hostile audience presupposes content assessment. Most often, the content of the speech in this context will be judged with an eye to possible counter-demonstrators, since the costs flowing from a containment of the hostile group and the protection of the applicant demonstrators might become high. To state a higher fee because the speech will possibly face a hostile reaction is unacceptable content-based regulation. In that way, the hostile audience doctrine intermingles with prior restraint doctrine, even overbreadth, since the overbroad language of the statute allows for improper discretion which results in disadvantaging groups which might expect a hostile audience reaction in the view of the administrator. On hostile audience per se, see Ch 3.

[59] In *Murdock v Commonwealth of Pennsylvania*, 319 US 105 (1943), the court held that the license fee levied on the distribution—because the Witnesses would ask for very little or even no money in exchange if the person interested did not have money, it is not really a solicitation—of religious literature was a flat tax imposed on the exercise of a fundamental right. The court also noted that 'the fee is not a nominal one, imposed as a regulatory measure and calculated to defray the expense of protecting those on the streets and at home against the abuse of solicitors'. 319 US 105, 113.

are constitutionally permissible'. The only discernible principle in *Forsyth* is that anticipated hostile audience reaction cannot result in a higher fee.[60]

ii. From Non-discrimination to Content-neutrality: How Prior Restraint Becomes Content-neutral Injunction

The Supreme Court spelled out in several cases that the administration of permits shall not be discriminatory, that is denied for some and granted to others, when both are basically in the same situation. This is, one might say, an application of the rule of content-neutrality to the context of prior restraint on assemblies, though in the early cases when the court has not yet developed the content-neutrality principle, the term used is non-discrimination. Basically, in each and every case mentioned so far, the court was checking if the permit scheme was administrated in a non-discriminatory way.[61]

In 1983, in accordance with the general trend to systematise speech jurisprudence in the units of content-based and content-neutral restrictions, the court adopted a new formulation of the test applicable to permit schemes. According to *US v Grace*, 'any permit scheme controlling the time, place, and manner of speech must not be based on the content of the message, must be narrowly tailored to serve a significant governmental interest, and must leave open ample alternatives for communication'.[62] There will be a separate discussion on content-neutral restrictions on assemblies later;[63] here it suffices to point to two developments. By the mid-1980s, doctrinal thinking about prior restrictions on assemblies changes from the prior restraint framework to content-neutrality framework. Thinking in terms of content-neutrality still shares with prior restraint thinking a complete lack of reflection, let alone responsiveness to a basic problem Edwin Baker and others remarked on 20 years ago: that the permit scheme essentially discriminates against those who want to use the streets for expressive purposes—that is uses constitutionally protected—while those who are not expressing any views are free to walk on the streets without need of a permit.

[60] Note that the court does not distinguish between fees exacted in anticipation of hostile audience, and fees exacted incident to the maintenance of order for reasons other than hostile audience. Probably, a fee adjusted to the expected size of the applicant demonstration would be considered content-neutral, and a fee adjusted to anticipated disorder by the applicants themselves would have to fulfill the *Brandenburg* criteria of imminent likely lawless action, since, compelling interest in strict scrutiny with regard to prevention of disorder must mean a high probability and immediacy of unlawful action. None of these, however, is indicated in *Forsyth*, what is more, *Forsyth* has not been refined in any later case.

[61] *Cox*: 'There is no evidence that the statute has been administered otherwise than in the fair and non-discriminatory manner which the state court has construed it to require'. 312 US 577, *Shuttlesworth* quoting the same at 394 US 147, 156.

[62] *United States v Grace*, 461 US 171, 177 (1983).

[63] See Chs 6–8.

A parallel development worth mentioning is the conundrum concerning injunctions which by the beginning of the 1990s started to interest not only scholars, but the Court itself. In a series of cases related to confrontational (often, but not always previously violent) anti-abortion speech, the Court approved injunctions restricting the right of protest in (limited) buffer zones around health facilities. The important case of *Madsen v Women's Health Center*[64] raised the question of whether the injunction was directed against anti-abortion speakers for their views, that is whether an injunction phrased regardless of the content of the speech could still qualify as content-based if it had an exclusive impact on only one side of the debate. Disputed among the justices was the question whether the injunction at hand was a prior restraint at all. Chief Justice Rehnquist, writing for the Court, argued in a footnote that the injunction prohibiting expression within a 36-foot buffer zone was not a prior restraint, since it did not limit whether the protestor could speak, and only limited the place of the speech. Also, it was not a prior restraint since it did not aim at the content of the speech, but it was issued because of protestors' prior unlawful conduct. Justice Scalia, dissenting, argued that the injunction was clearly a prior restraint,[65] and was clearly content-based. Here what occupies me is less this latter issue, or who was right in the *Madsen* case,[66] but rather, I want to point out that both opinions think the issue of prior restraint turns on, or, is at least closely related to whether the injunction was content-neutral or content-based. Clearly, prior restraint arguments have become increasingly infused, or even overwhelmed, by the content-neutrality principle and the attached variety of tests. The beginnings, however, can be found in early cases urging limited discretion to ensure fair and non-discriminatory use of permit schemes and other prior restraints.

A final development related to permits on assemblies came in 2002 in the case of *Thomas v Chicago Park District*, a unanimous decision.[67] Justice Scalia wrote the very short judgment, upholding the constitutionality of a permit scheme against a facial challenge. The ordinance at hand required a permit for events involving more than 50 persons, and the Park District had altogether 28 days to make a decision. The ordinance listed 13 grounds on which the permit could be denied, among them violation of a previous permit

[64] *Madsen v Women's Health Center, Inc*, 512 US 753 (1994).

[65] '[A]n injunction against speech is the very prototype of the greatest threat to First Amendment values, the prior restraint'. 512 US 797.

[66] Some commentators tend to find fault more with Scalia J than with the majority, eg Owen Fiss on the exact matter, but one can be sure Martin Redish would also not think injunctions should get a stricter scrutiny than criminal statutes. I personally find persuasive the critique by Scalia about assumed facts on the part of the majority—and that might change the outcome, but certainly would side with the mentioned authors on the question of injunctions as such, and especially would not accept Scalia's claim that the collateral bar rule of *Walker v Birmingham* justifies strict scrutiny.

[67] *Thomas v Chicago Park District*, 534 US 316 (2002).

and misrepresentation of facts in the permit request. What might have come as a surprise, was that the Court declared the procedural safeguards elaborated in *Freedman* as not constitutionally required in case of content-neutral regulations of permits for parks (this was advocated by Justice Harlan in *Shuttlesworth* though that was a case on vagueness).

This means most importantly[68] that no prompt judicial review is constitutionally required, or, it is left undecided whether the judicial review is to be commenced or determined promptly. Also, it was of no concern that the park authority had almost a month to decide on the granting of a permit. Thus, one might need to ask for a permit months before a planned demonstration with over 50 participants in any of Chicago's parks and other public property, if one was to be sure to go on with the demonstration on or around the planned date (ie judicial review included).

Thomas v Chicago Park district shows the rather distorted nature of the allegedly speech protective American law when it comes to freedom of assembly, largely caused by the content neutrality or time, manner and place doctrine.[69] Such an outcome is not possible in Europe since the *Baczkowski* judgment of the ECtHR, as will be explained below. Nonetheless, it has to be noted that lower courts in the United States are often willing to strike down permit schemes with long deadlines, and even notification regimes, especially when it comes to smaller or single-person demonstrations or performances.[70] If one adds to this that *Thomas* was a facial challenge, it cannot be excluded that in the near future the US Supreme Court will refine its stance on prompt issuance of permits and speedy judicial remedy.

It is also clear that the press freedom cases can have some application to freedom of assembly, this, however, happens through the wide understanding of the concept of the press, and not through a wide understanding of the ban on prior restraint. In *Lovell v Griffin*, the court spelled out that[71]

> [t]he liberty of the press is not confined to newspapers and periodicals. It necessarily embraces pamphlets and leaflets. These indeed have been historic weapons

[68] *Freedman*, 380 US 51, 58–59 (1965), requires that 'noncriminal process which requires the prior submission of a film to a censor avoids constitutional infirmity only if it takes place under procedural safeguards designed to obviate the dangers of a censorship system. First, the burden of proving that the film is unprotected expression must rest on the censor ... exhibitor must be assured, by statute or authoritative judicial construction, that the censor will, *within a specified brief period, either issue a license or go to court* to restrain showing the film ... the procedure must also assure a prompt final judicial decision, to minimize the deterrent effect of an interim and possibly erroneous denial of a license'.

[69] For a similar view, see Robert H Whorf, 'The Dangerous Intersection at "Prior Restraint" and "Time, Place, Manner": A Comment on *Thomas v Chicago Park District*' (2002) 3 *Barry Law Review* 1.

[70] See the discussion in Nathan W Kellum, 'Permit Schemes: Under Current Jurisprudence, what Permits are Permitted?' (2008) 56 *Drake Law Review* 381, especially 405–22, and Edan Burkett, 'Coordination or Mere Registration? Single-Speaker Permits in *Berger v City of Seattle*' (2010) *Brigham Young University Law Review* 931.

[71] *Lovell v Griffin*, 303 US 444, 452 (1938).

in the defense of liberty, as the pamphlets of Thomas Paine and others in our own history abundantly attest. The press, in its historic connotation, comprehends every sort of publication which affords a vehicle of information and opinion.

That means that ordinances which condition leafleting, handbilling, and similar activities—which often, even typically accompany demonstrations and protests—on a prior permit, are unconstitutional.

B. Germany: Only Notice and Strict Proportionality

Unlike in the United States, in Germany, prior restraint has not become a central issue in freedom of assembly, and I would say, neither that of free speech. This is somewhat peculiar regarding strong textual and historical aversion towards prior restraint. The guarantee of freedom of expression of opinion in article 5 I of the Basic Law (GG) sets out the prohibition of censorship, which is understood to solely cover prior limits. Article 8 I GG guarantees the right to assemble 'without notice or permit', though paragraph II allows for statutory limits in case of assemblies under the open sky.

The prohibition of censorship in article 5 I does not, so far, have an application to assemblies and demonstrations, and as to the scholarly literature, there does not seem to be any claims as to the applicability of the prohibition of censorship either.[72]

Article 8 I GG guarantees the right to assemble without permit or notification, but paragraph II allows for restrictions on the basis of law regarding assemblies under the open sky.

It follows first that a permit or notification regime, with regard to indoors assemblies, would be clearly unconstitutional, and any regulation can only aim at ensuring that no arms are brought to the assembly, and it remains peaceful. As to outdoor assemblies, however, this provision enabled the federal and—since regulating assemblies became a *Länderkompetenz*—land legislation to require prior notice. The deadline traditionally has been way shorter than—as we have seen—conceivable in the United States; in German federal law it has been 48 hours. Also, there are strong voices in the literature claiming that to introduce a permit system for outdoor assemblies would be contrary to the German Constitution.[73]

[72] Though I once heard Alexander Blankenagel contemplating the possibility of applying the art 5 I censorship rule against prior bans of Neo-Nazi demonstrations. This has not become the case, so far at least: see the Rudolf Hess memorial march decision of the Constitutional Court, BVerfGE 124, 300 (2009).

[73] Philip Kunig, 'Kommentar zu Art 8' in Ingo von Münch and Philip Kunig (eds), *Grundgesetz-Kommentar I*, 5th edn (München, Beck, 2000) ann 27, 592.

Advance *notice* of outdoor assemblies, on the other hand, has explicitly been found constitutional in the seminal *Brokdorf* decision of the German Federal Constitutional Court (GFCC). Advance notice is required because outdoor assemblies have external effects which many times necessitate special advance measures. The notice includes information which enables the authorities to gain insights as to what measures are to be taken in order to facilitate the undisturbed course of the assembly, and, on the other hand, as to how to protect interests of third parties and the public interest, or, how to coordinate the two.[74]

While upholding the constitutionality of advance notice, the court restricted the scope of constitutionally permissible interpretation of some statutory rules related to it. The Federal Assembly Law contained discretionary language allowing the official to disperse an unnotified assembly without any further condition. The court spelled out that the verb 'can' (*kann*) does not mean unfettered discretion: dispersal is constitutionally warranted only if it is necessary for the protection of equally weighty values. Also, the proportionality of the restriction must be respected. The sole fact of not having notified does not warrant the dispersal of the assembly,[75] but it might warrant a fine or other smaller sanction, as I see it. Also, the lack of notice decreases the threshold for intervention not automatically, but because, and to the extent it results in, a limited range of necessary information for proper policing.[76]

These general principles have been further elaborated with regard to so-called spontaneous and urgent demonstrations where the notice requirement has been constitutionally relaxed by the court. This will be discussed under exemptions, below. Here it suffices to note that the German approach is internally consistent, even if textually somewhat curious in light of the specific ban on prior notice in the guarantee of freedom of assembly.

C. United Kingdom: Notice Only for Processions

A novelty of the Public Order Act 1986 (POA) has been the introduction of the obligation of advance notice in case of public processions. (As mentioned, no such requirement is enacted for stationary meetings.) Advance notice is required, in general, except if it was not reasonably practicable to give any advance notice. The provision should have intended to exempt spontaneous processions, thus 'any' should not be interpreted as imposing undue burden, for example a telephone call five minutes before the

[74] BVerfGE 69, 315, 350 (1985).
[75] BVerfGE 69, 315, 315 (headlines) and 350.
[76] BVerfGE 69, 315, 350.

procession starts. What is reasonably practicable, in particular, is a question not yet really answered by the higher courts.

As to the scope, the provision, in section 11 of the POA 1986, applies to all processions which are held

> to demonstrate support or opposition to the views or actions of any person or body of persons, to publicise a cause or campaign or to mark or commemorate an event.

There is no duty to notify the police of processions customarily or commonly held, thus logically those commemorating processions which are customarily or commonly held are exempted too. Presumably, those cases are exempted since the police have been aware of them.[77] This also shows that the purpose of requirement is really just notifying and not obtaining an authorisation from the police. However, as Fenwick observes, the cases where the advance notice makes most sense, because the police might wish to impose conditions on the processions, that is which might 'disrupt the community', will be exactly the cases which the police will be aware of anyway.[78]

Thus, the notice requirement might be of little use. It requires further research to decide whether its introduction was induced by problems related to processions of which the police were not aware, or, simply by a tendency to make processions more difficult and more controllable. The sole purpose, made explicit by the government when introducing the bill, which is, according to DGT Williams, 'clear enough',[79] is that advance notice 'will trigger discussions between the police and the organisers; and that surely must be to the benefit of both'.[80]

In my view it is rather doubtful whether the exercise of a both politically, and 'individually' important right should be made dependent on the bargaining skills of the particular demonstrators. The 'discussion' is not one between equal partners. Besides, the police exercise discretion in bringing prosecutions in case of unnotified assembly. Discretion might, of course, result in rigorous enforcement against unpopular marches while being lenient with more conventional ones.

D. France: Notice Only for *Manifestations*

In France, demonstrations (*manifestations*) are subject to a notification regime, while *réunions* (meetings taking place not on a public route) can

[77] *Cf* Richard Stone, *Textbook on Civil Liberties and Human Rights*, 5th edn (Oxford, Oxford University Press, 2004) 347.

[78] Helen Fenwick, *Civil Liberties and Human Rights*, 4th edn (London, Routledge 2007) 456.

[79] DGT Williams, 'Processions, Assemblies and the Freedom of the Individual' [1987] *Criminal Law Review* 167–79.

[80] HL Deb 13 June 1986 vol 476, col 580, as cited by Williams, ibid.

be held without advance notice. Earlier, the original 1881 law prescribed notification also for *réunions*, but that was abolished in 1907, the motivation behind it being the protest of the Catholic Church.[81]

The piece of law prescribing advance notice for *manifestations* was a Decree-Law of 23 October 1935[82] supplemented by a 1995 law[83] which gave the opportunity for the Conseil Constitutionnel (CC) to declare freedom of demonstration protected by freedom of expression of opinions and ideas under article 11 of the Declaration of the Rights of Man and Citizen 1789 (DDHC).[84] In 2012, the 1935 Decree-Law and its modifications were codified into articles L 211-1–L 211-4 of the Code of Internal Security.[85]

The CC itself has not found problematic the requirement of advance notice as such. In legal scholarship, however, the difference between permit and notification is most explicit because it relates to a general view on repression versus prevention. French scholarship would dislike a permit system because it is a preventive type of regulation and as such, it is considered to be the highest danger to liberty. Repressive regimes are favoured over preventive regulation, just as advance declaration is favoured over preventive ban.[86] If one cannot even exercise a freedom because one is pre-empted or influenced in it as a default rule, then the freedom at hand is not really a freedom.[87]

Therefore, French lawyers are particularly sensitive to the requirement of advance notice in the case of demonstration. There is a general fear of

[81] Léon Duguit, *Traité de droit constitutionnel*, vol 5, *Les libertés publiques*, 2nd edn (Paris, Fontemoing-Boccard, 1925) 348.

[82] Decree-Law of 23 October 1935 (décret-loi portant réglementation des mesures relatives au renforcement du maintien de l'ordre public). A Decree-Law was a special type of legislation, issued by the government on the authorisation of the parliament. In the given case, the law authorised the government to take measures having the force of law in order to defend the franc. When in 1950 a court was asked to decide on the legality of the Decree-Law regulating liberty to demonstrate in order to *defend the franc*, it gave a rather curious reasoning. The Court of Appeals of Bordeaux found the Decree-Law was in accordance with the enabling law because it was in the general interest, as if everything which is in the general interest is capable of defending the franc. (Court of Appeals of Bordeaux, 18 July 1950, case *Izaute* as cited by Alain Boyer, 'La liberté de manifestation en droit constitutionnel français' (2001) 44 *Revue française de droit constitutionnel* 675, 693). It is almost certain that such an interpretation would be unacceptable under the Fifth Republic, since the limits of delegation of legislative power are much stricter than in previous Republics especially if it comes to 'fundamental liberties'. See also Marcel-René Tercinet, 'La liberté de manifestation en France' (1979) *Revue de Droit Public* 1009, 1914.

[83] Law no 95-73 of 21 January 1995.

[84] Decision no 94-352 DC, 18 January 1995.

[85] Book 1, Public order and security, ch 1, Prevention of attacks to public order during demonstrations and crowdings [*manifestations et rassemblements*], section 1, Demonstrations on the public road, inserted by Ordinance no 2012-351 of 12 March 2012.

[86] Claude-Albert Colliard and Roseline Letteron, *Libertés publiques*, 8th edn (Paris, Dalloz, 2005) 73–96.

[87] It is then 'the negation of freedom', ibid, 82, § 96.

'glissement vers l'autorisation',[88] that is, a slide towards authorisation. As there is, however, in the positive law or in the history of French constitutionalism nothing which would prohibit a permit system in the case of demonstration, scholars cannot help but warn against such a possible development of the law.

Some claim that already the system (*régime*) in place has basically become a *régime préventif* instead of a *régime répressif*.[89] What makes a system to be based on authorisation instead of simple advance notice is the possibility of prior ban at the occasion of the notification. If there is no notification requirement, then there cannot really be a prior restraint, since the authorities do not necessarily know in advance about the upcoming demonstration.

The notification has to be submitted between the fifteenth and the third day before the planned date of the demonstration. To hold a demonstration without notification is a delict under the Penal Code (article 431-9). There is no mention in the positive law about a possible different deadline in specific cases, such as that of an 'urgent' assembly. The authority—which is not the local authority, but the prefect,[90] the representative of the central government—is obliged to immediately give a receipt (*récépissé*) which would prove that the organisers did not breach the notification requirement.

Even though there is no notification requirement in the case of *réunions*, the prefect can authorise that a *réunion* take place on the public route. In that case, the organisers have to get into contact with the authorities in advance. This is, however, perceived not as a prior restraint, but as an extra possibility, therefore, it is also not subject to special guarantees.

E. European Court of Human Rights: Both Permit and Notice in Theory Acceptable

In line with the general merge between article 10 and article 11, the ECtHR's strong presumption against prior restraint[91] under article 10 applies to prior restraints on assemblies and demonstrations. This, however, does not invalidate, for example, permit requirements per se, but has made it increasingly difficult for a state to prove the necessity of blanket prior bans.

A notification, or even a permit required by national law, is as such not an unjustified infringement on freedom of assembly and demonstration, not

[88] Ibid, 504, § 675–76.

[89] Eg Frédéric Dieu, 'La "soupe au porc" et le juge des référés du Conseil d'État de France: la validité de l'interdiction d'une manifestation discriminatoire du fait de sa nature même' (2007) 71 *Revue trimestrielle de droits de l'homme* 885, 888.

[90] CÉ, 23 July 1993, *M Saldou*, no 107126.

[91] *Observer and Guardian v United Kingdom*, Application no 13585/88, Judgment of 26 November 1991, Series A 216, 14 EHRR 153, § 60: 'the dangers inherent in prior restraints are such that they call for the most careful scrutiny on the part of the Court'.

even if it involves a mandatory permit fee. In *Andersson*,[92] the applicant claimed that a 60 Swedish Krona permit fee to hold a demonstration was in violation of his article 10 rights (he claimed article 10 because although originally some other people were planning to come to the demonstration, actually it was only the applicant who demonstrated). The Commission held the application manifestly ill-founded. It stated that even if we suppose that the permit on payment was interference, it was necessary for the proper regulation of traffic and to otherwise maintain order in public places. Also, the low amount of the fee made the claim of disproportionate interference implausible.

The European Convention on Human Rights (ECHR) organs have not deemed the distinction between permit and notification relevant or important, and have not required a number of persons necessary to qualify as an assembly that should be notified. For example, in the *K v Netherlands*[93] case the Commission found the claims manifestly ill-founded that the requirement of prior permission to make a *one-person*-demonstration by upholding a banner at the Amsterdam railway station was contrary to article 10. The applicant was protesting against the Netherlands' candidature for the 1992 Olympic Games by holding a banner on the platform, when she was removed by the authorities. She did not ask for permission, even though Dutch law prohibited,

> the display of objects at a railway station without prior permission by the railway authorities in order to prevent disturbance of the order, safety or the good running of operations.

The Commission, in tune with its general weak review in freedom of protest and assembly cases, did not consider fatal that the applicant evidently did not pose any danger of 'disturbance of the order, safety or the good running of operations'. Rather, it emphasised that the applicant was not prosecuted, and she was not prevented from protesting at another place. Thereby, the interference was not considered disproportionate.

The case of *Oya Ataman v Turkey*[94] is a more recent case involving protest of human rights advocates against so-called F-type prisons. The applicant took part at an unnotified demonstration which was dispersed by tear gas, and on the occasion of which also 39 demonstrators, among them, the applicant, had been arrested. The Court declared a violation on the ground that the demonstrators, though convened unlawfully, did not pose any danger of disturbance to public order, not even to the regular flow of traffic.

[92] *Andersson v Sweden*, Application no 12781/87, Decision on admissibility, 13 December 1987, DR 59 171.

[93] *K v Netherlands*, Application no 15928/89, Decision on admissibility, 13 May 1992.

[94] *Oya Ataman v Turkey*, ECHR 2006-XV, Application no 74552/01, Judgment of 5 December 2006.

By actually requiring some chance of some substantive harm, these Court judgments imply a detour from the Commission's earlier more dismissive approach. In addition, in *Oya Ataman*, the ECtHR also emphasised the advance notice's role in facilitating for the police 'to enable the assembly to occur', that is the mentioned paternalistic argument which in my view logically implies only a voluntary notification regime.

More novel is the idea—borrowed from the Venice Commission—that prior notice or permit allows 'not to use powers that [the police] may validly have (for instance, of regulating traffic) to obstruct the event'.[95] Thus, prior notice is not only or not at all an interference, but eventually an important tool in safeguarding or promoting freedom of assembly, and, controlling police themselves.

Meanwhile, the usefulness, and general admissibility of prior notice and permit systems under the Convention, do not imply that a demonstration which had not been notified, or authorised, and, thus, had been even banned, is deprived of Convention protection. The status of such prior bans, together with prior set conditions is a question which will be discussed next.

III. PRIOR BAN AND CONDITIONS

In what cases an assembly can be banned in advance is certainly among the most sensitive issues, as that would prevent the exercise of the right altogether. Jurisdictions are split on the question, the United States having no special rule elaborated in jurisprudence, while the United Kingdom has introduced different threshold criteria for processions on public property, and for meetings on private land (a very broad category in the United Kingdom). In France, general public order fears justify a prior ban if applied proportionately, while in Germany there is a jurisprudentially imposed system of mutual cooperation, with gradually enhancing intervention powers in case of disregard. Conditions are related to ban in the jurisdictions, which still differ about the prerequisites for imposing them. France and Germany are most explicit about the dangers of governmental conditioning, that is the problem of changing the message of assemblies by conditions.

[95] § 16 of the judgment, quoting § 29 of the Opinion of the European Commission for Democracy through Law (the Venice Commission) interpreting the OSCE/ODHIR guidelines on drafting laws on freedom of assembly with regard to the regulation of public meetings, adopted at its 64th plenary session (21–22 October 2005).

A. United States: No Special Doctrinal Rules

It follows from the previous discussion under 'Advance notice or permit' that in the United States, constitutionally acceptable grounds for prior ban and conditions include content-neutral ones, basically any (not vaguely defined) significant interest which is unrelated to the suppression of speech, if protected in a way that leaves open ample alternative channels of communication, a criterion not exactly clarified in jurisprudence.

Content-based grounds are only permissible if *Brandenburg*[96] criteria are fulfilled, that is imminent lawless action is likely to occur unless the ban or condition is put in place, see below in chapter three. Naturally, states (and even municipalities) have different rules which could not be traced here, but all of them are controlled by US Supreme Court jurisprudence discussed above, which boils down to the doctrine of content neutrality, and the prohibition of unfettered discretion in regulating assemblies in advance. A spectacular example of the potentially mischievous operation of these facially innocent and well-argued doctrines has been the controversy around a New York City march against the impending Iraq War, where only a stationary assembly instead of a march was allowed, leaving out such important symbolic locations as the UN Headquarters. This has been found constitutional under *Ward* and *Forsyth*.[97]

B. United Kingdom: Vague Conditions, Prohibited Zone, Loose Review and the Human Rights Act

In UK law, the regime is split into processions and stationary meetings also with regard to bans and conditions. The Public Order Act 1986 authorises the police to impose conditions on any sort of meetings, and marches, in other words also on those where there is no obligation of advance notice.[98] Section 12 of the Act empowers the police—the Chief Officer of Police if considering in advance, or the constable at the scene if decided during the meeting—to impose conditions in a much wider range than it was possible under the Public Order Act 1936.

As to processions, the police officer can impose conditions in one of four cases. The first three are where the officer 'reasonably believes' that there will be: (i) 'serious public disorder', (ii) 'serious damage to property', or

[96] *Brandenburg v Ohio*, 395 US 444 (1969). See Ch 3, text accompanying nn 32–38.

[97] *United for Peace and Justice v City of New York*, 243 F Supp 2d 19 (SDNY 2003), citing *Ward v Rock Against Racism*, 491 US 781 (1989) and *Forsyth*, above n 53. In more detail, see Suplina, 'Crowd Control', above n 48.

[98] In spite of contrary statements in *DPP v Jones* [2002] EWHC 110 by Gage J. *Cf* also Neil Parpsworth and Katharine Thompson, 'Imposing Conditions on a Public Assembly' (2002) 166 *Justice of the Peace* 424.

(iii) 'serious disruption to the life of the community' caused by the procession.[99] The first two are obviously much clearer than the third.

Serious disruption to the life of the community, as a condition for restriction of rights, is extremely vague in numerous respects. For instance, the smaller the community is to be understood, the wider the possibility of imposing conditions: virtually any demonstration will disrupt the life of a small number of people to some extent. The vagueness of the requirement is to some extent diminished by judicial interpretation: in *Reid*[100] the court stated that the conditions should be strictly interpreted.

The fourth case which authorises imposition of conditions[101] is related to the purpose of the meeting. If the officer reasonably believes that the purpose of the assembly is the 'intimidation of others with a view to compelling them not to do an act they have a right to do or to do an act they have a right not to do', he or she might impose some condition to avoid such a result. For the imposition of conditions both coercive and intimidatory purpose is required which in the interpretation of the courts seems to be a rather stringent condition. It was determined, for instance, that shouting and raising arms might cause discomfort, but it does not amount to intimidation.

If any of the above four triggers occur, the police officer is entitled to impose *any* condition which might be necessary for the prevention of the occurrence of the mischief. The conditions can include practically everything (including but not limited to changing the planned route or time) except for banning the whole procession. In *DPP v Baillie*[102] the Divisional Court affirmed that the effect of overly burdensome conditions might amount to a ban, which is unlawful under sections 12 and 14, since a banning power only arises under more severe circumstances according to sections 13 and 14A (see below).

Section 14 authorises the police to impose conditions on *stationary meetings*. The preconditions for doing so are essentially similar to the section 12 conditions which are valid for processions, that is some probability of disorder, damage, disruption or intimidation is required. On the other hand, the conditions which might be imposed on meetings are limited, not 'everything that is deemed necessary by the officer' can be imposed, but only directions as to the place, as to the duration, and as to the number of participating persons,[103] that is issues which in the German, but depending

[99] Section 12 (1)(a) POA 1986.

[100] Reid [1987] *Criminal Law Review* 702.

[101] Section 12(1)(b) of the 1986 Public Order Act.

[102] *DPP v Baillie* [1995] *Criminal Law Review* 426.

[103] The condition also has to be communicated to the demonstrators, ie it has to be heard by them, otherwise they will not be liable. Nonetheless, the mentioned widening of the field of applicability of the provision from those assemblies where at least 20 people are present, to those where at least two are present, severely compromises this apparent moderation of the legislator.

on the exact wording, in the US understanding as well, would qualify as modality or content-neutral restrictions.

The reason for the limited scope of imposable conditions on meetings, as opposed to processions, has been stated by the White Paper preceding the adoption of the POA: 'meetings and assemblies are a more important means of exercising freedom of speech than marches'.[104] Discussion is considered superior to potentially pressuring expression.

Case law on imposition of conditions also dealt with the difference between stationary meetings and processions. In *DPP v Jones*,[105] a 2002 Divisional Court case, there was an animal rights demonstration planned at Huntingdon Life Services premises. The police got advance notice, and imposed some conditions, including the route from the place where the demonstrators would disembark to the place of the demonstration proper. Jones was found to be outside the designated area when trying to get back to the road, and arrested for not complying with the imposed conditions. The court found that under section 14 there is no power for the police to impose conditions as to the route the participants should reach the place of the demonstrations, since, at most, the *movement* of persons could qualify as a public procession, and thus, it would fall under section 12, which, if at all, could be made conditional only in a different notice. What is more, the going from the disembarkation point to the place of assembly cannot be placed under conditions at all, since Gage J thinks that the power of imposition of conditions in section 12 refers only to such processions where advance notice is required.[106]

As indicated above, this is probably a false interpretation of the POA. Nonetheless, there is much sense in the view of Gage J that going to an assembly would not normally qualify as a public procession. At the least, there is certainly no inherent necessity of that. Meanwhile, the police are entitled to fix the entrance and exit points of a demonstration under a section 14 notice.

The decision can be criticised for the almost untenable distinction of processions and stationary meetings. Meetings can easily become processions, and vice versa. Every beginning, and every conclusion of a march, consists of stationary gathering, while every stationary assembly is preceded by a movement of people, most of the time in groups, to the place. Should the police then really issue a notice under section 14 and another one under section 12 if they want to cover the whole event? This would invite claims of disproportionate burdening on a fundamental right,[107] and would

[104] Home Office, *Review of Public Order Law* (Cmnd 9510, 1985).

[105] *DPP v Jones* [2002] EWHC 110. This is *not* the 1999 *DPP v Jones and Lloyd* case, the famous trespassory assembly case of the House of Lords discussed later.

[106] *DPP v Jones* [2002] EWHC 110, § 28.

[107] Beth Cook, 'Moving On' (2003) 153 *New Law Journal* 1279.

question the sense of having these two kinds of regulatory regimes in the POA as both should apply in every case.

At the same time, the decision should be welcome for at least not widening the already large discretion the police have in imposing conditions. It is always beneficial from the perspective of fundamental right if the police have to justify one by one the steps they take. On the other hand, the court reasonably acknowledged that, if the directions of the notice are severable, there is no need to invalidate the whole notice if some of the directions turn out to be illegal.[108]

A demonstrator incurs liability if he or she knowingly fails to comply with the conditions imposed by the police on a procession or meeting. Organisers cannot be made liable for a breach arising out of circumstances beyond their control, that is the organisers are liable for their own conduct, including inciting others to breach the imposed conditions. However, the incitement—just as the conditions—must actually come to the notice of the demonstrator who is incited to act upon it,[109] and must contain an element of persuasion;[110] otherwise the organiser will not incur liability, both according to earlier case law.

A more recent case, *Broadwith*[111] dealt with another aspect of liability for breaching the conditions. There were two assemblies notified which were supposed to follow each other. The police issued a condition that the second could not start earlier than a given time. Broadwith approached the closed area before the given time, and was warned not to enter. When he did, he was arrested. The issue was whether the police order imposing conditions only applied to those who participated at the first assembly, since there was no evidence that Broadwith did, or, it applied to everybody who could be reasonably believed to intend to participate at the second procession. The court agreed with the police and the lower court that the conditions applied to Broadwith. Rose LJ here ignored the possibility of a situation where someone does not intend to take part at the protest and also did not take part at the preceding protest. Possibly, it was not the case with Broadwith, nonetheless, the rules on burden of proof and standard of proof as to such questions could have been clarified by the court.

A post-HRA case, relating to a monthly Critical Mass procession coinciding with the opening of the London Olympic Games, is also characteristic of the light touch review courts exercise with regard to police and assembly. Critical Mass is exempted from the notice requirement,[112] but, as it turns

108 *Cf* Parpsworth and Thompson, 'Imposing Conditions', above n 98, 425.

109 *Krause* (1902) 18 TLR 238.

110 *Hendrickson and Tichner* [1977] *Criminal Law Review* 356.

111 *Broadwith v Chief Constable of Thames Valley Police* [2000] *Criminal Law Review* 924.

112 See below under section IV.A.

out, still can be the subject of conditions imposed by police. What is more, though the Critical Mass does not have a predetermined route—a fact confirmed and accepted by the House of Lords—police are still entitled to determine the route it takes by conditions under section 12 POA, although it was only the police who claimed that the cyclists could disrupt the Olympic ceremony.[113] Police arrested 182 people, but only interviewed five, and they were only charged for violating a section 12 order (fear of serious disruption to the life of the community). It looks as if the power under section 12 served as a pretext to pre-emptive detention of persons feared to become 'protestors'. Courts found it raised no problem.[114] The case is typical of the view where, if something is perceived as protest, then it appears somehow more acceptable for it to be subject to limits than when it is only an everyday activity.[115] If the right to assembly and protest is a human right, then it should be the opposite.

All in all, it appears from the discussed cases that at least before the Human Rights Act 1998 (HRA) codifying the European Convention of Human Rights came into force, the UK law had only allowed for review for procedural errors and unreasonableness in cases of conditions imposed by the police on marches and meetings, or, more precisely, the law had not encouraged a strict review of policing demonstrations. The courts had lacked both the clear power of substantive review,[116] and the willingness to interfere with the exercise of statutorily granted police discretion.[117] As the HRA imposes a duty to interpret UK law in harmony with the ECHR if it is possible, courts are required to read into the police discretion of sections 12 and 14 a duty of proportionality in the fashion of the ECHR. Thus, courts are currently entitled to review both as to the substance, and to the form, the decisions of police officers, the terms of the POA being vague enough to make possible an interpretation that conforms to the Convention. Still, not every decision appears to take seriously the human rights implications of public order law, as recent cases discussed above testify.

As to the banning powers, the regime is split as well: marches can be banned under the 1986 Act under special circumstances. If the Chief Officer of Police reasonably believes that the powers under section 12 (imposing conditions) are not sufficient to prevent the holding of an assembly from resulting in serious public disorder, he or she must apply to the council for

[113] See, eg the views of some cyclists on this: http://www.theguardian.com/uk/2012/jul/29/critical-mass-police-arrest-three.

[114] *Powlesland v DPP* [2013] EWHC 3846 (Admin).

[115] http://www.theguardian.com/environment/bike-blog/2013/mar/18/police-activism.

[116] *Cf Secretary of State for Education and Science v Tameside* [1977] AC 1014, as cited in Fenwick, *Civil Liberties*, above n 78, 461.

[117] *Cf Secretary of State for the Home Department, Ex p Nothumbria Police Authority* [1989] QB 26, as cited in Fenwick, *Civil Liberties*, above n 78, 461.

issuance of a prohibiting order. The council may make an order as requested or modified with the approval of the Secretary of State. The police officer must reasonably believe in the occurrence of a serious public disorder—neither serious damage to property, nor serious disruption to the life of the community is sufficient, unlike in the case of conditions. Secondly, once the officer apprehends such a danger, there is no discretion on the part of the police: the decision is compulsively conferred on a higher level to the council and the Secretary of State. This certainly reduces to some extent the possibility of arbitrariness and discriminative enforcement.

However, compared to the imposition of conditions, the banning order will have an extremely serious effect: it is possible that in a whole area no processions whatsoever might be held for a period of as long as three months, which can even be further prolonged. The provision is clearly overbroad: it catches not only those marches which might turn violent or disorderly, but any kind of processions to take place in the area, even though the rationale of the banning power is admittedly the prevention of serious disorder.

In *Kent v Metropolitan Police Commissioner*[118] the court refused to quash a banning order under a similar provision of the Public Order Act 1936. The court declared that the ban could only be quashed if there was no reason whatsoever to impose it, and that the Act provided sufficient remedy insofar as it allowed the revocation of the ban. Obviously, it is not possible to challenge an order just by establishing that one particular procession will not turn violent if a ban is already in effect, but a revocation can only be applied for if the applicant can show that no danger of public disorder exists both in terms of area and time and possible processions.

In other words, a banning order shifts the burden of proof in such a way as to render it practically impossible for even unquestionably peaceful demonstrators to march in a given area for a given period of time if they face opposition from a hostile police officer. Fenwick mentions that the government rejected the possibility of a more specific banning order regime which would only target the 'real' target, that is violent marches, because it would allegedly have put too great a burden on the police. The argument is that same marchers could then convene under another name, but with the same violent purpose. Actually, Fenwick proposes a 'compromise solution' according to which marches with a similar political message to what was the message of the banned march could also be banned.[119] Nonetheless, I do not quite see why it is too much to expect from the police, council and Secretary of State to make an individual evaluation in each case, or why police cannot be trusted to form a good case-by-case evaluation, reviewable by courts.

[118] *Kent v Metropolitan Police Commissioner, The Times*, 15 May 1981, as cited by Fenwick, *Civil Liberties*, above n 78, 463.

[119] Ibid.

The current system of ban on processions is thus certainly quite restrictive. Even though bans are rarely issued, the banning power can be easily used as a strategic weapon in negotiating with the demonstrators.[120] It also seems that in practice there is not much control on the police. The more discretion the police are statutorily granted, the less other organs that have some say in the banning decisions will be willing to interfere: the council and Secretary of State will not risk serious disorder, and the court, as it is obvious from *Kent,* will also be reluctant to question the evaluation by the police.[121]

As to stationary meetings, the law is less restrictive because it only applies to private land. The Criminal Justice and Public Order Act 1994 introduced the notion of trespassory assemblies, or, more precisely, a statutory, more or less comprehensive regulation of possibilities of banning a meeting on *private* land. By amending the Public Order Act, it established a banning power for meetings parallel to that for processions.

The circumstances which might lead to a ban are the following: the police must reasonably believe that the assemblers intend to assemble in a place (to which they have either no, or only a limited, right of access) probably *without the consent of the owner* and this may result in 'serious disruption to the life of the community' [or 'in significant damage to the land, building or monument of historical, architectural, archaeological or scientific importance'].[122]

Thus, though similar, there are some differences in the two kinds of banning powers. Banning is only possible with regard to stationary assemblies taking place on private land, the amount of which, however, considerably increased in recent decades.[123]

Additionally, banning assemblies is possible on the condition that they would cause serious disruption to the life of the community, while with marches it is only possible for the prevention of serious public disorder. What a serious disruption to the life of the community might be is a question for the police officer, and, on review, for the magistrates' court to decide. It is certainly much less than danger to property or life or limb.

The regulatory technique is otherwise almost the same: the chief officer of the police applies to the council of the district for a banning order which, with the consent of the Secretary of State, will make such or a modified order. The difference is that the police have discretion in launching the process. The similarity is that the order applies to a designated area (delineated in a radius around a specified point) for a specified period of time, thus

[120] Ibid.

[121] Stone, *Textbook*, above n 77, 350.

[122] s 14A(1)(b)(i) and (ii) POA, as inserted by the Criminal Justice and Police Order Act 1994 'CJPOA'.

[123] Fenwick, *Civil Liberties*, above n 78, 464.

again—possibly—also catching assemblies which are not likely to cause serious disruption to the community. What is more, the police are entitled to stop any person within five miles around the prohibited place (the specified centre of the radius) who are reasonably thought to be going to that place. Non-compliance with such a stopping order might result in arrest and fine.[124]

Section 14A was the basis for a banning order in the leading House of Lords case *DPP v Jones and Lloyd*,[125] which to some extent interpreted the law more favourably to freedom of assembly. The order prohibited demonstrating, or, more precisely, trespassory assemblies, within a four miles radius around Stonehenge. Jones and others, however, were assembling on the highway around Stonehenge within the prohibited area, since they wished to protest against the order. The police told them to disperse, and when they failed to comply, the defendants were arrested. It was clear that the protesters were neither violent, nor disorderly, and it was not likely in any case that they would cause any disturbance. The question thus arose whether they had committed a trespassory assembly by assembling peacefully in the area to which a section 14A banning order was in force.

The issue was whether the right of the public on a highway was in a sense limited in that it excluded holding peaceful assemblies there while a section 14A order was in effect. Precedents seemed to support two interpretations of the rights related to the highway. Reasonable and usual activity on the highway should not be punished under the first interpretation,[126] while only activity which is ancillary to passing and repassing the highway is reasonable under the second.[127] Lord Irvine took the first view for the following reasons: first, he cited Collins LJ in *Hickman v Maisey*[128] according to which the use of the highway was given a 'reasonable extension' in modern times. Such extensions are allegedly 'in accordance with the enlarged notions of people in a country becoming more populous and highly civilised'. That is a kind of general reason given by an at most authoritative (100-year-old case from a lower court) decision that the common law might change with changes in society.

Secondly, the other reason for including other reasonable activities in the scope of legitimate use of the highway was for Lord Irvine the absurdity of the rigid, exclusively right-to-passage view.[129] Only allowing activities

[124] s 14C.

[125] *DPP v Jones and Lloyd* [1999] 2 AC 240.

[126] Lord Esher in *Harrison v Duke of Rutland* [1893] 1 QB 142, 146 ff.

[127] Lopes LJ in *Harrison v Duke of Rutland* [1893] 1 QB 142, 154, and Lord Slynn of Hadley in *DPP v Jones and Lloyd* [1999] 2 AC 240, 259–66.

[128] *Hickman v Maisey* [1900] 1 QB 752.

[129] 'In truth, very little activity could accurately be described as "ancillary" to passing along the highway: perhaps stopping to tie one's shoe lace, consulting a street-map, or pausing to catch one's breath. But I do not think that such ordinary and usual activities as making a sketch, taking a photograph, handing out leaflets ... would qualify'. *DPP v Jones and Lloyd* [1999] 2 AC 240, 255 ff per Lord Irvine.

incidental to passage would render many common activities unlawful, though 'the law should not make unlawful which is commonplace and well accepted'.[130] In other words the respect is due to usage and public acceptance, not to a fundamental right, as often happens in English law.

The last reason is again a highly technical one: to allow only uses of the highway which are incidental to passage would create discordance between the law of trespass and the law of obstruction.[131]

Clearly, there is no 'right' to freedom of assembly here in the usual sense of the term. It is similarly unnecessary to invoke article 11 of the ECHR, because the common law is sufficiently clear.[132] The law is simply[133]

> that the public highway is a public place which the public may enjoy for any reasonable purpose, provided the activity in question does not amount to a public or private nuisance and does not obstruct the highway by unreasonably impeding the primary right of the public to pass and repass: within these qualifications there is a public right of peaceful assembly on the highway.

What is reasonable, is a question to be decided by the magistrates' court on a case-by-case basis, no further instructions can be given in that regard. That means that an assembly, though amounting neither to nuisance nor to obstruction, nor being unlawful in other respects, still may turn out to be an unreasonable use of the highway if the magistrates deem it, for instance, because it is neither 'commonplace', nor 'well-accepted'. The right to passage prevails over other uses of the highway, since it is the primary one. Still, the House of Lords found the assembly a reasonable use of the highway, a clear step forward.

C. France: Substantive Values as Troubles to Public Order and Proportionality

Despite the general aversion and caution towards 'preventive regimes', French jurisprudence—similarly to the German where that aversion is largely absent—does not differentiate between the justifiability standards of prior, as opposed to post, restrictions on freedom of assembly. Therefore, much of what will be discussed next in relation to prior bans and conditions will actually display the substantive values to be explored in chapters three to five below. I will still follow this framework since the other jurisdictions do show some differences.

A demonstration can be banned if the authority estimates that the planned demonstration is capable of disturbing public order.[134] Earlier, this

[130] *DPP v Jones and Lloyd* [1999] 2 AC 240, 256 per Lord Irvine.
[131] Ibid, 258 ff.
[132] Ibid, 259.
[133] Ibid, 257.
[134] Art L 211-4 Code of Internal Security, replacing art 3 Decree-Law of 23 October 1935.

requirement was not checked strictly by courts, the Conseil d'État having found the reality of a threat to public order sufficient.[135]

Later on, however, the Conseil d'État has brought its jurisprudence in relation to demonstrations in harmony with that of *réunions publiques*, and basically found the *Benjamin* necessity review applicable. When police banned a demonstration against the visiting Chinese President organised by the Tibetan community in France, courts and the Conseil d'État declared that if it is possible to secure public order by less intrusive measures than a ban, then that is the way to be chosen.[136] Therefore, the police have to evaluate in each case whether the measures planned are 'justified by the necessities of maintaining public order'.[137] To avoid difficulties in the international relations of France is not a pertinent reason to justify restrictions on a demonstration, as that has to relate directly to public order. In a similar vein, the Paris Court of Appeals found a ban on a demonstration by police trade unions based on the 'discredit to the position' or public function of the police also void because of impermissible reason.[138]

Even though dangers to the integrity of international relations, or to the reputation of the police, do not fall under public order, the concept is quite broad. A more recent case on *référé-liberté*,[139] an extraordinary procedure for the safeguard of fundamental liberties, made clear that the freedom of demonstration can have its limits in the interest in anti-discrimination. In the famous '*soupe gauloise*' or '*soupe au cochon*' decision[140] the Conseil d'État had to decide whether the ban on food distribution organised by a radical right-wing group (SDF—Solidarité des Français, SDF is a common acronym for '*Sans domicile fixe*', ie homeless) with a probable racist animus was violating freedom of assembly. The organisers were advertising that they were distributing soup containing pork—the message being obviously that it was not intended for Jews and Muslims. The police banned the distribution and the organisers went to court claiming a 'grave and manifestly illegal violation' of their fundamental liberty to demonstrate, which has to be shown in the *référé-liberté* procedure. The administrative tribunal decided in favour of the applicants, but the Conseil d'État reversed the decision, relying basically on two major arguments.

First, the Conseil d'État accepted that risks associated with an assembly motivated by discriminatory intent qualify as 'troubles to public order' which exclude a grave and manifestly illegal violation. More precisely, the

[135] CÉ, 19 February 1954, *Union des syndicates ouvriers de la region parisienne CGT*, Recueil 113 as cited by Patrick Wachsmann, *Libertés publiques*, 3rd edn (Paris, Dalloz, 2000) 464.

[136] CÉ, 12 November 1997, *Ministre de l'Intériuer c Association, 'Communauté tibétaine en France et ses amis'*, Recueil 417 as cited by Wachsmann, ibid, 464.

[137] Wachsmann, ibid, 465.

[138] Administrative Court of Appeals of Paris, no 97PA00133, 7 March 2000.

[139] See art L 521-2 Code of Administrative Justice.

[140] CÉ, 5 January 2007, no 300311, Recueil Dalloz, 2007, 307.

risk stemmed from a possible *reaction* to what is *conceived as a demonstration capable* of infringing the *dignity* of the persons deprived of the offered aid (meaning the food).

The Conseil d'État did not make clear whether the reaction disturbing public order was meant to come from those homeless persons who—being Jews or Muslims—cannot eat pork, or from whomever saw this kind of undignified activity on the public route. Similarly, it remains unclear whether any sort of immediacy of a danger, or even some higher probability is required. The adjective 'susceptible', in other words capable, would imply that the sheer possibility is sufficient for justifying a restriction on freedom of demonstration. Frédéric Dieu interprets 'susceptible' here as implying intention on the part of organisers,[141] but this might be only because this kind of discrimination can be only intentional. What is more, here the intention seems to be presumed—or, the important factor is what others think about the intention of the organisers.

Furthermore, the *juge de référé* of the Conseil d'État also stated that respect for freedom of demonstration does not hinder an authority invested with the power of police to ban an activity if that is *the sole measure* to prevent troubles to public order (emphasis added). Therefore, the Conseil d'État does not grant unlimited discretion to the police in deciding about the existence of troubles to public order. Quite to the contrary, there seems to be a proportionality review, even if the Conseil d'État does not state the 'exact weighing' it pursued. If the measure has to be the sole measure which is capable to prevent the troubles to public order, then it seems that the Conseil d'État accepted on its own judgment that the distribution of the pork would have had a consequence of disorder.

The human dignity argument is thus not clearly self-standing; it mediates between the pork distribution and the disorderly or violent reaction. In this sense, the 'pork soup' decision might imply an argument analogous to 'fighting words', nonetheless, this evidently is an infinitely laxer requirement compared to that. Notably, the Conseil d'État left unclarified if the (perceived) infringement of dignity of persons was automatically, in any case, conducive to troubles to public disorder, or just in the specific case. Also, it is not clear how far discriminatory practices or views per se, where there is no apparent harmdoing, would forfeit assembly rights.

The Conseil d'État definitely found proven that the views of the demonstrators were discriminatory, the source for this being the website of the SDF. If one takes the wording seriously, it seems that the perception of (by the way indetermined) others as to the (intention of the organisers of) infringing human dignity is sufficient for the establishment of troubles to public order. Dieu rightly points out that it is embedded in earlier, even if not

[141] Dieu, 'La "soupe au porc"', above n 89, 895.

too early, jurisprudence that the 'dignity of the person' is part of the public order,[142] notably in the (in)famous decision *Commune de Morsang-sur-Orge* in relation to the consensual employment of little people (people living with dwarfism) for the purposes of entertainment.[143] As the police are entitled and obliged to protect public order, any (perceived and intended) attack on dignity is an attack to public order. It is another question, how to discover the existence of an attack to human dignity in a particular situation, and what the sufficient and necessary means are to counter it.

Secondly, the Conseil d'État also made a very interesting argument when it stated that the administrative tribunal could not uphold, without contradiction, that the distribution of pork on the public route was organised in a discriminatory manner, while at the same time find a grave and manifestly illegal violation of the fundamental liberty to demonstrate. Thereby, the Conseil d'État basically said that the discriminatory exercise of a fundamental liberty is not protected by the fundamental liberty, since being free from discrimination (by private persons!) is also a fundamental liberty. Organising a demonstration of discriminatory character is illegal, and, what is more, this illegality is a more serious violation than the interference flowing from the prohibition of the demonstration itself.[144]

Nonetheless, as under the *référé-liberté* procedure, only grave and manifestly illegal violations of fundamental liberties can be pursued, this decision shall not be deemed a decision on the ultimate limits of liberty of demonstration in the concrete sense of the word. As Dieu points out, however, the decision should be taken as delineating the principles to be considered while deciding a case at the level of facts.[145]

In another (ordinary administrative review) decision, the Conseil d'État found that previous intimidating and threatening conduct of anti-abortion protestors invading clinics could serve as a basis for a prior ban of another demonstration—notified before the Notre Dame, and not explicitly next to the neighbouring clinic—even if this previous conduct was not considered in the judgments of lower administrative courts.[146] In the weighing it was also relevant that the demonstration could have been held elsewhere, and no general ban was issued against the association. Previous disorderly conduct of the same association was also found sufficient for an advance ban of another demonstration in front of an abortion clinic by the Administrative Court of Appeals in another proceeding.[147]

[142] Ibid, 893.

[143] CÉ, 27 October 1995, *Commune de Morsang-sur-Orge*, Recueil, 372; RFDA 1995, conclusions Frydman.

[144] Dieu, 'La "soupe au porc"', above n 89, 889.

[145] Ibid.

[146] CÉ, 30 December 2003, *Association SOS TOUT PETITS*, no 248264.

[147] Administrative Court of Appeals of Paris, 23 March 2000, nos 98PA04534, 98PA04548, 98PA04549.

Apart from bans, the police have a right to impose conditions when they become aware of the upcoming demonstration, that is when the notification is submitted. Nonetheless, I could not verify the exact legal source for this power, thus it most probably is the general police power of municipal authorities (police, mayor or the prefect) as granted in the General Code on territorial units.[148]

As to *other* prior burdens, there seems to be consensus that they have to be justified under a *Benjamin* type necessity review, that is only those limitations are allowed which are the sole means for the prevention of troubles to public order. As in other cases, it does not mean a very high standard of probability of 'troubles', but it does mean some evidence in the hand of the police that actually some serious harm (disorder or violation of human dignity) might perceivably happen which they cannot handle unless the measure is taken.

The main decision of the Conseil Constitutionnel on prior restraints, other than banning, is the decision on video surveillance and search of vehicles.[149] The law at hand (before promulgation) regulated several questions related to video surveillance of public places (more precisely: the public route and places especially exposed to risks of aggression and theft), a provision of bringing and wearing arms and objects capable of being used as projectiles at a demonstration, and the possibility of search for vehicles for the purposes of finding arms or projectiles. The Conseil Constitutionnel found the procedures related to the installation of video surveillance sufficient to guarantee the 'individual liberty' protected by article 66 of the Constitution, that is in this regard it did not consider if there might be a danger to freedom of demonstration.

In finding the system constitutional, the Conseil Constitutionnel imputed importance to the fact that there would be proper and permanent information on the video surveillance, in other words it is not secret and everybody is, in fact, aware of it. Meanwhile, blatantly, there is no chilling effect consideration present in the decision in this regard. Apart from the proper information, the Conseil Constitutionnel found the video surveillance constitutional on procedural grounds (independent commission, right to remedy, restrictions on the storage of the recorded data, etc).

As to the freedom of demonstration restriction proper, the Conseil Constitutionnel held actually very little. It spelled out (third *considérant*) that the freedom of collective expression of ideas and opinions is constitutionally guaranteed. Individual liberty, and, freedom of movement (*liberté d'aller er venir*), mentioned together with collective expression in the very same sentence, are not likely to be relevant with regard to the

[148] Ch II: Municipal Police, General Code of Territorial Collectivities, arts L 2212-1–L 2212-10.

[149] Decision no 94-352, 18 January 1995.

demonstration, but refer in general to the person's rights when walking on the street. As the Conseil Constitutionnel also affirmed that the prevention of attacks to the public order, and notably to the security of the persons and goods is similarly of constitutional value, it admitted the legislator's competence to bring about reconciliation between these two sides.

As to the particular legislative provision, which authorises the prefectoral authority to prohibit the bringing and wearing of arms or objects capable of being used as arms, the Conseil Constitutionnel attached importance to the following. It weighed heavily that the law only allowed the prohibition in cases where the circumstances indicated that *grave* troubles to public order are to be feared, and that the prohibition can only be imposed in the 24 hours preceding the demonstration.

The Conseil Constitutionnel appears to have integrated a '*réservé que*' type of interpretation without explicitly saying so with regard to the spatial aspect of the ban.[150] It recalled, namely, that the authorisation of imposition is restricted to the place of the demonstration itself, its surroundings, and the entering points of the demonstration, and interpreted these to mean only immediate proximity.

Also, the Conseil Constitutionnel seems to have instructed lower authorities—and eventually the courts—that the extent of the prohibition shall be limited and proportional to the necessities which the circumstances require.

Further, with relation to the similar provision enabling the prohibition of bringing or wearing objects capable of being used as a projectile, the Conseil Constitutionnel held that the formulation is so general and imprecise that it violates the constitutionally guaranteed freedom of the individual (ie here the norm applied is article 66 of the Constitution 'proper'). Luchaire remarks, in this regard, that a similar imprecision and generality would also have been well discernible in the case of objects capable of being used as arms, since the Criminal Code (to which the law on video surveillance gives reference) is quite broad. The second paragraph of article 132-75 of the Criminal Code refers to objects which are used or meant (destined) to be used to kill and hurt by the perpetrator. Article 132-75 was, as such, referenced by the law on video surveillance, the second paragraph therefore also seems applicable. However, as the law authorises search of vehicles in every case where the imposition of prohibition is permitted, it would necessarily authorise search of vehicles for objects meant (destined) to be used to kill and hurt. As, this, however, is impossible to tell in advance, according to Luchaire, it should be interpreted in a restrictive way. Either the second paragraph does not count in the application to the prohibition and to the search of vehicles, or, it can only constitute an infraction of the law from

[150] Similarly François Luchaire, 'La vidéosurveillance et la fouille des voitures devant le Conseil constitutionnel' (1995) 111 *Revue du droit public et de la science politique en France et à l'étranger* 573, 583.

the point that it is used or meant (destined) as an arm, meaning only during the demonstration and not in advance.[151] Such a (re)interpretation would certainly be desirable.

As to the authorisation of search of vehicles for arms or objects capable of being used as arms and the seizure of these objects, the Conseil Constitutionnel took a strict approach. It found that to the extent that such a search and seizure would result in finding infractions and in the persecution of the perpetrators, the power to pursue search and seizure belongs to the judicial (as opposed to the administrative) police powers, controlled by the judiciary, and not by the executive, since the judiciary is supposed to protect individual liberty. As the law authorised the prefectoral authority for such a search and seizure provided that they notify (only) the prosecutors, it is unconstitutional. Here the value violated is not freedom of collective expression, but the individual liberty. Thus, this part of the decision also does not spell out a principle specifically related to demonstrations, but is more of a criminal-procedural argument, which nonetheless reinforces the line between preventive and repressive public order activities.

The law, which was finally adopted, authorises the prefect to ban the bringing and wearing—without a legitimate reason—of an object constituting arms in the sense of the Penal Code within a designated area around the place of the planned manifestation if *grave* troubles to public order are feared. The area cannot be larger than justified by public order necessities.[152]

The Conseil d'État, as highest administrative court, also handed down a number of judgments related to prior restraints in a similar manner. For instance, it did not consider disproportionate the temporary reintroduction of French–Spanish cross-border checks for one day at the occasion of an ETA *manifestation* planned in Bayonne, for the support of ETA members held in prison in France and in Spain, because there was ample evidence of danger of violence.[153] The demonstration to be held was part of a series of demonstrations, the two preceding ones having turned violent. In the second *considérant*, the Conseil d'État pointed out that there were street fights organised by separatists of Spanish citizenship, and that the expected fusion of this group, with a French movement, made the occurrence of violence again probable. The Conseil d'État accepted that the reintroduced cross-border check might have put a burden on the assembly rights of the applicants, because the procedure resulted in long queues and traffic jams, thus, some people who intended to go could not get to the demonstration. Nonetheless, the Conseil d'État apparently deemed such an indirect prior restraint as being proportionate to the danger of violence.

[151] Ibid, 584.

[152] Art 2 bis Decree-Law of 23 October 1935 was substituted by art L 211-3 Code of Internal Security in 2012.

[153] CÉ, 30 July 2003, no 237649.

D. Germany: Graduality of Cooperation, Conditions and Ban

Not a fully-fledged prior restraint, but the so-called duty to cooperate on the part of demonstrators and organisers, is well understood to impose limits on the freedom of assembly, even more than in the United Kingdom since in Germany it has been imposed by the (GFCC) itself. In the *Brokdorf* decision, the court claimed that the more the organiser shows cooperative spirit at the time of the advance notification, the higher the threshold of permissible state intervention for the protection of public security and order will be.[154] The court even advised the organisers to take one-sided measures, which build trust between them and the police, and that would have the same effect of raising the level of danger where intervention is constitutionally permissible. In addition, the court apparently invites, if not obliges, participants to take into account 'time-tested practices' (*bewährte Erfahrungen*) of former demonstrations.[155]

It remains unclear whether cooperation is an obligation, a *Pflicht* or just an *Obliegenheit*, this latter normally meaning non-enforceable duties or burdens. Still, as the court puts a very clear obligation to learn and adapt to former well-tried experiences on the police, and expects cooperation from the organisers, the conclusion that the court engages in a very dangerous '*Vestaatlichung*', 'state-isation' of a freedom, is well grounded.[156] A constitutionally imposed duty of cooperation transforms freedom of assembly into a curious right to 'co-form' matters of state competence,[157] a rather serious distortion of the function of fundamental rights. The problem is, of course, that true as it might be, this critique certainly remains without response in reality: de facto there will be a bargaining, and the level of 'friendliness' or at least 'correctness' induced by cooperation certainly will have an effect on the legal evaluation of both the conduct of the police, and that of the demonstrators.

One of the reasons for the acceptability of advance notice is to enable the authorities to impose conditions in case of foreseeable likely direct endangering of public security. Demonstrators have a right to self-determination with regard to date and time of their planned assembly, but practical concordance requires the protection of the rights of others and other substantive constitutional values, such as public security, as much as possible. Such protection might result in imposing conditions on the timing or the route of the assembly.[158] On one occasion, the Federal Administrative Court found lawful an obligation of would-be demonstrators to report to the police so

[154] BVerfGE 69, 315, 357 (1985).
[155] Ibid.
[156] Kunig, above n 73, ann 20. Art 8, at 589.
[157] Ibid.
[158] BVerfG, 1 BvR 961/05, 6 May 2005.

that those likely to be violent could have been prevented from travelling *abroad* to the G8 summit.[159]

Even mass detention of demonstrators before the G8 summit in Heiligendamm was permissible under German law (the complaint was rejected without examination by the GFCC), while the ECtHR found it violated the European Convention on Human Rights.[160] Thus, though in theory the threshold is the concrete danger of violent conduct on an upcoming assembly, and previous violence also weighs in the assessment of danger, the concreteness and likeliness can be rather attenuated.

Risk of violation of *other* substantive values—as has already been discussed under Part II B—might also serve as a ground justifying conditions, and—if conditions are not suitable—a ban. These include commonsensical ones such as damage to life, limb or property, then coercion in a reasonably narrow sense, and finally human dignity mediated by 'public peace'.

A characteristic of German law is the graduality of duties: the more willing the organiser is to cooperate, the higher the threshold for police intervention for first imposing conditions, and if they are not sufficient or suitable, a ban (or dispersal). This is very much in harmony with the doctrines of proportionality, balancing and practical concordance. Graduality is not required, but prohibited in one case: when the condition would change the message of the assembly. In that case, a ban might be constitutional if other criteria are fulfilled, while a condition is unconstitutional, at least in theory.

E. European Court of Human Rights: Strong Substantive and Procedural Protection

As mentioned above, a demonstration which was held, even though it had been banned or not authorised, is not deprived of article 11 protection. Since only unpeaceful assemblies fall out of the scope of article 11, unlawfully convened assemblies are still protected.

As a default rule, in a case of denial of authorisation, or, any kind of measure having the effect of prior ban on assembly, the ECHR requires that the authorities give proper grounds. The Court exerts substantive review, and it appears now settled that a prior ban cannot be justified unless incitement to

159 BVerwG, 6 C 39/06, 25 July 2007.

160 *Schwabe and MG v Germany*, Application nos 8080/08 and 8577/08, Judgment of 1 December 2011.

violence or rejection of democratic principles would otherwise occur with some (unclear) level of probability. In *Stankov* it is stated:[161]

> Sweeping measures of a preventive nature to suppress freedom of assembly and expression *other than in cases of incitement to violence or rejection of democratic principles*—however shocking and unacceptable certain views or words used may appear to the authorities, and however illegitimate the demands made may be—do a disservice to democracy and often even endanger it. (Emphasis added)

These two concerns were reaffirmed in *Güneri*,[162] and thus it appears settled that a prior ban on substantive grounds can only be justified if either incitement to violence,[163] or a rejection of democratic principles, would occur on the banned assembly. The required probability is not exactly clear, just as what amounts to 'rejection of democratic principles'—secessionist speech according to *Stankov*[164] does not, while, for example 'seeking the expulsion of others from a given territory on the basis of ethnic origin is a complete negation of democracy'.[165]

Among more recent cases on prior restraint, the *Baczkowski v Poland*[166] ruling is of foremost significance. The judgment is quite unique because the Court managed to overcome rather serious preliminary objections and declare violation of freedom of assembly, the right to effective remedy with respect to assembly, and discrimination in the same regard basically by discussing at length the role of freedom of assembly and demonstration in a democracy as a tool of protecting vulnerable minorities and furthering pluralism.

The decision is full of statements of principle, which serve as an answer to the government's technical objections. In a maximalist fashion, the Court reversed the government's preliminary objections into substantive violations of the ECHR.

In the case, contrary to *Güneri*, the banned assemblies did take place despite the ban, and the police even protected the demonstrators. Also, the reviewing administrative authority quashed the first instance bans, and even the Constitutional Court—in review for compatibility initiated by the Ombudsman—ruled that some of the provisions the bans were based on were unconstitutional. Still, the ECtHR declared a violation of article 11 on

[161] *Stankov and the United Macedonian Organisation Ilinden v Bulgaria*, Application nos 29221/95 and 29225/95, Judgment of 2 October 2001, ECHR 2001-IX, § 97.

[162] *Güneri and Others v Turkey*, Application nos 42853/98, 43609/98 and 44291/98, Judgment of 12 July 2005, § 79.

[163] In *Stankov*, above n 161, § 102 the Court reminds us of its statement in *Incal* according to which 'the mere fact that a message read out at a commemorative ceremony to a group of people—which already considerably restricted its potential impact on national security, public order or territorial integrity—contained words such as "resistance", "struggle" and "liberation" did not necessarily mean that it constituted an incitement to violence, armed resistance or an uprising (loc. cit., pp. 1566-67, § 50)'.

[164] *Stankov*, above n 161, reaffirming: *United Macedonian Organisation Ilinden and Others v Bulgaria (No 2)*, Application no 34960/04, Judgment of 18 October 2011, citing *Stankov (No 1)*, § 36.

[165] *Stankov*, above n 161, § 100.

[166] *Baczkowski v Poland*, Application no 1543/06, Judgment of 3 May 2007.

the ground that the bans were not prescribed by law since they were imposed unlawfully.

The case is important in various regards. First is the status of the 'victim' as a requirement for standing before the Court. The government claimed that the applicants were not 'victims' since they did not suffer any moral or pecuniary damages, since the assembly did take place, and no sanction was applied against them. Besides, the government also claimed that there was no interference in the applicants' rights to freedom of assembly for the same reasons. The Court rejected both of these claims and held the following:[167]

> [T]he applicants took a risk in holding them given the official ban in force at that time. The assemblies were held *without a presumption of legality*, such a presumption constituting a *vital aspect* of effective and unhindered exercise of the freedom of assembly and freedom of expression. The Court observes that the refusals to give authorisation could have had a *chilling effect* on the applicants and other participants in the assemblies. It could also have discouraged other persons from participating in the assemblies on the ground that they did not have official authorisation and that, therefore, no official protection against possible hostile counter-demonstrators would be ensured by the authorities. (Emphases added)

This quote is highly significant—especially if understood in the context of the case. The assemblies at stake were demonstrations organised by the Equality Foundation in order to alert the public to the issue of discrimination against minorities and women. The banned assemblies were those which were organised by members of NGOs protecting the rights of various sexual minorities. On the same day, other assemblies were authorised, which basically wished to convey a counter-message (eg protest against partnerships, 'paedophilia', pro 'Christian values', etc).

Secondly, there was another preliminary issue raised by the government, namely that of exhaustion of domestic remedies. The government argued that the applicants failed to exhaust remedies because they did not submit a constitutional complaint whilst the ECtHR ruled in a previous judgment that the Polish constitutional complaint might qualify as an effective remedy under the ECHR. The Court rejected this objection basically relying on the importance of timing in the freedom of assembly and expression context. This is one of the occasions when freedom of expression considerations successfully made their way into article 11 case law.

As the Court did not specify why the dates the assemblies were planned to be held on were of special importance, in essence it ruled that any remedy which cannot be obtained before the planned date of an assembly is ineffective, and, therefore, does not need to be exhausted.[168] What is more, regarding

[167] Ibid, § 67.

[168] This interpretation was approved again in *Patyi v Hungary (No 2)*, Application no 35127/08, Judgment of 17 January 2012, § 23, and *Szerdahelyi v Hungary*, Application no 30385/07, Judgment of 17 January 2012, § 31.

article 13, the Court even declared a violation of the right to remedy for basically the same reasons (§ 82 of the judgment):

> [S]uch is the nature of democratic debate that the timing of public meetings held in order to voice certain opinions may be crucial for the political and social weight of such a meeting. Hence, the State authorities may, in certain circumstances, refuse permission to hold a demonstration, if such a refusal is compatible with the requirements of Article 11 of the Convention, but cannot change the date on which the organisers plan to hold it. If a public assembly is organised after a given social issue loses its relevance or importance in a current social or political debate, the impact of the meeting may be seriously diminished. The freedom of assembly—if prevented from being exercised at a propitious time—can well be rendered meaningless.

It seems, therefore, to be the state of the law that organisers are the sole masters of the timing of assembly in the sense that if they say that the timing is important, it should be unquestionably considered part of the content of their message, and as such, cannot be restricted.

This stands in sharp contrast to the lenient review of the removal of the protester from the Amsterdam Central Station in the Dutch case,[169] where the Commission considered the fact that the applicant had the possibility to protest at other places (most probably somewhere where the Olympic delegation, the target of the protest, would not have seen her), as one factor rendering the interference proportionate.

Again, one might observe a strengthening of the ECHR protection in the last decade, which might also be due to the different degree of restriction in the Dutch case, on the one hand, and in the Polish case on the other, but it might also result from the increasingly rights protective mood of the Court. In any case, these strong procedural guarantees are a far cry from the lenient standard declared by the US Supreme Court in *Thomas v Chicago Park District* as discussed above.[170]

IV. EXEMPTIONS, DEROGATIONS FROM THE NOTIFICATION REQUIREMENT

A. Traditional Processions: Content Discrimination or a Reasonable Exception?

The jurisdictions examined all carve out exceptions from the notification or permit requirement for assemblies traditionally held. The particular

[169] *K v Netherlands,* above n 93.
[170] Above text accompanying nn 67–70.

formulation and, thus, scope of the exception is naturally diverging from country to country.

In France article L 211-1 of the Code of Internal Security (replacing identical regulation in the Decree-Law of 23 October 1935) exempts processions (this time the expression used is '*sorties*') *conforming to local usage* from the advance notice, having first of all religious processions in mind, and it applies largely to those still today.[171] Nonetheless, within this scope, the interpretation is quite generous as even a 70-year interruption does not prevent a procession from qualifying as conforming to local usage.[172] Such *manifestations* are also exempted from the ban of disguising the face.[173] Légifrance does not yield any search results which are not about religious processions, thus the conclusion that French legal practice hereby de facto institutes a content-based exemption for religious processions appears inevitable. This, however, seems to raise no controversy in the country, and it is possible also that whenever a group would claim its *manifestation* should be considered conforming to local usage, courts will accept it.

In German law, there is a more complicated controversy around traditional or religious processions. Article 17 of the Federal Assembly Law[174] exempts from the notice requirement (and indeed from ban and conditioning) open air worships, masses, religious processions, funeral and wedding processions and traditional popular festivals. The apparent privilegisation of such assemblies over political ones resulted in scholars claiming the regulation unconstitutional,[175] others in need of an interpretation to conform to the Constitution.[176]

Since 2001, however, as the GFCC appeared settled on a narrow (or enlarged) concept of assembly, which in any case restricts the scope of article 8 GG to public matters,[177] some of the authors argue that article 17 of the Assembly Law does not even cover assemblies protected by article 8 GG.[178] Thus, the regulation does not privilege them: to the contrary, these assemblies are subject to general police law with a wider range of intervention possibilities than it is the case with article 8 assemblies.[179]

[171] Colliard and Letteron, *Libertés Publiques*, above n 86, 503.

[172] CE, 11 February 1927, *Abbé Veyras*, Recueil 176, no 585 as cited by Colliard and Letteron, above n 86, 503, fn 2.

[173] See Ch 7.

[174] On its status see Ch 1, n 138.

[175] Eg Sieghart Ott and Hartmut Wächtler, *Gesetz über Versammlungen und Aufzüge*, 6th edn (Stuttgart, Boorberg, 1996) § 17.

[176] Alfred Dietel, Kurt Gintzel and Michael Kniesel, *Versammlungsgesetz*, 15th edn (Köln, Carl Heymanns, 2008) § 17.

[177] BVerfGE 104, 92 (2001), see the discussion on the notion of assembly in German law in Ch 1.

[178] Eg Dietel, Gintzel and Kniesel, *Versammlungsgesetz*, above n 176, § 10, 349.

[179] *Klein* DVBl 1971, 241 n 101 as cited by Volkhard Wache, '§ 17 VersG' in Georg Erbs and Max Kohlhaas (eds), *Strafrechtliche Nebengesetze*, 185. Ergänzungslieferung (München, Beck, 2011).

This approach, however, strikes back from the opposite end: most of these processions should certainly enjoy basic rights protection because of the applicability of freedom of religion, simple freedom of action (with its easier limitability) will not do. It is hard to see why one basic right (freedom of assembly within the narrow notion) and another (freedom of religion) should be subject to different regimes when the activity is actually the same (procession). The problem has thus, in my view, become moot neither because of the mentioned decision of the GFCC, nor because the regulation of assemblies became a competence of the Länder. Saxony's new Assembly Law contains an identical regulation,[180] while the Bavarian Assembly Law exempts such assemblies from the ban on disguising the face and of bringing 'protective weapons'.[181]

The UK POA section 11(2) dispenses with the notice requirement for *processions commonly or customarily held* in the given area, and also funeral processions 'organised by a funeral director acting in the normal course of his business'. 'Commonly or customarily held' includes traditional May Day or Good Friday processions,[182] but the category is not limited to it as the rationale of the exemption is that police are aware anyway.

A 2008 House of Lords judgment in *Kay*[183] on Critical Mass cycle rallies in Central London found that a 12-year practice certainly qualifies as customary, thus the notice requirement does not apply. The court has not clarified how long a practice below 12 years will suffice, but the case affirms that the exception as applied does not relate to the content of the message, but really to its recurring nature. The House of Lords disagreed with the Divisional Court[184] about whether the route of the procession needs to be known to police in advance in order for the notice to be dispensable. Though Critical Mass does not have a predetermined route, the House of Lords decided that it is still the same procession, in other words it falls under the exemption. This generous understanding, however, did not prevent the Divisional Court from subsequently finding that police are still entitled to impose conditions as to the route of the Critical Mass, despite the fact that it does not have any predetermined route.[185]

As to funeral processions, the somewhat meticulous formulation of 'organised by a funeral director acting in the normal course of his business' appears to exclude mass funeral processions which normally are political,

[180] Law about Assemblies and Processions in the Free State of Saxony of 20 January 2010, *SächsGVBl* S 2 § 17.

[181] Bavarian Assembly Law of 22 July 2008 (*GVBl* S 421), BayRS 2180-4-I, § 16 IV. For the notion of protective weapons and disguising identity, see below Ch 7.

[182] Usual examples in UK textbooks on civil liberties, eg Stone, *Textbook*, above n 77, 260.

[183] *Kay v Commissioner of Police of the Metropolis* [2008] UKHL 69.

[184] *Commissioner of Police for the Metropolis v Kay* [2007] EWCA Civ 477, [2007] 1 WLR 2915.

[185] *Powlesland v DPP* [2013] EWHC 3846 (Admin).

and might be a source of danger and occasion—for example in Northern Ireland—of intergroup conflict. However, regulations regarding Northern Ireland simply exempt 'funeral processions' from advance notice, without further specification.[186] This same regulation still contains a hint on the specific history: it does not exempt customarily or commonly held processions from advance notice,[187] though the Secretary of State can regulate in an order those processions which are exempted.[188]

In the United States the situation of exemptions for traditional assemblies is unclear. Traditionally, funeral processions were exempted by laws and regulations in some of the states and municipalities.[189] Early state court cases sometimes struck down such regulations for being discriminatory.[190] However, there not only funeral, but some other processions were also exempted, and the court had even left open the possibility of later allowing for a funeral procession exemption.[191]

The US Supreme Court has not exactly ruled on this issue. Major assembly cases of the US Supreme Court, such as *Shuttlesworth* involved ordinances exempting funeral processions, but this was not the main reason for their unconstitutionality. In *Shuttlesworth*, the exception only appears in a footnote, only for the sake of being precise.[192]

Although such regulations are clearly content-based, and thus would fall under strict scrutiny, the widespread practice in state and municipal laws to exempt funeral processions from the permit requirement either indicates that such exemptions would pass strict scrutiny, or that it raises no controversy.

[186] Art 3(4)(a) of The Public Order (Northern Ireland) Order 1987.

[187] Neil Jarman, 'Regulating Rights and Managing Public Order: Parade Disputes and the Peace Process' (1995–98) 22 *Fordham International Law Journal* 1415, 1422.

[188] Art 3(4)(b) of The Public Order (Northern Ireland) Order 1987.

[189] Eg Edwin Baker found 9 of 18 examined regulations containing such exemption, see Edwin Baker, 'Unreasoned Reasonableness: Mandatory Parade Permits and Time, Place, and Manner Regulations' (1983) 78 *Northwestern University Law Review* 937, text accompanying nn 32–34, also citing examples from as early as 1888. An internet search for 'exemptions from permit requirement for funeral procession' (without quotation marks) also shows the exemption being widespread all over the United States.

[190] *Commonwealth v Mervis*, 55 Pa Super 178 (1913); *Commonwealth v Curtis* 55 Pa Super 184 (1913).

[191] 'It may well be urged that there is something distinctive in a funeral procession. It is not only a work of charity but of necessity as well, that we bury the dead. These occasions are attended by a solemnity all their own; and experience has taught us there is, usually at least, little about them to encourage the presence of large bodies of citizens, while there is much to keep in serious and orderly mood those who may take part in them. When the question arises whether such an exception alone, to the general character of an ordinance such as we have before us, would amount to undue discrimination, it may be properly dealt with'. *Commonwealth v Mervis*, 55 Pa Super 178, 3 (1913).

[192] *Shuttlesworth v City of Birmingham*, 394 US 147, 151, fn 1 (1969).

B. Spontaneous and 'Urgent' Assemblies

A demonstration can be unnotified for several reasons. Unnotified demonstrations form a special category in freedom of assembly literature. They are usually perceived to be potentially more dangerous or disturbing; nonetheless, in some sense the worthiest of protection since they are presumably prompted by some important event, and are thus spontaneous, somehow genuine.

In addition, it often happens that organisers do not give prior notice because they are sure that the authorities would ban the demonstration unlawfully. Therefore, the leniency which is required in the handling of such assemblies functions as a safety check, or a last resort built-in guarantee of freedom of assembly. As it can be seen on the example of the *Baczkowski* case, local authorities might well render freedom of assembly meaningless by constantly rejecting permit requests or issuing clearly biased bans in the guise of upholding traffic regulations. Though second instance administration and the courts were eager to quash the first instance ban, even they could not effectively remedy the lost opportunity to protest at the right time and right place. In some cases, however, even higher instance authorities or courts are not willing, or are—as a matter of positive law—not able, to correct the first instance bias or mistake. If such official conduct can be taken for granted, protestors might wish to risk an unnotified assembly rather than a banned one.

For this, and the proper spontaneous protest situation, the ECtHR spelled out general principles in the *Oya Ataman v Turkey* case, mentioned above,[193] and in the *Bukta v Hungary* case.[194]

In *Oya Ataman,* the human rights protest of the applicants—historically and theoretically at the core of freedom of assembly as essentially political protest, a form of petitioning the government in the interest of the most vulnerable: maltreated prisoners[195]—had not been notified, and was dispersed within half an hour by tear gas. In the view of the applicant, the dispersal took place in order to prevent the reading out of a press statement protesting against the isolation and possible maltreatment of prisoners.[196]

The Court did not find evidence that the demonstrators posed a danger to public order, apart from minor disruption to traffic, and was 'particularly struck by the authorities' impatience in seeking to end the demonstration, which was organised under the authority of the Human Rights Association. As a statement of principle, the Court declared:[197]

[193] *Oya Ataman v Turkey*, above n 94.

[194] *Bukta and Others v Hungary*, 51 EHRR 25, Application no 25691/04, Judgment of 17 July 2007.

[195] For the situation in F-type prisons in Turkey, see eg the Human Rights Watch reports and materials available at http://hrw.org/english/docs/2001/05/11/turkey123.htm.

[196] *Oya Ataman v Turkey*, above n 94, § 34.

[197] Ibid, § 42.

> [W]here demonstrators do not engage in acts of violence it is important for the public authorities to show a certain degree of tolerance towards peaceful gatherings if the freedom of assembly guaranteed by Article 11 of the Convention is not to be deprived of all substance.

Therefore, it concluded that there was a violation of freedom of assembly, since the state failed to show the necessary tolerance in handling an unlawful, but peaceful demonstration.

The Court had the opportunity to reiterate and further elaborate on its stance on unnotified assemblies in the 2007 case of *Bukta and Others v Hungary.*[198] The facts of the case are closest to a spontaneous demonstration proper, though, in German terms, it might still qualify only as *Eilversammlung*, urgent demonstration, and not a spontaneous one.[199]

In *Bukta*, the applicants held a protest in front of a hotel where the Hungarian Prime Minister participated at a reception given by the Romanian Prime Minister on the occasion of a national holiday which commemorates the 1918 declaration of transfer of Transylvania from Hungary to Romania. The Hungarian Prime Minister made public the day before the event the fact that he intended to participate. Thus, applicants, wishing to protest against the participation of the Hungarian Prime Minister at such an event, did not, and could not, adhere to the three days notice required by the Assembly Act, but held the protest without prior notification. The police dispersed them, relying first of all on the Assembly Act, the text of which did not grant discretion to the police if facing an unnotified demonstration, though also mentioning a sharp noise heard which might be a danger for the delegation in the hotel. That every unnotified demonstration is unlawful under the Assembly Act, and will be dissolved, was confirmed on appeal by the domestic courts. Though the Hungarian Government tried to argue at Strasbourg that there was a detonation heard, and that was the cause of the dissolution, the ECtHR dismissed this argument, as domestic courts did not rely on it either. Rather, it pointed out that if special circumstances justify an immediate response to a political event in the form of a demonstration, it is disproportionate to disband the ensuing peaceful assembly solely because of the lack of prior notice.[200]

That means that there is an obligation flowing from the ECHR to guarantee the possibility of spontaneous demonstrations. Nonetheless, it is also clear that it does not mean more. Prior notice is not contrary to the ECHR,

[198] *Bukta and Others v Hungary*, above n 194.

[199] See BVerfGE 85, 69, 75 (1991): 'Unlike in the case of spontaneous assemblies, in the case of urgent assemblies it is not the notification as such, but only the observation of the deadline is impossible. Therefore, in such a case, there is no need to dispose with the notification, rather there is only the need to shorten the deadline for notice in a way which accounts for the special nature of the assembly.'

[200] *Bukta and Others v Hungary*, above n 194, § 36.

and it cannot be considered redundant unless: (i) special circumstances justify an (ii) immediate response to a (iii) political event. If these conditions are fulfilled, the lack of prior notice is not a sufficient reason to disband an otherwise peaceful and orderly assembly.

Recently, a demonstration blocking a central bridge in Budapest for several hours was understood (not decided, as that was not the issue) to be clearly illegal by the ECtHR. [201] The issue to be decided was the dispersal of a later demonstration—in support of the dispersed bridge blockade, both in protest against election results pronounced two months before—halting vehicular traffic and public transport in and around a main square. The Court found that it was proportionate, especially as the demonstrators could express their solidarity with the illegal bridge blockade, as their demonstration was only dispersed after several hours,[202] despite the fact that it seriously disrupted traffic and was not notified.

Bukta does not mean that 'the absence of prior notification can never be a legitimate basis for crowd dispersal'.[203] The exact contours of the exemption remain to be clarified, such as the issue of urgent assemblies or '*Eilversammlungen*', eventual permissibility of delayed notice requirement, or the proportionality of measures other than dispersal.

Some of those issues are clarified in German law, the apparent origin of the doctrine of spontaneous assembly. According to the GFCC spontaneous demonstrations are those which form instantaneously from an actual occasion.[204] Literature differentiates between several sorts of spontaneous assemblies. According to a dominant categorisation, spontaneous assemblies in the wider sense include: (i) instantaneous, (ii) urgent and (iii) flash assemblies.[205]

Instantaneous assemblies are spontaneous assemblies in the strict sense, as it is only in their case that the determination of holding an assembly and its realisation cannot be separated, but coincide. In the case of urgent and flash assemblies, the moments of determination and the demonstration itself are separate, though the assembly follows shortly after the determination.[206]

The difference is legally relevant, as in the case of urgent assemblies, the court has not dispensed with the duty of notification, it has just acknowledged a shortening of the deadline for notification. In the case of genuinely spontaneous assemblies, to give notice is impossible, as there are no organisers, and as there is no time anyway: the decision to hold an assembly and holding it actually coincide. Thus, so to speak, spontaneous

[201] *Éva Molnár v Hungary*, Application no 10346/05, Judgment of 7 October 2008, § 10 and § 41.
[202] Ibid, § 42.
[203] Ibid, § 37.
[204] BVerfGE 69, 315, 348 (1985), BVerfGE 85, 69, 75.
[205] Dietel, Gintzel and Kniesel, *Versammlungsgesetz*, above n 176, 247.
[206] Ibid.

(instantaneous) assemblies are exempted because of the factual impossibility of notifying in lack of planning and organising.

Urgent (or rapid) assemblies are, however, planned and have an organiser, but their goal would be endangered if the organisers adhered to the deadline.[207] Thus, here the constitutionally acceptable solution is to allow for a shortened deadline for advance notice which should be given in any form (phone, fax, email, etc)[208] without delay immediately after the decision to hold an assembly was made.[209]

An assembly which is meant to surprise is not considered 'spontaneous', because it was planned in advance by its initiators. What is more, it seems that such demonstrations are even considered to be malicious, as 'pretended spontaneous actions'.[210] Maliciously unnotified assemblies, however, are to be dispersed, at least according to some commentators and courts.[211]

In my view, it is possible—and regularly the case with flash mobs, for example—that an assembly is not spontaneous in the strict sense, but still would lose its sense if it were notified. At the same time, most such assemblies do not cause any sort of disturbance, and do not require any policing. The surprising intent in itself is neither consequentially nor even symptomatically related to direct dangers to public safety or order as required by the law on assemblies. Therefore, here legislator and courts seem to engage in an obscure moralising by disapproving 'pretension'. In the meantime, I was not able to clearly verify to what extent this interpretation of unnotified flash mobs as malicious assemblies is really applied in practice apart from a single OLG (Oberlandesgericht) Düsseldorf case.

The French Conseil Constitutionnel has not yet adopted a stance on spontaneous or urgent assemblies. According to the Code Pénal, a manifestation held without prior notice is an illegal demonstration, punishable by six months imprisonment or a fine.[212] The law which reformed the Code and inserted this crime was adopted in 1992, but it was not submitted for review to the Conseil Constitutionnel. Some writers would claim that every unorganised demonstration is an *attroupement*.[213] Thus, it would follow that the spontaneous demonstration being unorganised, therefore, is an *attroupement*, and as such illegal. Such a view runs clearly counter to both *Oya Ataman* and *Bukta*.

[207] BVerfGE 85, 69, 74.

[208] Dietel, Gintzel and Kniesel, *Versammlungsgesetz*, above n 175, ann 22 to § 14 VersG, 249.

[209] BVerfGE 85, 69, 74.

[210] Dietel, Gintzel and Kniesel, *Versammlungsgesetz*, above n 175, ann 19 to § 14 VersG, 248.

[211] Ibid, ann 122 to § 15 VersG, 299 refers to OLG Düsseldorf, NStZ 1984, 514, in this regard affirming.

[212] Art 431-9 Penal Code.

[213] Eg Bernard Stirn, *Les libertés en Question*, 6th edn (Paris, Montchrestien, 2006), § 37.

In US Supreme Court jurisprudence there is no explicit discussion on spontaneous or urgent assemblies. *Shuttlesworth,* of course, exempts from the duty to notify (ask for a permit), if the permit scheme is unconstitutionally vague.

Apart from Harlan J's remark in concurring to *Shuttlesworth*,[214] arguments related to spontaneity came up in 2002 in the case of *Watchtower*,[215] where an ordinance requiring permit (basically registration) for door-to-door canvassing was found unconstitutional by the US Supreme Court, partly because such a system effectively prevents spontaneous expression.[216] Nonetheless, the Supreme Court has not elaborated further on this issue and it has not developed a proper doctrine or test. Especially seen in the light of *Thomas v Chicago Park District*, decided the same year, *Watchtower*'s emphasis on the importance of spontaneous speech might be inapplicable to demonstrations. Lower courts, including circuits, nonetheless sometimes carve out an exception for spontaneous expression, especially in cases of smaller or even one-person demonstrations or performances.[217]

In the United Kingdom, section 11 POA 1986 requires advance notice of processions 'unless it is not reasonably practicable to give any advance notice'. This exemption is meant to cover spontaneous and urgent processions, such as that in front of an embassy prompted by the news of execution of a political prisoner within 24 hours, or a demonstration campaigning for a 'pedestrian crossing outside a school after a fatal road accident'.[218] Considering that literature has not indicated any significant controversy related to the interpretation of 'reasonably practicable', the conclusion might be drawn that UK law is the most generous among the examined jurisdictions with regard to notice and exemptions.

[214] '[W]hen an event occurs, it is often necessary to have one's voice heard promptly, if it is to be considered at all'. *Shuttlesworth v City of Birmingham*, 394 US 147, 163 (1969) (Harlan J concurring).

[215] *Watchtower Bible and Tract Society of New York, Inc v Village of Stratton*, 536 US 150 (2002).

[216] Ibid, 167.

[217] Eg *Santa Monica Food Not Bombs v City of Santa Monica*, 450 F 3d 1022 (9th Cir 2006), or *Grossman v City of Portland*, 33 F 3d 1200 (9th Cir 1994), *Arizona Right to Life PAC v Bayless*, 320 F 3d 1002, 1008 (9th Cir 2003), *Parks v Finan*, 385 F 3d 694, 701–03 (6th Cir 2004) all as cited and discussed in Kellum above, n 70, 410–12, and Burkett, above n 70.

[218] See Home Office, *Review of the Public Order Act 1936 and Related Legislation* Cmnd 7891 (Green Paper, 1980) § 68, as cited by David Bonner and Richard Stone, 'The Public Order Act 1986: Steps in the Wrong Direction?' [1987] *Public Law* 202, 216.

3

From Violence to Public Disorder to Crime Prevention

I. THE PEACEFULNESS REQUIREMENT: A DETERMINANT OF SCOPE OR A LIMIT

NO CONSTITUTION OR human rights instrument protects the right to unpeaceful assembly. There is always a requirement—mostly already included in the concept and scope of the right—of peacefulness. Criminal codes through time and place regularly punish armed participation at a demonstration, that is even legally possessed arms cannot be taken to an assembly.

Apparently it is assumed that an assembly should be about expression and not about threat or violence. Of course, quite a few assemblies are about violence, threat, or coercion in one way or the other, and they are still protected by the constitution. It is a fiction of the law that the would-be Skokie marches, or the Neo-Nazi rallies in Germany, are not about violence. In some sense, the sit-ins and mass protests organised by Martin Luther King Jr were equally about violence. Some of them were occasions of civil disobedience, and most of them could count on the violent reaction of the Southern racists. This was actually the strategy of the civil rights movement: to shock the conscience of the nation by forcing the racists to manifest their violence openly. Hidden forms of violence which pervaded the south well into the post-War period were not perceived as violence until the civil rights protesters provoked open violence.[1] The extent to which 'provocation' is condemned or confirmed by constitutional jurisprudence, will accordingly also be explored later, the doctrines most relevant being 'heckler's veto' and 'fighting words'.

The peacefulness requirement only aims at preventing the most violent, the most threatening, and the most coercive assemblies, or, one is tempted to say, openly displayed or openly attempted violence. The general problem posed by violence for law, or, the other way round, the problem posed by law for violence cannot be resolved here. Clearly, demonstrations are sites of confrontation and often in the sense of challenging state authority.

[1] For a good analysis of the tactics and the reactions to the Civil Rights protests, see James A Colaiaco, 'Martin Luther King, Jr and the Paradox of Nonviolent Direct Action' (1986) 47 *Phylon* 16.

There is arguably already an imbalance in the prohibition of arms at an assembly, since the police do dispose of some arms (though rather tools for crowd control and dispersal). This imbalance is, however, only the usual Hobbesian imbalance flowing from the state monopoly on violence, which I do not intend to question or theorise, just to note here.

The most interesting exception in this regard is the United States where weapons are not *eo ipso* banned at public assemblies. What counts as unpeaceful is otherwise also diverging among the jurisdictions, just as the concrete notion of violence and its watered down pair concept of public order prevailing over freedom of assembly.

A. Germany: Peaceful and Without Arms

The German Basic Law (GG) defines the scope of freedom of assembly as 'peaceable and without arms'.[2] Peaceful or peaceable is according to commentators an assembly which does not take a 'violent or subversive' turn.[3] The language stems from the Federal Law on Assemblies and Processions, which allows for preliminary ban in case there is evidence that the organiser, or his or her supporters, strive for a violent or subversive course.[4]

In particular the adjective 'subversive' (*aufrührerisch*) sounds rather vague and problematic from a constitutional point of view, and there is no echoing parlance by the German Federal Constitutional Court (GFCC) to this effect. Instead, in the court's formulation these are 'acts of a certain dangerousness, such as aggressive excesses against persons or things or other violent acts [*Gewalttätigkeiten*]' that turn the assembly unpeaceful, thus it requires some intensity and concreteness. By distinguishing different sorts (or degrees?) of coercion, the court emphasises that 'a mere obstruction [*Behinderung*] of third persons'[5] does not deprive the assembly of its peaceful nature. Passive

[2] GG art 8 I: 'friedlich und ohne Waffen'.

[3] Hans D Jarass, 'Kommentar zu Art 8', ann 7 in Hans D Jarass and Bodo Pieroth, *Grundgesetz für die Bundesrepublik Deutschland. Kommentar,* 8th edn (München, Beck, 2006), Philip Kunig, 'Kommentar zu Art 8' in Ingo von Münch and Philip Kunig (eds), *Grundgesetz-Kommentar I,* 5th edn (München, Beck, 2000) ann 23.

[4] § 5 Nr 3 Assembly Law of 15 November 1978 (*BGBl I S 1789*), modified by Art 2 of the Law of 8 December 2008 (*BGBl I S 2366*).

[5] BVerfGE 104, 92, 106 (2001), *Sitzblockaden III.* However, a long, ideologically and doctrinally complex debate revolved around obstruction of third persons, which will be covered below, under *Nötigung* in Germany, Ch 4. Here it has to be borne in mind that though every peaceful assembly falls under the scope of freedom of assembly in Germany, it does not mean that the assembly itself cannot be constitutionally restricted if restrictions are justified under the triple test of basic right limitation (proportionality in brief). In this sense, German constitutional interpretation often displays a tendency to allow a wide scope of protection in the first step, including as wide range of conducts as conceivable under the basic right, even if the restrictions imposed by the legislator are easily justified in the second phase of review, ie justifiability of limitations. That is how the broad understanding of peaceful is regarded in its proper context.

resistance, some level of implied coercion, does therefore not in itself deprive the conduct of constitutional protection.

The prohibition on bringing arms to an assembly includes weapons in the technical sense of the word, and in this case it is irrelevant why they are brought to the assembly. Other dangerous tools which are capable of taking the life of another are also constitutionally prohibited from assemblies, though it is unclear whether non-traditional arms fall under the ban on arms or unpeacefulness.[6]

The literature is virtually unanimous that gas masks, helmets, and similar protective covers (which in German are casually called protective weapons, '*Schutzwaffen*') do not fall under the ban on arms, though their wearing can be constitutionally restricted for other reasons if the requirements of proportionality are met.[7]

Probably more interesting is the clear stance the scholarly literature takes on individual responsibility at a demonstration. The general view is that the assembly remains 'peaceful', thus, protected, even if there are unpeaceful, violent 'elements' present, as long as the violence of the individual troublemakers is not supported by the solidarity of the majority who are thus supposed not to become either active or silent accomplices. The organiser is especially required to disavow violence, though the exact moment where the organiser's omission is already beyond the limit, is disputed.[8]

All in all, police are allowed to intervene first only against individual troublemakers whose conduct is thus outside the scope of freedom of assembly. If such an intervention fails or is insufficient, then the police can only take measures against the assembly itself if the conditions under article 8 II GG, are fulfilled, in other words the intervention would have to pass constitutional muster, including the proportionality test.[9]

B. United States: No Ban on Guns

The First Amendment also only guarantees the right of the people peaceably to assemble. What peaceably exactly means has not been the subject of extensive Supreme Court jurisprudence.

[6] *Cf* Roman Herzog, 'Kommentar zu Art 8' in Roman Herzog, Theodor Maunz and Günter Dürig (eds), *Maunz-Dürig Grundgesetz* (München, Beck, 2005) ann 66; and Wolfram Höfling, 'Kommentar zu Art 1' in Michael Sachs (ed), *GG–Grundgesetz Kommentar,* 5th edn (München, Beck, 2009) ann 36.

[7] See also Ch 7.

[8] Wolfgang Hoffmann-Riem, 'Kommentar zu Art 8' in Erhard Denninger, Wolfgang Hoffmann-Riem, Hans-Peter Schneider and Ekkehard Stein (eds), *Kommentar zum Grundgesetz für die Bundesrepublik (AK-GG)* (Neuwied, Hermann Luchterhand Verlag, 2001) ann 28, is somewhat more stringent than Kunig, 'Kommentar zu Art 8' above n 3, ann 24.

[9] BVerfGE 69, 315, 360 f (1985), Herzog, 'Kommentar zu Art 8' above n 6, ann 117; Helmuth Schulze-Fielitz, 'Kommentar zu Art 8' in Horst Dreier (ed), *Grundgesetz. Kommentar,* Vol I, 2nd edn (Tübingen, Mohr Siebeck, 2004) ann 110.

This is in a sense the result of the dogmatic structure of constitutional law in the United States. Unlike in the European Convention on Human Rights (ECHR) or Germany, the American understanding does not differentiate between scope of the right, and permissible limitations on the right, which would then in the particular case allow for restriction. Rather, traditionally at least, the American jurisprudence is more categorical: either something is protected or unprotected. Thus, it does not need to differentiate between unpeaceful assembly and for other reasons unprotected assembly. The kind of very obvious or inherent limits to freedom of assembly which are comparable to other jurisdictions' peaceability criteria can be seen in such quotes as, for example, the following in *Cantwell v Connecticut*:[10]

> No one would have the hardihood to suggest that the principle of freedom of speech sanctions incitement to riot, or that religious liberty connotes the privilege to exhort others to physical attack upon those belonging to another sect. When clear and present danger of riot, disorder, interference with traffic upon the public streets, or other immediate threat to public safety, peace, or order appears, the power of the State to prevent or punish is obvious.

A more significant difference in the United States, compared to other jurisdictions, is the lack of explicit, general ban on carrying guns and weapons to a demonstration. This does not mean that various gun control laws may not affect the legality of bringing arms to a demonstration, but certainly the federal constitution does not restrict it as such. The passivity of police in handling demonstrations of visibly and openly armed persons also testify, to a general view, that this is constitutionally protected. Even in cases where permit for assembly is required, bringing guns to a demonstration will not by far result in denying the permit for grounds of unpeacefulness.[11]

The Supreme Court has not ruled specifically on the issue of carrying guns to a protest or demonstration yet, but the 2008 case of *District of Columbia v Heller,*[12] spelling out the constitutional right to keep and bear arms, probably points also in the same direction as the intensifying practice of the open-carry movement to bring guns to demonstrations and protests.

There does not, so far, seem to be any concern that guns in the mass might be significantly more dangerous than elsewhere, let alone how wearing a gun to a demonstration might efficiently silence counter-speech.

[10] *Cantwell v Connecticut*, 310 US 296, 308 (1940).

[11] See Ann Gerhart, 'Militia Movement Packing Heat at Gun Rally on the Potomac', *The Washington Post* (19 April 2010) available at www.washingtonpost.com/wp-dyn/content/article/2010/04/18/AR2010041802391.html?sid=ST2010041803839. Gerhart's article includes a link to the 26pp permit issued for the Gravelly Point and Fort Hunt Park gun rallies: api.ning.com/files/YH9bc-rAzt9SVhE8yFztXjMEZZelXEaB652XM95uHcdxr*nDt9HjBkILttqi*Zcw5gYKWvLIyTPEZQtKcc*ZrSilwwYjtXsN/Permitp.2to26.pdf.

[12] *District of Columbia v Heller*, 554 US 570 (2008).

I do think, however, that whatever might be the merits of a constitutional principle of possible armed self-defence against the government, it certainly should not apply to speakers of opposite view, or to other addressees or targets of a demonstration. In this regard, however, the US Supreme Court might have a precedent, as *Virginia v Black*[13] allows for restriction of speech which aims at intimidation as falling under the category of true threat. A case-by-case approach, intervening only in cases of intimidating 'gun wearing' would probably be the most consistent with the rest of the free speech doctrine.

C. United Kingdom: Not a Thematised Separate Question

Unlike in Germany and under the ECHR, in the United Kingdom the question of peacefulness does not arise separately as a preliminary question of scope (at least in traditional, domestic, pre-Human Rights Act (HRA) understanding).

As we have seen, the Public Order Act (POA) 1986 allows for banning in cases of apprehension of serious public disorder, serious public disorder is thus certainly the antithesis of 'peaceful'. Different forms of mob or street violence (riot, affray, destruction of property, other ordinary violent crimes, etc), as criminalised in many provisions of statutory and common law, are also clearly beyond any claim to freedom of assembly, just as in the other jurisdictions.

Apart from this, English law shows an increasingly alarming spectrum of other criminal or administrative provisions threatening freedom of assembly in anti-terrorist and anti-harassment legislation and legislation on antisocial behaviour. These latter ones will be dealt with in the relevant sections in the following pages, at least to the extent they were interpreted by higher courts. David Mead's significant 2010 book on the new law of peaceful protest,[14] as in so many other respects, is recommended for its coverage of the many details—dangers and challenges—involved in these provisions. This book aspires to keep repetitions to a minimum, instead providing a broader comparative aspect.

D. France: *Attroupement* and Group Violence

Definitely, in France, both *manifestation* and *réunion* are only protected in their peaceful version. The 'peacefulness' criterion figured in a few early

[13] *Virginia v Black*, 538 US 343 (2003).

[14] David Mead, *The New Law of Peaceful Protest. Rights and Regulations in the Human Rights Act Era* (Oxford, Hart Publishing, 2010).

constitutional documents which, however, did not make a lasting impact on French constitutionalism.[15]

Hubrecht claims that among all the notions surrounding the law of demonstration, the notion of *attroupement* is defined with most precision, thus he even suggests deriving the notion of *manifestation* from (the negation of) *attroupement.* As an *attroupement* is an assembly of individuals with arms or capable ('susceptible') of troubling the public peace,[16] it is certainly true that an assembly is supposed to be peaceful. Wearing guns at a *manifestation* or *réunion publique* is punishable with three years imprisonment or a €45,000 fine according to article 431-10 of the Criminal Code, a rather serious punishment.

The Conseil Constitutionnel (CC) affirmed the constitutionality of a law enabling the prefectoral authority to prohibit the bringing or wearing of arms and objects capable of being used as arms to and at a demonstration, but struck down a provision—basically on overbreadth or rule of law grounds—which would enable the imposition of a similar ban with regard to objects capable of being used as *projectiles*.[17]

The 2010 law against 'group violence'[18] was also found constitutional in its aspects relevant for our discussion.[19] The new provision punishes those who knowingly participate in a group, even if temporary, which aims at preparing voluntary violent acts against persons or goods, provided that the aim is supported by material facts.[20]

The CC found the provision does not violate freedom of assembly (*réunion* or *manifestation*), is clear and precise, and prescribes a proportionate punishment, thus it does not fail to observe the principle of legality and proportionality of punishments. Again, characteristically for the judicial treatment of freedom of assembly, the CC cites that the applicants claimed violation of both *liberté de réunion* and *liberté de manifestation*, but answers only that the law does not realise any violation of 'the freedom

[15] The Constitution of 1791 affirms in Title I, § 2 that the 'Constitution guarantees as natural and civil rights ... the liberty of the citizens to assemble peacefully and without arms, in accordance with the laws of police'. This formula was repeated in a Declaration of Rights before the Montagnard Constitution of 24 June 1793. After that, liberty of *réunion* was not mentioned in constitutional documents until the 1848 Constitution whose art 8 again guaranteed freedom of peaceful assembly within the limits of rights of others and public security. However, all these documents were rebutted later, and none of them serves as point of reference in contemporary constitutional discourse either. See also Ch 1 above.

[16] Hubert G Hubrecht, 'Le droit français de la manifestation' Pierre Favre (ed), *La manifestation* (Paris, Presses de Sciences Po, 1990) ch 5, 186.

[17] Decision no 94-352 DC, 18 January 1995.

[18] Law no 2010-201 of 2 March 2010 (loi renforçant la lutte contre les violences de groupes et la protection des personnes chargées d'une mission de service public)

[19] Decision no 2010-604 DC, 25 February 2010.

[20] Art 222-14-2 Criminal Code.

of movement or of the collective expression of ideas and opinions' (*considérant* 30). That is all the Conseil Constitutionnel says about the assembly aspects of the law, clearly considering the law unproblematic in this respect. Therefore, it is likely that the Conseil Constitutionnel—if it were to explicitly reason in terms of scope first, and limitations second—would simply consider the activities punished by the group violence law as completely outside the protection of freedom of assembly.

Nonetheless, and importantly, the Conseil Constitutionnel interpreted the 'knowing participation' criterion as requiring that it be proven, both that the person participates with a view to commit the violence, and that this intention is supported by one or more material facts (*considérant* 12). On the one hand, the Conseil Constitutionnel has not annulled this pre-emptive law which might, in theory, be applied against protestors who have never committed, and will never commit, any violent acts. On the other hand, it gave a narrow interpretation which still binds penal responsibility to proven individual acts, thereby depriving the law of its dangerous tendency to establish 'guilt by association'.

E. European Court of Human Rights: Systematic, Intentional Violence

Article 11 of the ECHR protects only the freedom of peaceful assembly. The European Court of Human Rights (ECtHR) exerts substantive review in this regard; the *Stankov*[21] decision testifies to such an approach.

In *Stankov*, the Bulgarian Government argued that the ban on demonstrations organised by the United Macedonian Organisation Ilinden was not an interference since the planned demonstrations would not have been of a peaceful nature. The ECtHR reiterated that article 11 only protects peaceful assemblies, but the peaceful character is only foregone if the organisers and participants have violent intentions. On the facts of the case the Government could not reasonably conclude that the planned demonstrations were to be unpeaceful.

The *Stankov* decision is one of the examples of substantive review which appears to stand in contradiction to several earlier inadmissibility decisions handed down by the Commission. *Chappell*[22] and *Pendragon*,[23] for example, both included complete blanket bans around Stonehenge for the period around the midsummer solstice. The Commission did not find it

[21] *Stankov and the United Macedonian Organisation Ilinden v Bulgaria*, ECHR 2001-IX, Application nos 29221/95 and 29225/95, Judgment of 2 October 2001.

[22] *Chappell v United Kingdom*, Application no 12587/86, Decision on admissibility, 14 July 1987.

[23] *Pendragon v United Kingdom*, Application no 31416/96, Decision on admissibility, 19 October 1998.

problematic that the cause of danger of disturbance lay outside the sphere of action of the applicants. Therefore, their right to freedom of assembly (and religion) was interfered with without any fault on their part. Remarkably, the Commission did not adhere to the relevant dicta of *Plattform Ärzte für das Leben*,[24] according to which states are required to take reasonable measures to prevent the violent behaviour of others threatening an assembly which is in itself peaceful. The *Chappel/Pendragon* line of inadmissibility cases seems also to conflict with earlier decisions of the Commission itself: in a 1980 case, *Christians against Racism and Facism (CARAF) v United Kingdom*[25] it stated that:

> The possibility of violent counter-demonstrations or the possibility of extremists with violent intentions, not members of the organising association, joining the demonstration cannot as such take away that right. Even if there is a real risk of a public procession resulting in disorder by developments outside the control of those organising it, such procession for this reason alone does not fall out of the scope of Article 11(1) of the Convention.

In this case, a planned anti-fascist procession was caught up by the general ban on processions in a certain area of London. The Commission accepted the ban as justified because earlier protests by the National Front resulted in serious damage to persons and property which even large contingents of police could not prevent. Here, therefore, the peaceful anti-fascists were restricted in their assembly rights because of previously unpeaceful others. Unlike in *Chappell* and *Pendragon*, the application was not found to be outside the scope of article 11.

That such an application would be manifestly ill-founded today is also unlikely because of the *Ezelin*[26] jurisprudence: the Court requires that a person be punished only if he himself committed some reprehensible act, since reaffirmed, for example, in *Galstyan v Armenia*.[27] *Ziliberberg v Moldova* is a case at hand which involved a demonstration gradually turning violent, but where there was no indication that the applicant participated in violence, and he was still fined for participating. The Court emphasised that[28]

> an individual does not cease to enjoy the right to peaceful assembly as a result of sporadic violence or other punishable acts committed by others in the course of the demonstration, if the individual in question remains peaceful in his or her own intentions or behaviour.

[24] *Plattform Ärzte für das Leben v Austria*, Application no 10126/82, Judgment of 21 June 1988.

[25] *Christians against Racism and Fascism (CARAF) v United Kingdom*, Application no 8440/78, Decision on admissibility, 16 July 1980, DR 21, 138.

[26] *Ezelin v France*, 14 EHRR 362, Application no 11800/85, Judgment of 26 April 1991.

[27] *Galstyan v Armenia*, 50 EHRR 25, Application no 26986/03, Judgment of 15 November 2007.

[28] *Ziliberberg v Moldova*, Application no 61821/00, Decision on admissibility, 4 May 2004.

How sporadic is sporadic is of course open to interpretation, and one should not be rushing to conclude, for example, that only such demonstrations can be dispersed where each and every participant is violent.

Furthermore, under *Plattform Ärzte für das Leben*[29] the possibility of violent counter-demonstrations is not a reason to ban the demonstration, thus the Court went further than the 1981 *CARAF* decision. '[T]he authorities have a duty to take appropriate measures with regard to lawful demonstrations for in order to ensure their peaceful conduct and the safety of all citizens'.[30]

It is also settled case law that an unlawful situation does not justify an infringement of freedom of assembly,[31] certainly there is then no possibility to interpret unpeacefulness as simple unlawfulness.

II. THE WOULD-BE DISORDERLY: JUDICIAL DOCTRINES OF RISK-ASSESSMENT

The following discussion will include some of the most important decisions on freedom of speech or opinion, even though they were actually delivered in the context of an assembly. They are therefore not only interesting because they display vividly the differences among the compared jurisdictions, but also for the similarity of merging speech and assembly doctrines, even in cases where the plurality of the participants is crucial. The following discussion could be structured in different ways; I have chosen a division according to the source of the perceived threat, because that division suits every jurisdiction at least in part. Accordingly, first the judicial handling of demonstrators as perpetrators or (more commonly) instigators will be examined, and I will then turn to doctrines related to hostile audience and counter-demonstration.

A. Differently Dangerous Demonstrators

i. United States: Imminence, Likelihood

In the United States, after half a century of hesitation, which cannot be dealt with on these pages,[32] the US Supreme Court 'finalised' its doctrine

[29] *Plattform Ärzte für das Leben v Austria*, 13 EHRR 204, Application no 10126/82, Judgment of 21 June 1988.

[30] *Oya Ataman v Turkey*, ECHR 2006-XV, Application no 74552/01, Judgment of 5 December 2006, § 35.

[31] Ibid § 39, referring to *Cisse v France*, ECHR 2002-III, Application no 51346/99, Judgment of 9 April 2002, § 50.

[32] For an early critical comment, see Hans A Linde, '"Clear and Present Danger" Re-examined: Dissonance in the *Brandenburg* Concerto' (1970) 22 *Stanford Law Review*

applicable to speech which intends or risks a harmful consequence in the 1969 case of *Brandenburg v Ohio*.[33] The *per curiam* opinion held that the First Amendment protects speech unless it incites to imminent lawless action which is very likely to occur, and claimed that this is a reformulation of the clear and present danger test as elaborated by Justices Holmes and Brandeis. The concurring Justices Douglas and Black dismissed the clear and present danger test, and advocated a distinction between speech and overt acts.[34] Brandenburg was the leader of a Ku Klux Klan group, convicted under Ohio's criminal syndicalism statute on the basis of films shot at a Ku Klux Klan 'organisers' meeting'. The films showed hooded figures with firearms, burning a large cross, making derogatory remarks of blacks and Jews. Speeches in the footage included very strong sentences such as:[35]

> We're not a revengent organisation, but if our President, our Congress, our Supreme Court, continues to suppress the white, Caucasian race, it's possible that there might have to be some revengeance taken ... We are marching on Congress July the Fourth, four hundred thousand strong. From there we are dividing into two groups, one group to march on St. Augustine, Florida, the other group to march into Mississippi ... Personally, I believe the nigger should be returned to Africa, the Jew returned to Israel.

The US Supreme Court reversed Brandenburg's conviction, stating that[36]

> [t]he Constitutional guarantees of free speech and free press do not permit a state to forbid or proscribe advocacy of the use of force or of law violation except where such advocacy is directed to inciting or producing imminent lawless action or is likely to incite or produce such action.

Later cases made clear that imminence and intent must both be present. For example in *Hess v Indiana,* the court reversed a conviction because the evidence failed to show that the 'words were intended to produce, and likely to produce, imminent disorder'.[37] In this case, Hess was arrested during an anti-war demonstration on a college campus for loudly stating, 'We'll take the fucking street later (or again)'. According to the US Supreme Court, the statement could be understood at best as 'counsel for present moderation'; at worst, as 'advocacy of illegal action at some indefinite future time', in other words intent might have been present, but not immediacy of danger. Also, as Hess—though facing the crowd—was not addressing a particular

1163, for a general historical sketch of the development of the test, see, eg John F Wirenius, 'The Road to *Brandenburg*: A Look at the Evolving Understanding of the First Amendment' (1994) 43 *Drake Law Review* 1.

33 *Brandenburg v Ohio*, 395 US 444 (1969).

34 Ibid, 456.

35 Ibid, 446 f.

36 Ibid, 447.

37 *Hess v Indiana*, 414 US 105 (1973).

group or a particular person, the utterance cannot be taken as advocacy of action proper.[38]

It appears impossible to find a case where the *Brandenburg* criteria have been found by the Supreme Court to be fulfilled.[39]

Less on the incitement side, but more on the distinction between violence and protected speech, the court developed in *NAACP v Claiborne*[40] a doctrine of individual liability. In the case, a boycott of white merchants was proclaimed in order to further civil rights causes. The boycott was accompanied by speeches and non-violent picketing, but there were sporadic acts and threats of violence. The white merchants sued the NAACP and the boycott's main organiser, Charles Evers, for lost income for the period of the boycott, 1966–72. The Supreme Court held that non-violent elements of the boycott were fully protected. A person cannot be held responsible for being a member of the body organising the boycott; civil liability arises only in the case where personal participation in violence or threat of violence is proven.

Finally, jurisprudence is unclear about whether *previous violence* might be a ground for limiting freedom of assembly of the same group. *Kunz v New York*,[41] in which a prior restraint decision was quashed on grounds of overly broad official discretion, clearly indicates that previous violence cannot form the basis of prior restraint. However, in an earlier labour picketing case[42] Justice Jackson found that a large-scale industrial conflict, where violence is neither episodic nor isolated, does provide sufficient grounds for a preliminary injunction on future assemblies. The abortion clinic protest cases decided decades later (and post-*Brandenburg*) also appear to accept injunctions for reasons of previous violent conduct, even injunctions applicable to people who were not enjoined.[43]

ii. Germany: Direct Endangerment, but Low Probability Standard

In Germany, the threshold for intervention is thematised, but is less elaborated than in the United States. The GFCC has spelled out some principles, though the ultimate yardsticks remain proportionality and deciding each case on its particular circumstances.

The *Brokdorf*[44] decision dealt also with the powers of prior ban and dissolution as authorised by the Federal Assembly Law. These provisions allow

[38] Ibid, 107–09.

[39] None of the 54 US Supreme Court cases, including reference to *Brandenburg* in Westlaw, is such.

[40] *NAACP v Claiborne*, 458 US 102 (1982).

[41] *Kunz v New York*, 340 US 290 (1951).

[42] *Milk Wagon Drivers Local 753 v Meadowmoor Dairies*, 312 US 287 (1941).

[43] See Chs 2 and 8.

[44] BVerfGE 69, 315 (1985), *Brokdorf*.

for restriction in case circumstances suggest that public security or public order is *directly endangered* by the assembly or procession.

In the interpretation developed in police law, public security means protection of such central legal values (*Rechtsgüter*) as life, health, freedom, honour, property or estates of the individual, integrity of the legal order or of state institutions. For an endangerment of public security, there must be a danger of a criminally proscribed offence against any of these values.[45] Public order, on the other hand, in police law, equals to the whole of unwritten norms whose observance is—according to prevailing social and ethical considerations—indispensable for the ordered living together of humans within the confines of a territory.[46]

This interpretation has been narrowed down by the GFCC in two ways.

First, in accordance with the principle of proportionality, a ban or dissolution is only constitutional if less intrusive means of imposing conditions has already been tried and exhausted.[47] In addition, not only the discretion as to the means, but also as to the substance of the authority is limited: not every sort of interest might justify a restriction on the right to freedom of assembly. Importantly, burdens flowing from the characteristic of assemblies as mass phenomena which cannot be eliminated without endangering the aim of the particular assembly itself are to be tolerated by third persons.[48]

Secondly, ban or dissolution is only allowed if public security or order is directly, immediately endangered. Thus, the requirement is stricter than in general police law. It necessitates in every case a probability assessment which should be based on facts, circumstances and other details, not on mere suspicion or assumptions.[49]

However, the GFCC expressly left the details to the ordinary courts, implying that anything more concrete would intrude upon their competences. Ordinary courts would normally check whether police offered sufficiently precise factual evidence which would suggest that public order or security would be endangered.[50]

Instead of more concrete tests, the *Brokdorf* decision includes a long contemplation on constitutional requirements flowing, not so much from the duty to protect the exercise of the right, but from procedural and

[45] Ibid, 352, with reference to Bill Drews, Gerhard Wacke, Klaus Vogel and Wolfgang Martens, *Gefahrenabwehr*, Vol 2, 8th edn (Köln, Heymanns, 1977) 130 and 177.

[46] BVerfGE 69, 315, 352.

[47] Ibid, 353.

[48] Ibid.

[49] Ibid.

[50] See, eg VGH (Administrative Court) Mannheim, 28 August 1986, 1 S 3241/85, NVwZ 1987, 237 (confirming the unlawfulness of a police ban of a meeting where David Irving was going to talk because unsubstantiated allegations that a counter-demonstration would result in disturbances).

organisational guarantees which should facilitate exercising freedom of assembly.

As mentioned already,[51] the GFCC imposes the obligation on both the police and demonstrators to adhere to 'time-tested practices' (*bewährte Erfahrungen*), such as cooperative and moderate behaviour and timely dialogue, which presumably helps prevent or calm down potential tensions. This, in relation to prevention of violence, means that the more cooperative the organisers are, the higher the threshold for potential police intervention lies.[52]

As can be seen from these formulations, the standards pronounced in *Brokdorf* are very principled, but abstract, and they faithfully mirror all the relativities (or flexibilities) of proportionality.

In relation to *mass* demonstration specifically, the decision offers some examples which would constitutionally justify police intervention. Such is the case when, for example, a demonstrator commits violent acts during the demonstration, or approves someone else doing so. A prior ban is justified only if it is predicted by a high probability that the organiser, or their supporter, intends to commit violent acts, or at least approves of such conduct.[53] This observation, it seems to me, necessitates a soft reading of the directness or immediacy requirement mentioned earlier in the decision, because it only requires a probability of intent to commit or of intent to approve, not also a probability of actual violence occurring. This differentiates the German approach from the US standard as pronounced in *Brandenburg*.

Nonetheless, one has to bear in mind the very different underlying facts of the mentioned cases. Neither in *Brandenburg* or *Hess* was there any violence, while in *Brokdorf* it was considered relevant that in previous such demonstrations acts of violence did occur. In this regard, the *Brokdorf* situation is closer to *NAACP v Claiborne*, as sporadic violence occurred in both cases. However, they are still hardly comparable as *Claiborne* related to a boycott which lasted years, while *Brokdorf* involved a 50,000 strong demonstration. Also, the courts were asked to decide on completely different issues: in *Brokdorf* the issue was the constitutionality of the prior ban and dissolution powers, in *Claiborne* the issue was liability for damages resulting from the boycott.

Later decisions of the GFCC have also not specified very precisely the level of risk necessary for restrictions to be justified. An appearance of 'readiness to violence' or a 'provocation to create a climate of violent demonstration' were found to be sufficient for restriction, at least if coupled with violations

[51] See above Ch 2.

[52] BVerfGE 69, 315, 356 f.

[53] Ibid, 360—in case of such prognosis, the assembly will qualify as unpeaceful, thus being completely deprived of constitutional protection.

of 'fundamental social and ethical views conforming to the Basic Law', in other words a constitutionally strengthened concept of public order.[54]

In addition, the court found constitutional the ban on uniforms expressing common political attitude as they are capable to excite 'suggestive-militant effects in the direction of intimidating, uniform militancy'.[55]

On the other hand, the court declared unconstitutional provisions of the new Bavarian Assembly Law which would make organisers liable to pay an administrative fine (*Bußgeld*) if they fail to take 'appropriate measures' to 'prevent' or 'stop' (*verhindern*) 'violent acts' (*Gewalttätigkeiten*, an expression by the way used by the GFCC itself) arising 'out of the assembly' (*aus der Versammlung heraus*) for rule of law considerations analogous to vagueness.[56] The court equally struck down the provisions rendering a fine for 'participating at an assembly in a way which contributes to the fact that the assembly appears from the outside to be of paramilitary nature or otherwise communicating readiness to violence, and thereby an intimidatory effect arises'.[57]

A G8 protest case, where German courts affirmed a six-day preventive detention of would-be demonstrators, reached the ECtHR recently, which decided that it violated both article 5 and article 11. The GFCC denied intermediary measures, and then also summarily declined to examine the complaints on their merit.[58] Article 11 was involved in two regards, the demonstrators were prevented from holding up banners with the slogan 'Free the prisoners', and were prevented from actually going to the place of the demonstration. Characteristic of German law—not so much thematised in German *assembly* literature—is the possibility of mass detention for preventive purposes. Those 'prisoners' whose liberation was at stake on the banners were 1,112 would-be demonstrators, whose detention went before the courts in 628 cases, out of which only 113 were found lawful ex post facto.[59] There was some violence at protests on the occasion of previous G8 summits, and also there was to be violence on the protest which could not be attended by the applicants. One of the applicants had previously been convicted for disturbing rail traffic at the occasion of anti-nuclear protests. German authorities in the present case claimed the banners would have realised incitement to prisoner liberation (prisoner liberation being a crime) while applicants

[54] See Ch 6 for more on this.

[55] For more on this see Ch 7.

[56] BVerfGE 122, 342 (2009) § 122.

[57] Art 7(2), sanctioned by a fine by art 21(7). Only the provisions for the fines, not the prohibitions themselves, were struck down for prudential and practical reasons, even though the constitutional objection of indeterminacy, unpreciseness or vagueness clearly relate to the substantive prohibitory rules, not to the provisions on the fines.

[58] 2 BvR 538/08 and 2 BvR 164/08 as cited by *Schwabe and MG v Germany*, ECHR 2011-IX, Application nos 8080/08, 8577/08, Judgment of 1 December 2011, § 36.

[59] Ibid, § 10.

claimed they called on the government, not other demonstrators, to free the detained. One applicant refused to identify himself, and later was fined €200. Charges of incitement to crime were later dropped for reasons of insignificance. Still German courts found the six-day detention lawful, the GFCC also apparently believing public security was directly endangered by the would-be demonstrators. This is a case showing strong parallels to *Laporte*[60] in the United Kingdom, discussed below, and seen in that light calls the rights-protective reputation of German law seriously into question.

Thus, though traditional police law notions of public safety and public order were considerably narrowed down by German constitutional law, courts, including the GFCC, are actually satisfied with a probability standard much lower than is constitutional in the United States, or, as it will be seen below, permissible in UK or ECHR law.

iii. United Kingdom: Unclarity as to Imminence

In relation to prevention of violence and disorder, cases related to the common law concept of *breach of the peace* are most characteristic of the judicial approach, traditionally oscillating between a very weak and a more rigorous standard. Two central cases involved conviction not for breach of the peace itself (which is not an offence in English law), but for obstructing an officer in executing his duties related to prevention of breach of the peace.

In the 1882 case of *Beatty v Gillbanks*[61] Salvation Army members were charged with unlawful and tumultuous assembly to the disturbance of the peace as Skeleton Army members were accompanying their marches shouting and disorderly. The Divisional Court ruled the disorder was not 'the natural consequence of their [ie the Salvation Army's] acts',[62] as it came from the rival group.

In contrast, a weak review was applied in the 1936 case of *Duncan v Jones*[63] which was a case relating to a speech to be held in front of a

[60] *R (on the application of Laporte) v Chief Constable of Gloucestershire* [2007] 2 All ER 529, [2006] UKHL 55.

[61] *Beatty v Gillbanks* (1882) 9 QBD 308.

[62] Note the similarity with the early US speech test, 'bad tendency', which was superseded by the more speech protective 'clear and present danger', and now *Brandenburg*.

[63] *Duncan v Jones* [1936] 1 KB 218. A member of the National Unemployed Workers' Movement wanted to stand upon a box to deliver a speech in front of an unemployed training site when she was asked by police to hold the meeting elsewhere. When she refused, she was arrested for unlawful and willful obstruction of an officer in the execution of his duty. There was no incitement, or other sign or probability of a breach of the peace alleged, although in the previous year a speech by the same person was followed by some disorder. The Divisional Court had explicitly found the right of public meeting and assembly inapplicable. It also accepted that a breach of the peace was reasonably apprehended by the officer because of the disorder in the previous year, and that the offence was realised when obstructing the officer in taking measures—ie the order of relocation—in reaction to such an apprehension.

training site for the unemployed. The court accepted the police officer's apprehension of a breach of the peace—based on a disorder a year before—as reasonable, not requiring any weighing of actual probability of ensuing disorder, nor providing any clarification as to what counts as disorder.

Breach of the peace since *R v Howell* (1981) is understood to occur when 'harm is actually done or likely to be done to a person or, in his presence, his property or is put in fear of being harmed through an assault, affray, riot, unlawful assembly or other disturbance'.[64] In *Steel v UK* the ECtHR accepted that the notion of breach of the peace as put forward in *Howell* fulfilled the requirement of 'lawful' for article 5 purposes,[65] thus it also satisfies the prescribed by law requirement in article 11(2).

More recently, a 2006 House of Lords judgment in *Laporte*,[66] on breach of the peace, examined the concept for its compatibility with Strasbourg jurisprudence in other respects, shedding light on the mechanisms of the Human Rights Act, while also clarifying to a considerable extent the tensions between freedom of assembly and public 'peace' in English law.

What is probably the most peculiar feature of the concept of peace is the duty—though imperfect, in other words not directly sanctioned per se—of the general public, of every citizen, to uphold the 'Queen's peace' and, if necessary, to assist the police in maintaining it (ie preventing a breach of the peace).

The *Laporte* case involved a demonstration planned by anti-war protesters at an RAF base also used by the US Air Force at Fairford in Gloucestershire. Ms Laporte intended to attend the demonstration against the war in Iraq, and thus started in a coach organised for this purpose from London to Fairford. However, as the Fairford police officer, Mr Lambert, also learned from intelligence sources that members of a violent anti-war group, the so-called 'Wombles' might be present in the coaches, he ordered the three coaches to be stopped and searched at a lay-by at Lechlade, some miles away from Fairford.[67] The police found some objects and instruments (masks, shields, etc) in the coaches which were rather inconsistent with the purpose of a peaceful demonstration; these instruments were seized. The police also discovered eight members of the Wombles among the 120 passengers, though unable to verify the identity of some other persons who, like Ms Laporte—perfectly lawfully—failed to identify themselves. Mr Lambert instructed the police at Lechlade to turn back the coaches to London and not to allow the passangers to get off the vehicles. Thus,

[64] *R v Howell* [1982] QB 416, 427 as cited in *R (on the application of Laporte) v Chief Constable of Gloucestershire* [2004] EWHC 253 (Admin) [20].

[65] *Steel v UK*, Application no 24838/94, 28 EHRR 603, Judgment of 23 September 1998, § 55.

[66] *Laporte*, above n 60.

[67] S 60 of the Criminal Justice and Public Order Act authorises such a stop and search.

it happened that Ms Laporte, together with more than 100 other persons, were not only prevented from attending the meeting, but also forced to stay in the coaches until they again reached London, that is for several hours altogether. Certainly, Mr Lambert did not apprehend an imminent danger of breach of the peace—he himself made it clear that was the reason why he did not order to arrest anyone at Lechlade. Still, he believed that there might be some disturbance if the coaches arrived at Fairford, thus, he ordered sending back as a measure short of arrest.

The Law Lords all agreed that there was no power to send the coaches back, and, thus, the measure adopted by the police did not have a basis in law, in other words it was not prescribed by law for the purposes of the ECHR. They similarly agreed that the premature and indiscriminate measure was in any event unjustified, because it was a disproportionate infringement of the right to freedom of speech and assembly. The correct interpretation of the common law is that there has been no power to apply measures, short of arrest, against persons if there is no imminent danger of breach of the peace, though there are differences in evaluating the precedents.[68] According to Lord Bingham, *Howell* is instructive regarding the legal concept of a breach of the peace. For the Court of Appeal in *Howell*, and for Lord Bingham in *Laporte*, the essence of the concept was to be found in 'violence or threatened violence'.[69] 'It is for this breach of the peace when done in his presence or the reasonable apprehension of it taking place that a constable, or anyone else, may arrest an offender without warrant'.[70] Nonetheless, Lord Bingham observes, that a 'breach of the peace is not, as such, a criminal offence, but founds an application to bind over'. According to Lord Brown,[71] however, this latter statement of Lord Bingham refers to the 'concept of a breach of the peace' in the sense that the breach itself possibly would come from someone other than the person to be bound over. The leading authority on the measures to be adopted in case of a breach of the peace is Lord Diplock's ruling in *Albert v Lavin*.[72] In that case, which was later applied in numerous other cases, Lord Diplock stated that

> every citizen in whose presence a breach of the peace is being, or reasonably appears to be about to be, committed has the right to take reasonable steps to make the person who is breaking or threatening to break the peace refrain from doing so; and those reasonable steps in appropriate cases will include detaining him against his will. At common law this is not only the right of every citizen,

[68] *Cf Piddington v Bates* [1961] 1 WLR 162, 169; *Moss v McLachlan* [1985] IRLR 76 [24]; *Minto v Police* [1987] 1 NZLR 374, 377.

[69] *Laporte*, above n 60, § 27.

[70] *R v Howell* [1982] QB 416, 427.

[71] *Laporte*, above n 59, § 111.

[72] *Albert v Lavin* [1982] AC 546.

> it is also his duty, although, except in the case of a citizen who is a constable, it is a duty of imperfect obligation.

Lord Bingham,[73] however, himself formulated a rule in *Laporte* which is clearer, and it was repeated by Lord Brown:[74]

> Every constable, and also every citizen, enjoys the power and is subject to the duty to seek to prevent, by arrest or other action short of arrest, any breach of the peace occurring in his presence, or any breach of the peace which (having occurred) is likely to be renewed, or any breach of the peace which is about to occur.

There is quite an agreement, therefore, that there is no way to prevent a breach of the peace except if it is either: (i) actual, or, (ii) already happened and likely to be renewed, or, is (iii) about to occur. That means, in the particular case, that there was no power to apply a measure even short of arrest against Ms Laporte and others since no breach of the peace was about to even occur. In other words, the police or citizens are neither entitled nor obliged to take reasonable steps to prevent a breach of the peace '*from becoming to occur*' as Lord Brown quite aptly formulated.[75] Consequently, the test is not simple reasonableness even in common law, even without regard to the Convention, but a stricter one.

There is, however, some disagreement as to the question of imminence on the ground of another earlier case, *Moss v McLachlan*.[76] In *Moss*, brought about in the midst of the miners' strike, the police prevented a group of striking miners from picketing places which were, or were in the near vicinity of, the area where some miners (apparently in opposition to the strike) worked. The court considered the situation as one in which a breach of the peace was imminent and therefore found the preventive action taken by the police reasonable.

In the *Laporte* case, the House of Lords differed on *why* they considered imminence was not fulfilled compared to the *Moss* situation. Lord Bingham was of the opinion that the facts of the present case differed so much that though *Moss* was good law, there was no application to the *Laporte* case—in *Moss* there was an imminent breach of the peace but in *Laporte* there was none. Lord Rodger, however, would have accepted that there was an imminent breach of the peace at Lechlade, had the police, that is Mr Lambert, been of that opinion (and he was not). This might indicate a willingness to defer to police discretion as to the existence of imminence. Lord Mance, to the contrary, considered that, even in the circumstances of *Moss*, there was no imminent breach of the peace, thus, it was wrongly decided. Obviously, he would require more concrete and clear evidence.

[73] *Laporte*, above n 60, § 29.
[74] Ibid, § 110.
[75] Ibid, § 115.
[76] *Moss v McLachlan* 149 JP 167, [1985] IRLR 76.

As the Lords do not agree on the threshold of imminence, the significance of the *Laporte* ruling from the viewpoint of freedom of assembly is considerably reduced: the application might be quite narrow.

Imminence which was defined as 'about to happen',[77] 'going to happen in the near future'[78] in *Laporte,* was understood as 'likely to happen' in 2011 by the Divisional Court, quite a different question.[79] Even that was, however, further weakened on appeal, when the Court of Appeal basically found the courts were not entitled to review the existence of imminence, but have to check only whether police could reasonably apprehend that a breach of the peace was imminent.[80]

The Lords in *Laporte* cited several times[81] *Redmond-Bate v DPP,*[82] a decision describing the changes brought about by the Human Rights Act as a 'constitutional shift'. Nonetheless, some statements in *Laporte* draw attention to the caution the Lords exercised towards parliamentary sovereignty, as it is in harmony with their HRA mandate to interpret the law in conformity with the ECHR only as long as it is possible, that is no statute can be invalidated if it is contrary to the Convention. Thus, for instance, Lord Brown explicitly maintained the possibility that primary legislation can confer a power to the police 'to prevent entirely innocent citizens from taking part in demonstrations already afoot',[83] though this seems to conflict with Strasbourg jurisprudence. What is more, Lord Rodger even emphasised that the common law goes further than ECtHR jurisprudence as of today in making persons acting entirely lawfully responsible if a breach of the peace is imminent. The ECtHR affirmed the conformity with the Convention of a police power to arrest a protestor if the target of the protest (a disrupted grouse hunter) might react violently in *Steel v UK.*[84] However, Lord Rodger[85] considered that in common law such a power, or, even a duty, exists also in a situation where the demonstrators' 'lawful and proper conduct' would naturally result in violent reaction, not on the part of the targeted audience, but by third parties. The judgment as a whole leaves open whether this is a power of last resort, or, easily flows from the duty of every citizen to preserve the peace unbroken.

UK courts—and by now the ECtHR—decided another type of police measure, kettling or cordoning, under breach of the peace law. *Austin v*

[77] *Laporte*, above n 60, §§ 49, 100.
[78] *Laporte*, above n 60, § 67.
[79] *R (on the application of Moos) v Commissioner of Police of the Metropolis* [2011] EWHC 957 (Admin) [56].
[80] *R (on the application of Moos) v Commissioner of Police for the Metropolis* [2012] EWCA Civ 12.
[81] *Laporte*, above n 60, §§ 34, 93, 122.
[82] *Redmond-Bate v Director of Public Prosecutions* (1999) 163 JP 789.
[83] *Laporte*, above n 60, § 132.
[84] *Steel v UK,* above n 65, §§ 58–61.
[85] *Laporte*, above n 60, § 78.

Commissioner of Police of the Metropolis,[86] a much criticised decision, involved a seven-hour cordon at Oxford Circus catching up several thousands, including the applicants, who consisted of a protestor at a 2001 May Day anti-capitalist demonstration and three bystanders. Austin, the demonstrator, was throughout peaceful and Saxby, another applicant of the case, was on a business trip in London that day and had no intention to demonstrate. The House of Lords—to simplify a complicated decision—found there was no deprivation of liberty, as that was neither the police's motive nor purpose, and circumstances mandated that the cordon was necessary.[87] Applying a circumstantial, balancing standard already in examining the scope of article 5 which, according to scholars, was hitherto unknown,[88] the Lords found there was no deprivation of liberty (the Court of Appeal found article 11 inapplicable as well, a finding questionable in light of *Ezelin* and other decisions emphasising that disorderliness of others does not pre-empt a peaceful protestor from relying on article 11).[89] This was upheld by the ECtHR, as will be discussed later.

A more recent case[90] found another instance of kettling justified on even more attenuated grounds. Police and the court accepted that the claimant (a Palestinian solidarity protestor) did not intend a breach of the peace. Still, his words could—in the view of the police—be understood by others as suggesting an intention to approach the car of the Israeli President (who was not yet even on the scene). Thereby, the court not only further weakened the imminence requirement, but also departed from the abovementioned 1882 case, *Beatty v Gillbanks*[91] which categorically rejected 'that a man may be convicted for doing a lawful act if he knows that his doing it may cause another to do an unlawful act'.[92]

Pre-emptive detention of would be protestors is also becoming increasingly a way to prevent any disruption of public events by preventing the protest from taking place at all.

The London Olympics saw the arrest of 182 cyclists participating at a monthly Critical Mass ride, out of whom only 12 were interviewed by

86 *Austin v Commissioner of Police of the Metropolis* [2009] UKHL 5, [2009] 1 AC 564 (HL).

87 David Mead, 'Of Kettles, Cordons and Crowd Control—*Austin v Commissioner of Police for the Metropolis* and the Meaning of "Deprivation of Liberty"' (2009) 3 *European Human Rights Law Review* 376, 394.

88 Ibid, 385 f, Helen Fenwick, 'Marginalising Human Rights: Breach of the Peace, "Kettling", the Human Rights Act and Public Protest' (2009) *Public Law* 737, 746 f.

89 The point is also made by Fenwick, ibid, 744 f.

90 *Wright v Commissioner of Police for the Metropolis* [2013] EWHC 2739 (QB).

91 *Beatty v Gillbanks* [1882] 9 QBD 308.

92 See Seamus Burns, 'Time for Courts to Put a Lid on Kettling? Pt II' (2013) 177 *Criminal Law and Justice Weekly* 724.

police.[93] Five were later convicted for not following section 12 conditions[94] imposed by police which was later affirmed by the Divisional Court.[95] Most spectacularly, a 'known anarchist' was pre-emptively detained before the royal wedding based on intelligence data unrelated to his person. This was found justified by the court.[96]

iv. France: Proportionality Unclarified

The French approach has not been made concrete in many high court decisions, which is perfectly consistent with the general outlook of the legal system. The main source of legal 'precedent' is, again, the *Benjamin* judgment in this regard. The reasons for intervention are the same: if the officer apprehends disturbance of public order then he or she can take proportional measures. The concept of public order is understood in quite an abstract sense which also includes, for example, human dignity. Therefore, the French allow for intervention way before any risk of violence has been assessed, and there is no calculus of probability prescribed by higher courts, let alone the Conseil d'Etat or Conseil Constitutionnel.

However, as *Benjamin* is a strict administrative proportionality requirement, there can be cases of reversal of police measures if courts find that the measure went beyond what was commanded by the situation. Also, in case there is no violation of dignity, disturbance to public order must mean some disorder, violence, intimidation or threat, and then that must be assessed properly, where overreaction of police can be considered disproportionate.[97] Bans of assemblies (*réunions publiques politiques*) of the National Front were quashed by the Conseil d'État because no disturbance of public order was expected which could not have been averted by adequate policing.[98] The Conseil d'État only mentions that the record does not show a high risk of disturbance to public order, but it does not go into any details.

French jurisprudence is not explicitly split according to the standard of justifiable limits between prior and post restraint, despite the aversion towards 'preventive regimes'. Thus, much of what was said regarding a prior ban and conditions displays these same substantive values—public order, including human dignity, previous intimidation or threats by an association, etc—and procedural standard (proportionality), although seen from another angle, is still useful here for the sake of comparison.

[93] Ruth Brander, 'Out of Order?' (2012) 162 *New Law Journal*, 19 October 2012, www.newlawjournal.co.uk/nlj/content/out-order-0.

[94] In more detail, see Ch 2 on prior restraint.

[95] *Powlesland v DPP* [2013] All ER (D) 96, [2013] EWHC 3846 (Admin).

[96] *R v Hicks* [2012] ACD 102, [2012] EWHC 1947 (Admin).

[97] See especially Ch 2, text accompanying nn 137–38.

[98] CÉ, 29 December 1995, no 129759, CÉ, 29 December 1997, no 164299.

French cases which reached the ECtHR provide some room for additional speculation. In *Ezelin*,[99] post-disciplinary sanction of a lawyer, peacefully participating at an originally peaceful demonstration which turned somewhat violent, was considered legal by French courts while impermissible by the ECtHR.

In *Cisse*, French courts found the evacuation of a church—occupied by protesters and hunger strikers with the consent of church authorities—was lawful as it was not an assembly and threatened public order for reasons of deteriorating sanitary and health conditions, but also because some of the barriers erected blocked traffic.

Thus, all these might qualify as components of public order,[100] and French courts do not differentiate more precisely their relations to each other, or the importance of any of these components. This less concrete, less scrutinising approach might be a result of the fact that the occupiers had already spent two months in the church, and the measure at hand was not a prior, 'preventive' measure, but a repressive one, just as in *Ezelin* the demonstration actually turned violent, and that is what French authorities understood compelled the disciplinary sanction. In both of these cases tangible harm, even if averted out of partially paternalistic or reprimanded for sheer 'reputational' reasons, has indeed occurred.

v. European Court of Human Rights: Disorder Concept in Flux, Probability Unclarified

As to the ECtHR, a good starting point is that freedom of expression jurisprudence is applicable also as to the protection of annoying or offensive assemblies. The Court has reiterated several times, for instance, in *Öllinger v Austria*,[101] that:

> [Freedom of assembly] also extends to a demonstration that may annoy or give offence to persons opposed to the ideas or claims that it is seeking to promote ... If every probability of tension and heated exchange between opposing groups during a demonstration was to warrant its prohibition, society would be faced with being deprived of the opportunity of hearing differing views.

It is less clear what sort of and how intensive a danger justifies interference with freedom of assembly. In the abovementioned case of *Steel v UK*, the ECtHR has actually accepted a concept of breach of the peace by

[99] *Ezelin v France*, above n 26.

[100] See the decision of the Court of Appeals of Paris of 23 January 1997 as cited by *Cisse v France*, above n 31, § 17.

[101] *Öllinger v Austria*, 46 EHRR 38, Application no 76900/01, Judgment of 29 June 2006, § 36, with reference to *Stankov* above n 20, § 86, and *Plattform Ärzte für das Leben* above n 24, § 32.

omitting any immediacy or imminence requirement,[102] in other words it basically lowered the threshold of national law, certainly then positioning the European standard below the English.

Earlier, the Commission regularly rubber-stamped government allegations on public disorder without requiring any standard of probability, in one case basing inadmissibility on that ground when it was not even thought to be so by domestic police.[103] Unhindered flow of traffic (in a pedestrian area!),[104] or avoiding excessive noise[105] exemplify the breadth of the traditional interpretation of prevention of disorder.

The Court used to take a similar stance, for example in *Cisse,* where the forcible evacuation of a church occupied by protestors with the consent of religious authorities was considered a measure pursuing the legitimate aim of preventing disorder.[106] *Steel v UK,* though an article 5 case, found the arrest of a protestor lawful who—in protest against a grouse shoot—'walked in front of a person who was armed with a gun, thus preventing him from firing', as such behaviour 'might provoke others to violence'.[107]

Prevention of disorder is often referred to instead of prevention of crime, another mentioned limit in article 11(2), without any discussion on the difference.[108] In *Ziliberberg* (2004) the application under article 11 was found inadmissible for the simple reason that the criminal provision relied on by the government claimed to protect public order.[109] Thereby the court avoids taking a stance both on the serious issue of defining the limits of a fundamental right out of a criminal law, and on the estimation of danger. Necessarily, this stance also prevents the court from actually reviewing whether the measure taken was capable of furthering the legitimate aim. In *Ezelin v France,*[110] a *post*-disciplinary sanction, imposed *after* the assembly was long over, was considered to be furthering the legitimate aim of the *prevention* of disorder.

Although in some cases, the Court does not accept the alleged legitimate aim, it does not correct the relevant jurisprudence either. In *Alekseyev*, the Moscow gay pride case, the Court explicitly did not decide on the issue of whether there was a legitimate aim, by finding that the ban was in any case disproportionate.[111] In a similar vein, in another decision involving Russia,

[102] Similarly Mead, *The New Law of Peaceful Protest*, above n 14, 361.

[103] *Rai, Allmond and Negotiate Now! v UK*, Application no 25522/94, Decision on admissibility, 6 April 1995.

[104] *GS v Austria*, Application no 14923/89, Decision on admissibility, 30 November 1992.

[105] *S v Austria*, Application no 13812/88, Decision on admissibility, 3 December 1990.

[106] *Cisse v France*, above n 100 § 46.

[107] *Steel v UK*, above n 65, § 60.

[108] Also Mead, *The New Law of Peaceful Protest*, above n 14, 90.

[109] *Ziliberberg v Moldova,* above n 28.

[110] *Ezelin v France*, above n 26.

[111] *Alekseyev v Russia*, Application no 4916/07, Judgment of 21 October, 2010, § 79. See Paul Johnson, 'Homosexuality, Freedom of Assembly and the Margin of Appreciation

where a peaceful opposition speaker was arrested after a demonstration, the Court left the question of legitimate aim undecided. Instead, it claimed that 'the questions of lawfulness and of the existence of a legitimate aim are indissociable from the question whether the interference was "necessary in a democratic society"', which clearly it was not.[112]

In *Oya Ataman* (2006), the dispersal of an unnotified demonstration was found—though in pursuance of the legitimate aim of prevention of disorder—unjustified, as 'there [was] no evidence to suggest that the group in question represented a danger to public order, apart from possibly disrupting traffic'.[113] Also, since *Oya Ataman*, it reoccurs in assembly jurisprudence that

> where demonstrators do not engage in acts of violence, it is important for the public authorities to show a certain degree of tolerance towards peaceful gatherings if the freedom of assembly guaranteed by article 11 is not to be deprived of all substance.[114]

Soon after, in *Bukta*,[115] the ECtHR did not accept that the sound of a detonation would be sufficient reason to disperse an unnotified (spontaneous or urgent) demonstration, though largely because national courts have not relied on this argument, and not because the ECtHR found such a danger to be vague or immaterial. In *Patyi (No 1)*—where a 20-strong demonstration on a 5m wide pavement was banned in advance—the ECtHR first nominally accepted that the measure pursued the legitimate aims of preventing disorder and protecting the rights of others, but found it was unnecessary for absence of any showing of potential disruption.[116] This does not mean, however, that any intensity of potential disruption would surely justify restrictions, because the Court—at least lately—regularly emphasises that a certain amount of disruption inheres in basically every assembly.

Particularly in a number of Turkish and other Eastern European cases the Court would go as far as to substantially review if there was any danger to public order, and delineates simple disruption from disorder.

Stankov, as discussed above,[117] uses especially strong language, when arguing for the permissibility of even secessionist speech; a type of expression, characteristically, either solely or combined with assembly. The Court

Doctrine of the European Court of Human Rights: *Alekseyev v Russia*' (2011) 11 *Human Rights Law Review* 578.

[112] *Nemtsov v Russia*, Application no 1774/11, Judgment of 31 July 2014.

[113] *Oya Ataman v Turkey*, above n 30 § 41.

[114] Ibid, § 42.

[115] Ironically, though, the government has not claimed prevention of disorder, but protection of rights of others as a legitimate aim, still the Court mentions prevention of disorder as a legitimate aim pursued by the Government. See *Bukta v Hungary*, Application no 25691/04, Judgment of 17 July 2007, §§ 28 and 30.

[116] *Patyi v Hungary*, Application no 5529/05, Judgment of 7 October 2008, §§ 41–43.

[117] *Stankov*, above n 21, § 97, see also Ch 2, text accompanying nn 161–65.

basically rules that a prior ban is only permissible if *incitement to violence or rejection of democratic principles* would occur. What amounts to rejection of democratic principles is not exactly defined, but it does include, for instance, advocating ethnic segregation, but not advocating secession.

Incitement of violence and rejection of democratic principles are relatively narrow criteria, but they might not apply to restrictions on freedom of assembly other than prior bans. If one compares the loose concept of disorder with the strong language in *Stankov*, the contrast might be explicable by an untheorised perceived difference between prior ban and other sanctions. ECtHR proportionality jurisprudence is, in general, especially marked by consideration of the severity of the imposed sanction, thus it is possible that, for example, an administrative sanction might be permissible while criminal punishment for the same deeds which led to the administrative sanction is not. Seeing the danger in such an approach the Court has emphasised that a mild sanction does not justify an interference otherwise deemed not 'necessary in a democratic society'.[118]

Dispersal, especially violent or speedy dispersal by the police, is another issue where the ECtHR appears to have strengthened the protection: lack of prior notice is not sufficient to justify dispersion (*Bukta*), and forceful or even violent dispersion of a peaceful but unlawful assembly is also regularly held disproportionate since the mid-2000s. *Oya Ataman* and *Balçik* both found no reason for the speedy dispersal of unnotified, but peaceful assemblies, within half an hour after the start.[119] In *Aldemir (No 2) v Turkey*,[120] an unnotified trade union meeting in an area where it was not permitted to demonstrate was dispersed by tear gas and truncheons. Initially the meeting was peaceful, though blocking Atatürk Avenue, where demonstrators attempted to walk to the Prime Minister's residence. Police forcibly dispersed the assembly for being unlawful. During the course of the dispersal, some protestors became violent and several police officers and protestors ended up injured. The ECtHR found police intervention 'caused tensions to rise, followed by clashes', and thus was disproportionate. From the formulation 'there is no evidence to suggest that the group in question initially presented a serious danger to public order'[121] one could conclude that a *serious* danger to public order is at minimum required for a dispersal to be found justified. Though *seriousness* is certainly below a *Brandenburg*-type

[118] *Ezelin*, *Galstyan*, *Vajnai*, *Csánics* and *Kuznetsov* might be examples of the latter approach, while earlier Commission inadmissibility decisions, and *Ziliberberg* and *Lucas* for the former. See in more detail with further references, Mead, *The New Law of Peaceful Protest*, above n 14, 105.

[119] *Oya Ataman v Turkey*, above n 30, § 41; *Balçik v Turkey*, Application no 25/02, Judgment of 29 November 2007, §§ 50–53.

[120] *Nurettin Aldemir and Others v Turkey*, Application nos 32124/02, 32126/02, 32129/02, 32132/02, 32133/02, 32137/02 and 32138/02, Judgment of 18 December 2007.

[121] Ibid, § 45.

imminence, it still shows an increased willingness to actually require some probability of harm. The requirement in *Vajnai* of a 'clear, pressing and specific social 'need'[122] might be also referred here to the same effect, at least in the context of political protests, where 'the containment of a *mere speculative danger*, as a *preventive* measure for the protection of democracy, cannot be seen as a 'pressing social need'.[123]

As to prevention of crime, *Schwabe v Germany*, the preventive detention case, confirms the *Vajnai* approach. The ECtHR found the offence which was feared to be committed was not 'sufficiently concrete and specific', as the opinion was domestic courts diverged. Also, the banners could be understood to request authorities, and not fellow citizens to free prisoners by force (referring to *Vajnai* on symbols with multiple meanings). The six days detention imposed on this basis, instead of, for example, seizing the banners, was found not necessary to prevent the offence—understood thus at most as a *negligent* incitement to violence by the ECtHR—to occur.[124]

Austin v UK,[125] the kettling case discussed above,[126] received a different treatment at Strasbourg than the preventive detention case against Germany. The ECtHR basically sided with the House of Lords, despite strong criticisms that it was inconsistent with earlier case law.[127] Especially criticised is that the ECtHR added *'context'* to the threshold considerations which engage article 5, that is whether there was a deprivation of liberty at all.[128] Strictly an article 5 decision, on which there certainly will be much more comment to come, from my focus here it perhaps shows the ECtHR to be more restrained with regard to actual crowd control than with regard to longer running preventive efforts.[129] There clearly were disturbances in London that day, and some of the protesters in and outside the cordon were clearly intent on causing disorder. A similar approach, perhaps, is found in the *Giuliani and Gaggio* case[130]—much cited in *Austin v UK*—which found the shooting and killing

[122] *Vajnai v Hungary*, 50 EHRR 44, Application no 33629/06, Judgment of 8 October 2008, § 51.

[123] Ibid, § 55.

[124] *Schwabe and MG v Germany*, above n 58, §§ 77–78 and §§ 115–18.

[125] *Austin and Others v UK*, Applications nos 39692/09, 40713/09 and 41008/09 [GC] Judgment of 15 March 2012.

[126] Above nn 86–89.

[127] David Mead, 'The Right to Protest Contained by Strasbourg: An Analysis of *Austin v UK* and the Constitutional Pluralist Issues it Throws Up' at ukconstitutionallaw.org/2012/03/16/david-mead-the-right-to-protest-contained-by-strasbourg-an-analysis-of-austin-v-uk-the-constitutional-pluralist-issues-it-throws-up/.

[128] Michael Hamilton, 'Guest Post on *Austin and Others* Grand Chamber Judgment on "Kettling"' 23 March 2012, echrblog.blogspot.com/2012/03/guest-post-on-austin-and-others-grand.html.

[129] Or, feels more threatened by UK resistance and a general attack on the Court, see Mead, 'The Right to Protest', above n 126.

[130] *Giuliani and Gaggio v Italy* [GC], Application no 23458/02, Judgment of 24 March 2011.

of protestors on the violent Genoa G8 protest proportionate under article 5. What distinguishes these cases from the others discussed is actual disorder taking place on the spot or its close proximity.

As to what other than serious danger of disorder can found dispersal and other sanctioning powers, certainly the *Stankov*-conditions justifying advance ban—incitement to violence and rejection of democratic principles—are equally applicable. *Vajnai* explicitly adds or includes in this list actual *totalitarian propaganda*,[131] a level of harm significantly below the American standard, but still possibly higher than some European standards.[132]

B. Hostile Audience, Counter-demonstration

The following enquiry aims to unveil the different emphases on different aspects of *reactive violence* by the jurisdictions. I will not discuss jurisdictions separately, since the previous section provides the general background country-by-country, but according to specific issues. In the United States, there is vast jurisprudence on relevant subquestions of reactive violence, while elsewhere they are less litigated. I first discuss the fighting words doctrine as that is particular to the US Supreme Court, and then continue with the other, doctrinally more commonly shared themes.

i. Fighting Words

Fighting words means speech which 'by [its] very utterance inflict[s] injury or tend[s] to incite an immediate breach of the peace'.[133] This has been part of the early list of low value speech, excluded from First Amendment protection in *Chaplinsky v New Hampshire* (1942).

Chaplinsky distributed Jehovah's Witnesses literature in the streets of Rochester, while denouncing all religions as 'rackets'. Citizens complained to the City Marshal, who said that Chaplinsky was lawfully engaged, but warned Chaplinsky about the crowd's beginning unrest. Later, a police officer led Chaplinsky away from the scene. On the way to the police station they had met the City Marshal who was hurrying to the scene as he was informed that a riot was unfolding. It was at this point of crossing each other's way when Chaplinsky told the City Marshal he was a 'God

[131] *Vajnai*, above n 122, § 56.

[132] A follow-up case to *Vajnai*, *Fratanoló* affirmed as 'already established' that 'for the interference to be justified, the Government must show that wearing the red star exclusively means identification with totalitarian ideas' (§ 27), and it is problematic—with (*cf*) reference to *Vajnai*—that domestic courts have not discussed whether there has been any 'intimidation', an expression not actually used in *Vajnai* (§ 27). *Fratanoló v Hungary*, Application no 29459/10, Judgment of 3 November 2011.

[133] *Chaplinsky v New Hampshire*, 315 US 568, 572 (1942).

damned racketeer' and a 'damned Fascist'. These latter two utterances were the only issue the court decided on, accepting that they are not protected by the First Amendment. 'Resort to epithets or personal abuse is not in any proper sense communication of information or opinion safeguarded by the Constitution, and its punishment as a criminal act would raise no question under that instrument'.[134]

Fighting words are deprived of constitutional protection if a 'man of common intelligence' who is addressed in the particular situation understood them as being an injury, or would react to them violently. As can be seen from this formulation, the fighting words doctrine originally set a lower standard than (the later accepted) *Brandenburg*-test in two regards. The first condition does not explain what speech inflicts injury in itself, and from the second one, tendency to incite immediate breach of the peace, it is clear that the first was not meant to be about violent reaction. Secondly, what the average person might consider fighting words, the actual person might not—actual harm is not necessary. Therefore, some authors argue that the fighting words doctrine is incorrect.[135]

In my view, however, the Supreme Court later narrowed down the doctrine approximating the *Brandenburg* standard. Already in 1949, in *Terminiello v Chicago* the Supreme Court had reversed a conviction based on a jury instruction saying that 'breach of the peace consists of any misbehavior which violates the public peace and decorum', and that the

> misbehavior may constitute a breach of the peace if it stirs the public to anger, invites dispute, brings about a condition of unrest, or creates a disturbance, or if it molests the inhabitants in the enjoyment of peace and quiet by arousing alarm.[136]

The Court has not reached the question whether Terminiello's speech—in a meeting which occasioned a turbulent protest of 1,000 persons outside the building—indeed constituted fighting words, but struck down the lower decisions for reasons of overbreadth of the instruction.

Later, in *Street v New York,*[137] the early flag burning case, the court reversed a conviction reasoning that the First Amendment protects uttering whatever derogatory opinion on the American flag; therefore, such speech does not constitute fighting words.[138] Here the Court quoted from *Chaplinsky* only that 'fighting words' are those which are 'likely to

[134] *Cantwell v Connecticut*, 310 US 296, 309 f, as cited in *Chaplinsky v New Hampshire*, 315 US 568, 572.

[135] Eg Michael J Mannheimer, 'The Fighting Words Doctrine' (1993) 93 *Columbia Law Review* 1527; Wendy B Reilly, 'Fighting the Fighting Words Standard: A Call for its Destruction' (2000) 52 *Rutgers Law Review* 947.

[136] *Terminiello v Chicago*, 337 US 1, 4 (1949).

[137] *Street v New York*, 394 US 576 (1969).

[138] Note that the holding appears limited to words, not to the act of burning the flag, and even so the majority opinion is accompanied by strong dissents from Warren, Black, White and Fortas JJ.

provoke the average person to retaliation, and thereby cause a breach of the peace',[139] in other words it left out the reference for speech 'inflicting injury in itself'.

Probably the most important case, bringing fighting words and advocacy to near-equal footing, is *Cohen v California* from 1971. Cohen was observed in a courthouse wearing a jacket which said 'Fuck the draft' as a protest against the Vietnam War, and convicted for 'behavior which has a tendency to provoke *others* to acts of violence or to in turn disturb the peace'.[140] The Supreme Court reversed the decision, stating, inter alia, that the jacket inscription did not constitute fighting words—'those personally abusive epithets which, when addressed to the ordinary citizen, are, as a matter of common knowledge, inherently likely to provoke violent reaction'.[141] Note the narrowing language compared with *Chaplinsky*. Also, Justice Harlan made clear that Cohen's communication was not fighting words because, obviously, it was not directed against the person of the person who saw it.

In a following decision, *Gooding v Wilson,*[142] the Supreme Court read conjunctively the infliction of injury and/or incitement to an immediate breach of the peace conditions as apparently stated disjunctively in *Chaplinsky*. In *Gooding*, a state law banning 'opprobrious words or abusive language' was found to be unconstitutional, because it did not require the probability of immediate violent reaction, neither in the text of the statute, nor as applied.

Also on overbreadth grounds, the court invalidated a statute in *Lewis v City of New Orleans*[143] which criminalised as breach of the peace 'to curse or revile or to use obscene or opprobrious language toward or with reference to a police officer while in actual performance of his duties'[144] irrespective of whether in the instant case Lewis' speech indeed consisted of fighting words.[145]

All in all, the fighting words doctrine requires a personal insult which is likely to lead to immediate violent reaction. Thus, it basically applies the same threshold as to the harmfulness of the speech as the *Brandenburg* test. The difference is that the *Brandenburg* test takes into account the actual audience's reaction, while the standard of *Chaplinsky* on the man

[139] *Street v New York*, 394 US 576, 592, citing *Chaplinsky v New Hampshire*, 315 US 568, 574 (1942).

[140] *Cohen v California*, 403 US 15, 16 (1971).

[141] Ibid, 20.

[142] *Gooding v Wilson*, 405 US 518 (1972).

[143] *Lewis v City of New Orleans*, 415 US 130 (1974).

[144] Ibid, 132.

[145] A later important decision, *RAV v City of St Paul*, 505 US 377 (1992), invalidated a statute on the grounds of content neutrality, again irrespective of whether the actual speech—burning a cross on a black neighbour's yard—might be proscribable under the fighting words doctrine. *RAV* does not question the validity of the fighting words doctrine as such.

of common intelligence has not been modified. Similarly to *Brandenburg*, there has been no Supreme Court case (except for *Chaplinsky*) which found that the criteria of fighting words had been fulfilled. In this regard, it might not be too far to conclude that fighting words are extremely hard to regulate in a manner that the Supreme Court would not find overbroad, vague, or content-discriminatory.

ii. Heckler's Veto and Heckler's Speech

Heckler's veto refers to a situation when the speaker—typically at a demonstration—is prevented from talking, conveying his or her message, by another person or persons, the heckler(s), by extreme noise or other disorderly or violent conduct or threat of it. What counts as heckler's veto is not obvious: I think the best way is to define it narrowly, for example, throwing eggs will not in itself be considered heckler's veto. I will only deal with heckler's veto in relation to the right of assembly and protest, but will not specifically discuss the status of heckler's veto in public schools in the United States which has become an intense, highly controversial subject of much of American jurisprudence and writing.[146]

Harry Kalven, who popularised the term 'heckler's veto', describes the harm done in this way: 'If the police can silence the speaker, the law in effect acknowledges a veto power in hecklers who can, by being hostile enough, get the law to silence any speaker of whom they do not approve'.[147] Two main concerns, however, complicate the picture. First, though it seems quite clear that government is there to protect the speaker from heckler's veto, it is also quite clear that there might be cases when disruption and violence cannot be prevented or stopped in any other way than by both restricting the speaker and the heckler, at least for the moment. Freedom of assembly is especially an area where it is well imaginable that a heckler might cause violence which endangers the speaker and/or the audience, and police do not have any other option than to remove (also) the speaker from the scene, disperse the meeting, etc. Secondly, a more principled concern is the extent of the free speech rights of the hecklers themselves.

In the United States, *Feiner* is the first decision on heckler's veto, largely rewritten, but never overruled in later jurisprudence. Feiner held a speech

[146] See, eg just from 2009, John E Taylor, 'Tinker and Viewpoint Discrimination' (2009) 77 *University of Missouri at Kansas Law Review* 569; Kevin H Theriot, 'Prince or Pauper? Religious Proselytizing and the First Amendment' (2009) 3 *University of St Thomas Journal of Law and Public Policy* 46; Joan W Howarth, 'Teaching Freedom: Exclusionary Rights of Student Groups' (2009) 42 *University of California, Davis, Law Review* 889; Matthew Baker, 'A Teacher's Right to Remain Silent: Reasonable Accommodation of Negative Speech Rights in the Classroom' (2009) *Brigham Young University Law Review* 705.

[147] Harry Kalven Jr, *The Negro and the First Amendment* (Columbus, Ohio State University Press, 1965) 140.

in front of a 'mixed', that is both black and white crowd, making derogatory statements regarding several public figures, and urging the blacks to 'rise up in arms and fight for equal rights'.[148] The crowd reacted with some excitement, there was some shoving and pushing, and milling, and one member of the audience was threatened with violence if the police did not step in. Thus, the police approached Feiner, and tried to persuade him to stop talking and help break up the crowd. When he ignored these requests, he was arrested, and later convicted for breach of the peace. The Supreme Court upheld his conviction, by applying the 'clear and present danger' test. The Court accepted lower courts' factual findings that there was indeed a danger of violence erupting in the crowd unless the police intervened. As Chief Justice Vinson, apparently unaware of any possible problem, put it: '[the] Petitioner was thus neither arrested nor convicted for the making or the content of his speech. Rather, it was the reaction which it actually engendered'.[149] Justice Black, in a famous dissent both does not see from the record that the danger of erupting violence was really clear and present, and, more importantly, criticises the majority for putting the consequences on the speaker, instead of, evidently, arresting the one who threatened violence, if this really is the way to prevent violence. This is a quite straightforward argumentation, which now, especially since *Brandenburg,* can be taken to be accepted by the US Supreme Court.

Nonetheless, Justice Black in *Feiner* hints that there might be cases when the police cannot but also restrict lawful speech for the protection of the speaker and others. He says: 'The police of course have power to prevent breaches of the peace. But if, in the name of preserving order, they ever can interfere with a lawful public speaker, they first must make all reasonable efforts to protect him'.[150] It is thus implied that when, but only when, every other means fail, interference with 'lawful speaking' might be constitutional.

A few important cases testify what the US Supreme Court perceives as not amounting to such ultimate situations. *Edwards v South Carolina*[151] is a classic civil rights protest case where 187 peaceful protestors were arrested and convicted for breach of the peace after not obeying an order to disperse. The dispersal order was made while 300 onlookers were watching, some of them recognised by the officer as potential troublemakers, but none threatened violence. When police ordered the dispersal, protesters started singing religious and patriotic songs while stamping their feet and clapping their hands.[152] The US Supreme Court reversed the decision, saying the record only shows 'that the opinions which they were peaceably expressing

[148] *Feiner v New York*, 340 US 315, 317 (1951).
[149] Ibid, 319 f.
[150] Ibid, 326 (Black J, dissenting).
[151] *Edwards v South Carolina*, 372 US 229 (1963).
[152] Ibid, 233.

were sufficiently opposed to the views of the majority of the community to attract a crowd and necessitate police protection'.[153] In the particular case, there was 'ample' police protection on the scene according to the testimony of a police officer, thus the court again did not have opportunity to specify what the limits of constitutionally mandated police protection are in case of a hostile audience. In *Gregory v Chicago*,[154] a case decided in the same year as *Brandenburg*, the court reversed the conviction for disorderly conduct of peaceful civil rights demonstrators who disobeyed dispersal orders issued because onlookers behaved in an unruly manner, and police feared they would not be able to prevent impending civil disorder. The Justices agreed that unruliness of onlookers is not a proper ground for restricting the right to assembly, but resolved the case on overbreadth grounds,[155] and again did not specify the extent of the obligation of the police to first deal with the hostile audience. In a more recent case, *Forsyth County v Nationalist Movement*, the Supreme Court ruled explicitly that the reaction of listeners is not a content-neutral basis for regulation of speech.[156] In the case, a county ordinance on use of public property vested discretion in the county administrator to impose a fee 'incident to the ordinance's administration and to the maintenance of public order'.[157] The Nationalist Movement was given a $100 fine for a demonstration organised against the Martin Luther King Jr federal holiday. The Supreme Court held the ordinance facially invalid because its application implied taking into consideration the audience's reaction to a demonstration, which necessarily includes enquiry into the content of the message. Again, this decision solidifies the principle that the burdens stemming from a heckler's veto cannot be imposed on the speaker. The extension of the principle is not qualified by the Supreme Court, though some district court decisions can be cited to the effect that police/local government are liable in civil suit for not protecting demonstrators against hostile audiences.[158]

US Supreme Court cases dealt much less with the possible free speech protection granted to hecklers and onlookers, though the question itself has been on the table for quite a while.[159] Numerous nineteenth-century

[153] Ibid, 237.

[154] *Gregory v Chicago*, 394 US 111 (1969).

[155] The jury was only instructed to consider whether demonstrators made 'improper noise' or a 'diversion tending to a breach of the peace' or 'collect[ed] in bodies or crowds for unlawful purposes, or for any purpose, to the annoyance or disturbance of other persons'. Ibid, 122 (Black J, concurring).

[156] *Forsyth County v Nationalist Movement*, 505 US 123, 134 (1992).

[157] Ibid, 123.

[158] See, eg *Dunlap v City of Chicago*, 435 F Supp 1295, 1301 (ND Ill 1977); *Cottonreader v Johnson*, 252 F Supp 492, 497 (MD Ala 1966); *Glasson v City of Louisville*, 518 F 2d 899, 901 (6th Cir 1975), as cited by Cheryl A Leanza, 'Heckler's Veto Case Law as a Resource for Democratic Discourse' (2007) 35 *Hofstra Law Review* 1305, 1310.

[159] For a relatively early commentary, see Eve H Lewin Wagner, 'Heckling: A Protected Right or Disorderly Conduct?' (1986) 60 *Southern California Law Review* 215.

lower court cases can be found interpreting limits to 'disturbance to assemblages',[160] of course, not necessarily with a constitutional focus. In *re Kay*,[161] a 1970 case culminating at the California Supreme Court, was about clapping and shouting for 5–10 minutes during the speech of a Congressman candidate. The clapping and shouting did not stop the speaker from finishing his speech, and later he even testified that he was not disturbed by the protest. Still, a few testimonies pointed that around the protestors the speech of the candidate could not have been heard clearly, though you could walk away to other parts of the park where it could. The Supreme Court of California held that the state can constitutionally proscribe hecklers' or counter-speakers' conduct only if it 'substantially impaired the conduct of the meeting by intentionally committing acts in violation of implicit customs or usages or of explicit rules for governance of the meeting, of which he knew, or as a reasonable man should have known'.[162] This, what might be called, 'substantial impairment test' has never been tested at the US Supreme Court, nor has anything else on speech rights of hecklers. Justice Douglas, alone, would have granted *certiorari* in a case where there was a non-disruptive protest against Richard Nixon's talk at a religious meeting, and the organiser of the protest was convicted for disturbing a religious meeting.[163]

In my view, in cases where the heckler does not make it impossible for the primary speaker to convey his or her message, a heckler's speech should also be constitutionally protected. All the more so if the primary speaker is a politician, or is backed by the state in one way or another, for example, as in *Reynolds* the speaker who was 'heckled' was Richard Nixon, or in *re Kay* where the town was invited to a celebration of the candidate of one party, but not the other. Nobody has a right to speak and be spared from (non-violent) reactions. Parallel to this, of course, if the heckler makes it impossible for the primary speaker to convey his or her message, then that would mean that one person's right to speech was privileged against the other's. Rightly understood, in my view, it is only for this 'absolute silencing' situation where the Supreme Court has developed the principle of 'no heckler's veto' as described above.

In Germany, the question arises as to who counts as participator and who as heckler. The Constitutional Court stated that not only sympathisers, but

[160] A custom digest search performed in Westlaw for citing references to '133 *Disturbance of Public Assemblage* 133k1 k. *Nature and elements of offenses*' brought up a 1,682 lines long document with case references, earliest being *Bell ads Graham*, 1 Nott & McC 278, SC Const (1818) which held that disturbing a religious assembly, during worship is indictable.

[161] In *re Kay*, 1 Cal 3d 930, 464 P 2d 142, 83 Cal Rptr 686 (1970).

[162] Ibid, 943.

[163] *Reynolds v Tennessee*, 414 US 1163 (1974).

also those with opposing views are constitutionally entitled to participate at a demonstration, and exercise criticism.[164]

However, there is no right to participate at a demonstration with the sole purpose to coercively prevent or hinder it.[165] This latter case is then the closest to heckler's veto. In a case where a party called 'Republicans' held a public meeting in a restaurant in Freiburg, people, who tried to enter the meeting while shouting 'This old Nazi S … masked as Republican should be interdicted here' or, 'Let us inside, and then the assembly is over', etc, were lawfully prevented from accessing the place.[166] An interesting aspect of the case—that the incriminating sentences were only said after the police had already closed the entry to the assembly—was not considered problematic by the Court because the issue was not the police blocking the entry, but the police's prohibition of the petitioner from entering the meeting which was issued after the petitioner had shouted the phrases mentioned. The GFCC rejected the argument that behaviour aiming to prevent an assembly would be covered by the scope of the right; only other rights and the prohibition of arbitrariness of official behaviour apply. Constitutionally protected participation necessitates a willingness to accept the assembly as it is, and to limit the pursuit of diverging goals to communicative means only. Those who seek intentionally to hinder an assembly cannot rely on article 8 GG even if they are numerous.[167]

The extent to which communicative means can be used for disturbance remained unclarified, that is the difference between criticism, protest and disturbance. The logic of the mentioned decision would probably suggest that the decisive element is intent: if the person shouts in order to be heard, then he is a participant; if he shouts in order to make it impossible for the primary speaker to be heard, he is a disturber, a 'heckler'. Similarly to the US jurisprudence, German courts also have come to the conclusion that one cannot be burdened for another's hostile speech. Thus, in a case where the demonstration's location was changed, because a counter-demonstration was to be expected, the added administrative costs could not constitutionally be imposed on the organisers of the primary demonstration.[168]

The ECtHR has not specifically dealt with heckler's speech cases—only sporadic references to heckler-like situations have been discussed. *Chorherr v Austria* involved a military parade where applicants went in with placards to protest against Austria's acquisition of interceptor fighter planes. It is questionable whether this can be qualified as heckler's veto, as the pacifists interfered with the view of a few parade-watchers only slightly, and if they

[164] BVerfGE 92, 191, 202 f (1995).
[165] BVerfGE 84, 203, 209 f (1991).
[166] Ibid.
[167] Ibid.
[168] OVG (High Administrative Court) Koblenz, 16 May 2006, 7 A 10017/06.

moved away, they could see fully. The ECtHR nonetheless accepted that the Austrian authorities acted within the ECHR when removing the pacifists from the scene and sanctioning them. The restriction fell within the margin of appreciation, and was considered non-excessive to the potential disturbances Mr Chorherr 'must have realised', and also because the measures were imposed 'to prevent breaches of the peace and not to frustrate the expression of an opinion'.[169] This very deferential decision did not rely on the idea that Mr Chorherr allegedly blocked the view of the public, this way 'heckling' the participation in an assembly.

The more recent case of *Vajnai v Hungary* is the only decision where the expression 'heckler's veto' comes up at all at the ECtHR:[170]

> [R]estrictions on human rights in order to satisfy the dictates of public feeling—real or imaginary—cannot be regarded as meeting the pressing social needs recognised in a democratic society, since that society must remain reasonable in its judgement. To hold otherwise would mean that freedom of speech and opinion is subjected to the heckler's veto.

Here the hecklers are the 'public' whose feelings—in this case towards the mere display of the red star—have been recognised in the Criminal Code, thereby sanctioning irrationality. This might also point in the direction that heckling is what goes beyond the frames of rationality, probably rational discourse, in the sense that it shuts down other's rational contribution to an ongoing debate without engaging it.

iii. Counter-demonstration

I employ the notion of counter-demonstration—as distinguished from heckling which can be the performance of a single individual—to cover situations where two opposing groups are present next to each other, both wishing to communicate their own message. Normally, the counter-demonstration refers to the group which came to protest the primary demonstration or primary event. Alhough some claim counter-demonstration to be organised,[171] I see no reason to exclude the frequent case of spontaneous counter-demonstrations from the discussion.

Counter-demonstrations are often assumed to be first of all a source of tensions. Still, courts do also accord protection to counter-demonstrations, and, in my view, rightly so. The following discussion will concentrate on two separate issues which nonetheless often intermingle: (i) whether there is a right to counter-demonstration; and (ii) how the risk of erupting violence

[169] *Chorherr v Austria*, Application no 13308/87, Judgment of 25 August 1993, §§ 31–32.

[170] *Vajnai*, above n 122, § 57.

[171] Eg Kevin Francis O'Neill and Raymond Vasvari, 'Counter-Demonstration as Protected Speech: Finding the Right to Confrontation in Existing First Amendment Law' (1995) 23 *Hastings Constitutional Law Quarterly* 77, 80.

as a potential result of clashing demonstrators and counter-demonstrators is handled by the courts.

a. United States

The US Supreme Court has—similarly to speech protection of heckling—not explicitly stated the constitutional right of counter-demonstration. Nonetheless, under any principled assessment of American jurisprudence, counter-demonstration should be as protected as the primary demonstration or event. All the rationales of protection apply equally to counter-demonstrators, just as the principle of content neutrality, the duty of the police to protect the unpopular speaker, the doctrines of vagueness and overbreadth, etc are equally valid.[172]

As to the anticipation of violence, the *Skokie* controversy could have offered the most famous example of constitutional risk-taking in situations of clashing groups; nonetheless, the courts for procedural reasons avoided (probably had to avoid) exactly this issue. In a sequence of denied permit applications, $350,000 permit fees, and court proceedings, the Village of Skokie tried to prevent the National Socialist Party of America from rallying in full Nazi paraphernalia wearing swastika in a mostly Jewish neighbourhood of a Chicago suburb, where Holocaust survivors also lived. There was ample evidence that various Jewish and other anti-Nazi organisations had planned a 12,000–15,000 strong counter-demonstration. People testified that they would be extremely hurt by the Nazi march, one witness claiming that though he did not intend to use violence, he was not sure if he could control himself. *Opinion* of the Mayor—formed after discussion with leaders of community and religious groups—that bloodshed would occur if the march took place had also been introduced.[173] Thus, the Village of Skokie sought to enjoin the Nazi marchers from wearing and displaying the Nazi symbols, and other material which 'incites or promotes hatred' against religious or ethnic groups, clearly a European sort of argument which would already restrict incitement to hatred, not first incitement to violence. An injunction was granted, and the appellate courts were unwilling to stay the injunction pending appeal on the merits. This refusal of a stay was reversed by a divided US Supreme Court.[174] On appeal, the Illinois appellate court modified the injunction so as only to enjoin displaying the swastika.[175] The appellate court held that a march cannot be prevented though 'there was and is a virtual certainty that thousands of irate Jewish citizens would physically attack the

[172] For a detailed description, see ibid, 100–13.

[173] See *Village of Skokie v National Socialist Party of America,* 51 Ill App 3d 279, 284, 366 NE 2d 347, 351 (1977).

[174] *National Socialist Party of America v Village of Skokie*, 432 US 43 (1977).

[175] *Village of Skokie v National Socialist Party of America*, 51 Ill App 3d 279, 366 NE 2d 347 (1977).

defendants'.[176] Underlying precedents were the hostile audience cases discussed above, from *Terminiello* to *Edwards* and *Gregory*. As there was no suit against, or initiated by, the organisations wishing to protest the Nazi march, there is no decision on the issue whether the 'virtual certainty of violence' arising from their (the counter-demonstrators') presence would deprive *them* of the right to assembly. Further in the Nazi suit, the Illinois Supreme Court also held the rest of the injunction invalid under the symbolic conduct doctrine.[177]

Meanwhile, a parallel suit was launched as the Village had enacted ordinances requiring an extraordinary permit fee, banning military uniforms and incitement to hatred against religious and ethnic groups on public assembly. The Seventh Circuit[178] struck down the ordinances, and the US Supreme Court denied *certiorari*.[179] Circuit Judge Pell found that the case was not governed by *Brandenburg v Ohio* because the Village—despite that it 'introduced evidence in the district court tending to prove that some individuals, at least, might have difficulty restraining their reactions to the Nazi demonstration'[180]—before the Circuit Court did not rely on a possibility of responsive violence.[181] Compare this with the 'virtual certainty' evidence in the injunction proceedings. Thus, the Seventh Circuit did not reach the question of protection of counter-speech either.

The Supreme Court mentioned 'counter-demonstration' in one single decision, and even there it is just an example.[182]

Lower courts have dealt with the protection granted to counter-demonstration, and some accept that counter-demonstration can be segregated from the demonstration, as a 'time, manner and place' restriction.[183]

In one case, however, the Ohio Supreme Court very clearly upheld the right to simultaneous counter-demonstration as applied to a Jewish organisation and Ku Klux Klan demonstration in front of John Demjanjuk's house.[184] However, the limits of the right to counter-demonstration are

[176] 51 Ill App 3d 279, 287, 366 NE 2d 347, 353.

[177] *Village of Skokie v National Socialist Party of America*, 69 Ill 2d 605, 373 NE 2d 21 (1978).

[178] *Collin v Smith*, 578 F 2d 1197 (1978).

[179] *Smith v Collin*, 439 US 916 (1978).

[180] *Collin v Smith*, above n 177, 1203.

[181] The rest of the reasoning relies on symbolic speech and captive audience doctrines which will be discussed in Ch 7.

[182] *Carey v Brown*, 447 US 455, 469 (1980).

[183] Eg *Grider v Abramson*, 180 F 3d 739 (6th Cir 1999) (Ku Klux Klan rally on courthouse steps and contemporaneous counter-demonstration); *Olivieri v Ward*, 801 F 2d 602 (2d Cir 1986), cert denied, 480 US 917 (1987) (Catholic gays organisation's demonstration in front of St Patrick's Cathedral in New York during the gay parade was separated temporally from anti-gay Catholic groups' demonstration at the same place. Nonetheless, both demonstrations were allowed to proceed simultaneously with the gay parade).

[184] *City of Seven Hills v Aryan Nations*, 76 Ohio St 3d 304, 667 NE 2d 942 (Ohio Supreme Court, 1996) (Ku Klux Klan and Jewish organisation demonstrating simultaneously in front of John Demjanjuk's house).

not clarified by this holding as there was clearly no probability of violence, either on the present enjoined demonstrations, or in the past on the part of the *particular Ohio branch* of the KKK. Both sides of the would-be demonstrators testified that they could contain themselves if the other side did not incite violence.[185] This testimony was fully accepted by the Ohio Supreme Court. That court thus relied on the principle that *Brandenburg* applied without alteration to simultaneous demonstrations of diametrically opposed groups, that is without intent, imminence and likelihood proven, restrictions were deemed unjustified. In my view, this is quite a consistent application of the general principles of First Amendment jurisprudence of the federal Supreme Court.

b. Germany

Germany's twentieth century has been manifestly full with both violent and peaceful counter-demonstrations. Ever since the Weimar era, opposing groups from the political far right and the left have been in constant clash. The reunification of Germany has brought a new wave of Neo-Nazi marches especially in the Eastern Länder which again drew a sometimes violent reaction from the centre or far left circles of German civil society.

Unlike, for instance in the United States, the protection accorded to counter-demonstration is an ever present, hotly debated topic.[186] The principles of the German constitutional jurisprudence look pretty straightforward. As there is a right to participate critically or even opposing at a demonstration,[187] there is clearly a right to counter-demonstration. The dividing line between critical participation and counter-demonstration remains disputed. As already mentioned with regard to the heckler's veto, there is no right to participate at a demonstration with the sole purpose to coercively prevent or hinder it.[188]

[185] Ibid, 307–09.

[186] See, eg the August 2010 scandal surrounding the decision of the Hannover administrative court allowing for a Neo-Nazi 'Mourning March'—commemorating the mistreatment of detainees in the interrogation centre of the British occupation forces in Bad Nenndorf between 1945–47—while banning the counter-demonstration organised by the German Federation of Trade Unions (DGB). *Neonazi-Demo erlaubt—Gegendemo verboten*, Mitteldeutsche Zeitung, 13.08.2010. www.mz-web.de/servlet/ContentServer?pagename=ksta/page&atype=ksArtikel&aid=1281678346714, *Gericht erlaubt Neonazi-Demo—Gegendemo verboten,* Stern, 12.08. 2010, www.stern.de/politik/ausland/gericht-erlaubt-neonazi-demo-gegendemo-verboten-1592720.html. In legal terms, the significance is maybe best characterised in comparing the results of the Westlaw search (one Supreme Court case mentioning counter-demonstration, 54 documents altogether, including articles and jurisprudence) with that of Beck online search for *Gegendemonstration* which shows 300 results, out of which 186 are case law, while the rest is articles, commentaries, notes, etc.

[187] BVerfGE 92, 191, 202 f (1995).

[188] BVerfGE 84, 203, 209 f (1991).

There is no right to prevent a demonstration, but there is always a right to organise a counter-demonstration, adhering to the regular notice requirement, duty to cooperate and so on. Clearly, police are obliged to protect demonstrators against violent counter-demonstrators,[189] and here it should not be of relevance which group counts as counter and which as primary.

As a default, a demonstration cannot be restricted because of a counter-demonstration, but 'if it is sufficiently likely that the authority—because of fulfilling paramount state duties and eventually despite involving additional external police force—is not capable to protect the notified assembly',[190] then restrictions on the duly notified primary assembly might be possible, and to countergo restrictions might give rise to liability in police law (so-called *Nichtstörerhaftung* in case of *Polizeinotstand*, policing emergency). German police law also knows another concept, '*Zweckveranlasser*', meaning someone who occasions a law-breaking even though she herself is not behaving unlawfully. The GFCC has left open the applicability of this, certainly problematic, concept to (opposing) assemblies, but in any case strongly limited its potential scope: beyond the sheer content of the message (ie Neo-Nazis and their counter-demonstrators expressing opposing views and even maybe wishing the outgroup to become violent) it requires specific accompanying elements of provocation.[191] Considering the generally more cautious stance German law takes on prevention of violence, the threshold for intervention would in any case likely remain below the threshold of US-style fighting words.

c. United Kingdom

In the United Kingdom, the 1882 case of *Beatty v Gillbanks,*[192] discussed above, was about Salvation Army members being charged with unlawful and tumultuous assembly to the disturbance of the peace because Skeleton Army members were accompanying their marches shouting and disorderly. The Divisional Court ruled the disorder was not 'the natural consequence of their [ie the Salvation Army's] acts', as it came from the rival group, and rejected 'that a man may be convicted for doing a lawful act if he knows that his doing it may cause another to do an unlawful act'.

Thus, as a general principle, a demonstrator cannot be punished for a disorder caused by counter-demonstrators either. Any further than that, however, the issue of counter-demonstration has not merited specific legal regulation and has not become the object of specific judicial doctrines.

[189] BVerfG, 1 BvQ 23/00, 18 August 2000.
[190] BVerfG, 1 BvQ 14/06, 10 May 2006.
[191] BVerfG, 1 BvQ 24/00, 1 September 2000, § 18.
[192] *Beatty v Gillbanks* (1882) 9 QBD 308.

Nonetheless, the very characteristic British regulation of protest, starting in the Public Order Act 1936, was actually essentially shaped by an instance of clashes between a march and a massive counter-march. In the so-called Battle of Cable Street, a Fascist (Mosleyan) march was prevented by counter-protestors from walking through a Jewish neighbourhood as planned. Police tried to protect the Fascists—who themselves became disorderly—but finally gave up. English collective memory appears to proudly cherish the event as one where people stood up against fascism and anti-Semitism, and there is no reason to doubt it.[193]

Legally, however, it has not unequivocally reinforced the protection accorded to assemblies, as the Public Order Act 1936 introduced, not only the ban on uniforms, but also the possibility of banning processions in a given area for three months (renewable)—and that basically made possible that no processions took place in inner London for years before the Second World War.[194]

Thus, it might well be that banning orders are regularly used to prevent clashes between opposing groups, within the general framework, and so no separate discussion arises.

d. France

In the mentioned *Association SOS Tout Petits* decision on ban of anti-abortion demonstration in front of Notre Dame, next to a hospital, the Conseil d'Etat also found that the Administrative Tribunal lawfully disregarded the objection that 'the risk of counterdemonstration could not justify the ban as it has not materialised, because it referred to a circumstance subsequent to the decision'.[195] With regard to another ban of protest of the same association in front of an abortion clinic, the Administrative Court of Appeal affirmed that the sole fact of a counter-demonstration does not justify a prior ban, but previous violence of demonstrators can, provided that it does not amount to a general ban on demonstrations by the association.[196]

Another ban was found lawful because previously at the same place, an assembly organised by the same association 'gave occasion [*donné lieu aux*

[193] Audrey Gillan, 'Day the East End said "No pasaran" to Blackshirts', *The Guardian* (30 September 2006), www.guardian.co.uk/uk/2006/sep/30/thefarright.past; 'Fascist march stopped after disorderly scenes', *The Guardian* (5 October 1936) www.guardian.co.uk/theguardian/1936/oct/05/fromthearchive.

[194] Rachel Vorspan, '"Freedom of Assembly" and the Right to Passage in Modern English Legal History' (1997) 34 *San Diego Law Review* 921, 1000, referring to Home Affairs Committee, *Fifth Report: The Law Relating to Public Order* (HC 1979–80, 756-I & II) 13.

[195] CE, 30 December 2004, *Association SOS Tout Petits*, no 248264, considérant 5.

[196] The reasoning is so sparse that it does not allow for verifying exactly what previous disorder looked like. Wikipedia describes several waves of incidents through a decade of forcible entrance into hospitals performing abortions, ensuing criminal convictions and even the introduction of a new crime, but it could not be verified. fr.wikipedia.org/wiki/Commandos_anti-IVG.

affrontements violents—note that it is unclear who actually was violent] to violent clashes during which several persons were injured', and the ban was not simply based on the fear of a potential counter-demonstration.[197] This is the closest case of a substantive review to be found on Légifrance, the French legal database maintained by government, on 'contre-manifestation', that is counter-demonstration.[198]

Though French courts do not theorise much on counter-demonstration, it appears de facto protected and in principle two opposing demonstrations are to be freely held in parallel, and police are obliged to protect against possible violence, from whichever side it might come. Nonetheless, there is no anti-heckler's veto principle pronounced so far in jurisprudence, is the extent of police protection clarified precisely.

e. European Court of Human Rights

ECtHR jurisprudence on counter-demonstration shows a similar trend—as seen above in general with regard to disorder and probability. Earlier, challenges to blanket bans were found inadmissible,[199] intergroup tensions and previous violence justifying a general ban. Though in *CARAF* the Commission specifically argued that the possibility of violent counter-demonstration does not take out the demonstration automatically of the scope of article 11, it still found the ban justified.[200] The case of *Stankov*[201] broke with this general caution towards interethnic and separatist contexts, while other cases, closer to counter-demonstration proper, have also redefined the jurisprudence. The case of *Plattform Ärzte für das Leben*—again about events of an anti-abortion organisation and counter-demonstrations—though about article 13, has in effect affirmed a right to counter-demonstration, and the obligation of police to accommodate and protect both opposing events.[202] In *Öllinger*,[203] Austrian authorities banned a protest demonstration against Comradeship IV, an organisation mainly of former SS-members

[197] Administrative Court of Appeals of Paris, 12 May 2005, no 01PA02401.

[198] Three out of the four hits on légifrance for '*contre-manifestation*' relate to *SOS Tout Petits*. The fourth one is a decision in *référé liberté*, where the Conseil found the École Normale Supérieure could lawfully prevent—disallow—a series of assembly events during a so-called 'Israeli Apartheid Week', properly balancing *liberté de réunion* with that of prevention of disturbance to public order and of counter-demonstrations. Clearly here the institutional setting was relevant, just as the École's willingness to offer room for discussions on the Middle East, while keeping political events out of the building. CÉ, = March 2011, no 347171, considérant 5.

[199] *Rai*, above n 103, *Rassemblement jurassien and Unité jurassienne v Switzerland*, Application no 8191/78, Decision on admissibility, 10 October 1979, DR 17, 108, and *CARAF* above n 25.

[200] See above, text accompanying n 25.

[201] *Stankov*, above n 21.

[202] *Plattform Ärzte für das Leben* above n 24.

[203] *Öllinger*, above n 101.

commemorating the death of SS soldiers in the Second World War on All Saints' Day at the Salzburg Municipal Cemetery. The commemoration counted as popular celebration and as such was exempted from the authorisation requirement.[204] Domestic authorities partly argued that the ban was necessary to protect Comradeship IV's event, while at the ECtHR the government mainly relied on the justification that Öllinger's protest would disturb cemetery-goers other than Comradeship IV, and thus the restriction served their rights. As the Constitutional Court had already added, even freedom of religion of others was involved. Austrian courts also accepted, as sufficiently weighty, the prevention of disturbances as in previous years there had been protests against Comradeship IV's commemoration, and those protests had caused 'considerable nuisance' to other cemetery-goers on this important religious holiday.[205] As the Government at the ECtHR argued: 'the authorities had also been able to rely on experiences from previous years in which assemblies like the one planned by the applicant had annoyed visitors, had led to heated discussions and had required police intervention'.[206]

The Government maintained that to allow and protect both events (a commemoration and a counter-demonstration) would require such policing which on its own would disturb 'the peace required for a cemetery on All Saints' Day'.[207] The ECtHR did not accept these arguments. Clearly Austrian law privileged one demonstration over the other, both by the exception for 'public celebration', an awkward label for an SS commemoration, and consequently also by the sheer acceptance that the SS commemoration would be happening anyway, and it was only Öllinger's protest which could have been prevented. The ECtHR faults Austria for not taking into account that Öllinger was a Member of Parliament who wanted to protest against the commemoration taking place, in other words, his would have been core political speech. Also, the ECtHR noted that there was no previous violence, neither would the protest have been noisy, or in other ways directed against, cemetery-goers' beliefs. Citing *Stankov*, it was affirmed in *Öllinger*: 'If every probability of tension and heated exchange between opposing groups during a demonstration was to warrant its prohibition, society would be faced with being deprived of the opportunity of hearing differing views'.[208] Thus, the rights of cemetery-goers, Comradeship IV and Öllinger should all be accorded proper weight in the balance, also because positive obligations flowing from article 11 require so.

[204] To its merit the Constitutional Court expressed doubts, nonetheless, it upheld the ban for reasons mentioned in the main text.

[205] *Öllinger*, above n 101, §§ 18–20.

[206] Ibid, § 29.

[207] Ibid, § 39.

[208] Ibid, § 36.

4

From Coercion to Direct Action to Disruption

IN RELATION TO freedom of assembly, coercion-related concerns have always enjoyed a special status. Importantly, both early psychology and legal history have assumed that assemblies of people tend to become mobs. Picketing, for a long time, was considered intolerable coercion, and so-called direct action protests still raise this question. The doctrine of captive audience also emerges from time to time in relation to marches and rallies.

One of post-War Germany's most spectacular identity struggles has been fought for decades within the legal framework of coercion or duress (*Nötigung*), about which Peter Quint wrote an entire monograph, the detail and quality of which is certainly not possible to reproduce here.[1]

In the US, courts have issued injunctions and affirmed restricted 'protest zones' next to abortion clinics, pursuing interests akin to prevention of coercion.

Other types of zoning, in and around parliaments, courts, prisons, and military areas might be justified since coercing the state might appear to undermine the already attenuated legitimacy of representative governments.

In this chapter I will examine those situations where the state intervenes in order to prevent protestors in coercing others, non-state actors, individuals, companies, and so on. Zoning proper (state buildings, cemeteries, and residential areas) will be examined under time, manner and place restrictions, partly because of the difference between coercing your fellow and the state, partly because these restrictions are typically framed as time, manner or place restrictions (TMPs).

It has to be noted that much of what follows could be reinterpreted—and accordingly vastly supplemented—from the broader angle of *civil disobedience*, an undertaking sadly not attempted here for reasons of limited space.

[1] Peter E Quint, *Civil Disobedience and the German Courts. The Pershing Missile Protests in Comparative Perspective* (London, Routledge-Cavendish, 2008).

I. *NÖTIGUNG* IN GERMANY

In Germany there has been a long debate about the constitutionality of sit-down demonstrations or sitting blockades. The issue arose out of protests against nuclear missiles stationed in Germany by the United States during the Cold War era.

Reaching through two decades, three diverging decisions of the German Federal Constitutional Court (GFCC) were handed down regarding a criminal offence for which demonstrators were usually prosecuted.

According to section 240 I of the Criminal Code, coercion (*Nötigung*) exists if someone illegally coerces another into an act, a default or an omission by way of force or threat of a palpable harm (*mit einem empfindlichen Übel*). According to section 240 II, the act is illegal if the use of force or the threat of the harm is considered 'reprehensible' (an expression which had replaced its Nazi-era variant: 'contrary to the healthy feelings of the people').

Ordinary courts, including the Federal Court of Justice, gradually developed an interpretation of *force* which revolves, not so much around the perpetrator's actions, as on the psychological state of the victim—as the purpose of the criminalisation is understood to be the protection of freedom of will. Accordingly, force need not be a 'direct exertion of bodily force' rather it suffices if the perpetrator actuates 'even with only little bodily effort a psychologically determined process' in the victim.[2]

As applied to demonstrations, this meant that the mere presence of the demonstrator, at a place which another wanted to occupy or cross, amounted to coercion if the presence of the demonstrator psychologically inhibited the other from realising his or her will.

In its first decision on *Nötigung*[3] in 1986, the GFCC split four/four on several issues, but was unanimous on the question of vagueness. Accordingly, neither the notion of force in section 240 I, nor the criterion of reprehensibility in section 240 II, is unconstitutionally vague. Though para II grants discretion to the interpreting court, it does so in a way that restricts the application of para I.[4] A vague limitation on a not-vague determination of criminal conduct does not violate *nullum crimen* principles.

Though the judges thus agreed on the constitutionality of the text of the statute itself,[5] they disagreed on the constitutionality of its *application*. Four judges accepted the wide understanding of force (where psychological

[2] *Laepple* decision of the Federal Court of Justice, BGHSt 23, 46, 54 as cited by BVerfGE 92, 1, 15.

[3] See BVerfGE 73, 206 (1986) *Sitzblockaden I*.

[4] Ibid, 238 ff.

[5] Ibid, 234 ff.

inhibition is enough as long as there is physical presence), while four other judges rejected it as violating the prohibition of analogy in criminal law.

In general, the court found that the scope of article 8 of the Basic Law (GG) extends to sit-down blockades. However, administrative or even criminal sanction is justifiable under article 8 II. In particular, as the sit-down blockade's *purpose* is to obstruct third persons, and the obstruction goes beyond the incidental by-product necessarily accompanying every demonstration, the conduct is proscribable.[6]

In the second (1995) decision, in reverse, the majority found the 'immaterialisation' of the notion of force unconstitutionally vague thus violating the principle of *nullum crimen*.[7] The Federal Court of Justice attempted to restrict the interpretation of force by requiring that it be of *significant weight* in order to qualify as 'reprehensible'. According to the GFCC this created more uncertainty than it resolved, because the notion of weight or significance of inhibition of will is no less vague than the notion of inhibition of will.[8] A strong dissent argued first that to block a road by one's body does indeed amount to physical force, as the body is a physical object, physically obstructing the way.[9] Furthermore, the interpretation of the ordinary courts was foreseeable as it has been followed by the courts for more than 100 years.[10]

In the lead opinion there is no reply to the dissent's argument that the human body as a physical object does actually hinder the movement of the car, and any sort of psychological inhibition is only the *consequence* of the physical obstruction, that is dependent on it. If there is no demonstrator sitting on the road, the drivers would not think they might kill the demonstrator unless they stop. Thus, the dissent apparently means that the interpretation is not extensive as the courts require regarding the use of physical force, thus it is not 'immaterialised'. On the other hand, the dissent does not react to the main argument of the majority about vagueness and inconsistent judicial understanding of the notion of force through time and through different crimes.

The question, to my mind, is which is more relevant: the difference between bodily effort and its effects as the majority sees it; or the dependency of the effects on the bodily effort as the dissent emphasises it. The majority could be read to imply that sitting on a road cannot be criminalised, because the demonstrator is obviously weaker than the car, so the demonstrator does not coerce the driver. Note, though, that the majority explicitly dismisses attempts to differentiate as to the weight of the pressure.

[6] Ibid, 250.
[7] BVerfGE 92, 1, 15–16 (1995), *Sitzblockaden II*.
[8] Ibid, 16.
[9] Ibid, 21–22.
[10] Ibid, 23–24.

The dissent explicitly finds the demonstrator's body on the road as an object which needs to be countered by physical effort, so the demonstrator is coercive.

Both opinions reflect categorical thinking, where either there is or there is no coercion. Meanwhile it is clear both that in reality there is no clear-cut boundary, and that in criminal law there ought to be one.

A way out of this has come in the third[11] decision to sitting blockades in 2001. Here the GFCC maintains that solely psychological coercion (*psyhologischer Zwang*) does not amount to force (*Gewalt*). Nonetheless, if the psychological coercive effect (*Zwangswirkung*) results from arranging *a physical obstacle* or impediment, it amounts to force.[12] Such is the case when protestors chain themselves by locks and metal chains to the entrance gates of a nuclear waste facility, as the chaining is the physical obstacle,[13] going beyond a simple psychological pressure which would be present if the protestors were standing there freely. More easily, parking different vehicles on both lanes and the side-lane of a highway, making it impossible without risk of self-injury to drive through it, is a physical obstacle resulting in psychological force.[14]

Still, according to the GFCC, the scope of article 8 GG extends to such 'forcible' actions as long as their aim is participation in formation of opinion and raising attention to public matters, and not 'the coercive or otherwise self-helplike [probably more as vigilantes] assertion [*Durchsetzung: assertion or implementation*] of own claims'.[15]

Thus, ordinary courts have to decide whether an event (sitting blockade or blockade of the highway in these cases) aims to raise attention and participate in the formation of opinion on public matters, or rather aims at 'enforcing [or extorting—*Erzwingen*]'[16] one's own (one is tempted to read it as individual, or, even, 'private') plans, preferences or wishes.[17] These latter categories notably do not fall under article 8.

This is, however, not the end of the story: although forcible actions with the aim of raising awareness to a public issue are covered by the scope of article 8, an intervention still might be justified, if it fulfills the requirements of proportionality. During this latter balancing exercise, the significance of contribution to debate on public matters must be assessed against the burden imposed on

[11] It is actually the fourth, but normally qualified as third in German literature.

[12] BVerfGE 104, 92, 101 (2001), *Sitzblockaden III*.

[13] Ibid, 102.

[14] Ibid, 103.

[15] Ibid, 105.

[16] Ibid, 105.

[17] Quint notes in this regard that the distinction mirrors that of Dworkin between persuasive and non-persuasive forms of civil disobedience. Quint, *Civil Disobedience*, above n 1, 254, referring to Ronald Dworkin, 'Civil Disobedience and Nuclear Protest' in Ronald Dworkin, *A Matter of Principle* (Cambridge, Harvard University Press, 1985) 109.

others by the action, and also in the light of the potential sanction. This happens by interpreting the criterion of reprehensibility (that makes the conduct unlawful according to section 240 II of the Criminal Code, see above) in a way that conforms to the Constitution, where it might matter, for example, if the public issue at hand also affects those burdened by the action. (In the concrete cases, the convictions were not finally reversed by the GFCC.)

This new compromise concept of *Nötigung* has not remained without critique: as a commentary argues, the physical force is hypothetical: the forcing effect comes not from the impossibility to physically get through the blockade, but from the '(ab)use of the principle of solidarity' which—clearly psychologically and not physically—disapproves getting through the blockade by driving over others.[18] Certainly the GFCC tries here to accommodate the Federal Court of Justice (BGH)'s broader understanding of coercion after the scandal the 1995 second GFCC decision evoked.[19] At the end of the day, direct actions without use of tools—chains, cars, etc—do not qualify as coercion, and even those which do might be so important for debate on public matters that a restriction cannot be justified.

II. UNITED KINGDOM: DISRUPTION, OBSTRUCTION AND MANY MORE

In the United Kingdom there are many common law and statutory provisions which aim to avert direct action, disruption or obstruction, from harassment laws to anti-social behaviour to aggravated trespass and fur ther to anti-terrorism legislation and so on, and clearly it is impossible to discuss each of them in detail.[20] Thus, this discussion aims only at clarifying where English law draws the line between permissible pressure and impermissible coercion on the example of aggravated trespass and obstruction of the highway, as the two are characteristic of the English approach.

Section 68 of the Criminal Justice and Public Order Act 1994 (CJPOA), as amended by section 59 of the Anti-social Behaviour Act 2003 (ASBA), criminalises aggravated trespass. Originally, it applied only to activities taking place in the open air until the ASBA cancelled the reference to open air from the provisions. It is an arrestable offence),[21] nonetheless arrest can

[18] Arndt Sinn, 'Gewaltbegriff—quo vadis?' (2002) *Neue Juristische Wochenschrift* 1024.

[19] See Quint's very thorough account on this, including the discussion on the *Tucholsky* and crucifix decisions, handed down the same year, and read together with the sitting blockade decision by conservative or more statist currents of German intelligentsia. Quint, *Civil Disobedience*, above n 1, 184–202 and 203–50.

[20] Mead spends almost 70 pages on direct action: see David Mead, *The New Law of Peaceful Protest. Rights and Regulations in the Human Rights Act Era* (Oxford, Hart Publishing, 2010) 237–310.

[21] s 68(4) CJPOA.

only be made in a case where the police reasonably suspect that a person is committing the trespass, that is there is no preventive power of arrest, unlike, for example, in breach of the peace. Aggravated trespass is committed by anyone who

> trespasses on land and, in relation to any lawful activity which persons are engaging in or are about to engage in on that or adjoining land, does there anything which is intended by him to have the effect (i) of intimidating those persons or any of them so as to deter them or any of them from engaging in that activity; (ii) of obstructing that activity, or (iii) of disrupting that activity.

Lawful activity means anything which does not constitute an offence or a trespass. Thus, there must be a trespass, and an intention to achieve the result; nonetheless no occurrence of the intimidation/obstruction/disruption of the lawful activity is necessary. At the end of the day, everything turns on the interpretation of the terms 'intimidation, obstruction, and disruption'.

Aggravated trespass as a complex offence requires therefore: (i) trespass on land and doing there anything (ii) intended to have (iii) intimidating, obstructing or disrupting effect on a (iv) lawful activity in which others are engaged or are about to engage. It was originally meant to be used against hunt saboteurs, but is also applied to anti-war demonstrators.[22] The already quite broad provision (eg simple disruption) is not interpreted narrowly by courts.[23]

The pre-Human Rights Act (HRA) case of *Winder v DPP*[24] dealt with hunting 'sabotage' where appellants were running after the hunt, but where it was proven that *by running* they did not intend to disrupt the hunt. The court found it sufficient that the protesters originally intended to disrupt the hunt, and they would have intended concretely disrupt the hunt had they had the opportunity to get closer to the hunt. This was prevented by the police arresting them. Thus, for the court, though the protestors did not intend to disrupt at the point when they were running and caught, they were already 'intending to intend' to disrupt in the future. Being a: (i) trespasser with an (ii) intention of disrupting and (iii) doing an act towards that end were sufficient, if proven, to establish liability under section 68 CJPOA. For the court, the intention could be a general one, a future one, and in the present case, running was 'more than a merely preparatory act' to disruption, thus it was close enough to the offence in the 'wide interpretation' of the court.

The 'more than mere preparation' is the statutory test for attempts.[25] Its application is problematic as there is no liability for attempt in the case of

[22] *Cf R v Jones (Margaret)* [2005] QB 259; *Ayliffe and Others v DPP* [2005] EWHC 684, [2005] 3 All ER 330, [2005] 3 WLR 628, [2005] Crim LR 959, now all affirmed by the House of Lords in the joint case *R v Jones et al* [2006] UKHL 16.

[23] Helen Fenwick, *Civil Liberties and Human Rights*, 4th edn (London, Routledge, 2007) 484.

[24] *Winder v DPP* [1996] 160 JP 713, *The Times*, 14 August 1996.

[25] Criminal Attempts Act 1981, s 1(1).

summary offences such as aggravated trespass, unless liability is specifically provided for in the criminalising statute.[26] The CJPOA does not provide for criminalising the attempt of aggravated trespass. Despite this, the court in *Winder v DPP* in effect criminalised an act where the most important element of an attempt, namely actual specific intent, was lacking. In other words, even if the attempt of aggravated trespass incurred liability under the CJPOA, there would be no way to punish the appellants since usually there is no attempt in lack of intent. The court, however, using the statutory test for attempts, made appellants liable for committing the offence itself. This remarkable legal *legerdemain* is facilitated mostly by deference to the magistrate's fact finding as to the remoteness or, more precisely, the sufficient connection between running and disrupting. General intention suffices, thus, and most probably, if general intention to disrupt, etc is established, then even mere presence will qualify to be an act towards the end of disruption.[27] *Winder* also renders basically moot the next section (section 69), empowering police to remove a person who—according to the reasonable apprehension of the officer—'is committing, has committed or intends to commit the offence of aggravated trespass on land'. The judgment leaves no room for a phase where the person is only intending to commit aggravated trespass, in other words where he or she is intending to intend to disrupt, obstruct or intimidate, which is exactly the case in section 69.[28]

Another case shows the further blurring of sections 68 and 69 in judicial interpretation. In *Capon v DPP*,[29] fox hunting protesters who trespassed on land where a fox was chased into a hole were prosecuted. The protestors planned to observe and record the digging out of the fox with a video recorder in order to see if any separate crimes were committed. They were entirely peaceful and they intended to avoid disruption of the hunt. Nonetheless, the police officer arrested them following a rather ambiguous conversation.[30] The officer told them to leave and threatened arrest for aggravated trespass. As the protesters knew that trespass requires an intention to disrupt, they remained completely peaceful and stated their intention not to disrupt. As they tried to work out why the police wanted to arrest them, or where there could be a legal problem in their conduct, they were arrested. In the later proceedings the police consistently referred to section 69, and there was no mention of aggravated trespass (section 68). The court, unfortunately, did not consider this to be a major flaw. The court of course

[26] *Cf* Criminal Attempts Act 1981, s 1(4) as referred to by Fenwick, above n 23, 484.

[27] Kevin Kerrigan, 'Freedom of Movement, Case comment to *Winder and Others v DPP*' (1996) 1 *Journal of Civil Liberties* 256, 257.

[28] Ibid, 258.

[29] *Capon and Others v DPP*, ILR 23/3/98 QBD, *The Independent*, 23 March 1998.

[30] Transcript available at David Mead, 'Will Peaceful Protesters be Foxed by the Divisional Court Decision in *Capon v DPP*' [1998] *Criminal Law Review* 870.

realised that the appellants neither intended nor committed an offence under section 68, nonetheless, it was affirmed that the officer could reasonably believe that they were intending to commit aggravated trespass, and thus, the police officer was entitled to remove, and, failing that, to arrest them under section 69. It is to be emphasised that section 69(3) (power to arrest) only applies if a person *knows* a direction under subsection (1) above has been *given* which *applies* to him. In the *Capon* case it is quite apparent that the protestors did not know that a direction under section 69 was given to them since the officer threatened to arrest them for *aggravated trespass* (section 68—ie no direction under section 69 was given) which they knew they did not commit; that is why they repeatedly explained their non-disruptive intention. Section 69 and the decision in *Capon* is a clear realisation of the fears of Phil Scraton and others before the introduction of the POA 1986 which applies a regulatory technique similar to the CJPOA 1994. Scholars had early on prophesised that by penalising, not only the harmful act, but also resistance to a police officer falsely apprehending the danger of the harm, the government would effectively be circumventing judicial review.[31] This is one instance which clearly shows the vulnerability of the reasonableness standard coupled with police discretion.

More recent aggravated trespass cases dealing with anti-war protestors show similar tendencies, nonetheless the reasoning of the defendants is usually much weaker. There was a considerable stream of protest and civil disobedience in the months preceding the outbreak of the Iraq War. Quite a few protestors were charged with aggravated trespass (section 68 CJPOA) for entering a military base by cutting a hole in the perimeter fence, chaining themselves to gates, and for criminal damage (section 1 Criminal Damage Act 1971) for destroying fuel tankers and bombers. Defendants mainly argued that they had a defence because they intended to disrupt an unlawful activity, namely, the Iraq War, to their minds a crime of aggression. The House of Lords jointly decided in *R v Jones et al*,[32] that appellants cannot rely on the defence that they wanted to prevent the commission of a crime of aggression, and that is why they committed aggravated trespass and criminal damage. The disrupters, and those who damaged military objects, claimed that their conduct fitted within section 68(2) of the CJPOA (prevention of offence by trespassing on land where unlawful activity is going on and disrupting, etc that activity), and section 3 of the Criminal Law Act 1967 (reasonable use of force for the prevention of crime), respectively.

Perhaps as no surprise, the House of Lords was unwilling to rule that the defence under section 3 of the Criminal Law Act 1967 was applicable

[31] Phil Scraton, '"If You Want a Riot, Change the Law": The Implications of the 1985 White Paper on Public Order' (1985) 12 *Journal of Law and Society* 385, 390.

[32] *R v Jones et al* [2006] UKHL 16.

to this international law crime.[33] The Court only marginally dealt with the aspect of the case that it was about a protest, even on a core political matter. Lord Bingham pointed out that as hindering the military activities of the government can establish charges of treason in some cases, it would be 'strange if the same conduct could be both a crime and a defence'.[34] This argument, while evident, is still formulated in an unsatisfactory manner: the question is, of course, how to discover the boundary where the right to protest ends and treason begins. Here, again, it would have been useful to consider the differences between disruption (or, as we have seen, 'reasonable' belief of a police officer about the (general) intention to disrupt an activity) and active destruction of property, since it is doubtful that the first could ever establish charges of treason.

Lord Hoffmann conceptualises the issues within the framework of self-help and use of force, no mention of protest and passive disruption occurs in the whole judgment. Again, the rather different defences to different offences were all dealt with uniformly as if there were no difference between intention to disrupt, and active damaging. That is why the reasoning is fixated on section 3 of the Criminal Law Act and not on the underlying provision: section 68(2) of the CJPOA. Drawing on a Court of Appeal precedent, Lord Hoffmann was willing to accept that in the construction of section 3 of the 1967 Act defence, the belief as to the existence of a crime being about to be committed should only be honest, but not necessarily reasonable. However, according to him, this does not mean that the defendant can use force which he deems reasonable though objectively it is unreasonable. Translated to the facts of the case this would mean that since defendants honestly believed that the United Kingdom was about to commit the crime of aggression, there was no need to examine whether this belief of theirs was reasonable or not. Nonetheless, it needs to be examined further if the force they used was reasonable in the light of objective standards.

[33] The Law Lords unanimously rejected that the defences in s 68(2) CJPOA and s 3 Criminal Act 1967 would include prevention of the crime of aggression. Among the arguments, the most important was the argument from democracy, or, parliamentary sovereignty, according to which new criminal offences can only be made by those representing the people, ie Parliament, and it is neither for judges (since a unanimous House of Lords decision in *Knuller (Publishing, Printing and Promotions) Ltd v DPP* [1973] AC 435) nor for the executive. Secondly, there is the usual argument for judicial restraint in the case of prerogative power in foreign policy. This self-restraint is connected with a particular factor of discomfort: courts shall not adjudicate on crime of aggression since this would involve a judgment on the state itself of which the courts form part. Though this argument is mostly destroyed by previous precedent, and, by a general trend of making individuals responsible for crimes under international law, Lord Bingham did not engage in any further discussion, just stated the problem of 'discomfort' as a self-evident necessity. The inconsistency of such a stance with previous precedent is explained in Clive Walker, 'Defence: Appellants Protesting against War in Iraq—Defendants Committing Offences of Damage or Aggravated Trespass at Military Bases' [2007] *Criminal Law Review* 66, 69.

[34] *R v Jones et al*, above n 32, [31].

> The crucial question ... is whether one judges the reasonableness of the defendant's actions as if he was the sheriff in a Western, the only law man in town, or whether it should be judged in its actual social setting, in a democratic society with its own appointed agents for the enforcement of the law.[35]

Lord Hoffmann cites Max Weber in support of the view that the state claims monopoly of the legitimate use of force and individuals can only use force to the extent that the state *permits it*.[36] He even cites the famous passage on the state of nature from the *Leviathan*.[37] Certainly, there is not much to object to such an argument in relation to active destruction of property of military forces, but aggravated trespass might need to be handled differently. After having envisioned the disasters of returning into a Hobbesian state of nature, Lord Hoffmann moves on to draw the conclusion about use of force not in the interests of the acting person, but in the interest of the community. If self-help is already limited in the case of imminent personal danger, then its use is even more circumscribed for the safety of the community. Note this is the opposite of what the German court argued in relation to sitting blockades. One commentator put it this way: 'public policies are for public forums or officials to settle',[38] in the words of Lord Hoffmann:[39]

> The right of the citizen to use force on his own initiative is even more circumscribed when he is not defending his own person or property but simply wishes to see the law enforced in the interests of the community at large. The law will not tolerate vigilantes. If the citizen cannot get the courts to order the law enforcement authorities to act ... then he must use democratic methods to persuade the government or legislature to intervene.

What is meant by 'force', and, 'democratic methods', however, has to be defined within the legal system. There is some room for the use of force; there are some cases when people are entitled to resort to force, a fortiori to protest. What form that protest might take should not be disposed of by an across-the-board Hobbesian reference, but is a question which requires further consideration. In the present case, it is obvious from the opinions of the Law Lords, that the first recommended remedy, that is the judicial way, is moot, since courts are simply not willing to interfere with questions of legality of warfare. The Law Lords in the same judgment, including Lord Hoffmann, made quite an effort to prove that they, as judges, are not willing to interfere with questions of the legality of warfare. This argument appears almost hypocritical if read in connection with further paragraphs of the judgment.

[35] *R v Jones et al*, above n 32, [34].
[36] Ibid, [76].
[37] Ibid, [77].
[38] Walker, 'Defence', above n 33, 68.
[39] *R v Jones et al*, above n 32, [83].

Under the part on 'civil disobedience' Lord Hoffmann condemns, in strong terms, the new phenomenon of 'litigation as continuation of protest', in a way somewhat irreconcilable with his previous view about the role of the courts. As to the democratic process, it can react quite belatedly, just as we might observe in relation to the Iraq War. In every other jurisdiction the protestors would have argued that that is what they actually tried to do: to influence the democratic process—in accordance with the prime function of the right to protest and assembly. The Law Lords have not had any thought about freedom of assembly, or even expression in general, and missed the opportunity of delineating more thoroughly disruption that has to be tolerated as the exercise of freedom of expression, and force which might not be.

All in all, English courts so far do not see a reason to differentiate permissible from impermissible disruption. The broadening of aggravated trespass in *Winder* and *Capon* might even diminish the progress brought about by *Jones and Lloyd*[40]—the trespassory assembly case declaring that assembly might be a reasonable user of the highway—because the unlawfulness of 'more than mere preparation' via aggravated trespass then turns the assembly into an unreasonable use of the highway.[41]

The other provision applied to direct action protestors, which gave rise to jurisprudence showing the characteristics of English protest law in operation, is obstruction of the highway. Here again protestors can go unpunished only if they show they somehow fit within the exceptions of the norm: a clash frozen halfway between a privilege and a right. The norm, section 137 of the 1980 Highways Act—similarly to previous statutes—reads: 'if a person, without lawful authority or excuse, in any way wilfully obstructs the free passage along a highway he shall be guilty of an offence'.

Lawful authority means, for example, a permission to hold a market, and so on. Lawful excuse is vaguer, thus it was the main object of litigation related to freedom of assembly. The most important case appears to be *Hirst and Agu*[42] from 1986. Hirst and Agu were animal rights activists, participating at a protest in front of a shop selling furs. The protesters gathered in groups, handed out leaflets, held banners, etc. They were charged with wilful obstruction of the highway, convicted, and their appeal dismissed by the Crown Court. The Crown Court's main reason was that their use of the highway was unreasonable, thus, lacking lawful excuse, since it was not incidental to the right to passage. The Divisional Court, on appeal, rejected

[40] *DPP v Jones and Lloyd* [1999] 2 AC 240. See Ch 2 on prior restraint, text accompanying nn 125–33.

[41] Similarly, Mead, *The New Law*, above n 20, 261.

[42] *Hirst and Agu v Chief Constable of West Yorkshire* (1987) 85 Cr App R 143.

the incidental to passage reasoning, and held, relying on *Nagy v Weston*,[43] that the correct approach was to check the following:[44]

1. whether there was an obstruction of the highway, which included any occupation, unless *de minimis*, of part of a road thus interfering with people having the use of the whole road;
2. whether the obstruction was wilful in the sense of deliberate; and
3. whether the obstruction was without lawful authority or excuse, which covered activities otherwise lawful in themselves which might or might not be reasonable depending on all the circumstances.

The magistrates' court is required to check, and, more importantly, the prosecution to prove, whether a deliberate obstruction—with regard to its time, place, purpose and actuality/potentiality—amounted to an unreasonable use of the highway. The activity of which the obstruction consists should be inherently lawful. Thus, *Hirst and Agu* makes clear that protest and assembly which 'obstruct' the free passage might still be reasonable in all the circumstances if it is otherwise lawful. Otton J remarked in dicta that freedom of protest on issues of public concern should be given the recognition it deserves.

In *Stephen Birch v DPP*[45] the Divisional Court had to examine whether *sitting on a road* as part of a demonstration had a lawful excuse.[46] The sitting caused traffic blockage, also obstructing vehicles unrelated to the business going on on the protested premises. The Divisional Court distinguished the facts from *Hirst and Agu*, and stated that handing out leaflets (the case in *Hirst and Agu*) is lawful, while lying down in the road so as to obstruct the highway, is not overtly a lawful activity.[47] This is a circular reasoning: lying down in the road is only made unlawful by section 137 Highways Act if other conditions are also fulfilled. Among those other conditions the 'otherwise' unlawfulness is explicitly stated in *Hirst and Agu*. The court in *Birch v DPP* apparently mistakes the result for the ground of the result. Thereby, the court does not feel forced to engage in serious discussion of the argument of the defendant, according to which protest and assembly can

[43] *Nagy v Weston* [1965] 1 All ER 78. In *Nagy*, the defendant was parking a van at a bus stop with the purpose of selling hot dogs, and was charged and convicted. The Divisional Court upheld the conviction, though it stated that 'excuse and reasonableness were really the same and, while there must always be proof of unreasonable user of the highway, such user was a question of fact in each case, depending upon all the circumstances including the length of time the obstruction continued, the place where it occurred, the purpose for which it was done, and whether it amounted to an actual obstruction'.

[44] *Hirst and Agu*, above n 42.

[45] *Birch v DPP* [2000] *Criminal Law Review* 301, *The Independent*, 13 January 2000.

[46] Birch participated at a demonstration in front of the premises of SARP UK, near a busy main road. Together with other demonstrators he sat down on the road in order to obstruct the access of vehicles to the SARP premises.

[47] *Birch v DPP*, above n 45 [8].

be a reasonable lawful excuse. In rejecting that argument on its surface, the court has ample material to cite from the trespassory assembly case of the House of Lords, *DPP v Jones and Lloyd*.[48] In *Birch* the weaknesses of *Jones* have become obvious: the primary right is travelling; the assembly cannot in any way obstruct that right. The other escape, the court finds from dealing with the assembly aspect, is a recurring tool in UK jurisprudence. As in the 2006 House of Lords case on aggravated trespass, *R v Jones et al*,[49] the court in *Birch* also tends to blur two defences: it applies the same reasoning to *lawful excuse* in case of obstruction of the highway on the one hand, and, to the logically more demanding *general defence for use of force* in case of prevention of (serious and imminent) crime, on the other.

In each of these cases UK law is structured in a way which disadvantages protest and demonstration, and only allows for accommodating that in the form of specifically justified exceptions in a given case. Thus, the level of criminalised (often only potential) disruption and obstruction, and, within my categories, the threshold of what counts as impermissible coercion is in result quite low in UK law.

III. UNITED STATES: INCONSISTENCY MASKED BY CONTENT-NEUTRALITY

Cases touching upon coercive expression by the US Supreme Court can usefully be studied in three groups. A bulk of the relevant jurisprudence relates to labour picketing, another one to civil rights movement and black/white tensions, and a third one to abortion clinic protests. The three topics are also three time periods, and social movement literature would roughly affirm that relevant jurisprudence came out coinciding with or right after the heyday of each topical movement.

Labour protests and picket cases started to come to courts in the nineteenth century,[50] but it was only in the first decades of the twentieth century that picketing came to be seen as coercion by most courts and commentators.[51] It took till 1940 for the US Supreme Court to find in *Thornhill v Alabama* that picketing is protected by the First Amendment,[52] and even

[48] *DPP v Jones and Lloyd* [1999] 2 AC 240. See above, and Ch 2 on prior restraints, text accompanying nn 125–33.

[49] See above, *R v Jones et al*, above n 32 and text accompanying nn 32–40.

[50] See, eg *Commonwealth v Hunt*, Metcalf 111, 45 Mass 111, (1842) WL 4012 (Mass), 38 Am Dec 346 (1842); or *Vegelahn v Guntner*, 35 LRA 722, 167 Mass 92, 44 NE 1077, 57 Am St Rep 443 (1896), as cited by Mark D Schneider, 'Peaceful Labor Picketing and the First Amendment' (1982) 82 *Columbia Law Review* 1469, 1477.

[51] Or, maybe more precisely, 'an act of coercion in its tendencies'. See the numerous references in Edgar A Jones, 'Picketing and Coercion: A Jurisprudence of Epithets' (1953) 39 *Virginia Law Review* 1023.

[52] *Thornhill v Alabama*, 310 US 88 (1940).

after this decision literature and the courts remained divided on the issue.[53] It seems quite clear that after all the Supreme Court more or less settled on: (i) rejecting that picketing as such amounts to coercion, but on (ii) recognising that specific circumstances can amount to it, and for those cases the legislator has the power to regulate undisturbed by the First Amendment.

In more recent decades the picketing/coercion issue took another turn related to so-called secondary picketing. Secondary picketing means that the employees picket not their own employer, but another who is in contractual relationship with their employer. There has been a wave of legislation restricting secondary picketing which gave rise to considerable litigation. The Supreme Court decided that statutory text prohibiting secondary protests that would 'threaten, coerce, or restrain' any person is vague and not specific enough.[54]

As to the civil rights movement, interestingly, sit-in cases are not so much shaping the law as one would expect, probably because the demonstrators were either completely peaceful or they deliberately engaged in civil disobedience. Typical of the handling of the sit-in cases is *Barr v City of Columbia.* A restaurant had a whites only policy for its lunch counter. A group of black students sat at the lunch counter and waited for service. When they refused to leave they were arrested and convicted for breach of the peace. The US Supreme Court reversed the decision for lack of evidence: as the demonstrators were entirely peaceful, quiet and polite, and 'the only evidence … is a suggestion that petitioners' mere presence seated at the counter might possibly have tended to move onlookers to commit acts of violence'.[55] Note, however, that three justices would have upheld the conviction for trespass for the same act,[56] as in so many other cases pointing out the difficulties in finding 'state action', thus the equal protection clause applicable to 'privately owned places of public accommodation'.[57]

[53] The *Harvard Law Review* published several articles in 1943 and the *Virginia Law Review* in 1953 discussing whether and under what circumstances picketing amounts to coercion or speech. Ludwig Teller, 'Picketing and Free Speech' (1943) 56 *Harvard Law Review* 180; E Merrick Dodd, 'Picketing and Free Speech: A Dissent' (1943) 56 *Harvard Law Review* 513; Ludwig Teller, 'Picketing and Free Speech: A Reply' (1943) 56 *Harvard Law Review* 532. Edgar A Jones, 'Picketing and Coercion: A Jurisprudence of Epithets' (1953) 39 *Virginia Law Review* 1023; Charles O Gregory, 'Picketing and Coercion: A Reply' (1953) 39 *Virginia Law Review* 1053; Edgar A Jones, 'Picketing and Coercion: A Reply' (1953) 39 *Virginia Law Review* 1063; Charles O Gregory, 'Picketing and Coercion: A Conclusion' (1953) 39 *Virginia Law Review* 1067.

[54] *NLRB v Drivers, Chauffeurs, Helpers, Local Union No 639*, 362 US 274, 290 (1960), as cited by Kate L Rakoczy, 'On Mock Funerals, Banners, and Giant Rat Balloons: Why Current Interpretation of Section 8(B)(4)(Ii)(B) of the National Labor Relations Act Unconstitutionally Burdens Union Speech' (2007) 56 *American University Law Review* 1621, 1628.

[55] *Barr v City of Columbia*, 378 US 146, 150 (1964).

[56] Black J, with whom Harlan and White JJ jointly dissented from the reversal of the trespass convictions. *Barr v City of Columbia*, 378 US 146, 151 ff.

[57] Webster McKenzie, Note, 'The Warren Court's Struggle with the Sit-in Cases and the Constitutionality of Segregation in Places of Public Accommodations' (2001) 17 *Journal of Law and Policy* 373. See also Michael Klarman, 'An Interpretive History of Modern

The idea that a sit-in might be 'coercion' has not even arisen, sit-ins are considered a property-discrimination clash, but are disposed of on procedural and other grounds. Indeed, sit-in demonstrations in courts were not even conceptualised as involving the First Amendment, let alone freedom of assembly. In effect, it was implied that sit-ins are as such illegal; nonetheless, only mild sanctions were found acceptable.[58]

As to *leafleting* and coercion—just as in the United Kingdom in *Hirst and Agu*—however, there was an important case in the 1960s: in *Keefe*[59] leaflets were distributed against a real estate broker who apparently persuaded white people to sell their flats in neighbourhoods which he managed to portray as becoming 'black'. The court does not make clear if it accepts the lower court's characterisation of the leaflets as having a *coercive impact*, but it makes a generous speech protective statement:[60]

> The claim that the expressions were intended to exercise a coercive impact on respondent does not remove them from the reach of the First Amendment. Petitioners plainly intended to influence respondent's conduct by their activities; this is not fundamentally different from the function of a newspaper.

NAACP v Claiborne Hardware, the famous boycott case reaching the US Supreme Court in 1982, is also a case in point. There the boycott of white, pro-segregationist merchants, supervised by civil rights activists was considered constitutionally protected. The court, however, relied more on the substance of the boycott (to realise constitutionally mandated equality) than on questions of coercion. '[A] nonviolent, politically motivated boycott designed to force governmental and economic change and to effectuate rights guaranteed by the Constitution itself'[61] cannot be restricted. The court reminded that though fragmented acts of violence and threats of violence occurred, this was no sound basis to impose liability for *all* damages and losses occurred. *A contrario*, damages and losses proximately resulting from violence, intimidation and coercion could be constitutionally awarded. The court did not have the occasion to clearly state what counts as coercion, because it found proven that (a significant parcel of) damages were awarded for constitutionally protected activity.[62] In any case, the

Equal Protection' (1991) 90 *Michigan Law Review* 213, and Brad Ervin, 'Result or Reason: The Supreme Court and the Sit-in Cases' (2007) 93 *Virginia Law Review* 181.

58 Bruce Ledewitz, 'Perspectives on the Law of the American Sit-in' (1995) 16 *Whittier Law Review* 499.

59 *Organization for a Better Austin v Keefe*, 402 US 415 (1971).

60 402 US 419.

61 *NAACP v Claiborne Hardware*, 458 US 886, 914 (1982).

62 An earlier case, *Meadowmoor,* was distinguished by saying that there violence was pervasive. To that decision Black J attached a dissent, opining that the injunction was overbroad because it not only restrained violent acts, but also expressed agreement with the views of those enjoined. *Milk Wagon Drivers Union of Chicago, Local 753 v Meadowmoor Dairies*, 312 US 287 (1941).

possibility for regulating coercive expression was left open in these cases; but the strong language in both *Keefe* and *Claiborne Hardware* suggests that the threshold for intervention is quite high.

Another, but rarely applied, doctrine in US law would be captive audience. To recall, in the landmark *Skokie* case from the end of the 1970s, the Seventh Circuit[63] struck down a Village of Skokie racial slur ordinance which made it a misdemeanour to promote or incite racial or religious hatred. It had been intended to apply the ordinance to a Nazi march with swastikas and military uniform planned by the National Socialist Party of America in a mostly Jewish neighbourhood which included Holocaust survivors. The US Supreme Court denied *certiorari*.[64] Circuit Judge Pell's reasoning relied mostly on the content-discriminatory nature of the ordinance and the lack of clear and present danger in the sense of *Brandenburg v Ohio*. The alleged infliction of psychic trauma, on the other hand, is insufficient to prohibit speech since there is no way to distinguish in principle such a harm from speech that is highly protected under the First Amendment, namely speech which 'invite[s] dispute ... induces a condition of unrest, creates dissatisfaction with conditions as they are, or even stirs people to anger'.[65] Offensiveness—including thus infliction of psychic trauma—is not a reason for restricting speech but rather a reason to protect it.

Skokie also argued that the planned march would invade residents' privacy, thus the march would produce a regulable captive audience situation.[66] Judge Pell responded that there need be no captive audience since residents could avoid the Village Hall for the 30 minutes of the march if they wished. *Skokie* thus seems to stand for the doctrinal stance that if one can avert his eyes from viewing a message, then he is not captive, and the speaker can rely on the First Amendment. Earlier cases also support this stance, and it has been strongly reinforced recently in *Snyder v Phelps*, in which a father of a soldier killed in Iraq could not claim in tort against Westboro church picketing during the funeral as it was 1,000 feet away and out of sight of the mourners, even assuming that the protest was tortious.[67]

An example of the situation when the eye cannot be averted is in *Virginia v Black* (2003),[68] a good contrast to *Skokie* in emphasising delineation between coercion and free speech. In this case the court accepted that

[63] *Collin v Smith*, 578 F 2d 1197 (1978).

[64] *Smith v Collin*, 439 US 916 (1978).

[65] *Collin*, 578 F 2d at 1206, citing *Terminiello v Chicago*, 337 US 1, 4 (1949).

[66] The cases referred to are: *Erznoznik v City of Jacksonville*, 422 US 205, 209 (1975); *Rowan v Post Office Department*, 397 US 728 (1970), and *Lehman v City of Shaker Heights*, 418 US 298 (1974).

[67] *Snyder v Phelps*, 131 S Ct 1207, 1220 (2011), more on the circumstances and the arguments, see Ch 8.

[68] *Virginia v Black*, 538 US 343 (2003).

cross-burning can be prosecuted if committed with the intent to intimidate, as an instance of *true threat.*

Captivity was found—unlike in *Snyder*—sufficiently severe to justify restriction in *Frisby v Schultz*, where the US Supreme Court upheld that offensive and disturbing picketing focused on a 'captive' *home* audience can be restricted.[69] This decision is among the first relating to the abortion protest controversy, which radically changed the legal environment of protest in the United States.

The main cases concerning protests next to abortion clinics (not to doctor's homes as in *Frisby*) are *Madsen*,[70] *Schenck*,[71] and *Hill*,[72] also discussed above under prior restraint[73] and below under place restrictions.[74] In these strongly criticised cases the US Supreme Court upheld restrictions on protest and counselling activities in 36 and 15 feet buffer zones around clinics and restrictions on noise as content-neutral, a view really hard to share at closer inspection.[75] Captive audience was referred to as justifying the noise restrictions,[76] in my view in harmony with general First Amendment logic.

The abortion protest jurisprudence is more surprising in the aspect that it allows restrictions on conduct much less serious than obstruction, intimidation or threat, in a quintessential forum (public street), in fact it allows for restrictions on simply entering an area. As to the content-neutrality, Justice Scalia in *Madsen* quotes the judge who issued the injunction making very clear that the injunction should apply—indeed it was applied—to persons who are not aware of the injunction, and who have come to the area the first time, as they are acting 'in concert' with organisations (cited in the injunction, like Operation Rescue, a violent pro-life group) if they express an anti-abortion view.[77]

[69] *Frisby v Schultz*, 487 US 474, 484–88 (1988).

[70] *Madsen v Women's Health Center, Inc*, 512 US 753 (1994).

[71] *Schenck v Pro-Choice Network of Western New York*, 519 US 357 (1997).

[72] *Hill v Colorado*, 503 US 703 (2000).

[73] See Ch 2.

[74] See Ch 8.

[75] From the many critical voices, eg Timothy Zick, 'Property, Place, and Public Discourse' (2006) 21 *Washington University Journal of Law and Policy* 173, Darrin Alan Hostetler, 'Face-to-Face with the First Amendment: *Schenck v Pro-Choice Network* and the Right to "Approach and Offer" in Abortion Clinic Protests' (1997) 50 *Stanford Law Review* 179.

[76] *Madsen*, 512 US 767 ff.

[77] 'At an April 12, 1993, hearing before the trial judge who issued the injunction, the following exchanges occurred: Mr. Lacy: "I was wondering how we can—why we were arrested and confined as being in concert with these people that we don't know, when other people weren't, that were in that same buffer zone, and it was kind of selective as to who was picked and who was arrested and who was obtained for the same buffer zone in the same public injunction". The Court: "Mr. Lacy, I understand that those on the other side of the issue [abortion-rights supporters] were also in the area. If you are referring to them, the Injunction did not pertain to those on the other side of the issue, because the word in concert with means in concert with those who had taken a certain position in respect to the clinic, adverse to the clinic. If you are saying that is the selective basis that the pro-choice were not arrested when

All in all, the relatively consistent and generous jurisprudence governing sit-ins and coercive speech clearly breaks with the abortion protest cases, hardly masked by claims of content-neutrality. A similar,[78] or even worse,[79] trend might be established with regard to 'animal rights' or environmental protests, facilitated by this jurisprudence.

IV. FRANCE: PRESSURE INHERENT IN STRIKE

French law accords strong protection to the right to strike,[80] a consideration of a certain importance to the relation between freedom of assembly (in the broad sense) and 'coercion'. Though the right to strike is the right of the salaried, and 'political strikes' are explicitly not included in the concept of strike,[81] the limits of the right to strike probably would equally, if not even more strictly, apply to demonstrations, or any direct action type protest.

The Conseil Constitutionnel specifically accepted that to prevent or disturb rail traffic by *a positive action*, going beyond sheer stoppage of work, such as placing an object on the tracks, is not protected by the right to strike.[82] The positive action outside constitutional protection would thus

pro-life was arrested, that's the basis of that selection...." Tr. 104–105 (Appearance Hearings Held Before Judge McGregor, Eighteenth Judicial Circuit, Seminole County, Florida (emphasis added)). And: John Doe No. 16: "This was the first time that I was in this area myself and I had not attempted to block an entrance to a clinic in that town or anywhere else in the State of Florida in the last year or ever. I also understand that the reason why I was arrested was because I acted in concert with those who were demonstrating pro-life. I guess the question that I'm asking is were the beliefs in ideologies of the people that were present, were those taken into consideration when we were arrested? ..." "When you issued the Injunction did you determine that it would only apply to—that it would apply only to people that were demonstrating that were pro-life?" The Court: "In effect, yes". Ibid, at 113–116 (emphasis added). And finally: John Doe No. 31: "... How did the police determine that I was acting in concert with some organization that was named on this injunction? I again am a person who haven't seen this injunction. So how did the police determine that I was acting in concert?" The Court: "They observed your activities and determined in their minds whether or not what you were doing was in concert with the—I gather the pro-life position of the other, of the named Defendants". Ibid, at 148 (emphasis added). These colloquies leave no doubt that the revised injunction here is tailored to restrain persons distinguished, not by proscribable conduct, but by proscribable views'. Madsen, 512 US 795–97, Scalia J, dissenting in part and concurring in part.

[78] Michael Hill, Note, '*United States v Fullmer* and the Animal Enterprise Terrorism Act: "True Threats" to Advocacy' (2011) 61 *Case Western Reserve Law Review* 981.

[79] Dane E Johnson, 'Cages, Clinics, and Consequences: The Chilling Problems of Controlling Special-Interest Extremism' (2007) 86 *Oregon Law Review* 249.

[80] § 7 of the Preamble to the 1946 Constitution, incorporated in the block of constitutionality by Décision n° 71-44 DC du 16 juillet 1971, affirmed specifically as to the right to strike by 79-105 DC du 25 juillet 1979 by the Constitutional Council.

[81] Louis Favoreu, Patrick Gaïa, Richard Ghevontian, Jean-Louis Mestre, Otto Pfersmann, André Roux and Guy Scoffoni, *Droit constitutionnel*, 3rd edn (Paris, Dalloz, 2000) 254, § 297.

[82] Decision no 81–127 DC, 20 January 1981, considérants 20–21, in effect limiting the interpretation by excluding the proscribability of disturbance and prevention of railroad traffic by simple stoppage of work.

presumably include, for example, lying down on the rails, or other similar, non-violent action where the body itself is obstructing some lawful activity. Though no detailed discussion on the question was possible to find, this seems to be somewhat below the German standard.

Besides, the right to strike includes picketing, but the Penal Code prohibits interference with the freedom of work by concerted and menacing behaviour,[83] including blocking the entrance,[84] but strictly only against co-workers.[85]

A classic form of direct action, blockade of the highway, has come before the ECtHR. In that case, French courts—though not all of them—found that halting the traffic by halting vehicles was unlawful, while driving at a very low speed (10km/hr) appears still within the right to strike (more precisely, within industrial action as voted by the trade union).[86]

V. EUROPEAN COURT OF HUMAN RIGHTS: NO VIOLATION

The Commission declared the German anti-missile sit-down cases inadmissible in earlier cases,[87] embracing some sort of a speech-action theory in emphasising that

> the applicant had not been punished for her participation in any demonstration as such, but for particular behaviour in the course of the demonstration, namely the blocking of a public road, thereby causing more obstruction than would normally arise from the exercise of the right of peaceful assembly.

This argument is still cited by the court.[88] Thus, though some level of disruption (eg to traffic) has to be tolerated according to the ECtHR, purposeful blocking, especially for several hours, is certainly not required to be tolerated under article 11 ECHR.

Recently, a demonstration blocking a central bridge in Budapest for several hours was understood (not decided, as that was not the issue) to be clearly illegal by the ECtHR.[89] The issue to be decided was the dispersal of a later demonstration—in support of the dispersed bridge blockade—halting vehicular traffic and public transport in and around a main square.

[83] Art 431-1 Penal Code. This same provision also prohibits the interference with freedom of demonstration.

[84] Cass Soc, 16 May 1989, no 87-42300.

[85] Cass Crim, 23 April 2003, no 02-84375.

[86] *Barraco v France*, Application 31684/05, Judgment of 5 March 2009, §§ 12–17.

[87] *CS v Germany*, Application no 13858/88; *G v Germany*, Application no 13079/87, Decision on admissibility, 6 March 1989.

[88] *Barraco* above n 86, § 46. See *G v Germany*, Application no 13079/87, Decision on the admissibility, 6 March 1989, DR 60, 256.

[89] *Éva Molnár v Hungary*, Application no 10346/05, Judgment of 7 October 2008, §§ 10 and 41.

The Court found that proportionate, especially as the demonstrators could express their solidarity with the illegal bridge blockade as their demonstration was only dispersed after several hours,[90] despite the fact that it seriously disrupted traffic and was not notified.

Similarly, a suspended jail and fine was found not to violate article 11 for at least sporadically blocking and entirely slowing down a French highway for five hours, causing a traffic jam for 10 hours. In *Barraco* the fact that the applicant had several times halted his vehicle was the main consideration to find that the burden caused 'went beyond the simple inconvenience occasioned by every demonstration on the public route'.[91] Thus, it is left open to what extent slowing down, but not halting, vehicular traffic would be protected under the ECHR. The Court in both the Hungarian and the French case emphasises the relevance of police tolerating the disturbance for several hours.

Sometimes, however, not even an actual blockade is required for the permissibility of restrictions. In a 2003 case, removal (dispersal probably), a four-hour detention and a £150 fine were found proportionate restrictions in a case where the applicant demonstrated at the entrance to a naval base in protest against the United Kingdom retaining a nuclear submarine. Testimonies diverged about whether there was any vehicular traffic blocked by the applicant, the arresting officer saying there was none. Still, the ECtHR declared it inadmissible.[92] Thus, the actual threshold for proscribable direct action protests under the ECHR might be quite low.

The ECtHR's cautious stance might well be due to the fact that European states—certainly the ones examined here—are also not clear and consistent about where coercion starts and freedom of assembly ends, but provide a very fragmented picture. Though the German compromise appears quite clear, it is anything but principled. The US Supreme Court, at least in the last few decades, does not fare any better either, protecting interests far below coercion or intimidation, even obstruction. This must mean at the same time that my focus on coercion is inadequate to the structure—if there is any—of law in this field. But what else should be the central principle structuring human rights jurisprudence if not that of the boundary between freedom and coercion? Some would say it is dignity; thus that is where I now turn.

[90] Ibid, § 42.

[91] *Barraco* above n 86, § 47.

[92] *Lucas v UK*, Application no 39013/02, Decision on admissibility, 18 March 2003.

5

Dignity as Peace, Truth and Love

TO WHAT EXTENT an assembly—intuitively, but far from exclusively, in the form of demonstration—is capable of violating human dignity is a very abstract question, nonetheless a question some courts aspire to answer. The concept of dignity, especially in law, is very controversial, but might sound more important or more precise than, for instance, public order. Dignity in comparative constitutional law is a genuinely German concept, which nonetheless has been conquering the world of global constitutionalism ever since the German Federal Constitutional Court (GFCC) started its operation. The following pages enquire whether the protection of human dignity can form a reasonable, tangible basis for restricting assembly and protest rights.

I. GERMANY: DIGNITY AND ITS SUBSTITUTE 'PUBLIC PEACE'

As is well known, the German Basic Law (GG) recognises as its highest (and inviolable) value[1] human dignity in its very first article, and makes respect for, and protection of dignity the duty of all state organs. It is unconditionally protected, cannot even be waived, and cannot be limited; in other words every interference within the scope of the *right* to human dignity is in itself a violation. There is thus no possibility to find a balance or compromise whenever human dignity is at stake. Human dignity is probably the most frequent among so-called *verfassungsimmanente Schranken* (constitution-inherent limits), that is constitutional limits not named as such in the provision of a particular basic right. For example, the seemingly illimitable assemblies which are not under the open sky are still subject to the limit of human dignity. Human dignity is also the ultimate candidate to anchor the protective duty of the state and the radiating indirect horizontal effect of

[1] On textual grounds, some authors question the normative character of human dignity, but these views remain marginal to the mainstream opinion of both scholarship and courts. See, Angelika Herdemerten, 'Kommentar zu Art 1' ann 45 in Ingo von Münch and Philip Kunig (eds), *Grundgesetz-Kommentar I*, 1st edn (München, Beck, 1974) and, for view of a proper basic right character Philip Kunig, 'Kommentar zu Art 1' ann 1 in Ingo von Münch and Philip Kunig (eds) *Grundgesetz-Kommentar I*, 5th edn (München, Beck, 2000), and Wolfram Höfling, 'Kommentar zu Art 1' in Michael Sachs (ed), *GG–Grundgesetz Kommentar,* 5th edn (München, Beck, 2009) ann 1 with further notes.

other basic rights—both can be used to constitutionalise the interest that is counterbalanced against freedom of assembly. What is more, human dignity itself appears to be directly binding, even among private persons, in horizontal relations[2] but even if not, the highly respected German Civil Code has in any case been transposing to private law most of what would follow from the direct effect of article 1 I,[3] especially in relation to expressive activities. Thus, rightly or wrongly, human dignity can pose a 'real threat' to freedom of assembly from various angles.

It is useful to follow the court's division of dignity arguments in German freedom of expression law into those related to either assertions of facts or expression of opinions. Opinion involves an evaluation, taking a stance, a value judgement, and as such it enjoys definitely more protection than factual statements. These latter ones are either true or false, and no personal stance is seen in their utterance, in other words factual assertions are not so close to an individual's personality as are opinions. I will start out the discussion with factual statements, and then continue with opinions.

The most important decision regarding a factual statement's potential to violate dignity is still the *Holocaust Denial* decision from 1994,[4] where the court found a prior ban justified by a future likely violation of human dignity. The occasion was a meeting (ie not an open-air assembly) on the 'blackmailability' of German politicians, organised by the Bavarian branch of the National Democratic (sic!) Party of Germany (NPD) in Munich. David Irving was also invited as a speaker, and it was likely that Holocaust denial would occur. The local authority in Munich imposed a condition on the organiser to guarantee that no denial of the Holocaust would happen at the meeting, or to dissolve the meeting if it did happen. The imposition of the condition was intended to be less restrictive than an outright ban, because the law allows for prior ban if the commission of criminal acts is to be expected with high probability. Denying the Holocaust involved the crimes of incitement of the people),[5] defamation,[6] and disparagement of the memory of the dead[7] in the interpretation of ordinary courts.

The main issue before the German Federal Constitutional Court (GFCC) was whether that interpretation was constitutional, or, more precisely, whether denying the Holocaust was outside the protection of the Constitution. First, the court had to decide which right was applicable here at all. As explained above,[8] as is typically the fate of freedom of assembly,

[2] Kunig, ibid, ann 27.
[3] Ibid.
[4] BVerfGE 90, 241 (1994).
[5] Art 130 Strafgesetzbuch (StGB) (Criminal Code), *Volksverhetzung*.
[6] Art 185 StGB, *Beleidigung*.
[7] Art 189 StGB, *Verunglimpfung des Andenkens Verstorbener.*
[8] See Ch 1 under Demonstration and the relation between freedom of assembly and freedom of opinion.

the court distinguished article 8 of the Basic Law or Constitution (GG), and relied solely on freedom of opinion. That this really is a strained view of the Constitution is intensified by the fact that article 5 does not appear to protect factual statements, and what is more, it is interpreted not to really cover them, unless they form the basis of an opinion. If that is not enough, before the Holocaust denial decision, factual statements proven false were considered clearly outside the scope of article 5 because, false factual assertions cannot form the basis of opinions.[9] However, the Holocaust denial decision states that, though such lies on their own are not protected, when they are 'inextricably connected to opinions',[10] article 5 I will cover the expression. While Holocaust denial—as knowingly proven false factual statement—is in itself outside constitutional protection, as many commentators emphasise,[11] I think it is unrealistic for it ever to happen without being connected to opinions.

In any case, the imposition of the condition interfered with an exercise of a constitutional right in the Munich meeting with David Irving. The interference is, however, justified because denying the Holocaust would violate the dignity of Jews living in Germany, especially survivors of the Holocaust or their descendents. It violates their dignity, because, as the Federal Court of Justice (BGH) stated and GFCC quotes with affirmation:[12]

> The historical fact that human beings were separated in accordance with the descent criteria of the so-called Nuremberg laws and were robbed of their individuality with the objective of their extermination gives to the Jews living in the Federal Republic a special personal relationship to their fellow citizens; in this relationship the past is still present today. It is part of their personal self-image that they are seen as attached to a group of persons marked out by their fate, against which group there exists a special moral responsibility on the part of everyone else and which is a part of their dignity. Respect for this personal self-image is for each of them really one of the guarantees against a repetition of such discrimination and a basic condition for their life in the Federal Republic. Whoever seeks to deny those events denies to each of them individually this personal worth to which they have a claim. For those affected, this means the continuation of discrimination against the group of human beings to which he belongs, and with it against his own person.[13]

Some might find the suggestion that the Shoah (the decision only talks about persecution of Jews) is part of the identity of Jews living in Germany somewhat stigmatising, but I take that there has been an overwhelming

[9] BVerfG, 1 BvR 824/90, 9 June 1992.

[10] BVerfGE 90, 241, 253 (1994).

[11] Eg Giso Hellhammer-Hawig, *Neonazistische Versammlungen. Grundrechtsschutz und Grenzen* (Aachen, Shaker, 2005) 31 ff with further notes.

[12] BVerfGE 90, 241, 251 ff, (English translation) in the website of the University of Texas School of Law, www.utexas.edu/law/academics/centers/transnational/work_new/ (copyright Professor BS Markesinis).

[13] BGHZ 75, 160, 162.

political—or moral even—consensus in Germany that mandates such a label. After all, no critique of this identity denial theory could be found, neither asking how courts are entitled to such construction, nor why only Jews living in Germany appear to be the victims. Doctrinally, to limit the circle of defamable persons is important from both a criminal law and a constitutional law viewpoint. In criminal law, for a defamation charge to stand, there needs to be a particular, clearly definable circle of persons. Women, Christians, etc would surely not be sufficient.[14] The GFCC in the *Tucholsky* or *Soldiers are Murderers* ruling[15]—of which there will be more discussion below—also made clear that though a certain concept of group libel is not inconceivable under the Basic Law, it is not any vague or general group about which a negative statement can form the basis of restriction on expression.

The *Holocaust Denial* case left some doubts about whether it relies on the personal honour clause in article 5 II (GG), which would mean that the dignity rationale is a value argument underpinning the personal honour restriction, or it takes the dignity right of article 1 I (GG) as a separate restriction inherent in the constitution. The question is important because of content neutrality issues. The prohibition of Holocaust denial is clearly a viewpoint-based restriction. Article 5 II lists as limits of the right 'general laws', and thus the question arises as to whether laws protecting personal honour are to be general laws as well. This question was not unequivocally decided in my view until the 2009 *Wunsiedel-Rudolf Hess March* decision, which clarified that protection of personal honour can also only be pursued in general laws.[16]

The requirement of a general law was already included in the Weimar Constitution, and the GFCC still appears to combine the somewhat conflicting scholarly views of the time. General law thus first cannot be a *Sonderrecht* (special law) against freedom of opinion, that is the law ought not differentiate between opinions 'solely because of their intellectual direction'.[17] Secondly, a general law regulates 'regardless of a specific opinion',[18] and, thirdly, the social good protected by the general law is one which ranks higher than freedom of opinion.[19]

[14] Valerius, BeckOK StGB § 185, ann 8–10.1 in von Heintschel-Heinegg (ed), *Beck'scher Online-Kommentar StGB*, 15th edn (Beck online, 2011) with references to several decisions of the Federal Court of Justice (BGH) and other courts.

[15] BVerfGE 93, 266 (1995).

[16] BVerfGE 124, 300, 326 (2009) *Rudolf Heß Memorial March* or *Wunsiedel*.

[17] Häntschel, HdbDStR II, 659 as quoted by Rudolf Wendt, 'Kommentar zu Art 5' ann 69 in Ingo von Münch and Philip Kunig (eds), *Grundgesetz-Kommentar I*, 5th edn (München, Beck, 2000).

[18] Rothenbücher, VVDStRL 4, 20 (1928) as quoted by Wendt, ibid.

[19] Smend, VVDStRL 4, 52 (1928) as quoted by Wendt, ibid.

All these three appear in the *Lüth* decision of the GFCC in one sentence divided by commas,[20] complemented by the so-called interdependency or mutual reaction doctrine (*Wechselwirkungslehre*). This latter one prescribes that the limit of 'general law' itself is to be interpreted in the light of the significance of the right to freedom of opinion. Furthermore, *Lüth* reinforced the imperative of *ad hoc* balancing, that is a fine-tuning of restrictions according to the particular facts of the case.[21]

On this basis, one can take the *Holocaust Denial* decision as saying either that the limit on freedom of opinion here is the higher-ranking human dignity (ie the prohibition of Holocaust denial is a general law in the third sense above), or that in terms of the *Wechselwirkungslehre*, the value of the expression of a statement made with knowledge of its falsehood is so little that it cannot exert a significant counter-effect on the limit of personal honour itself.

What is sure is that the *Holocaust Denial* judgment decided on the constitutionality of Holocaust denial as *defamation*, subsumed under article 185 of the German Penal Code, an offence against the person, not against public order. The GFCC explicitly declined to address the rest of the grounds on which the condition was based (including article 130, incitement of the people). However, after the decision of the GFCC, the legislature added a new offence, article 130 III, to the Penal Code,[22] penalising approval, denial or belittlement of the genocide committed under the Nazi rule if it is committed in a manner capable of disturbing the public peace. Note that article 130 III does not refer to human dignity, and the crime is placed among offences against public order.

The GFCC has not scrutinised article 130 III, in other words the Holocaust denial provision, but again everybody appears to take it for constitutional. If so, then the implied reasoning must be the following: expressing approval, denial or belittlement of the genocide committed under Nazi rule is in itself a violation of human dignity or personal honour of Jews living in Germany, and thus, no other condition is constitutionally required. That the legislature included in article 130 III, the requirement that the manner of the expression be also capable of disturbing the public peace, is

[20] BVerfGE 7, 198, 209 ff (1958), *Lüth*.

[21] Ibid, 208.

[22] Law on fighting criminality, 28 October 1994 (Verbrechensbekämpfungsgesetz). A commentator explains that the new provision was added—redundantly, as Holocaust denial has been subsumed (and prosecutable without private motion) under defamation since 1985—after the Federal High Court (the BGH) overturned a decision because the lower court erred in classifying an incident of Holocaust denial under incitement of the people by calumnious agitation instead of defamation. See, Günter Bertram, 'Der Rechtsstaat und seine Volksverhetzungsnovelle' (2005) *Neue Juristische Wochenschrift* 1476, 1476, fn 4. Still I think it is fair to note that the clear benefit of the provision of incitement of people over defamation is the more severe sanction, but also that there is no defence of proof, ie the deniers cannot abuse the court system to actually further promote their agenda.

fully within its power, as the provision is thus a less extensive restriction than would be constitutionally permissible.[23] Therefore, human dignity appears here as a self-standing limit on expression (and, thus, assembly).

Denying the Holocaust is not the only way that dignity arguments find their way into discussions on assemblies and demonstrations. As I said above, value judgements and opinions can also sometimes amount to a violation of dignity, or personal honour. Earlier case law on freedom of opinion would be applicable against symbolic displays at assemblies which aim at *vilification* (*Schmähkritik*) of a particular person. For instance, a placard showing a person—even a politician—as a copulating pig would be violating human dignity for its 'bestial' nature and 'depersonalisation'.[24] However, this does not go as far as to prohibit calling a politician a 'coerced democrat' and a 'strongman' whom some Germans admire just as they embraced the Führer.[25] In a different political setting, an NPD election campaign placard with the slogan 'Stop the Polish invasion!' displaying two crows extending a leg towards Euro banknotes was found constitutionally proscribable as a violation of dignity, it appears, again because of the equation of humans with animals.[26]

In contrast, the court found the slogan 'Send foreigners back home—for a German Augsburg worth living in' (*Aktion Ausländer-rückführung—Für ein lebenswertes deutsches Augsburg*) as not violating human dignity.[27] The slogan could not only be interpreted as expressing an opinion of the worthlessness of foreigners because a city with foreigners is not worth living in. Rather, the sentence can—and then constitutionally is required to—be understood also as part of a more general agenda of creating a German city worth living in. Though even understood this way, foreigners are certainly portrayed as a problem, but they are not denied their right to life and equal worth in the community. The court was criticised for reconstructing the meaning this way (as very often happens),[28] but praised for keeping the scope of 'killer argument' human dignity narrow.[29]

[23] *Cf* also the BGH's decision affirming the condemnation of an Australian for putting online in Australia material denying the Holocaust. BGHSt 46, 212—*Volksverhetzung im Internet*. The issue was only whether public peace can be disturbed via the internet. The court declared that the internet posting posed a 'threat suitable to severely disturb the thriving coexistence of Jews and other population groups and to prejudice their reliance on legal certainty'. (My translation). Ibid, 220.

[24] See BVerfGE 75, 369 (1987) *Political Satire* or *Copulating Pig* case.

[25] See BVerfGE 82, 272 (1990) *Stern-Strauss* or *Zwangsdemokrat* case.

[26] BVerfG, 2 BvR 2179/09, 24 September 2009.

[27] BVerfG, 1 BvR 369/04, 4 February 2010.

[28] See the many references in Kirsten Teubel, 'Deutung einer Äußerung—willkürliche Rechtsanwendung? (2005) *Neue Juristische Wochenschrift* 3245.

[29] See, eg Friedhelm Hufen, 'Meinungsfreiheit für rechtsextremistische Parolen?—Verfassungswidrige Verurteilung wegen Volksverhetzung' (2011) *Juristische Schlung* 88, 90.

Another aspect of the problem of statements disparaging groups is the definition of a group. The most important case in this regard remains the already mentioned *Tucholsky* or *Soldiers are Murderers* cases,[30] related and joined cases about different persons claiming at different occasions in pamphlets, on armbands and banners, in a newspaper, etc that soldiers are murderers or trained or potential murderers.[31] The GFCC found the expressions protected by artice 5 (GG), but maintained both the fact/opinion distinction and the possibility of group rights prevailing over expression. In contrast to the *Holocaust Denial* case, it earned less agreement among the German judiciary and academia.[32]

Having remanded the case for lack of sufficient weight accorded to freedom of expression in the balance, the GFCC did not strike down the norm itself, article 185 of the Criminal Code criminalising *Beleidigung* (insult, libel, defamation), for example, for vagueness. The court also expressly approved the applicability of libel provisions to defamation against *state authorities*, because 'without a minimum social acceptance, state institutions cannot carry out their duties'.[33] This protection, however, does not go as far as to shield institutions from public criticism,[34] which is 'especially guaranteed' by article 5 (GG). The court emphasises the importance of *ad hoc* balancing, fine-tuned to the interests at stake in the given case, but laid down guiding principles. First, human dignity always prevails over freedom of opinion, and the weighing also must ensure that due weight is given to human dignity as the underlying, ultimate value for every fundamental right and the whole constitutional system. Further, freedom of opinion also has to yield to honour protection in the case of vilifying insults or formal defamation (eg the case with the copulating pigs),[35] which nevertheless has to be interpreted quite narrowly, and has almost no applicability in discourse which essentially affects the public. Thirdly, the

[30] BVerfG, 1 BvR 1423/92, 25 August 1994, *Soldaten sind Mörder I*, and BVerfGE 93, 266 (1995) *Soldaten sind Mörder II*.

[31] The discussion of the *Tucholsky* rulings draws on, Orsolya Salát, *Interpretative Approaches to Freedom of Expression in Germany, the United States and Canada: The Impact of Free Speech Theories on Adjudication* (LLM thesis, Central European University, Budapest, 2006) 68–71.

[32] For critique of being overly speech protective, see Herdegen, NJW 1994, NJW Jahr 1994 Seite 2933 f; Sendler, ZRP 1994, ZRP Jahr 1994 Seite 343 ff; Steinkamm, NZWehrR 1994, 45 ff; Stark, JuS 1995, JUS Jahr 1995 Seite 689 ff; Dreher/Tröndle, o Fußn 6) § 193 Anm 14c, dd, for being underprotective of speech, see Gounalakis, NJW 1996, NJW Jahr 1996 Seite 481, all as cited by Walter Schmitt Glaeser, 'Meinungsfreiheit, Ehrenschutz und Toleranzgebot' (1996) *Neue Juristische Wochenschrift* 873, 874, nn 11 and 12.

[33] BVerfGE 93, 266, 290.

[34] Eg the GFCC overturned a condemnation for disparagement of the state when a person in strong words recalled the 1980 Oktoberfest attacks (13 deaths and 200 injuries), intimating that the criminals were a Nazi group, and the state deliberately omitted prosecution because of still existing sympathies with Nazism, 1 BvR 287/93, 29 July 1998.

[35] BVerfGE 75, 368 (1987).

court recites the obligation to assign an objective meaning to the utterance, taking into account the context in which it was made. As to the 'soldiers are murderers' statements, the court emphasises the difficulty of drawing a line between violation of the personal honour of members of a collective on the one hand, and legitimate and highly protected criticism of social institutions, such as the military, on the other. Therefore, it is not enough that the defamatory statement refers to an identifiable group, but it is also necessary that the group be 'conceivable', that is not so large, or otherwise indefinite, that the defamation cannot be seen as directed at an individual member of the group. The examples mentioned of a group unsuitable to be victims of libel are Catholics, Protestants, trade-union members and women. This much is an affirmation of the criminal law jurisprudence of the BGH. The GFCC adds that[36]

> in the case of accusations addressed to large collectivities, it is mostly not individual misbehaviour or individual traits of group members that are concerned, but the unworthiness of the collectivity and of its social function from the point of view of the speaker.

Note that at the same time the court also implies that group libel can be asserted in case of vilification or formal defamation. This, however, will be a rather rare case, since it requires personal insult pushing the issue of discussion completely to the background. This might occur especially if the disparaging assertions relate to 'ethnic, racial, physical or mental characteristics from which thus the inferiority of a group supposedly derives'.[37] This thought clearly underlies the *Polish Invasion* and other cases which I discussed before the *Tucholsky* rulings.

The German court thus very clearly sees the problem that dignity arguments might spill-over to discussions of matters of public interest or core political speech, but instead of directly declaring that public persons and collectivities do not have much personality rights, or that the state has no protectable honour in any sense—as the US Supreme Court basically declared—it tries to find a more sophisticated distinction between public matters and attacks against a person. I am somewhat hesitant whether that is possible, but clearly here one faces a perimeter issue, as some would claim in the United States such statements are controlled by general social norms of decency, while in Germany they are controlled by law. Also, it is remarkable that the German court explicitly upholds the honour of state institutions as a possible interest worthy of protection. One might speculate that the German court fears leaving the state unable to protect itself against subversion, or even perhaps expresses some sort of militant–democratic fears. Similarly to the stance of the GFCC on flag disparagement,[38] here a window

[36] BVerfGE 93, 266, 300.
[37] Ibid, 304.
[38] See Ch 8.

is left open for even worse times, when law might need to be used more openly for holding together the state itself. This is both very unprincipled and risks being misused, also because the Basic Law provides other means for militant democracy, but I see no other reason why the court would explicitly stress the 'defamability' of state institutions. Note also that the court explicitly reconstructs the contested expression as referring to soldiers of the world, and not only to soldiers of the Bundeswehr (ie the post-Second World War West German army banned from actively participating in armed hostilities)—the latter would be conceivable enough to be protected against defamation,[39] notwithstanding the fact that the army is a state institution par excellence, and there is no world military. The *Tucholsky* rulings also suffer from an artificial reconstruction of whether 'soldiers are murderers' is a factual statement or an opinion. I think it clearly is both (as basically most controversial statements are), but the GFCC struggles to explain that the murder is not meant in the way criminal law understands it,[40] and also, that it cannot be a factual statement, as everybody knows that the Bundeswehr has not killed anyone.[41] Clearly, this in no way excludes the meaning that soldiers—on occasion[42]—necessarily (would) kill as that is the nature of the job: a factual statement.

This complicated and rich jurisprudence discussed so far is still not the end of the constitutional story of expression and dignity-like arguments in Germany. Or, one might say, because many considered the reach of the dignity argument to be seriously restricted by the GFCC, other types of arguments were brought up, first by other courts, and most recently, in the *Hess Memorial March* decision, by the GFCC itself.

With regard to Neo-Nazi demonstrations, there was a long and unusually stern controversy between the High Administrative Court of North Rhine-Westphalia (OVG NRW) and the GFCC. The OVG stubbornly held that Neo-Nazi demonstrations, as such, are either not protected by the Constitution at all, or can be constitutionally banned.[43] It claimed that the Constitution includes inherent limits that *ex ante* prohibit the promotion of National Socialism and thus permit a prior ban on Neo-Nazi marches. These limits include not only human dignity, but also structural principles[44] of democracy, federalism, and the rule of law, the right to resist (all these permanently entrenched by the eternity clause of article 79 III).

[39] BVerfGE 93, 266, 302.

[40] Ibid, 306.

[41] BVerfG, 1 BvR 1423/92, 25 August 1994, *Soldaten sind Mörder I*, NJW 1994, 2943, 2944.

[42] Georgios Gounalakis, 'Soldaten sind Mörder' (1996) *Neue Juristische Wochenschrift* 481, 485.

[43] Which one of the two is not clear even to an author who wrote a whole doctoral dissertation on this subject: Giso Hellhammer-Hawig, *Neonazistische Versammlungen. Grundrechtsschutz und Grenzen* (Aachen, Shaker, 2005) 48 ff.

[44] Art 20 I GG (Basic Law) refers to the federal state (*Bundesstaat*), not exactly federalism, as implied by the OVG.

Furthermore, the de-Nazification provisions of article 139, and article 26 I(1),[45] which proclaim that actions capable of disturbing and intended to disturb the peaceful coexistence of peoples, in particular the waging of a war of aggression, are unconstitutional, also bear relevance to the Neo-Nazi marches. All these limits were rejected by the Federal Constitutional Court in several decisions,[46] and in this sense the controversy is only politically interesting. Two ramifications which might relate to it still need to be noted. The first one is the federalism reform which transferred the competence to regulate freedom of assembly to the Länder in Germany, and second, the *Hess Memorial March* decision of the GFCC from 2009.

The federalism reform from 2006 resulted in the possibility for each Land to adopt a fully new regulation on assemblies, or a partial one where the Federal Assembly Law remains valid in the unaffected provisions, or not to adopt any Land law at all. In this latter case, the Federal Assembly Law remains effective in its entirety. A few Länder had already introduced regulations of both sorts,[47] and the Federal Constitutional Court has even already decided on the constitutionality of the Bavarian Assembly Law.[48] Most of the changes relate in one way or another to extreme right wing activities, which have been on the rise ever since German reunification, especially, but far from exclusively, in the eastern Länder. Legislative reactions can be understood as attempts to find new ways of fighting 'extremism'. The Constitutional Court's jurisprudence has been thus presumably found to be of little help not only by the OVG NRW.

The federal legislator also tried to enhance protection against Neo-Nazi marches. In anticipation of Neo-Nazi marches around the Brandenburg Gate and the Holocaust Memorial for the sixtieth anniversary of the end of the Second World War for Germany on 8 May 2005, a new paragraph IV on incitement of others was added to article 130 of the Criminal Code. The new provision renders punishable by a fine or up to three years of imprisonment anybody who publicly, or in an assembly, disturbs the public peace by approving, glorifying or justifying the tyrannical and despotic National Socialist rule [*nazionalsozialistische Gewalt- und Willkürherschaft*] in a way which violates the dignity of the victims.[49]

[45] Art 26(1) GG (Basic Law).

[46] BVerfG, 1 BvQ 8/01, 26 January 2001, BVerfG, 1 BvQ 13/01, 24 March 2001, BVerfG, 1 BvQ 19/01, 12 April 2001. But see the interesting jurisprudence on Holocaust Memorial Day in Ch 6.

[47] For an overview, see Johannes Lux, 'Die Bekämpfung rechtsextremistischer Versammlungen nach der Föderalismusreform' (2009) *Landes- und Kommunalverwaltung* 491.

[48] BVerfG, 1 BvR 2492/08, 17 February 2009. For an overview of the Bavarian law, see Khwaja Mares Askaryar, 'Das bayerische Versammlungsgesetz—Überblick über wesentliche Änderungen gegenüber dem Bundesversammlungsgesetz' (2009) 4 *Kommunaljurist* 126.

[49] New para 4 to art 130, Criminal Code, introduced by law of 24 March 2005 (*BGBl I S 969*).

The Constitutional Court found the provision constitutional, albeit not on grounds of dignity, despite the fact that the text itself includes the requirement of violation of human dignity. The occasion for the Court's judgment was a series of banned marches in memory of Rudolf Hess in Wunsiedel with mottos such as 'He chose honour over freedom'. The prior bans were based on the likelihood that criminal offences under article 130 IV would occur, which then could be prevented by applying article 15 of the Assembly Law. The Constitutional Court issued preliminary decisions not to suspend the ban on the marches before substantive review. The decision on the merits came out in 2009,[50] after the applicant had eventually died. The Court decided the case for reasons of general constitutional significance despite the death of the applicant, and I think quite rightly so, as it found a whole new basis for dealing with recurring shadows of the past.

The Court found that the provision is in none of the above senses a general law, and, thus it cannot be justified under article 5 II (GG). It also made clear that the personal honour, as limit to freedom of opinion, can only be interpreted in connection with the requirement of a general law. It then follows that human dignity can also only be protected by general laws according to article 5 II.[51] In the discussion of what counts as general law, the court introduces—or reaffirms as it claims[52]—a version of content-neutrality where viewpoint discrimination is not permitted. Laws which refer to the content of an expression of an opinion have to be phrased in a sufficiently abstract and open way to be capable of subsuming different ideological views on the subject,[53] in order to qualify as general laws. I think this more or less coincides with the differentiation in US law between subject matter restriction and viewpoint-based restriction. Clearly then article 130 IV does not qualify as a general law under article 5 II, as it only penalises glorification of the National Socialist tyranny.[54] That would explain why it is to no avail that the provision also requires a violation of human dignity, the highest value in German constitutional law. Human dignity thus does not authorise 'special law', *Sonderrecht* (at least in cases of opinion, as opposed to false factual statements), which is, I think, a normatively correct clarification by the Constitutional Court. In this regard, it still has to be noted that the Court in the last part of the opinion basically reads the element of a violation of human dignity out of the statute. Possibly, this serves

[50] BVerfGE 124, 300 (2009) *Rudolf Heß Memorial March* or *Wunsiedel*.

[51] Ibid, 326.

[52] Ibid, 324, referring to BVerfGE 47, 198, 232 (1978).

[53] BVerfGE 124, 300, 324.

[54] It remains unclear to me if the viewpoint discriminatory nature of the provision lies in the glorification element or in the fact that it is only national socialist tyranny which is in focus, not, eg communist tyranny or any totalitarian regime as well. Common sense dictates either both, or the latter, as no effort to criminalise denigration of national socialist rule is on the horizon of rational lawmakers.

twin purposes—not only to avoid overburdening authorities with the duty to repeatedly prove that the very stringent requirement is fulfilled (as the Court finds the restriction constitutionally justified for other reasons), but also to avoid dangerously watering down the concept of human dignity.[55]

If not human dignity, then what would justify such a non-general, viewpoint-discriminatory law, which clearly also goes against the prohibition of discrimination on the basis of political conviction spelled out in article 3 GG? The Court explains that the *Unrecht* (non-law or extreme injustice) and horrors that the National Socialist rule implemented in Europe and large parts of the world 'elude general categories', and the creation of the Federal Republic of Germany is to be understood as a counter-plan (*Gegenentwurf*) to that. Therefore, an exception from the requirement of general law is inherent in article 5 for provisions which aim at preventing a propagandistic affirmation of the National Socialist tyranny between 1933 and 1945.[56] It is as though the Court finds that the uniqueness of the 'radical evil' of the National Socialist regime is not graspable under the general rules of reason. More pragmatically, it adds that

> the advocacy of this rule in Germany is an attack on the identity of the polity with a potential to threaten the peace inside. To this extent it [the advocacy] is incomparable with other expressions of opinion, and last but not least is capable of causing profound disquiet also abroad.[57]

Still, it does not mean that the GG would contain a general fundamental principle against National Socialism. The militant democracy provisions of the GG[58] first kick in when an 'active fighting-aggressive stance against the free democratic basic order' is taken. Consequently, also in the realm of freedom of opinion, a merely intellectual endorsement will not suffice, but the violation of a concrete legal value (*Rechtsgutverletzung*) or a recognisable endangering situation is necessary for expression to be restrictable.[59] This is true even for the current exception of propagandistic affirmation of National Socialist rule from 1933–45, and thus, even though the requirement of general law is suspended, the law and its application still have to pass the normal proportionality review, that is the regulation has to be capable and necessary of achieving a legitimate aim, and the restriction has to be necessary to the aim pursued, and proportionately balanced with freedom of opinion.

[55] The technique applied is a textual distinction between human dignity in art 1 GG and dignity of the victims in art 130 IV Criminal Code, a somewhat surprising differentiation. BVerfGE 124, 300, 344.

[56] Ibid, 327.

[57] Ibid, 329.

[58] Arts 9 II, 18, 21 II. (Criminal associations, abuse and forfeiture of rights, party ban).

[59] BVerfGE 124, 300, 329.

Article 130 IV StGB protects the legitimate aim of public peace, which is however to be interpreted narrowly. Public peace is too broadly conceived if it is to grant protection 'against subjective disquiet of the citizens resulting from confrontation of provocative opinions and ideologies', and it is intended to preserve only 'social and ethical views considered fundamental'.[60] Note that the similarly defined public order is not accepted to justify content restrictions, only modalities according to a different strain of case law.[61] Disquiet caused by the content of an opinion is the 'other side of freedom of opinion', and its protection would eliminate the 'principle of freedom itself'.[62] Public peace, however, can be constitutionally interpreted to mean only the prevention of 'unpeacefulness'. Those opinions whose 'content is recognisably animated toward acts endangering legal values [*rechtsgutgefährdende Handlungen*], i.e. they are a transition to aggression and breach of law', are a violation of public peace. The preservation of public peace refers to the external effects of expressions of opinion, for example, by emotionalised appeals which evoke in the addressed audience 'a willingness to act' or which 'reduce inhibitions' or 'intimidate any third party directly', or so the Court asserts with illustrations.[63] Article 130 IV properly (*geeignet*) protects public peace when it criminalises the approval, glorification, etc not of ideas, but of the historically concrete National Socialist tyranny, with its real crimes (which are singular in history, and whose inhumanity [*Menschenverachtung*] is not to be outdone).[64] Approval, glorification and justification are intense enough to typically result in a danger to public peace. The Court goes on to find the restriction both necessary (no less intrusive means) and proportionate in the narrow sense, meaning it realises a 'careful balance' between freedom of opinion and public peace, and especially that the restriction does not penalise pure expression of right wing radicalism or ideas related to National Socialism.[65] The Court similarly upheld the interpretation of paragraph IV of article 130 as applied to the present case of a memorial march for Rudolf Hess. Hess was the 'substitute of the Führer', who was co-responsible for the massive human rights violations of the regime; thus, the glorification of his person is a glorification of the historical National Socialist tyranny.[66]

[60] Ibid, 333.
[61] See Ch 7.
[62] BVerfGE 124, 300, 333.
[63] Ibid, 334.
[64] Ibid, 336.
[65] Ibid, 337 ff.
[66] Thus, it was correct for the Federal Administrative Court to conclude that a march in his memory would realise approval of the national socialist tyranny. It raises neither questions under art 5, art 8, or under art 103 II, the *nullum crimen sine lege* guarantee. BVerfGE 124, 300, 342 and 345.

The decision was mildly criticised for the tension between the justification of the provision as non-general law, and the rejection of the existence of an anti-National Socialist founding principle.[67] Another author argues that finding a new 'inherent constitutional limit', outside paragraph II of article 5 GG, is both doctrinally and politically wrong.[68] Also, the difference, if any, between the stance of the OVG NRW and the GFCC appears to be blurred after the *Wunsiedel* decision,[69] even though the GFCC explicitly refers to the OVG NRW as being in error. The OVG NRW would exclude from constitutional protection the expression of a commitment to National Socialism, while the GFCC appears to carve out an exception 'only' for positive evaluation of the historical National Socialist tyranny, provided that it threatens to violate legal values covered by the concept of a narrowly understood public peace. Time will tell if in practice the purported or alleged narrowness of public peace indeed makes a difference, or if expressing a commitment to National Socialism necessarily requires (will be interpreted to require) intimidation, emotional appeal, transition to aggression, or any such allegedly concrete violation of public peace. These questions will resolve themselves in time.

Long-term questions arise though by the juridification of the claim that there are facts which go beyond generalisable categories of human comprehension. If human dignity is already an activist concept worth keeping narrow, then this overcompensates in the other direction—law is taking over in an area where law's logic is said not to operate. How can legal coercion be based on an argument out of incomprehension or inconceivability? Can the radical evil be consistently countered by a violation of the categorical imperative? At the practical level, the GFCC clearly tries to narrow the scope of article 130 IV. But is there really a difference between advocating National Socialist principles and advocating them with reference to the historically realised practice of National Socialism? A balance so strenuously sought here appears to be sought just for the sake of balance, so that it can be said that there is yet a more intrusive means, that is also banning the simple distribution of ideas, and if there is a more intrusive means, then the present solution is one where there is no less intrusive means.

[67] Uwe Volkmann, 'Die Geistesfreiheit und der Ungeist—Der Wunsiedel-Beschluss des BVerfG' (2010) *Neue Juristische Wochenschrift* 417. Similarly Mehrdad Payandeh, 'The Limits of Freedom of Expression in the Wunsiedel Decision of the German Federal Constitutional Court' (2010) 8 *German Law Journal* 929.

[68] Mares Askaryar, 'Die Entscheidung des Bundesverfassungsgerichts zu § 130 IV StGB. Zugleich ein Beitrag zur Anwendbarkeit verfassungsimmanenter Schranken auf Grundrechte mit qualifizierten Gesetzesvorbehalt' (2010) *Kommunaljurist* 405.

[69] Similarly Volkmann, 'Die Geistesfreiheit', above n 67, 419 and Payandeh, 'The Limits', above n 67, 940.

II. FRANCE: DIGNITY AS PUBLIC ORDER AND OFFICIALLY DECLARED TRUTH

In France, free speech in general is even more restricted than in Germany, and those restrictions equally apply to assemblies. For lack of a human rights conscious case law, it is very hard to decipher what constitutional value justifies the far-going and very diverse restrictions, which cannot all be described in this book.

In any case, an illustrative example is the remarkable combination of human dignity and public order as grounds of justification (where public order is the legitimate aim, and the proportionality of the restriction is enhanced because it protects human dignity). At least, this mixed argument appears both in a few decisions of the Conseil d'État, discussed below,[70] and, independently, in a scholarly analysis[71] contrasting French and American perspectives on Holocaust denial and officially declared truth.

Defamation on the basis of race or religion was criminalised in France in 1939, suspended by the Vichy Regime, and then reinstated in 1946. Since 1972, provocation to discrimination, hatred or violence against another person for reason of their origin, belonging or non-belonging to an ethnic, national, racial or religious group, has been punishable under the law on the press for the same reason as defamation.[72] In addition to public prosecutor and/or victim, the Minister of Justice and non-governmental organisations are also entitled to initiate proceedings. Also, the defence of truth was abolished with regard to such defamation.

More prominently, the Gayssot Law from 1990 penalises 'any racist, anti-Semitic or xenophobic act' and 'any discrimination based on someone's belonging or not belonging to an ethnic group, a nation, a race or a religion', and makes it a crime to

> contest or call into question the existence of one or several crimes against humanity as defined in Article 6 of the statutory regulations of the International Military Tribunal annexed to the August 8, 1945 London Agreement, and involving crimes committed either by members of an organisation declared criminal pursuant to Article 9 of the regulations or by a person convicted for such crimes by a French court or an international court.[73]

[70] CÉ, 5 January 2007, no 300311, *Gallic Soup*, CÉ, 9 January 2014, no 374508, *Dieudonné*.

[71] Russell L Weaver, Nicolas Delpierre and Laurence Boissier, 'Holocaust Denial and Governmentally Declared "Truth": French and American Perspectives' (2009) 41 *Texas Tech Law Review* 495.

[72] Law no 72-546 of 1 July 1972 (loi relative à la lutte contre le racism).

[73] Law no 90-615 of 13 July 1990, art 9, as translated and quoted by Weaver et al, 'Holocaust Denial', above n 71, 497, fns 18 and 19.

The Conseil d'État confirmed the dissolution of the associations '*Jeunesses nationalistes*'[74] (Nationalist Youth) and '*L'Oeuvre française*'[75] (French Oeuvre) which organise assemblies inciting to hatred, discrimination and violence of persons for reasons of their foreign nationality, origin, or their Muslim or Jewish religion.

'Public abuse', 'incitement to racial hatred', 'praising war crimes', 'trivialising crimes against humanity', etc are all criminalised in French law, and sentences are normally accompanied by heavy criminal fines.

French prosecutors often appear to use criminal provisions against political opponents of the government. For instance, two leaders of the extreme right wing party Front National have already been convicted under the Gayssot Law, and Jean-Marie Le Pen was also sentenced for other crimes such as 'public abuse', 'incitement to racial hatred', 'praising war crimes', etc.[76] These provisions could not give rise to any constitutional litigation (as the QPC procedure was not set up yet, and preliminary review was not initiated by either Members of Parliament or government, even though the Gayssot Law was very much debated among French intelligentsia), but international human rights forums such as the Human Rights Committee (*Faurisson*)[77] and the ECtHR (*Garaudy*,[78] *Le Pen*,[79] *Gollnisch*[80] in a different case than discussed below) found no violation of their right to freedom of opinion or even research (with Gollnisch and Faurisson). At the ECtHR, most of these cases are declared inadmissible, relying often on article 17 ECHR (abuse of rights), or just simply manifest ill-foundedness.

The Cour de Cassation, in 2010, decided—for lack of a serious question of constitutionality (!)—not to submit to the Constitutional Council a newer case involving the Gayssot Law in its very first decisions handed down in priority preliminary ruling of constitutionality, the QPC procedure.[81] In a one-paragraph reasoning (half of which is the description of the offence),

[74] CÉ, 25 October 2013, no 372319.

[75] CÉ, 25 October 2013, no 372321.

[76] Weaver et al, 'Holocaust Denial', above n 71, 504.

[77] HRC, *Robert Faurisson v France*, Communication No 550/1993, UN Doc CCPR/C/58/D/550/1993 (1996).

[78] *Garaudy v France*, Application No 65831/01, Admissibility Decision, June 24, 2003.

[79] Eg Le Pen was condemned under art 23 of the Law of 28 July 1881 on freedom of the press. Le Pen said that: 'The day when we will have, in France, not 5 million but 25 million Muslims, they will be the ones who will command. And the French will hug the wall, go down the sidewalk, looking down. When they do not, they are said, "What are you looking at me like that? Looking for a fight?"And you just have to run away otherwise you take a fight'. And later: 'Especially since when I say that with 25 million Muslims here, the French will hug the walls, people in the room tell me not without reason: "But Mr. Le Pen, it is already the case now!"' *Le Pen v France*, Application no 18788/09, Decision on admissibility, 20 April 2010.

[80] *Gollnisch v France*, Application no 48135/08, Decision on admissibility, 7 June 2011.

[81] The QPC is a form of concrete review introduced in French law in 2008. See Otto Pfersmann, 'Concrete review as indirect constitutional complaint in French constitutional law: a comparative perspective' (2010) 6 *European Constitutional Law Review* 223.

the highest French court sitting in civil and criminal matters simply declares that the law refers to texts orderly introduced to French law, is clear and precise, and *thus* is not in conflict with constitutional principles of freedom of expression and opinion.[82] Thus, there was absolutely no discussion in any sense of constitutional or human rights, no discussion of means and ends, proportionality, etc. What is more, any future assessment would be blocked as QPC may be initiated only once on any given provision.

This is all the more troubling because of the following. While some of the convictions under the Gayssot Law were handed down in clear cases of denying the existence of death camps or gas chambers,[83] other statements can hardly be qualified as denial. Gollnisch, the second most important figure in the Front National at the time, and a professor at the University of Lyon, was sentenced under the Gayssot Law because: (i) he claimed another professor of history was, though respectable, not impartial in preparing a report on racism and Holocaust denial at the University of Lyon as he was Jewish (a statement which in general falls under discrimination in French law), and (ii) because of a—later withdrawn—statement that the number of persons killed in the Holocaust should be an issue left for historians to freely discuss. This latter remark was the main catalyst of the controversy. He explicitly said he did not deny the existence of deaths in gas chambers.[84] He received a three-month suspended sentence, was fined €5,000, and was ordered to pay €55,000 in damages and also for the publication of the decision in newspapers. However, finally the Cour de Cassation annulled the sentence,[85] a move apparently unexpected in the so predictable French legal system where the judge is merely the mouthpiece of the law.[86] In the light of this annulment in 2009, it is really surprising that a year or so later this very same Court blocked the way to constitutional review in QPC. Lower courts themselves showed they were willing to construct a 'contestation of crimes against humanity' from statements explicitly 'denying' those crimes, on the one hand, and other statements which are critical of the law's reach in declaring an official truth, on the other. Still, the Cour de Cassation found the law was clear and precise and not in need of constitutional check.

A less questionable, but still characteristic conviction under the Gayssot Law relates to Le Pen's so-called 'detail' remark. He said that in books on the Second World War, the Holocaust takes up a few pages and gas chambers a few lines, and 'that's what one calls a detail'. Disgusting as it

[82] Cass, 7 May 2010, no 12008.

[83] This is the case with Faurisson, Court of Appeals of Paris, 9 December 1992, and *Pierre Marais v France*, Application no 31159/96, Decision of admissibility, 24 June 1996, DR 86-A, 184, all as cited by Weaver et al, 'Holocaust Denial', above n 71, 499, fns 31, 32 and 36.

[84] See Weaver et al, 'Holocaust Denial', above n 71, 499–504.

[85] Cass Crim, 23 June 2009, no 08-82521.

[86] See Weaver et al, 'Holocaust Denial', above n 71, for a total lack of a possibility of reversal.

might be, he did not deny the existence of either the Holocaust or the gas chambers, nor even said they were understandable or explicable events (no justification). Still, his words can be interpreted—and I suppose were meant to be—as a belittlement (*Verharmlosen*—trivialisation), that is something German law would also find reprehensible, though that is exactly where one can be doubtful if it were in line with the reasoning of the GFCC's *Holocaust Denial* decision. It is one thing to deny a part of one's identity, and another to say it was a small element during the War, the latter being clearly an opinion. In any case, these are of no concern to French courts, and it is not so easy to unequivocally establish what is.

As most of the decisions are not publicly available, and the ones that are have very sparse reasoning, here I turn to scholars (who also often rely on the press, even in cases where the decision was not ordered to appear in the press). Scholars think that such far-going restrictions are necessary first to protect the dignity of the victims,[87] and secondly because of public order fears[88]—a clear heckler's veto, as the French normally start disruptive protests when public persons, especially university professors, are saying such kinds of things. Finally, restrictions such as the Gayssot Law are said to be necessary to prevent French people from forgetting the Holocaust, and that fear is increasingly justified as survivors are ageing and passing away.[89] Human dignity seems strongest here, or it is closest to what can be conceived of as a right of another person in terms of the general limit in article 4 of the Déclaration des droits de l'homme et du citoyen. Bertrand de Lamy contemplates the refusal of the Cour de Cassation to transfer the Gayssot Law to the Conseil Constitutionnel and notes that human dignity is also embedded in the Preamble to the 1946 Constitution.[90] Public order also clearly acts as a limit to freedom of opinion in article 10. Most problematic is certainly the legally enforced official history in the third explanation. This is, however, widely practiced in France through the commemorative laws (*lois mémorielles*), which are largely without normative content apart from the Gayssot Law[91] and might in anyway be in harmony with the strong role of the state

[87] Ibid, 508.

[88] Ibid.

[89] Ibid, 509.

[90] Bertrand de Lamy, 'QPC: refus de transmission' (2011) *Revue de science criminelle* 178. The Preamble to the 1946 Constitution, referred to in the Preamble to the 1958 Constitution, and thus having constitutional value.

[91] Law no 83-550 of 30 June 1983 regarding the commemoration of the abolition of slavery (loi relative à la commémoration de l'abolition de l'esclavage), law no 2005-158 of 23 February 2005 on the colonisation (loi portant reconnaissance de la Nation et contribution nationale en faveur des Français rapatriés), law no 2001-70 of 29 January 2001 on the recognition of the Armenian genocide of 1915 (loi relative à la reconnaissance du génocide arménien de 1915), devoid of any normativity. The planned law criminalising denying the Armenian genocide was quashed as unconstitutional. Decision no 2012-647 DC, 28 February 2012, but that does not affect the validity of the Gayssot Law.

in framing the proper 'consciousness of the French' as has been visible, for example, in the Islamic veil debate, and lately in the burqa controversies.[92]

The Conseil d'État also makes use of the first two arguments, although it combines human dignity and public order in such a way that the latter includes the former. This kind of combination has been accepted in French law since the *Dwarf Throwing* (exact translation of the French *lancer de nains*)[93] decision. Accordingly, one cannot waive their human dignity, because it is part of public order, and even if one freely, in all liberty, wants to be the thrown person in a show of that kind, it is necessary and proportionate for the local authority to prohibit it because of disturbances to public order. In relation to freedom of demonstration, the Conseil d'État held that it can have its limits in the interest in anti-discrimination and human dignity, this latter being part of 'public order'. Recall that in the famous '*Soupe gauloise*' or '*Soupe au cochon*' decision[94] the Conseil d'État decided that the ban on food distribution organised by an extreme right-wing group (SDF—Solidarité des Français, SDF is otherwise a common acronym for '*Sans domicile fixe*', ie homeless) with a probable racist animus does not violate freedom of assembly.[95] The 2014 ban of a show of a comedian (Dieudonné) with anti-Semitic messages was found justified by the same mixture of dignity and public order reasons by the Conseil d'État.[96]

As both the *Gallic soup* and the *Dieudonné* cases and the numerous memorial laws testify, the threshold for expression to violate human dignity and equality is both lower in France and has a wider application to groups than in Germany. In addition, the Conseil d'État is not preoccupied at all with the problem of horizontal application of human rights, since it includes human dignity and anti-discrimination in the concept of public order without any further ado. The reference to public order appears to '*etatise*' or 'verticalise' the balancing, but it is nonetheless a fiat of will to say that public order includes this kind of protection against offensive speech, even without any further showing that actual disturbances to public order would otherwise occur. The lack of any demonstration of material harm contrasts nicely with the US approach, to which I now turn.

III. UNITED STATES: DIGNITY AS NON-ARGUMENT

In First Amendment jurisprudence, dignity does not have such a privileged status as in Germany or France, or, to be precise, dignity does not figure

[92] For my view that *laicité* (the French concept on separation of church and state) starts overpouring to the private sphere in a way not true to its traditions, see Ch 8.

[93] CÉ, 27 October 1995, *Commune de Morsang-sur-Orge*, Recueil Lebon, 372.

[94] CÉ, 5 January 2007, no 300311. Recueil Dalloz, 2007, 307.

[95] See the discussion in Ch 2, text accompanying nn 136–41.

[96] CÉ, 9 January 2014, no 374508.

as a legal value in relation to speech, especially political speech in public assemblies.

In comparisons of US and German free speech law, it is a well-known assertion—basically the only one, reiterated and restudied ad nauseam—that all the above-mentioned German cases which rely on dignity would fall under *New York Times v Sullivan*[97] or *Hustler v Falwell*,[98] including Holocaust denial or bestialising depiction of politicians or public persons, or claiming that soldiers are murderers, or offering Gallic soup (or, let's say, steak) to the homeless. Campus hate speech codes are a special, and extremely controversial, field of regulation whose analysis goes beyond the scope of this project. Situations similar to those conceived as involving speech–dignity clashes elsewhere are partly conceived under the fighting words doctrine, but largely are not seen at all as situations giving rise to restrictions on speech.

Regarding the proscribability of group libel, the US Supreme Court's jurisprudence consists of at most two cases, one of them likely to be obsolete. After the Second World War, the Court upheld a kind of group libel statute in an opinion written by Justice Frankfurter. In *Beauharnais v Illinois*[99] (1952) there was a call for 'whites to unite' in order to stop murder, rape, etc committed by blacks against whites and similar allegations. The statute, as construed by state courts, allegedly only limited fighting words, but not completely in the sense of *Chaplinsky*.[100] The most important characteristic of the *Chaplinsky* doctrine, that is the direct personal attack against an *individual*, was notably missing. The US Supreme Court, in a five/four decision, nonetheless upheld Beauharnais's conviction under the group libel statute. Justice Frankfurter's opinion stresses both the need for deference to the legislature in questions of scientific evidence about harmful effects of racial hatred and the need to protect both individuals and groups against libel. The relevance of the ruling is questionable, since both *Brandenburg v Ohio* and the *Skokie* cases rely on opposite premises and resulted in opposite outcomes.[101] Though *Beauharnais* was never overruled, its relevance seems to have eroded.

RAV v City of St Paul[102] from 1992 is the next case where the US Supreme Court struck down a group libel or hate speech statute, albeit on content neutrality grounds which I will examine below in chapter seven.

Here it suffices to emphasise the very characteristic feature of First Amendment doctrine, whose default reflex leads it to discuss cross burning

[97] *New York Times Co v Sullivan*, 376 US 254 (1964).
[98] *Hustler Magazine, Inc v Falwell*, 485 US 46 (1988).
[99] *Beauharnais v Illinois*, 343 US 250 (1952).
[100] *Chaplinsky v New Hampshire*, 315 US 568, 572 (1942).
[101] See Ch 2.
[102] *RAV v City of St Paul*, 505 US 377 (1992).

as fighting words, that is in terms of reaction of the target of the cross burning, and with absolutely no hint of human dignity. In *Virginia v Black*, the cross-burning case from 2003, the question of 'intimidation' arose, which was largely translated by the court as true threat.[103] Again, human dignity does not figure in the discussion at all, clearly because it is considered so vague, devoid of any requirement of material harm, that no justified restriction on the right to free speech can be constitutionally based upon it.

IV. UNITED KINGDOM: DIGNITY UNDER DIFFERENT NAMES

In the United Kingdom, dignity—as an explicit legal value, let alone a right—does not shape the law on protest either. Though free speech law in general is more restrictive than in the United States—for example stirring up racial and religious[104] *hatred* have been criminalised, not only incitement to unlawful action—UK law is focused on consequential harm.

However, (in part only until 2013), section 5 of the 1986 Public Order Act (POA) proscribed the use of 'threatening, abusive or insulting words or behaviour likely causing harassment, alarm, or distress', which was often applied to situations where German or French law would operate with the mixture of dignity and public order/peace.

Hammond v DPP[105] involved an evangelical Christian holding a sign inscripted with 'Stop immorality', 'Stop Homosexuality' and 'Stop Lesbianism'. The message was unwelcome to the audience who then threw mud and poured water on Hammond. Hammond's conviction was affirmed by the Divisional Court, which sought to test whether the expression was 'legitimate', and finding it was not.[106]

Norwood v DPP[107] was about a British National Party (BNP) politician displaying a poster from his own window stating 'Islam out of Britain' and 'Protect the British people' next to a photo of 9/11 twin towers in flame, and a crescent and star surrounded by a prohibition sign. Article 10 ECHR was found to be overstepped as the display was not an intemperate criticism of the tenets of Islam, but an 'insulting attack' on its followers. Again, Norwood was supposed to prove that his conviction was unreasonable or disproportionate, an undertaking which remained unsuccessful.

[103] *Virginia v Black*, 538 US 343 (2003).

[104] For an argument that the new offence introduced in the Racial and Religious Hatred Act 2006 is redundant, see Ivan Hare, 'Crosses, Crescents and Sacred Cows: Criminalising Incitement to Religious Hatred' [2006] *Public Law* 521.

[105] *Hammond v DPP* [2004] EWHC 69 (Admin).

[106] For more discussion, see David Mead, *The New Law of Peaceful Protest. Rights and Regulations in the Human Rights Act Era* (Oxford, Hart Publishing, 2010) 226–27.

[107] *Norwood v DPP* [2003] EWHC 1564 (Admin).

In these cases, remarkably deprived of any sense of the human rights approach, the audience (the 'victim' of insult) suffices to be a hypothetical onlooker.[108] In *Hammond* no concern regarding heckler's veto played a role either, and hostile audience reaction was instead seen as confirmation of the insulting character of Hammond's speech.

In *Abdul v DPP*,[109] the English *Tucholsky* case,[110] protestors against soldiers returning home from Iraq shouted 'murderers', 'burn in hell', 'rapists', 'baby killers' and 'terrorists', and were convicted under section 5 POA, for using insulting and abusive language. These utterances constituted 'a very clear threat to public order' according to the court,[111] despite the fact that neither arrest, nor any other police measure was taken at the demonstration, but only later, after having watched film shootage of the event.[112] It was considered relevant that the incriminated sentences were uttered in a crowd situation: during a military parade which was watched by protestors. Though there occurred no violence on the part of well-wishing parade watchers against protestors, the court imputed this to skilful policing (and not to the normal operation of a democratic society).

In light of *Norwood*, *Hammond* and *Abdul*, without relying on a specific interest or value of human dignity, UK law restricted hostile expression related to group identity to a greater extent than German, and perhaps even French law.

Since these cases were decided, however, the legislator changed the law, and deleted the 'insulting' part of section 5 POA.[113] Thus, in this segment, the democratic process ended up providing a higher protection to freedom of assembly than domestic courts, or, as it will be seen below, the ECtHR.

This legislative improvement left the 'abusive' part of the harassment provision in section 5 POA unaltered though, thus scenarios as in *Abdul v DPP* will continue to be prosecuted.

In addition, the 2014 Anti-social Behaviour Act allows for injunction in case of conduct likely to cause nuisance or annoyance, a material standard cutting even below the abolished 'insulting' standard in section 5 POA, coupled with a weakened standard of proof ('balance of probabilities').

[108] For more discussion, see Mead, n 106, 224–29.
[109] *Abdul v DPP* [2011] EWHC 247 (Admin), [2011] Crim LR 553.
[110] See above in relation to German law, text accompanying nn 25–31.
[111] *Abdul v DPP*, above n 109, [52] i.
[112] For more detailed comment, see Alex Bailin, 'Criminalising Free Speech?' (2011) 9 *Criminal Law Review* 705.
[113] Crime and Courts Act 2013, s 57(2).

No wonder scholars[114] and NGOs[115] urged 'no' to the introduction of this unusually vague provision; nonetheless, their voices remained unheard.

In sum, English law, despite abolishing the punishment of 'insulting behaviour' (and the Anti-social Behaviour Orders or ASBOs, not discussed here), continues to limit freedom of assembly in pursuance of unclarified, vague public order interests. These interests sometimes overlap with concerns elsewhere understood as dignity concerns or group identity concerns, but are all caught up within a comfortably cloudy understanding of public order which does not compel courts to seriously engage with arguments from human rights. More precisely, English courts do not even have to make the argumentative moves between dignity, group identity and public order, but are contented with cursory references to 'threats to public order'.

V. EUROPEAN COURT OF HUMAN RIGHTS: HATE SPEECH CHAOS

In the jurisprudence of the ECtHR, dignity does not figure explicitly as an important concept either, which is partly due to the fact the ECHR does not contain a right to human dignity. This does not mean that dignity-like interests are not very much protected in other areas of the jurisprudence, especially under article 8, sometimes in conjunction with article 14.

Nonetheless, quite clearly, the cases argued under dignity and public order/public peace in Germany and France would largely be inadmissible under the ECHR, for reasons of article 17,[116] prohibition of abuse of rights, or for simply being unfounded. For example the request of Solidarité des Français, the organisation distributing the pork soup was declared inadmissible.[117] *Norwood* was also declared inadmissible.[118] In general, 'gratuitously offensive speech' does not merit protection in Strasbourg.[119]

Lehideux and Isorni v France is, however, a case which suggests that the ECtHR accords greater protection to offensive speech than France. In that case, representatives of an association cultivating the memory of Maréchal

[114] In general: Kevin Brown, 'Replacing the ASBO with the Injunction to Prevent Nuisance and Annoyance: A Plea for Legislative Scrutiny and Amendment' (2013) 8 *Criminal Law Review* 623. Specifically related to freedom of assembly: David Mead, 'Anti-nuisance Injunctions—a Few Thoughts' 11 November 2013, protestmatters.wordpress.com/2013/11/11/anti-nuisance-injunctions-a-few-thoughts/.

[115] Liberty, *Liberty's Response to the Home Office's Proposals on More Effective Responses to Anti-Social Behaviour* (London, Liberty, 2011) 15, as cited by Brown, ibid.

[116] On Holocaust denial, see *Garaudy v France*, Application no 65381/01, Decision on admissibility, 24 June 2003, DR 2003-I.

[117] *Association Solidarité des Français v France*, Application no 26787/07, Decision on admissibility, 16 June 2011.

[118] *Norwood v UK*, Application no 23131/03, Decision on admissibility, 16 November 2004, 40 EHRR SE11.

[119] Eg *Giniewski v France*, Application no 64016/00, Judgment of 31 January 2001, 45 EHRR 23.

Pétain were found guilty of apology of the crimes of the collaboration, a criminal offence. The applicant endorsed the so-called double game theory by praising Pétain as 'supremely skilful', while condemning 'Nazi atrocities and persecutions' or 'German omnipotence and barbarism'.[120] The ECtHR found a violation of article 10 as there was no Holocaust denial, and the applicants' statements were rather to be interpreted as part of an ongoing debate in history and historical identity of the French, considering also that the prosecution withdrew from the proceedings.

The ECtHR, similarly to the Conseil d'État, confirmed in *Vona v Hungary* that associations intimidating ethnic minorities can be dissolved without violating article 11.[121] The Hungarian Guard certainly staged paramilitary-like threatening marches, which even in the United States would qualify as 'true threat'. It has to be noted though that the dissolution has not prevented newer versions of the Guard from reappearing and continue intimidation in the form of demonstrations.[122] This happens when the state fights against abuses of freedom of assembly within the framework of freedom of association, which reinforces my argument that the two rights must be properly delineated. Though the ECtHR mentions this problem, due to its international nature, it clearly is unable to solve it.

Other recent hate speech cases in Strasbourg—not in the context of an assembly, but principally applicable because of the fall-back nature of article 10—show a more alarming trend. *Féret v Belgium*,[123] *Le Pen v France*,[124] or *Vejdeland v Sweden*[125] are perhaps most notorious for a weakened standard which allow for limiting speech which is simply offensive or abhorrent, but does not specifically incite to hatred.[126] In this regard, there is notable tension within ECHR jurisprudence between these cases (against ethnic or sexual minorities), and the *Red Star* case, where it was declared that 'dictates of public feeling—real or imaginery' do not authorise the state

[120] *Lehideux and Isorni v France*, Application no 24662/94, Judgment of 23 September 1998, 30 EHRR 665, § 47.

[121] *Vona v Hungary*, Application no 35943/10, Judgment of 9 July 2013.

[122] See Orsolya Salát, 'Report on Freedom of Assembly in Hungary' in Anne Peters and Isabelle Ley (eds), *Comparative Study: Freedom of Peaceful Assembly in Europe Study Requested by the European Commission for Democracy through Law—Venice Commission* (Max Planck Institute for Comparative Public and International Law, 2014) www.venice.coe.int/files/Assemblies_Report_12March2014.pdf, 113–26.

[123] *Féret v Belgium*, Application no 15615/07, Judgment of 16 July 2009.

[124] *Le Pen v France*, Application no 18788/09, decision de recevabilité de 20 avril 2010 (inadmissible).

[125] *Vejdeland v Sweden*, Application no 1813/07, Judgment of 9 February 2012.

[126] See, Stefan Sottiaux, '"Bad Tendencies" in the ECtHR's "Hate Speech" Jurisprudence' (2011) 7 *European Constitutional Law Review* 40; Kiska Roger, 'Hate Speech: A Comparison between the European Court of Human Rights and the United States Supreme Court Jurisprudence' (2012) 25 *Regent University Law Review* 107; Stefan Sottiaux and Stefan Rummens, 'Concentric Democracy: Resolving the Incoherence in the European Court of Human Rights: Case Law on Freedom of Expression and Freedom of Association' (2012) 10 *International Journal of Constitutional Law* 106.

to restrict human rights, as 'society must remain reasonable in its judgement' for to count as democratic.[127]

To sum up: dignity-type arguments arise especially in Germany and France, in relation to the Holocaust, Jews, people of colour, immigrants and so on, in other words what is commonly called hate speech. Therefore, dignity in this part of human rights law acts like a buffer between different groups, it basically functions as protecting social identity, as a perimeter (and not, eg as an autonomy-enhancing argument). That is why in some jurisdictions, dignity appears to mingle with public order, also a dubious concept with at times identity, at times authoritarian, and again other times militant democracy overtones. German legal language here focuses on the individual, while in French law the focus on discrimination might signal a more collective identity-based approach.

Although English law is exempt from a specifically dignitarian argument, this chapter shows it embraces restrictions for similar scenarios often to a larger extent than German or perhaps even French law. The ECtHR's somewhat chaotic hate speech jurisprudence increasingly rubber stamps national restrictions in pursuance of interests way below the German standard. The US Supreme Court has unsurprisingly proved most resistant to explicit or implicit dignity like restrictions.

In the last three chapters, American jurisprudence will appear in a significantly worse light due to the distortious effects of content neutrality on assemblies. These chapters will deal with restrictions not on the content, but on the 'modality' of an assembly. The next chapter discusses restrictions related to the time of the assembly, which is a significant question despite not being in the spotlight in either jurisprudence or scholarship. Time restrictions will be followed by a chapter on restrictions related to the 'manner' of the assembly, where jurisprudence—contrary to 'time'—abounds. Finally, chapter eight will analyse restrictions on the 'place' of the assembly.

[127] *Vajnai v Hungary*, Application no 33629/06, Judgment of 8 July 2008, 50 EHRR 44, § 57.

6

Restrictions on the Time

I. SPECIAL DAYS OF THE YEAR: THE NOTION OF PUBLIC ORDER IN GERMANY

GERMANY IS THE prime example of where assemblies may not take place on special days of the year if additional conditions are fulfilled.

The Constitutional Court has accepted a postponing condition imposed on a Neo-Nazi march which was scheduled for the 27 January (the Holocaust Memorial Day in Germany). The justification accepted was that an extreme right wing march on that very day would disturb public order.

Public order is different from both public peace (which forms the basis of restricting assembly in pursuance of dignity-like interests, as discussed above),[1] and public safety. Public order is a concept normally less adequate for restricting basic rights than its related concept of public safety since the case of *Brokdorf*. It includes those 'unwritten rules that the currently predominate social and ethical views consider must be followed as an indispensable condition of an ordered human coexistence within a particular territory'. As such, it is not normally sufficient to justify a ban on an assembly.[2]

In the present case, however, the Court found that it is possible to rely on public order considerations if the restriction resulting is only a delay by one day of the planned demonstration. Such delays are constitutional as

> public order is affected if a particular day has such an unequivocal meaning in society with a significant symbolic force and the planned march would attack upon that very meaning in a way which at the same time significantly violates fundamental social or ethical views.[3]

Such was the case with an 'extreme right wing' march on the day of remembrance of the liberation of the Auschwitz concentration camp on 27 January 1945, proclaimed the official day of remembrance to the victims of National Socialism.

[1] Ch 5.
[2] BVerfGE 69, 315, 352 (1985), *Brokdorf*.
[3] BVerfG, 1 BvQ 9/01, 26 January 2001, § 15.

The decision, however, did not discuss in detail competing interests of the speaker, as the organiser of the march explicitly claimed he was not aware of the day's significance, and on his own also 'booked' the next day, 28 January, when it became likely that the march would not be allowed to go ahead on the 27 January. Thus, the Court declared that the organiser did not show 'an interest in need of particular protection' to march exactly on 27 January. Furthermore, the case went to the Constitutional Court for preliminary suspension of the ban ('condition'), and this expedited procedure only allows for correcting the most obvious mistakes committed by ordinary courts and authorities.

Thus, significantly, in the procedure before the German Federal Constitutional Court (GFCC) the argument was not raised and discussed that the date should be available for 'protest' exactly because the date means something. Still, the GFCC would probably find a 'delaying condition' constitutional even if the very purpose of a march would be (explicitly) to protest Holocaust Memorial Day itself, or any related topic.

In another decision the Court even declared that to avert endangering of public order, it is possible to restrict freedom of assembly if it is the *Art und Weise*, that is the manner or modality of the realisation of an assembly, and not the content which gives rise to concerns.[4] The Court sketched three examples. Accordingly, it is permissible to restrict 'aggressive and provocative conduct of participants which intimidate the citizens, through which demonstrators create a climate of violent demonstration and a climate of potential readiness to violence'.[5] The next example of the Court of more interest to us here is the extreme right wing march on Holocaust Memorial Day, provided in addition that 'from the manner and modalities of the realisation of the assembly provocations arise which significantly encroach upon the ethical sentiments of citizens'.[6] Note that the expression 'ethical sentiments' (or maybe ethical sensitivity: *sittliches Empfinden*) conspicuously diverges from the usual one in the definition of public order: 'fundamental social and ethical views' ('*grundlegende soziale und ethische Anschauungen*'). Here, the modality of the realisation of the assembly is not (solely) the time (ie Holocaust Memorial Day), but also the 'provocative way' the protestors behave.

The same applies, so the Court adds, 'when a procession in its overall outlook identifies with the rites and symbols of the Nazi tyranny, and intimidates other citizens through evocation of the horrors of the past totalitarian and inhuman regime'.[7]

[4] BVerfGE 111, 147 (2004), *Stoppt den Synagogenbau!* or *Inhaltsbezogenes Versammlungsverbot*.

[5] Ibid.

[6] Ibid, 157.

[7] Ibid.

Note that in the German understanding modality differs from content-neutrality as understood, for example, in US free speech law. Here the reason for restriction clearly relates to the content of the message of the demonstrators, as only a pro-Nazi viewpoint gives rise to the need for restriction. Still, if the restriction only affects the time of the demonstration, then it is still found to be a restriction on modality, and thus, there is no need to defend it on the basis of article 5 II of the Basic Law (GG), in other words no requirement of a general law is foreseen. However, the Court goes further, and declares that the next question is proportionality of official reaction, that is if possible, only a condition should be imposed, but if that is not enough to avert the danger, then a ban might also be constitutional.

In general it appears from the complicated jurisprudence[8] of the Court that public order can be the basis for restrictions on modalities, but not on the content of the expression, be it on an assembly or anything else.[9] Content can only be restricted if public safety, understood to include substantive legal values, is directly endangered. In this case, necessarily, a ban might also be constitutional,[10] and it is even preferred (mandated) over imposing a condition on content, as the state is forbidden from forcibly changing the substantive message. In the case of modalities, however, imposition of a condition will regularly be a less restrictive means if public order is endangered, and as the limit is public order, not public safety, there is no need to examine if the law restricting freedom of assembly is a general one in the sense of article 5 II GG.

In an even more curious decision from 2005 the German Court also found permissible a rerouting of a far right demonstration away from both the Holocaust Memorial and the Brandenburg Gate in Berlin on the day of the sixtieth anniversary of capitulation of Germany. This decision, discussed in detail below,[11] was however not decided on public order grounds but partly on human dignity, and partly on balancing competing rights of the youth organisation of the Nationalist Party and of the general public who wanted to attend a government-organised commemorative event at the Brandenburg Gate. Still, the special date played a role in the whole scheme, and the Court also found the date weighty as an argument in favour of restricting the rights of the young Nationalists, even though they were the first to notify the authorities about the planned march.

[8] To get a general sense of the conundrum around public order, see Ulrich Battis and Klaus Joachim Grigoleit, 'Rechtsextremistische Demonstrationen und öffentliche Ordnung—Roma locuta?' (2004) *Neue Juristische Wochenschrift* 3459. It is partly overridden by the decision related to the Rudolf Hess memorial marches, discussed above, Ch 5, text accompanying nn 47–59.

[9] Giso Hellhammer-Hawig, *Neonazistische Versammlungen. Grundrechtsschutz und Grenzen* (Aachen, Shaker, 2005) 29.

[10] Ibid, 29 and 135–56.

[11] See Ch 8, text accompanying nn 118–24.

II. DURATION, TIME LIMIT, FREQUENCY

An important question for the demonstrators might be how long and how often they are constitutionally entitled to demonstrate. From a theoretical point of view, the answer largely depends on the rationale of the protection of the right to assembly.

If assemblies (demonstrations) are simply about expression in the narrow sense, then the first and only time might suffice, and it would not need to take a longer time than what is sufficient to express the message. After all, we are all sensible persons and understand the message already the first time, with no need for repetition.

However, if assemblies are also, or foremost, about thematising a new issue, creating a new social meaning, 'raising awareness', setting an agenda or exerting political pressure, then they might need to take longer and might occur repeatedly, even if the message is the same throughout and every time.

How long and how frequently, though, are not questions answerable in the abstract. Maybe then it is no wonder that not many high court cases have dealt with this question.

A rights-friendly approach would probably require that as a default demonstrators can stay as long as, and return as often as, they wish, but the protection decreases with the increasing burdens or externalities such an enduring or repeating demonstration puts on the normal daily life of the community. In practice, the boundary is probably determined through negotiation between police and demonstrators, and it will depend on the particular circumstances of a locality, with all that this brings about in relation to non-mainstream groups. Very few points seem clear. Obstructive demonstrations, if they are tolerated at all,[12] will not be tolerated too long or too often.

As to frequency, in general, over all jurisdictions, previous unlawful action is a ground for denying permits, or imposing conditions, or issuing injunctions.

In this latter regard, recall the controversy in the United States about abortion protests, and especially who is bound by the injunction. In the United Kingdom, harassment provisions are applied to prevent repetition of protest events, well below the threshold of obstruction, even well below causing alarm or distress. Injunctions may be issued—and increasingly often are issued—against protests directed at unidentified persons who belong to 'loosely formed unincorporated organisations'[13] such as campaign groups.

[12] See Ch 2, section IV.

[13] David Mead, *The New Law of Peaceful Protest. Rights and Regulations in the Human Rights Act Era* (Oxford, Hart Publishing 2010) 276.

On the other hand, recurring yearly (or monthly, as with the Critical Mass) single cause demonstrations are common events in all jurisdictions, some of them, such as religious or other traditional processions, regularly exempted even from the notification requirement.[14] On its own, the recurring nature is not a problem anywhere.

As to duration, there is again likely to be a practical negotiation between the police and demonstrators, depending also on the nature of the place where the demonstration is to be held.

In case of demonstrations or marches on roads and streets, certainly traffic rerouting is unlikely to be mandated by human rights for a significant period of time. The famous *Schmidberger* decision of the European Court of Justice (ECJ)[15] is beyond the scope of this project, but is still notable. To allow for a 30-hour complete closure of the Brenner Pass, a vital transportation route in Europe, for an environmental demonstration, is certainly among the most extreme, and most unlikely scenarios to happen under the jurisdictions examined here. Also, it appears to me, that the ECJ would not (even cannot) go as far as to mandate such a restriction on the free movement of goods in order to protect freedom of assembly, thus the EU countries examined in this book have a certain national discretion in this regard.

Parks are arguably different, where there is no traffic; thus, demonstrators can stay longer, as they cause less of an inconvenience for others. As will be shown below, under 'modes and means of asthetic harm',[16] the US Supreme Court rejected the proposition that the First Amendment protects a demonstration for homeless people to continue through the night on the National Mall and Lafayette Park in Washington DC.[17] It is all the more ironic, and clearly shows the distortions of content neutrality and public forum doctrines, that the Occupy Wall Street protesters (ie a demonstration which was not attempting to specifically point out the plight of the homeless by the expressive activity of sleeping) could camp and sleep in Zuccotti Park in New York for almost two months, only because Zuccotti Park is privately owned. The demonstrators were finally removed by police for reasons of sanitary and safety hazards, and some possible criminal activity such as drug use. If there really was—and there probably was—a sanitary hazard, unaverted but caused by the demonstrators themselves, then at some point the state must step in, and two months appear a generous arrangement, especially given that the residents were also complaining, even staging a protest at the City Hall themselves

[14] See Ch 2.

[15] Case C-112/00, *Eugen Schmidberger, Internationale Transporte und Planzüge v Republik Österreich*.

[16] Ch 7, text accompanying nn 234–40.

[17] *Clark v Community for Creative Non-Violence*, 468 US 288 (1984).

against the passivity of police in handling the situation in Zuccotti Park.[18] Demonstrators were allowed to return after the park had been cleaned up, but they were not allowed to start camping again. This question, of course, entirely depends on the private owner of the park, and certainly no court would find unconstitutional a limitation on demonstration which is well below the one found constitutional in the homeless sleeping tent case by the US Supreme Court for *publicly* owned parks.

[18] 'City, Zuccotti Park owners order protesters to leave until park has been cleaned', *Associated Press* (15 November 2011) www.washingtonpost.com/national/city-zuccotti-park-owners-order-protesters-to-leave-until-park-has-been-cleaned/2011/11/15/gIQATLePNN_story.html.

7

Restrictions on the Manner

ACCEPTABLE REGULATION ON the 'manner of an assembly' refers to three main issues: first, and most famously, the many questions of symbolic expression from banned and protected symbols to masks and uniforms, inherently related to the relation (or difference) of freedom of expression and freedom of assembly;[1] secondly, the noise made either intentionally or necessarily by the demonstrations; and, finally, the litter and other aesthetic harm which is created on such occasions.

Although some of these issues might sound uninteresting, they are in fact part and parcel of a system of restrictions which often affect the essence of the freedom which is inherent in assemblies.

I. BANNED AND PROTECTED SYMBOLS: WHOSE IDENTITY?

Symbols at an assembly come in many varieties. Social movement history testifies that symbols play a, probably, more important role than anything else in making an efficient protest event. Symbols induce unity and a sense of strength, but they also convey the message in a compact form. They can be worn on clothes, brought with, drawn or printed on placards, and so on. What is more, not only material objects can bear or become symbols. Marching in formation, special gestures, dancing a special dance,[2] or the various uses of fire, itself a symbol of growing multiplicity, are also symbolic.[3] Symbols, valuable as they are to the protesters, often seem threatening to the authorities or the general public exactly because of their powerful unifying capacity. Also, symbols may hurt more than words as the recognition of the symbol immediately recalls a range of associations. Moreover, symbols are simplifying and far more apt to stir emotions than reasoned argument.[4]

[1] See Ch 1.

[2] Of course, chanting and singing are also symbolic, just as seeking symbolic places. I have grouped these other time, manner or place restrictions (TMPs) under different headings because the justification for restricting them are different.

[3] Elias Canetti, *Masse und Macht*, 5th edn (Hamburg, Claassen Hamburg, 1992).

[4] Cf Jackson J's statement: 'Symbolism is a primitive but effective way of communicating ideas. The use of an emblem or flag to symbolize some system, idea, institution, or personality is a short-cut from mind to mind'. *West Virginia State Board of Education v Barnette*, 319 US 624, 632 (1943).

Finally, there is a competition between symbols of protesting groups and state symbols, best exemplified by the flag desecration cases.

Therefore, it comes at least as no surprise, that courts tend to grant less protection to so-called symbolic speech than to the 'default' category of reasoned argument. The US Supreme Court's symbolic speech doctrine is a case in point where a court explicitly says so, while in the other jurisdictions the constitutionality of serious limitations, or selective outright bans on symbols at demonstrations are often not even questioned in and by courts.

Various symbols, though widespread in the practice of demonstrations everywhere, have attracted a differing amount of legislative and judicial attention in the different countries. These differences will be taken into account in the following discussion.

A. Symbolic Speech in the United States

Symbols have always been in use at assemblies, but until the middle of the twentieth century theoretical questions of symbolic speech had not come to the forefront of debate. The 1931 decision of *Stromberg v California,* for instance, is about a ban on displaying the red flag that is a symbol, although the decision does not revolve around what speech protection symbols should enjoy. The statute in *Stromberg* proscribed displaying a red flag in a public place or in a meeting place[5] 'as a sign, symbol or emblem of opposition to organised government, or as an invitation or stimulus to anarchistic action, or as an aid to propaganda that is of a seditious character'.

In this case, however, the question was not to what extent waving the red flag was expression, but whether displaying the red flag with any of the proscribed *meanings* was constitutionally protected. Thus, the court had to deal, not with the symbolic conduct part of the expression, but exactly with the content part (opposition to organised government, stimulus to anarchistic action, or propaganda of sedition). As such, it found that the latter two (incitement or solicitation) categories are proscribable, but the state cannot prohibit using the red flag as a symbol of opposition to organised government. The line is very thin in this pre- 'clear and present danger', and of course pre-*Brandenburg*[6] case, but it is nonetheless existing as between stating a view (opposition to organised government) and incitement to action. Thus, in *Stromberg*, the court has not yet questioned whether speech by symbolic conduct is speech, nor has it indicated that it would be worthy of less protection.[7]

5 *Stromberg v California*, 283 US 359, 361 (1931).

6 *Brandenburg v Ohio*, 395 US 444 (1969). See Ch 3, text accompanying nn 32–38.

7 It obviously could not have done so, as the statute at hand itself was based on the assumption that displaying the red flag was speech.

The symbolic speech doctrine has its origins proper in a later dispute over what counts as speech and what is conduct, unprotected by the First Amendment. Justice Black was the most prominent representative of the view that speech should be afforded absolute protection while conduct (or action) zero.[8] The court itself on many occasions made clear that though not subscribing to a rigid speech–action theory, it maintains a difference in the protection afforded to pure speech and 'speech plus'. In *Cox v Louisiana I*, the court per Justice Goldberg stated what later came to be cited many times:[9]

> We emphatically reject the notion urged by appellant that the First and Fourteenth Amendments afford the same kind of freedom to those who would communicate ideas by conduct such as patrolling, marching, and picketing on streets and highways, as these amendments afford to those who communicate ideas by pure speech … it has never been deemed an abridgment of freedom of speech or press to make a course of conduct illegal merely because the conduct was in part initiated, evidenced, or carried out by means of language, either spoken, written, or printed.

Note the remarkable lack of any reference to the right of the people peaceably to assemble with regard to marching and picketing. Even within the speech framework, what counts as 'pure speech'—if it exists at all—has never been defined. Almost all speech worthy of its name makes use of symbolism and includes some material element, or modality, even in our virtual world.

In the classic symbolic speech decision in 1968, in *United States v O'Brien*, the Warren Court upheld the criminal conviction for burning a draft card in opposition to the Vietnam War.[10] According to the newly enacted four-step standard,[11]

> government regulation is sufficiently justified if it is within the constitutional power of the Government; if it furthers an important or substantial governmental interest; if the governmental interest is unrelated to the suppression of free expression, and if the incidental restriction on alleged First Amendment freedoms is no greater than is essential to the furtherance of that interest.

Then the court went on to find that the registration system was certainly within governmental power and was useful in many regards, fulfilling substantial governmental interest. Jurisprudentially, the decisive point is that proscription of destroying the draft card is an incidental regulation on speech, and incidental regulation is subjected to less stringent constitutional requirements. Justice Harlan, concurring, adds that O'Brien had many other ways to convey his message other than by burning the draft card, and *a contrario*, if a message can only be conveyed in a way which violates an

[8] See, eg *Street v New York*, 394 US 576, 609 ff (1969) (Black J dissenting).
[9] *Cox v Louisiana*, 379 US 536, 555 (1965).
[10] *United States v O'Brien*, 391 US 367 (1968).
[11] Ibid, 377.

'incidental' regulation, then that would be found an unconstitutional burden. Clearly, the majority and the concurring do not find it important that to burn the draft card is certainly among the most effective and powerful ways of protesting against the war. Neither does it bother the court that in effect it imposes its own view on how to communicate a specific message.

However, in the following year, in *Tinker v Des Moines Independent Community School District,* the court did not rely on *O'Brien.* It found that wearing an armband for the purpose of expressing opposition to the Vietnam War is 'the type of symbolic act' protected by the First Amendment, and 'closely akin to 'pure speech'.[12] High school students were suspended for wearing armbands after the school board adopted a policy forbidding armbands in reaction to the rumours that some students were going to wear them. The case is therefore different from *O'Brien* as the regulation was not incidentally burdening speech, but aimed at preventing disruption resulting from speech feared by authorities.[13] In distinguishing this case from other scenarios, the court noted that the case 'does not concern aggressive, disruptive action or even group *demonstrations*. Our problem involves direct, primary First Amendment rights akin to "pure speech"' (emphasis added).[14] Is it then implied here that group demonstrations involve 'indirect', 'secondary' rights, akin to 'impure' speech?

Tinker does not cite *O'Brien*, and does not analyse the question of symbolic expression any further than the declaration that wearing a black armband is closely akin to pure speech. The only focus is the potential for disruption, which was found to be without any merit. As such, *Tinker* properly favours free expression and affirms the commonplace that symbolic conduct has meaning and should be constitutionally protected along the same lines as any other expression. *Tinker*, however, does not affect the precedential status of *O'Brien*, not overturned to this day.[15]

O'Brien has, however, been cited in the flag burning cases, but was found inapplicable. Clearly, flag burning or desecration touches more directly on state symbolism than the draft card in *O'Brien*. In a series of cases, the American flag was either burned, worn on trousers, or modified by affixation. In *Street v New York*, the appellant burned his own American flag in reaction to the news that James Meredith, a civil rights leader, was killed by a sniper. He said on the street corner next to the burning flag that 'We don't need no damn flag ... if they let that happen

[12] *Tinker v Des Moines Independent Community School District*, 393 US 503 (1969).

[13] Similarly John Hart Ely, 'Flag Desecration: A Case Study in the Roles of Categorization and Balancing in First Amendment Analysis' (1975) 88 *Harvard Law Review* 1482, 1489.

[14] *Tinker*, above n 12, 393 US 508.

[15] *O'Brien* finds notable application in the nude dancing and public nudity decisions, *Barnes v Glen Theatre*, 501 US 560 (1991) and *City of Erie v PAP's AM*, 529 US 277 (2000).

to Meredith'.[16] He received a suspended sentence under a flag desecration statute. The Supreme Court reversed the conviction, but did not decide on the issue whether burning a flag is an expressive activity protected by the First Amendment.[17] The four dissents attached to the Court's opinion are more interesting as they do not avoid the issue of whether flag burning amounts to protected speech. Among the dissents, one can find a whole range of reasons focusing on the flag, on the fire, and on the difference between speech and action which purport to deny that flag burning is protected. Justice Black thinks flag burning as conduct is outside First Amendment protection, Justice Fortas argues that the applicable statute is a general law which serves safety and undisturbed traffic, while Chief Justice Warren and Justice White, in separate dissents, strangely take for evident that flag desecration can be constitutionally criminalised.

In *Spence v Washington*,[18] the court faced a similar challenge, but again declined to decide the real issue. Spence was not burning a flag, but affixing on it a peace symbol in protest at the invasion of Cambodia, and the Kent State killing of four protesters by the police. This was found to be violating a flag misuse statute. The Supreme Court reversed the decision and found the statute *as applied* unconstitutional. The *per curiam* decision found *O'Brien* inapplicable, as it took the statute to be directly related to expression. Assuming *arguendo* that the state might have a legitimate interest in preserving the integrity of the flag, it found that there was no evidence that anybody would have taken Spence's modified flag to be endorsed by government.

The assumption part of the *Spence* decision was brought again before the court in *Texas v Johnson*, the penultimate case in the saga of flag desecration. Johnson burnt a flag in protest against the Reagan administration, and was convicted for 'damaging the flag … in a way that the actor knows will seriously offend one or more persons likely to observe or discover his action'.[19] The difference between this and the previous statutes is thus that here the (likely) reaction of the onlookers was the turning point. Whether one feels offended by the burning of a flag, however, can only be a result of communication of an idea. A flag burning by itself—for instance, as a result of a natural catastrophe—does not offend any reasonable person. The interest of the state of preserving national unity in the symbol of the flag is thus an interest not unrelated to expression. Therefore, *O'Brien* does

[16] *Street v New York*, 394 US 576, 579 (1969).

[17] Because the majority found the conviction could have been at least partly based on not what he did to the flag, but what he said about it. This is an uncommon way of seeing the lower court's judgment, as the issue was unanimously phrased as relating to burning the flag in the Court of Appeals. The majority was sharply criticised for this avoidance of the issue by the dissenters.

[18] *Spence v Washington*, 418 US 405 (1974).

[19] *Texas v Johnson*, 491 US 397 (1989).

not apply. As the protection of the flag's integrity is even a content-based restriction, it should be subjected to the most exacting scrutiny. In this light, the issue turns on the state's interest to prescribe what shall be orthodox or to protect the society against offensive ideas; and neither of these is a legitimate concern. In reaction, the Flag Protection Act was enacted which criminalised any person who 'knowingly mutilates, defaces, physically defiles, burns, maintains on the floor or ground, or tramples upon' a United States flag, except conduct related to the disposal of a 'worn or soiled' flag.[20] The government argued that unlike the statute in *Johnson*, this text aims only to protect the physical integrity of the flag, independent of any expressive conduct and without regard to the onlookers' reaction. The case of *United States v Eichman* invalidated the Act because the government could not show that the interest in protecting the flag's integrity is unrelated to suppression of expression. The interest in preserving the flag as a symbol for national ideals is implicated only 'when a person's treatment of the flag communicates [a] message'[21] inconsistent with the ideals. *O'Brien* thus does not apply, and under *Johnson* there is no uncertainty as to the unconstitutionality. The Flag Protection Act entails not only content-based, but even viewpoint-based discrimination, to use a later, but more precise doctrinal language.

At this point, it is worth recalling the *Skokie* controversy[22] and the *RAV*[23] and *Virginia v Black*[24] cases. In *Skokie* the would-be demonstrators wanted to march in full Nazi paraphernalia, wearing the swastika. In both *RAV* and *Virginia v Black*, a cross was burnt. Injunctions in *Skokie* against the march and the wearing of the swastika were found unconstitutional for failure to fulfil *Brandenburg* criteria.

As to the facts in *RAV*, the defendant burned a cross on a black family's lawn and was convicted under a Bias-Motivated Crime Ordinance, which prohibits display of a symbol which one knows or has reason to know 'arouses anger, alarm or resentment in others on the basis of race, color, creed, religion or gender'.[25] Although the Supreme Court of Minnesota claimed to have narrowed the scope of the ordinance to fighting words, it disregarded the fact that anger, alarm and resentment are not sufficient evils under the *Chaplinsky* doctrine (concurring opinion by Justice White).[26] Nevertheless, the majority did not reach this issue, deciding the case on

[20] Flag Protection Act of 1989, 103 Stat 777, 18 USCA § 700 (Supp 1990), as cited by *United States v Eichman*, 496 US 310 (1990).

[21] Ibid, 316.

[22] Ch 3, text accompanying nn 172–80.

[23] *RAV v City of St Paul*, 505 US 377 (1992).

[24] *Virginia v Black*, 538 US 343 (2003).

[25] St Paul Bias Motivated Crime Ordinance, St Paul, Minn Legis Code § 292.02 (1990).

[26] *Chaplinsky v New Hampshire*, 315 US 568, 571 f (1942) as cited by *RAV v City of St Paul*, 505 US 377, 399 (1992) (concurring opinion of White J).

content-neutrality grounds. The novelty of the reasoning is that even low value speech cannot be regulated on the basis of content unless one of the following criteria is met. First, 'the basis for the content discrimination consists entirely of the very reason the entire class of speech at issue is proscribable', or, secondly, the state is concerned only about the 'secondary effects' of the speech, or a 'particular content-based subcategory of a proscribable class of speech' is 'swept up incidentally within the reach' of the legislation, or, finally, 'the nature of the content discrimination is such that there is no realistic possibility that official suppression of ideas is afoot'.[27] Assuming *arguendo* that the ordinance, as applied, only prohibited fighting words, Justice Scalia finds that none of the four possibilities applies. Rather, the legislation is impermissibly content-based insofar as it prosecutes fighting words only on the basis of race, gender or religion and impermissibly viewpoint-discriminatory since it punishes fighting words based on intolerance but not those advocating tolerance in line with the state's commitment to equality. As Justice Scalia's example goes, using aspersions upon a person's mother in support of racial, religious, etc tolerance would not be covered by the statute.

The most radical implication of the *RAV* majority is that even within low value categories strict scrutiny applies. Therefore, *RAV* is decided on content-neutrality grounds, and not so much on symbolic speech grounds. Nonetheless, the underlying assumption is that symbols can amount to fighting words, but that symbols are only regulable if they actually constitute fighting words.[28]

In *Virginia v Black*[29] the court faced a very similar challenge. There was also cross burning, and a statute which made it a crime 'for any person ... with the intent of intimidating any person or group ... to burn ... a cross on the property of another, a highway or other public place', and specifies that 'Any such burning ... shall be prima facie evidence of an intent to intimidate a person or group'.[30] The court found in favour of the cross burners because the prima facie evidence provision was unconstitutional. Apart from that, however, it accepted that cross burning can be prosecuted if committed with the intent to intimidate. The evidence provision is unconstitutional because it takes away the very reason why the felony itself is constitutional. The majority of the Justices agreed on the proscribability of cross burning as an instance of true threat if made with an intent to intimidate. (Justices Scalia and Thomas also found constitutional the evidence provision, though they also had differences). True threats are low

[27] Ibid, 388–90.
[28] On the fighting words doctrine, see Ch 3.
[29] *Virginia v Black*, 538 US 343 (2003).
[30] Ibid (without citation reference for the Virginia statute).

value speech, therefore constitutionally regulable if one of the *RAV* criteria is met. In this case, according to the majority of the Justices, a ban on cross burning with an intent to intimidate falls under the first criterion. The basis for the ban 'consists entirely of the very reason the entire class of speech at issue is proscribable', because cross burning is a particularly virulent expression of intimidation.

The dissenters and literature maintain that the ruling is inconsistent with *RAV* and earlier doctrine.[31] It is easy to show that the statute is viewpoint-discriminatory, just like the ordinance in *RAV*:

> One could argue that cross burning is the most potent arrow in the white supremacist's quiver. Those who wish to deliver a message of racial harmony are extremely unlikely to use cross burning as their mode of communication. Consequently, when the state regulates cross burning, it is undoubtedly handicapping one side of the debate.[32]

As Justice Souter points out, for such cases the court applies strict scrutiny, and, since the state has failed to show a compelling interest in opting for such viewpoint-discrimination instead of a content-neutral statute proscribing any kind of intimidation, the statute is unconstitutional.[33] Justice Souter's main concern is that, under a statute banning a particular symbol, it is most likely that prosecutors and courts would find an intent to intimidate, though exactly what would be the question to be proven, basically independent of whether intimidation results from using a symbol or just plain words.

A few lessons can be drawn from this complex case law on symbols in the United States. Jurisprudence on flag desecration turns out to be the most straightforward. Here the state promotes a symbol, and as a symbol is by definition expressive, its promotion is also by definition expressive. Every conduct which uses the symbol *as symbol* is therefore also *necessarily* expressive, be it that of the state 'protecting' or that of a demonstrator 'criticising' the symbol.

It is true, on the other hand, that regulating the draft card is not *necessarily* expressive as the draft card is not *necessarily* a symbol. However, in my view the US Supreme Court deliberately ignored the fact that *anything* can become expressive or a symbol (what is more, especially a draft card or any other official paper). If something is used as a symbol, its use as a symbol ought not to be sanctioned, that is the principle behind the flag desecration cases. This does not mean of course that O'Brien could not have been obliged to compensate

[31] Eg Frederick Schauer, 'Intentions, Conventions, and the First Amendment: The Case of Cross-Burning' (2003) *Supreme Court Review* 197, 209; Guy-Uriel E Charles, 'Colored Speech: Cross Burnings, Epistemics, and the Triumph of the Crits?' (2005) 93 *Georgia Law Journal* 575.

[32] Charles, 'Colored Speech', ibid, 607.

[33] See 583 US 387 (per Souter J, partly concurring and partly dissenting).

for the cost of issuing a new draft card. Just as the unconstitutionality of flag desecration does not mean that you can tear down a flag from an official building of the state without being liable to pay for the cost of a new flag.

Cross burning and swastikas are similar to the flag in that they are necessarily symbols. However, contrary to the flag, they are symbols (of hatred) that the state 'dislikes' and does not identify with. Under content-neutrality, this cannot exactly make a difference: the state's view about a symbol is necessarily expressive, too, and thus, restrictions based on that view are content-based. That is why Justice Souter is right arguing for a total impermissibility of regulating symbols qua symbols.

US jurisprudence has failed, but struggled to recognise a unified principle regarding symbolic speech or conduct. European countries, discussed next, apply an even more contradictory approach towards banned and protected symbols.

B. Banned Signs in Germany and France

i. Germany

Symbols in general are protected speech under the Basic Law (GG), covered by article 5 on freedom of expression of opinion. This includes the protection of symbols on demonstrations.[34] There is no doctrinal disadvantagement of symbolic speech or conduct as it is observable in the US doctrine. Nonetheless, many more symbols cannot be displayed in Germany than in the United States. All the grand symbolic conduct cases, except for *O'Brien*, of course, would very likely turn out the other way round in Germany. The reasons and structure of the argument are very different, though common ground is that the simple dislike of the content of the message is not enough to restrict it. German doctrine also tries to uphold the principle of content neutrality, but there is a near universal consensus among legislators and courts that more important values can justify restrictions on the free use of some symbols if the restriction does not in itself target the idea which is expressed by the symbol. This criterion is accepted to be fulfilled if the banned symbol happens to be that of a constitutionally banned *organisation*.

The central norm—as luckily in German law there often is one—is article 86a of the German Criminal Code, criminalising the distribution and public use of symbols (rather: signs) of banned parties and organisations and their substitute organisations.[35] Banned organisations are those which have

[34] BVerwGE 72, 183.

[35] Substitute organisation can be a party or an association of which it is incontestably (*unanfechtbar*), ie at the final stage of review, established that it is a substitute for the banned one. Section 86 StGB (Criminal Code).

been, or are being, banned under the Basic Law's militant democracy[36] clauses,[37] but also those which were banned right after the Second World War.[38] The overwhelming majority of banned organisations are Nazi, neo-Nazi, or other extreme right wing organisations,[39] the GFCC (German Federal Constitutional Court) banned a Nazi (Socialist Reich Party)[40] and a Communist party.[41] Symbols according to article 86a of the Criminal Code include, in particular, flags, insignia, uniforms, slogans and forms of greeting, and also symbols which are so similar to the banned ones that they can be mistaken for them. As interpreted, a photo or *Abbildung* of Hitler is also a symbol for the purposes of article 86a,[42] but not that of Rudolf Hess who became a symbol of the extreme right wing only after 1945.[43]

As can be seen, the prohibition on symbols on a demonstration is not specific; but is regulated by the general laws realising militant democracy in Germany, not only in the political arena, but in general. The aim of article 86a is interpreted to avert 'social habituation' to symbols which might induce the revival of the banned organisations.[44] In the interpretation of the Federal Court of Justice (BGH, the highest ordinary court for civil and

[36] For the concept, see Karl Loewenstein, 'Militant Democracy and Fundamental Rights I' (1937) 31 *American Political Science Review* 417, and Karl Loewenstein, 'Militant Democracy and Fundamental Rights II' (1937) 31 *American Political Science Review* 638. For recent theoretical and comparative discussions see the contributions in András Sajó (ed), *Militant Democracy* (Utrecht, Eleven, 2004). On the German approach see, most recently, Markus Thiel, 'Germany' in Markus Thiel (ed), *The 'Militant Democracy' Principle in Modern Democracies* (Surrey, Ashgate, 2009) 109.

[37] Art 9(2) GG declares that '(2) Associations whose aims or activities contravene the criminal laws, or that are directed against the constitutional order or the concept of international understanding, shall be prohibited.' Under art 21(2), parties which by reason of their aims or the behaviour of their adherents, seek to undermine or abolish the free democratic basic order, or to endanger the existence of the Federal Republic of Germany, shall be banned by the Constitutional Court. (Translation of the constitutional texts is from Andreas Stegbauer, 'The Ban of Right-Wing Extremist Symbols According to Section 86a of the German Criminal Code' (2007) 8 *German Law Journal* 173, 177, fn 14).

[38] Gertrude Lübbe-Wolff, 'Zur Bedeutung des Art 139 GG für die Auseinandersetzung mit neonazistischen Gruppen' (1988) *Neue Juristische Wochenschrift* 1289, 1294, as cited by Stegbauer, above n 37, 177.

[39] Though FDJ-Westdeutschland, the West German branch of the GDR's only legal (and basically state-maintained) youth movement was also banned.

[40] BVerfGE 2, 1 (1952).

[41] BVerfGE 5, 85 (1956) *KPD-judgment*.

[42] BGH MDR 1965, 923; OLG München NStZ 2007, 97 as cited by Ellbogen, '86a StGB' in von Heintschel-Heinegg (ed), *Beck'scher Online-Kommentar* StGB, 15th edn (2011) ann 2.

[43] OLG Rostock NStZ 2002, 320; Bartels/Kollorz NStZ 2002, 298 as cited by Ellbogen, ibid. Ellbogen claims that speeches of Hitler are also punishable under art 86a, eg if displayed in the form of a ringtone of a cell phone.

[44] Consistently, there is an exception clause in § III covering the use of such symbols in art, scholarship, research and teaching. (For uncertainties in interpreting the limits of this so-called social adequacy clause, see Ellbogen, ibid, ann 12, and Fischer StGB § 86a ann 22, as cited by Ellbogen.)

criminal matters) the aim is also the maintenance of political peace.[45] As the BGH put it:[46]

> Thus, the aim of the criminal provision has to be understood not only as preventing a revival of the banned organisations or of their anti- constitutional endeavours, to which the prohibited sign symbolically refers. The provision also serves to preserve the political peace because it avoids even the appearance of such a revival. It also prevents foreign or domestic observers of political events in the Federal Republic of Germany from assuming that behaviour opposed to the constitution and the rule of law, as symbolised by the sign, is tolerated in German politics.

Political peace, though undefined, covers the post-Second World War value consensus in which National Socialist ideas do not have a place. The reputational interest of the Bundesrepublik is somewhat more concrete, and it is also a regular concern in relation to extreme right wing activities in Germany ever since the end of the Second World War.

The GFCC, on its part, does not refer to political peace regarding banned signs, but only to the prevention of revival of banned organisations and their endeavours. Rather, it states that the rationale of article 86a of the Criminal Code is to ban such symbols from the entirety of political life in Germany, and in effect to institute a 'communicative taboo'.[47] That is why the will behind displaying the symbols is irrelevant, or at least that seems to be the view of the GFCC. Critical uses of symbols thus can also be punished constitutionally.[48] The BGH appears settled in the opposite direction,[49] exemplifying a rare case where the ordinary court grants more freedom than the GFCC would require.[50] The BGH has since 1972 consistently remanded cases of conviction when the symbol is used 'clearly and unequivocally in a manner hostile'[51] to the ideology behind the symbol. Besides, satirical uses of banned symbols might fall under freedom of art and thus cannot be proscribed according to the GFCC either.[52]

[45] BGHSt 25, 30, 33 (1972) *Verwenden des 'Hitlergrußes' aus Protest gegen Polizeiaktion*. Stegbauer, 'The Ban of Right-Wing Extremist Symbols' above n 37, referred the author to this case.

[46] Ibid, BGHSt 25, 30, 33.

[47] BVerfG, 1 BvR 150/03, 1 June 2006, § 18.

[48] Ibid.

[49] At least when there is clear and unequivocal hostile tendency against the ideology referred to by the symbol. BGH, BGHSt 51, 244, 15 March, 2007 (reversing a conviction for selling articles displaying, eg the swastika, in a clearly Nazi hostile manner for punks, a left-wing subculture).

[50] I do not mean to imply that according to the Constitutional Court the Constitution prescribes, instead of allows, the prohibition of critical uses of these symbols.

[51] BGHSt 25, 30, 33 f, BGHSt 25, 128, 130 f, as cited by BGHSt 51, 244.

[52] BVerfGE 82, 1 (1990), *T-shirt mocking Hitler*. This ruling is consistent with BVerfGE 77, 240 (1987), reversing a conviction for using an emblem of FDJ (Freie Deutsche Jugend, the only recognised youth organisation in the GDR whose West German branch was banned in the FRG), on placards advertising the staging of a Brecht play, 'Herrnburger Bericht'.

As to the substitute similarity requirement, the GFCC has decided, despite scholarly views to the contrary,[53] that the slogan '*Ruhm und Ehre der Waffen-SS*' (fame and honour of the Waffen-SS) is so dissimilar to the '*Blut und Ehre*' slogan (blood and honour) of the Hitler Youth that it cannot be constitutionally prohibited.[54] Newly invented slogans which were never used by a banned organisation are within constitutional protection of free speech. That also includes using 'blood and honour' as a slogan in English, because it was never used by the Hitlerjugend in this form.[55]

This cursory discussion already shows that the condition of previously banned organisation is though content-based, at least is quite rigid, and many would claim even dysfunctional and alien to the challenges of real life.[56] As to viewpoint-discrimination, to use the US terminology, the BGH took a stance distinguishing hostile and sympathetic uses. This, however, does not prevent lower courts from recurrently sticking to the idea that article 86a cuts both ways,[57] an interpretation the GFCC would also not mind. This is indeed a serious question to which I do not see any principled answer, because the underlying approach is contradictory. The ambiguity of delineating banned symbols very clearly exposes the vulnerability of content-based restrictions which are justified by abstract and mediated dangers[58] of revival of a horrible past, and the law's inadequacy of dealing with such dangers.

ii. France

In French law it is a contravention (a less serious offence in the penal regime, next to crimes and delicts) to wear or display in public, uniforms, insignia or symbols which recall those of organisations or persons responsible for crimes against humanity.[59]

[53] Eg before the decision of the GFCC: Jan Steinmetz, '"Ruhm und Ehre der Waffen-SS"—Verwechselbares Kennzeichen iS des § 86a II 2 StGB?' (2002) *Neue Zeitschrift fur Strafrecht* 118, and after the decision came out, Andreas Horsch, 'Das BVerfG, die Ähnlichkeit i S des § 86a II 2 StGB oder: Zeit für die Entdeckung der Lebenswirklichkeit' (2008) *Die Rechtsprechung* 99.

[54] BVerfG, 1 BvR 150/03, 1 June 2006.

[55] BGHSt 54, 61. The ruling does not affect possible illegality on other grounds, among them, as displaying the symbol not of the Hitlerjugend but of Blood and Honour, a neo-Nazi organisation banned in Germany.

[56] Eg Horsch, 'Das BVerfG, die Ähnlichkeit im Sinne des § 86a II 2 StGB', above n 53.

[57] To their benefit it has to be noted that the BGH also held this view, though back in 1970. BGHSt 23, 267 (1970).

[58] Art 86a is a so-called *abstraktes Gefährdungsdelikt*, criminalising a 'conduct typically capable of bringing a dangerous situation into existence, even if in any given case the subject of protection is not actually exposed to the danger concerned'. Stegbauer, 'The Ban of Right-Wing Extremist Symbols', above n 37, 175, citing Troendle and Fischer, in *Strafgesetzbuch*, 53rd edn (München, 2006) § 13 ann 9. This, as must be obvious by now, is very far from even the loosest US standard as exemplified by *Virginia v Black*.

[59] Art R 645-1 of the Penal Code. French law widely employs an editorial technique compiling both legislative and regulatory level norms in one document, called a code. (Though the

Article R 645-1 of the Penal Code refers to organisations banned and persons convicted; in other words, the scope in this regard is reasonably narrow and similar to that in Germany. Exceptions are granted to films, spectacles (theatre performances) or exhibitions envoking history. 'In public' is understood broadly. (Public includes even the internet as has been the basis of the famous *LICRA v Yahoo!* controversy between French and US courts,[60] which is of no interest to us here apart from the fact that it displayed very clearly the unbridgeable gap between the First Amendment and the French understanding of free speech.) There is no controversy in France parallel to that discussed in Germany about the interpretation of '*rappelant*', that is what counts as a *similar* symbol, uniform, etc. Of course, the lack of awareness or sensitivity in this regard does not exempt French law from the problems inherent in such a regulation, as discussed with regard to analogous German law on the previous pages.

C. Flag Disparagement in Germany and France

i. Germany

As one commentator emphasises, and in contrast to the United States, the federal flag in Germany has not been an object of veneration, at least since the Second World War.[61] Still, according to article 90a (disparagement of the state and its symbols)[62] of the Criminal Code

> (1) A person who publicly, in an assembly, or through the dissemination of writings
>
> 1. insults or maliciously disparages the Federal Republic of Germany, one of its regional states, or its constitutional order or
> 2. disparages the colours, the flag, the coat of arms or the anthem of the Federal Republic of Germany or one of its regional states shall be punished by a term of imprisonment up to 3 years or with a fine.

concept is different from the original, rigorous and systematising understanding of code as in the Napoleonic Codes, or in the Civil or Criminal Code in Germany, etc.) This is the case with the Penal Code, whose first part is the legislative part, including crimes and delicts, and the second part is the regulatory, including contraventions. The R in the numbering of the article shows that the provision belongs to the regulatory part, ie it is a contravention.

[60] Finally settled in an interpretation sympathetic to French law, questioning extraterritorial effect of the First Amendment in US Court of Appeals for the Ninth Circuit, *Yahoo! Inc v LICRA and UEJF*, 443 F 3d 1199, 12 January 2006.

[61] Ute Krüdewagen, 'Political Symbols in Two Constitutional Orders: The Flag Desecration Decisions of the United States Supreme Court and the German Federal Constitutional Court' (2002) 19 *Arizona Journal of International and Comparative Law* 679.

[62] As translated on the website of the University of Texas School of Law, www.utexas.edu/law/academics/centers/transnational/work_new/german/case.php?id=632, Nomos Verlagsgesellschaft.

This again is a potentially endangering offence,[63] in other words, a doubly mediated 'endangering-endangering'.[64]

As the state does not have dignity, the protected object must be derived from something more particularly embedded in the Constitution. The GFCC had the occasion to examine this provision's compatibility with the Basic Law in the so-called *Federal Flag* decision from 1990. However, in the case it relied on freedom of art,[65] and not on freedom of expression or assembly, as the flag was portrayed disparagingly on the back cover of a book.[66] Thus, the result—reversing the conviction—is not automatically applicable to a demonstrator. Rather, it seems the court made an exception solely because freedom of art was at stake. Notably, it accepted that the provision itself is constitutional. The constitutional value served by the provision is explained in the following way:[67]

> The purpose of these symbols is to appeal to the citizens' sense of state [*Staatsgefühl* in original, translated as 'sense of civic responsibility' by the Institute of Transnational Law][68] ... As a free state, the Federal Republic relies rather on the identification of its citizens with the basic values represented by the flag. The values protected in this sense are represented by the state colours, stipulated in Art 22 GG. They stand for the free democratic constitutional structure.... The flag serves as an important integration device through the leading state goals it embodies; its disparagement can thus impair the necessary authority of the state. From this, it also follows that state symbols only enjoy constitutional protection in so far as they represent what fundamentally characterises the Federal Republic.

[63] Jan Steinmetz, 'StGB § 90 a Verunglimpfung des Staates und seiner Symbole Rn 2' in Wolfgang Joecks and Klaus Miebach (eds), *Münchener Kommentar zum Strafgesetzbuch*, Vol 2 (München, Beck, 2005), for the concept, see above n 58.

[64] '*Gefährdungs-Gefährdungsdelikt*': Herwig Roggemann, 'Von Bären, Löwen und Adlern—zur Reichweite der §§ 90 a und b StGB. Meinungs- und Kunstfreiheit im gesamtdeutschen Verfassungs- und Strafrecht- Verfassungskonforme Einschränkung oder Streichung der §§ 90 a und 90 b?' (1992) *Juristenzeitung* 934, 938. (Though at that point it is about art 90 b, entitled anti-constitutional disparagement of constitutional organs (such as legislative organ, government or constitutional court or its member in this capacity).)

[65] Freedom of art is guaranteed in art 5 III GG. Its specificity is that there is no mention of possibility of restricting freedom of art (similarly to the guarantee of indoor assemblies). Nonetheless, the court interpreted this and similar (so-called *vorbehaltslose*) provisions as still underlying limits inherent in the Constitution (*verfassungsimmanente Schranken*) itself. Thus, for example, in the *Mephisto* case it ruled that protection of dignity after death overrides (at least temporarily) freedom of art. BVerfGE 30, 173 (1971).

[66] BVerfGE 81, 278 (1990). In the ordinary courts, a producer of a pacifist book (*Laßt mich bloß in Frieden—Just Leave me in Peace*) was held responsible for a collage, where one part displayed a flag and the other part a urinating man's torso, put next to each other in a way that the urine was pouring upon the federal flag. (Unfortunately only the front page is available on this anarcho-syndicalist webpage: zuchthaus.free.de/syndikat-a/?p=productsMore&iProduct=1353&sName=an-Venske,-Ney,-Merian,-Unmck-%28Hg.%29-La%DFt-mich-blo%DF-in-Frieden.)

[67] BVerfGE 81, 278, 293 *et seq* (1990).

[68] The website of the University of Texas School of Law, www.utexas.edu/law/academics/centers/transnational/work_new/german/case.php?id=632, Nomos Verlagsgesellschaft.

Compared with the language of the US decisions, the striking difference is that maintenance and promotion of the authority of the state is a constitutional value, a value rooted in the Basic Law, a stance the US Supreme Court ultimately dismissed in *Texas v Johnson*[69] and *Eichman.*[70]

At the same time, most commentators interpret the aim of article 90a as being more the protection of free democratic basic order than authority of the state. Or, to be fair, these two intermingle, just as can be seen from the above quote. The German court also explicitly adds that 'the protection of symbols must not lead to an immunisation of the state against criticism and even against disapproval'.[71] However, as state authority and freedom of art are both protected by the Constitution, there is a conflict which can only be resolved by (*ad hoc*) balancing, the more *ad hoc*, more 'fine-tuned' to the particular circumstances of the case, the better. The GFCC appears to exercise rather rigorous review whether ordinary courts normally mandated to execute this balancing process[72] have properly done so.

In another decision decided on freedom of art grounds, the GFCC basically applied the same approach. In the case a left-wing[73] demonstration was organised where a song '*Deutschland muss sterben, damit wir leben können*' (Germany has to die so we can live) was sung.[74] The song included the following verse, whose reference to the flag's colours served as the basis for conviction:

> Black are the heavens, and the Earth is red,
> And gold the hands of those bastard fat cats,
> But the German eagle will crash down dead,
> For, Germany, we carry you to your graveyard bed. (trs Joseph Windsor)

The GFCC found a flaw in the application of law by the ordinary courts because they did not classify the song as protected by freedom of art. After a long discussion of what counts as art, which should not be of interest to us, the court found that the song was not more radical and critical–bitter than one of Heinrich Heine, and also it otherwise fulfilled the criteria of art. In a way, the court found that the song continued the tradition—so familiar in Central (and Eastern) Europe—of envisioning the doom of a country and death of a nation.[75] Furthermore, the refrain line is a reference to a

[69] *Texas v Johnson*, above n 19.
[70] *United States v Eichman*, above n 20.
[71] BVerfGE 81, 278, 294, as translated in the website of the University of Texas School of Law, www.utexas.edu/law/academics/centers/transnational/work_new/german/case.php?id=632, Nomos Verlagsgesellschaft.
[72] BVerfGE 18, 85, 92 (1964); BVerfGE 85, 248, 257 *et seq* (1992), BVerfGE 93, 266, 296 (1995).
[73] Environmentalist, antifascist, antimultinational companies, antimilitarist. The text of the song is reproduced in the decision: BVerfG, 1 BvR 581/00, 3 November 2000.
[74] Ibid.
[75] Ibid, § 23.

fight fought via memorials between those venerating the First (and possibly Second) World Wars and those who perceive them in a very different light.[76]

After stating these analogies, the court remanded the case, but made some unusual, important comments. As the lower court had not properly recognised the core message of the song, the GFCC did not find it necessary to decide whether the lower court misstated the limits of freedom of art by songs used as '*Kampfmittel*', warfare agent. It stated, however, that endangerment of the integrity (*Bestand*) of constitutional democracy can justify restriction on freedom of art. Nonetheless, it found doubtful whether a three-minute song, already apparently known to the 50 people listening to it, would realise the endangerment.[77] This is clearly a weakening of the abstractness of danger as normally understood in German criminal law, certainly a welcome development from the point of view of constitutional rights. (It is, though, still a far shot from simply finding, as the US Supreme Court did, after all, that flag disparagement was flat-out protected speech.)

Finally in 2008, the court had to explicitly address the issue of freedom of speech (not freedom of art) and flag disparagement. In the so-called *Schwarz–Rot–Senf* case a speaker at a right-wing demonstration referred to the black–red–golden coloured federal flag as black–red–*mustard*.[78] He was convicted for disparaging the flag. Ordinary courts have not mentioned or weighed the value of freedom of expression of opinion in their judgments. That this was going to be found problematic by the GFCC comes as no surprise. Free speech notably also belongs to the fundaments of the free democratic constitutional/basic order, now clearly a ruling concept in interpreting flag disparagement cases, as it facilitates constant *intellectual* interaction so necessary in a democratic state.[79] Thus, 'the reputation of the state and the right to criticise it stand in a relationship of tension that needs to be resolved in the individual case by way of practical concordance'.[80] As

[76] Ibid, § 30.

[77] Ibid, § 31.

[78] BVerfG, 1 BvR 1565/05, 15 September 2008. Extract from the speech: 'No, comrades, we do so simply because for us the fate of our German fatherland matters. We have all been born into this community of life and destiny. We cannot as easily unsubscribe. We cannot get a document on which there is—well, well, we are not Congolese or Siberians, no, we are now even German. From birth on. The question is—are we as Germans assholes who can be canned here by this system? Or will we stand by our flag? And by that I do not mean the black, red and mustard. Under these circumstances. Oh, sorry, black, red and gold, could I possibly be so misinterpreted. We stand by our flag. We're in this deep dark night of Germany. But just as on 21 December the nights start getting shorter and the days are longer, and just as after the deepest and darkest night is again a sunrise, so one day our people and our Reich will stand up in new splendour. And this is what we stand for, why we fight and what we can be proud of. The fact that we have been the first but not the last. Hail to our beloved Germany. Hail to the German Reich.' (Author's translation.)

[79] See, eg BVerfGE 7, 198, 208 (1958), *Lüth*.

[80] Valerius, '90a StGB' in von Heintschel-Heinegg (ed), *Beck'scher Online-Kommentar StGB*, 15th edn (2011) ann 13.

such a resolution was not attempted by ordinary courts, it was clear that the application of law is deemed not to pass constitutional muster.

Here again, the GFCC went further than simply remanding by stating that the ordinary court has to examine how free speech concerns counterbalance values promoted by article 90a of the Criminal Code. In a last paragraph the GFCC recognised—also citing sources from 1929, 1925/26 and 1997 as evidence—that *Schwarz-Rot-Senf* was a reference to the Weimar Republic where 'right-wing extremists' protested against the liberal republican state with this labelling of the flag. Still, in the court's view it is not evident that this historical reference is still 'present in the consciousness of the population', and thus it would be comprehended in this way in the particular situation. But, even if this historical reference is judged relevant and lively, it has to be thoroughly examined if to call the golden colour in the flag mustard means in the specific situation a 'sensitive vilification or a particular contempt capable of hollowing out and of undermining the respect of the citizens for the integrity of the rule of law democracy in the Federal Republic',[81] language recalling the 'Germany has to die' decision discussed above. This last paragraph can hardly be interpreted other than as a kind suggestion to the ordinary court of 'no punishment'.

All in all, the argumentation seems twisted. The court on the one hand sticks to the constitutionality of article 90a, not even discussing it on rule of law grounds,[82] but then does not let a rather clearly disparaging message be punished. In addition, the GFCC employs two types of audience in order to measure the endangerment which is necessary for so-called 'expression offenses' to be realised. First it refers to the 'average audience', then in the last mentioned paragraph it refers to the 'population', apparently apolitical and historically ignorant.[83] Recall that with such potentially endangering crimes this audience is anyway a 'virtual construct'.[84] Even if one assumes that no historical connection to Weimar would be typically established in the hearers, the 'objective sense' of the message was clear in the context, as one critique correctly points out.[85] It is very hard, even for a very ignorant listener, to understand the *whole* speech in question,[86] according to which birthright Germans 'not Congolese or Siberians' hail 'our German Reich' as not being 'contemptuous' for the rule of law democracy. The court would have been consistent with either striking down the norm itself or

[81] BVerfG, 1 BvR 1565/05, 15 September 2008, § 16.

[82] Somewhat similarly to US overbreadth and vagueness doctrines, uncertainty of criminal provisions might amount to violation of art 103 II GG, as hinted by a commentator, Mareike Preisner, '"Schwarz-Rot-Senf"—Aufregung angebracht?' (2009) *Neue Juristische Wochenschrift* 897, 898.

[83] Preisner's expressions, ibid.

[84] Stegbauer, 'The Ban of Right-Wing Extremist Symbols', above n 37, 178.

[85] Preisner, "Schwarz-Rot-Senf" above n 82, 898.

[86] See above n 78.

not questioning the clear meaning of the mustard message. Maybe future constitutional jurisprudence would tip the scales one way or another, and I would certainly prefer the former. Till then, upholding constitutionality of a norm, in effect disadvised ever to apply, is simply a twisted undertaking which invites police, administration, and ordinary courts to honestly not quite capture it.

ii. France

If the GFCC is running with the hare and hunting with the hounds, then the French Conseil Constitutionnel is simply deferring to legislative judgment. It is however true that the original legislative ban was more limited than the German law.

The ban from outraging the flag was introduced in a 2003 law[87] as a delict,[88] and rendered punishable to outrage the flag or the national anthem during a demonstration *organised or regulated by public authorities*. Demonstrations regulated by public authorities, as explained by the *travaux preparatoires*, and cited by the Conseil Constitutionnel,[89] are sports, recreational or cultural events where security and health regulations necessarily apply for reason of the number of participants.

The Conseil Constitutionnel[90] found the law constitutional, by referring to the constitutional provisions on both freedom of opinion, and on the flag and the anthem. Nonetheless, it emphasised that intellectual works (works of the spirit or mind—'*oeuvres de l'esprit*'), expressions uttered in private circles and demonstrations not organised or regulated by authorities are excluded from the scope of application.

In a 2005 case, during a street theatre festival, a 25-year-old climbed to the façade of the Mayor's office in Aurillac, tore down the flag and threw it onto the gathering of a few hundred people. Then he ignited the flag, and waved it until it was completely burnt. The delinquent said that he destroyed the flag out of protest against the government, as a symbol of the actual government, in a festive atmosphere, and did not mean to destroy the symbol of the nation, and he regretted his deed. The Riom Court of Appeals found that he had committed outrage of the flag, but considering his active repentance,

[87] Art 113 of Law no 2003-239, 18 March 2003, inserting art 433-5-1 into the Criminal Code, legislative part.

[88] A (penal) delict is a medium level serious criminal act between crimes and contraventions, the most and least serious offences. Contraventions are defined by the regulatory power, ie by decree in the Conseil d'Etat. See art 34 of the Constitution of 1958, but the punishments for the different classes of contraventions are determined by law, by the Parliament. The regulatory power is entitled to decide into which class a contravention should fall.

[89] Decision no 2003-467 DC, 13 March 2003, (loi pour la sécurité intérieure) Recueil, 211, considérant 104.

[90] Ibid, considérants 99–106.

only a moderate fine was inflicted.[91] This is a case which fell under a demonstration organised and regulated by public authorities, as the Court of Appeal emphasised. The webpage only displays the festival from 2010 and among the partners it mentions as logistical supporter the city of Aurillac.[92] It is not possible to discern from the decision whether anyone claimed in court that the festival was actually an artistic one, which seems to be taken out of the scope of the ban at least by the Conseil Constitutionnel. (Though it is also not completely clear if the Conseil Constitutionnel meant that artistic performances where authorities do need to provide organisational or logistical support for this reason get back under the ban. Or, maybe, the Conseil Constitutionnel would start distinguishing art, or, '*oeuvres de l'esprit*',[93] from cultural events.) It is also true that the person actually committing the outrage of the flag was not (and not claimed to be, as I understand) an artist, and the delict was not (claimed to be) part of an art performance.

The flag outrage ban was broadened in 2010. The topic became hot once again in spring 2010, when a photograph showing a man wiping his backside with the tricolour was widely circulated in the French media. The government reacted by enacting a fifth class contravention (most serious among the regulatory offences).[94] It bans the public destruction, deterioration or degrading use of the flag if committed with the intent to outrage the flag and in conditions capable of disturbing public order. The distribution of recording of such uses of the flag is also prohibited.

In December 2010, a young Algerian, in a hall of a prefecture, had broken and thrown a flag pole at a man out of anger about slow, inadequate, and at times, insulting or degrading public service.[95] It seems that there was no appeal against the decision of the Tribunal Correctionnel de Nice, the first instance court, where he was fined €750 (suspended) *and also convicted to citizenship training at his own cost.* A *stage de citoyenneté* is a proper mandatory course, where the convict gets familiarised with republican values of tolerance, and of respect of dignity of the human person,[96] a sanction introduced in 2004, and also imposed for wearing a burqa and other,

[91] Court of Appeals of Riom, 14 June 2006, no 06/00167.

[92] www.aurillac.net/index.php?option=com_content&view=article&id=157&Itemid=318&lang=fr.

[93] Decision no 2003-467 DC, 13 March 2003, considérant 104.

[94] Art R 645-15 Criminal Code, regulatory part, enacted by art 1 of Decree no 2010-835 of 21 July 2010.

[95] Decision of the Tribunal correctionnel de Nice of 22 December 2010. The decision cannot be found online, I have to rely on articles from the press: 'Première condamnation pour outrage au drapeau' *LeMonde.fr*, 22 December 2010, www.lemonde.fr/societe/article/2010/12/22/premiere-condamnation-pour-outrage-au-drapeau_1456880_3224.html, 'Un jeune homme condamné pour outrage au drapeau français' *Liberation.fr*, 22 December 2010, www.liberation.fr/societe/01012309542-un-jeune-homme-condamne-pour-outrage-au-drapeau-francais.

[96] Art R 131-35 of the second part of the Criminal Code, inserted by Decree no 2004-1021 of 27 September 2004.

apparently 'un-French' conduct. It is not hard to imagine how cynical this sanction might have appeared to the young man who actually protested against intolerant and disrespectful treatment by French authorities…

The differences between the delict examined by the Conseil Constitutionnel and the new contravention are important, though both can be considered more of a symbolic, than of a really repressive nature for reason of relatively loose sanctions. Some would argue the new contravention is unconstitutional because it takes away a factor which the Conseil Constitutionnel considered important when examining the proportionality of the delict. Notably, the contravention bans outraging the flag in public, and public is really broadly understood. This means that the French Government moved from the rationale of separating state and degrading the flag to excluding degrading the flag from the entirety of public life, real or virtual.

The Conseil d'Etat examined this provision,[97] and found it was valid, but significantly restricted—or, as French legalese has it, 'neutralised'[98]—its interpretation. Accordingly, only such physical or symbolic degradation of the flag can be punished which is capable of causing 'grave troubles to public security and tranquillity [*sic*]' and, secondly, which is 'committed with the sole purpose to destroy, vandalise or degrade it'. Thus, the sanction does not apply if the degradation of the flag is part of the 'expression of political or philosophical ideas' or 'artistic activity'. However, as commentators also point out, the decision leaves lower courts with the task of defining what qualifies as an *oeuvre de l'esprit* and what not.[99] In law, normally, *oeuvre de l'esprit* is a notion used in intellectual property law describing the objects protected by author's rights.[100] Hopefully, courts would not start interpreting the flag degradation contravention as excluding punishment only for art works protected by copyright.

D. Banned Signs and Flag Desecration in the United Kingdom

The United Kingdom has no ban on any symbols, neither does it accord (in any of the jurisdictions) legal protection against desecration of any of the official flags and other state symbols. This, seemingly liberal approach, is however compromised by the ban on uniforms, discussed below, which is interpreted very broadly and would, for example, certainly prevent several people from wearing the swastika during a demonstration. Thus, what is truly exceptional about the United Kingdom is only that flag desecration is not explicitly regulated.

[97] Under a jurisdiction for excess of power. CÉ, 19 July 2011, no 343430, *Ligue des Droits de l'Homme c/ ministère de la justice*.

[98] Ligue des Droits de l'Homme Toulon, 'Le Conseil d'État neutralise le décret sur l'outrage au drapeau tricolore', ldh-toulon.net/le-Conseil-d-Etat-neutralise-le.html, 1 September 2011.

[99] Eg Roseline Letteron, 'Outrage au drapeau et liberté d'expression', 7 July 2011, libertescheries.blogspot.hu/2011/07/outrage-au-drapeau-et-liberte.html.

[100] See art L 112-2 Code of Intellectual Property.

However, section 5 of the Public Order Act 1986 (POA) entitled 'Harassment, alarm or distress' has been applied to flag desecration. In *Percy v DPP*[101] an anti-proliferation protester daubed 'Stop Star Wars' across a US flag and waved it in front of a US Air Force base in England, then threw it onto the road in front of a US vehicle and trampled on it. She was convicted by the district judge under section 5 POA for using threatening, abusive or insulting words or behaviour likely to cause harassment, alarm, or distress. The district judge found there was a pressing social need 'to prevent denigration of objects of veneration and symbolic importance for one cultural group'.[102] The Divisional Court accepted this as legitimate aim, despite the irony of according a status to the US flag in the United Kingdom that would be unconstitutional in the United States. However, it found the criminal punishment disproportionate for failing to consider relevant other factors, such as whether[103]

> the behaviour went beyond legitimate protest; that the behaviour had not formed a part of an open expression of opinion on a matter of public interest, but had become disproportionate and unreasonable; that an accused knew full well the likely effect of their conduct upon witnesses; that the accused deliberately chose to desecrate the national flag of those witnesses, a symbol of very considerable importance to many, particularly those who were in the armed forces; the fact that an accused targeted such people, for whom it became a very personal matter; the fact that an accused was well aware of the likely effect of their conduct; the fact that an accused's use of a flag had nothing, in effect, to do with conveying a message or expression of opinion; that it amounted to a gratuitous and calculated insult, which a number of people at whom it was directed found deeply distressing.

These 'factors' are totally unable to provide guidelines on how to interpret section 5 in harmony with the Human Rights Act 1998 (HRA). Some of them are part of the offence itself, others are conclusions rather than premises,[104] all in all, they clearly do not make up an identifiable standard.

E. European Court of Human Rights: The *Red Star* Cases

The ECtHR's most important case at hand is clearly *Vajnai v Hungary*[105] in 2008, where the Hungarian Criminal Code's provision[106] relating to

[101] *Percy v DPP* [2001] EWHC Admin 1125, 166 JP 93.

[102] Ibid, § 5.

[103] Ibid, § 32.

[104] Andrew Geddis, 'Free Speech Martyrs or Unreasonable threats to Social Peace?—"Insulting" Expression and section 5 of the Public Order Act 1986' [2004] *Public Law* 853, 861.

[105] *Vajnai v Hungary*, 50 EHRR 44, Application no 33629/06, Judgment of 8 October 2008.

[106] On the tormented and problematic history of its adoption, see Gábor Halmai, A *véleményszabadság határai* (*Limits of Freedom of Opinion*) (Budapest, Atlantisz, 1994) 258–60.

totalitarian symbols was found applied in violation of article 10 of the European Convention on Human Rights (ECHR).

The applicant was a prominent member of the Workers' Party which operates legally, but never reaches the threshold to get to Parliament. He wore the red star on a demonstration, where he was a speaker. Vajnai was convicted on the basis of article 269/B of the Criminal Code prohibiting the 'dissemination, public use or exhibition of signs of totalitarian regimes, including swastika, an SS-badge, an arrow-cross, a symbol of the sickle and hammer or a red star, or a symbol depicting any of them'.[107] The provision was upheld by the Hungarian Constitutional Court in an abstract norm control proceeding, in a decision much criticised as being inconsistent with previous case law on freedom of expression.

The ECtHR found the conviction amounted to a disproportionate interference with the right to free speech. Restrictions on political speech need to be examined with utmost care, and blanket bans are especially concerning as they might overreach to speech which cannot be legitimately restricted. Most crucially, the court found the red star had multiple meanings, among them it is the symbol of the international workers' movement, and it was not established (nor claimed) that Vajnai advocated totalitarianism or defiance of the rule of law. Also, the party was not banned in Hungary, the demonstration was lawful, and no actual or even remote disorder triggered by the display of the red star was ever reported. In a way, the court applied US doctrines of overbreadth, and chilling effect, and hinted that the showing of some actual danger is required for restrictions on political speech to pass the test of the ECHR.

Apart from these similarities with American doctrines, the emphasis on the lawfulness of the party might imply that a German or French type ban, not blanket, but strictly linked to banned organisations, would get a more lenient treatment on the part of the court. Although even then it would need to be shown that the red star is displayed in a particular case in sympathy with a banned party, and, of course, the party ban would also need to pass human rights standards. In relation to this, taboo arguments of German courts are necessarily absent, too.

As to militant democracy, the court noted the basically insignificant support the party enjoyed in Hungary, and the assurances the Republic of Hungary has provided to victims of Communism. In a unique paragraph, the court stated that 'dictates of public feeling—real or imaginery—' do not authorise the state to restrict human rights, as 'society must remain reasonable in its judgement' for it to count as democratic.[108] Four follow-up cases

[107] As translated in § 15 of *Vajnai v Hungary*, above n 105.

[108] Ibid, § 57.

against Hungary based on the same facts merited condemnation at the ECtHR since the *Vajnai* judgment.[109]

In my understanding, the *Vajnai* judgment turns on the multiplicity of meanings of the red star, from which arises the need to examine every case of display carefully in its context, as context decides which meaning is salient in the particular instance. However, as every symbol has multiple meanings, a contextual examination is necessary in every case, and it needs to be shown that the use of a particular symbol either amounts to totalitarian propaganda (as the court seems to accept in both paragraphs 25 and 56), or creates an actual danger of disorder. The *Vajnai* arguments could also apply to the display of the swastika, and other Nazi symbols. Thus, the court would still check the context in which the symbol is displayed. However, it would be a rare scenario where, for example, a swastika is displayed without identification with totalitarianism.[110]

Other concerns, such as, for example, dignity of the victims, do not play an important role in the equation under the *Vajnai* approach. The categorisation of victims' concerns as 'irrational fears', 'sentiments' and 'feelings' might in effect imply a rejection of dignity claims.

All in all, the watermark is the one US jurisprudence also was struggling with: whether to draw a line between advocacy of ideology and advocacy of actions, and maybe adding to the latter some probability requirement. As long as that line is not clearly drawn, ECtHR jurisprudence would be exposed to the ambiguities of content-based restriction just as much as German (or, implicitly, French) is.

II. UNIFORMS AND MASKS: WHOSE FEAR?

A. Uniforms

Wearing uniforms is, under conditions, expressly prohibited on demonstrations in Germany, France, and the United Kingdom, and they are clearly allowed in the United States in light of the symbolic speech and content neutrality doctrines. The ECtHR has not discussed the issue so far.

[109] *Fratanoló v Hungary*, Application no 29459/10, Judgment of 3 November 2011; *Horváth and Vajnai v Hungary*, Application nos 55795/11 and 55798/11, Judgment of 24 September 2014; *Noé, Vajnai and Bakó v Hungary*, Application nos 24515/09, 24539/09, and 24611/09, Judgment of 24 September 2014; and *Vajnai v Hungary (II)*, Application no 6061/10, Judgment of 24 September 2014.

[110] But consider the Hindu movement in Germany to stop criminalising the use of the swastika, reasoning that they are entitled to use it as they were before Nazism appropriated it and provided it with a hateful meaning. Under the *Vajnai* logic, I think they would be free to display the swastika.

i. United Kingdom

In the United Kingdom, section 1 of the Public Order Act 1936 proscribes the wearing of uniforms associated with *political* organisations while section 2 proscribes *paramilitary* organisations. The new powers were mostly enacted in order to enable the police to handle properly the violence provoked by the Fascist movement in Britain. According to section 1

> any person who in any public place or at any public meeting wears uniform signifying his association with any political organisation or with the promotion of any political object shall be guilty of an offence.

The chief officer of police, with the consent of the Secretary of State might permit the wearing of a uniform on any ceremonial, anniversary, or other special occasion, if the occasion will not be likely to involve risk of public disorder. Apparently, the legislator chose the more restrictive way of regulation.

From a human rights perspective, the rule would be the permissibility of wearing uniforms, and only in the likelihood of public disorder a ban could have been introduced. As logically this must have been the rule before the 1936 Act came into force (at a time when, eg only common law breach of the peace powers were available), there must have been a serious fear of 'radicalisation' resulting from the Nazi paramilitary marches of the 1930s. The question which is left unclear by such across-the-board prohibition remains, of course, whether there would have been a real radicalisation of the UK population at large without this and other, more restrictive rules and practices, for instance that 'There was, in fact, an almost continuous ban on processions in London from 1937 until after World War II'.[111]

There is no legal definition of what counts as uniform, but there is one case which rendered the notion of uniform a little bit more concrete. In *O'Moran v DPP*[112] the demonstrators wore black berets, dark glasses and dark clothes, somewhat similar to Irish Republican Army (IRA) uniform. According to Lord Widgery, even the wearing of the beret in itself would amount to a 'uniform' in the sense of section 1 of the act, if worn by a number of persons appearing together, since it shows their association. The minimum criterion he established for 'wearing a uniform' was that it must be an article of cloth, thus, for instance, badges do not qualify. It might well be, but it is not necessary, that the article had been used in the past as a uniform by an organisation. But simply wearing a uniform, for example a beret, by a number of persons could also qualify if it indicates their association with each other, and if they 'by their conduct indicate that

[111] Rachel Vorspan, '"Freedom of Assembly" and the Right to Passage in Modern English Legal History' (1997) 34 *San Diego Law Review* 921, 1000, referring to First Home Affairs Committee, *Fifth Report: The Law Relating to Public Order* (HC 1979–80, 756-I and II) 13.

[112] *O'Moran v DPP* [1975] QB 864.

that beret associates them with other activity of a political character'. Apart from that, one has to look at all the circumstances. That might give rise to arbitrary selection of those against whom the ban is enforced, but the low number of cases might also suggest that British police are not making use of this discretionary power.[113] It is quite probable that its application would not survive an HRA/ECtHR challenge after *Vajnai*.

In addition to the Public Order Act 1936, a ban on uniform might come from the unexpected source of the Terrorism Act 2000. Section 13 introduced a new offence for wearing uniform of a proscribed organisation, where proscribed appears to include organisations proscribed before the law entered into force as well. Also, being a member is not necessary as wearing an item of clothing or displaying an article in a way arousing reasonable suspicion that the person is a member of such an organisation suffices. The law is thus the worst example of guilt by association, in fact, even guilt by non-association or ghost-association, and it lacks absolutely any show of material harm. Accordingly, in *Rankin v Murray*[114] the provision was found applicable to someone *wearing a ring* (!) with the inscription UVF, a common abbreviation for the Ulster Volunteer Force, a proscribed organisation. Absurd as it may sound, the court affirmed in a clear textualist fashion that even if the ring was received as a gift, that is indeed the beholder is not a member of the proscribed organisation, the provision still applies, as what matters is the objectively reasonable suspicion which already flows from the wearing itself. The court also rejected a kind of seriousness standard, which would not construe the provision as including foolish or out-of-bravado displays. This led David Mead to a remark worth quoting 'woe betide Mr and Mrs Anderson giving their daughter Isobel Rachel a coming-of-age bracelet engraved with her initials'.[115] Another commentator contemplates what might then happen to 'deluded youths' wearing swastikas on T-shirts as a 'post-modern iconic statement' or even 'in a kind of New Age way' referring to oriental mysticism, unlikely to be recognised by police officers.[116]

ii. Germany

In Germany, the ban on uniforms is twofold. First, there is a ban of wearing uniforms of banned organisations in public, as discussed above. This ban

[113] Similarly David Mead, *The New Law of Peaceful Protest. Rights and Regulations in the Human Rights Act Era* (Oxford, Hart Publishing 2010) 214.

[114] *Rankin v Murray* (2004) SLT 1164, see Andrew Lothian, 'Time, Gentlemen? Latest Criminal Cases, Including Sentencing Discounts; Non-disclosure by the Crown; Support for Proscribed Organisations; Circumstantial Proof; Road Traffic', 1 August 2004, *theJournal online*, the members' magazine of the Law Society of Scotland, www.journalonline.co.uk/Magazine/49-8/1000140.aspx.

[115] Mead, *The New Law of Peaceful Protest*, above n 113, 217.

[116] Lothian, 'Time, Gentlemen?', above n 114.

also includes symbols such as buttons or parts of uniforms as explained.[117] Apart from this, the old Federal Assembly Law has banned wearing 'in public or in an assembly uniforms, parts of uniforms or similar pieces of clothes as expression of a general political attitude' (*Gesinnung*).[118]

This latter provision has found application both to the extreme right and to a significant extent the left, anti-nuclear protestors, the Autonoms, etc a famous image being the 'Schwarzer Block'. Some claim the law overreaches itself as it not only regulates uniforms in assemblies, but generally in public.[119]

The GFCC never ruled on this problem of overreach. The ban itself was found unproblematic in a 1982 decision,[120] whose reasoning will be briefly set out here.

The starting point is that freedom of expression and assembly protect pictorial and suggestive collective manifestations of opinion. However, uniforms expressing common political attitude are capable not only of reinforcing the outer effect of collective expressions, but also of inciting 'suggestive-militant effects in the direction of intimidating, uniform militancy'.[121] This militancy inherently encroaches upon the 'free battle of opinions', and therefore, the Constitution does not prevent the legislator from inhibiting from the outset the public wearing of uniforms, including forms which are meant to evade this restriction.

Such '*Umgehungsformen*' are in particular civilian clothes which look essentially unitary and display references to historically known militant groupings in a recognisable fashion, especially if their wearing is accompanied by other such references, such as marching in formation or other militant conduct. The more visible the similarity to uniforms, the more relevance the assembly law's ban has even when members of groups show up in a seemingly scattered way.[122]

In spite of this decision, much confusion remained or even might have occurred following this judgment. It only seems to be clear that those who regularly wear uniforms, for example soldiers, are not allowed to wear the uniform at political demonstrations.[123]

Inversely, however, wearing a uniform of the Federal Army (available freely in commerce) during sports training does not fall under the ban, if the common *political* attitude is not apparent for the audience.[124]

[117] Above, text accompanying nn 34–58.

[118] Art 3 VersG. For the status of the Federal Assembly Law after the federalism reform, see above, Ch 1, n 138.

[119] Eg Alfred Dietel, Kurt Gintzel and Michael Kniesel, *Versammlungsgesetz*, 15th edn (Köln, Carl Heymanns, 2008) 19.

[120] 1 BvR 1138/81, 27 April 1982, NJW 1982, 1803, *I'm not a donkey*.

[121] Ibid.

[122] Ibid. Not literal, but close translation of the main paragraph of the decision.

[123] BVerfGE 57, 29 (1981), VG (Administrative Court) Wiesbaden, NVwZ, 2004, 635.

[124] BGH, 29 September 1983, 5 StR 811/83, NStZ 1984, 123.

The City of Konstanz Prosecutor's Office considered blue–yellow anoraks at an election campaign by members of the Liberal Party FDP fell outside the uniform ban, basically reciting the GFCC's grounds word-by-word.[125] The Osnabrück Prosecutor's Office, in a widely read decision, recently found that wearing transparent strike waistcoats did not qualify as uniform because the demonstrators' ordinary clothes were visible under the waistcoat. It did not qualify as a similar piece of cloth either because its single-use character prevented it from being perceived as an ordinary cloth. Thirdly, the office distinguished the trade union strike relating to a collective agreement as not being a political strike.[126] A commentary of the assembly law similarly claims that uniformed officers participating at a demonstration furthering 'professional' interests do not fall under the ban for lack of common 'political attitude'.[127]

From these instances it appears that the accepted scope of the uniform ban is quite narrow at least compared to the text.

First, the 1982 GFCC decision is understood to have narrowed the scope of the uniform ban to 'mass suggestive' and militant uses. What those LeBonian terms mean are naturally left to evaluation in the particular case. For OLG Koblenz, the reason for the ban is that uniform symbolises organised violence, and this court understands the GFCC by narrowing the applicability of the ban to such occasions.[128] The new Bavarian Assembly Law—whose different provisions were found preliminarily unconstitutional[129]—only bans intimidatory uniforms,[130] an even narrower term, which on its face might even satisfy US standards. Recall in addition that the GFCC argued that militancy hinders free battle of opinion—a different way of saying that you should fight on the level of reasoned argument and not by physical threats. Still, in my view if the GFCC had wanted to restrict limitation of uniform bans to intimidation and threat, it would have clearly said so. However, ordinary courts and policing authorities appear reasonably cautious when interpreting the grounds for a ban.

[125] StA Konstanz, 23 February 1984, 11 Js 16/84. Dietel, Gintzel and Kniesel, above n 122, 140, refers in this regard to LG Konstanz, MDR 1984, 692—ie to a court decision which I could not find.

[126] StA Osnabrück, 28 April 2006, 730 UJs 12661/06. StA Konstanz, 23 February 1984, 11 Js 16/84.

[127] Dietel, Gintzel and Kniesel, above n 119, 141.

[128] OLG Koblenz, 11 January 2011, 2 Ss 156/10.

[129] The GFCC in a preliminary expedited proceeding rendered inapplicable several important provisions of the law: *BVerfGE 122, 342* (2009). The Bavarian lawmaker has changed the law (law from 22 April 2010, *GVBl S* 190, entered into force on 1 June 2010), and the GFCC later declared inadmissible a challenge against it (BVerfG, 1 BvR 2492/08, 21 March 2012). The law modified art 7 on militancy ban, but it maintained the condition of intimidation relevant for my purposes above.

[130] Art 7 BayVersG. Khwaja Mares Askaryar, 'Das bayerische Versammlungsgesetz—Überblick über wesentliche Änderungen gegenüber dem Bundesversammlungsgesetz' (2009) 4 *Kommunaljurist* 126, 128.

Secondly, what counts as *common political attitude* is also limited in two ways. On the one hand, it has to be comprehended as such by the public, the audience, similarly to what was discussed above in relation to 'expression offences' in the Criminal Code.[131] On the other hand, '*political*' itself is narrowed down: it is doubtful on the basis of the above examples if, for instance, a labour strike would ever count as 'political'.

iii. France

French law does not have a demonstration specific ban on uniforms. It does have the mentioned ban on symbols and garments of organisations or persons responsible for crimes against humanity,[132] but apparently there is no belief that uniforms automatically enhance the potential for violence or militancy, as it is in the United Kingdom and Germany. The other general dress code, the recent burqa ban, could be conceived as a ban on uniform clothing, but the law itself only mentions concealing the face, and thus I will discuss it shortly under masks.

As to the reverse, in an interesting contrast to German law, French law prohibits wearing the uniform for reservists on any *political or syndical* event or demonstration.[133] Recall that German courts try to limit political as not meaning labour strikes. Here in France the idea is that the military uniform is the symbol of state, which should be outside or elevated over any debate of a certain intensity of interests.[134]

B. Masks

Masks can be removed by police in the United Kingdom, and are banned under conditions in Germany and France. The United States, strangely enough, has not produced a coherent jurisprudence on the issue of masks, and the Supreme Court does not appear to be willing to take a case. The ECtHR has not faced the issue of masks yet.

131 See above, text accompanying nn 34–58.

132 See above, text accompanying nn 59–60.

133 Order of 14 December 2007 (Arrêté du 14 décembre 2007 relatif au port de l'uniforme militaire par les réservistes de la réserve militaire, les anciens réservistes admis à l'honorariat de leur grade et les anciens militaires n'appartenant à aucune de ces deux catégories) art 1 II b, art 4 II b.

134 Order of 14 December 2007 (Arrêté du 14 décembre 2007 relatif au port de l'uniforme militaire par les réservistes de la réserve militaire, les anciens réservistes admis à l'honorariat de leur grade et les anciens militaires n'appartenant à aucune de ces deux catégories) art 1 II b, art 4 II b.

i. United Kingdom

In the United Kingdom, section 60AA of the Criminal Justice and Public Order Act 1994 (CJPOA) has authorised the police to 'require any person to remove any item which the constable reasonably believes that person is wearing wholly or mainly for the purpose of concealing his identity'. The next paragraph authorises the constable to seize such items. Those powers are quite often used, just as demonstrators often tend to wear masks, helmets, scarves and similar clothes to disguise their identity.

Nonetheless, none of the cases I found deal explicitly with possible problems inherent in prohibiting masks. In *R (on the application of Laporte) v Chief Constable of Gloucestershire*[135] there was such a seizure under section 60AA, because the police found some masks. However, the House of Lords judgment only mentions the removal and seizure of disguises among the facts, and pursued no further, normative examination in that regard. In *Austin v Metropolitan Police Commissioner*,[136] the Queen's Bench Division made reference to *Laporte*, again without challenging the order for removal and seizure, and in neither case did any of the judges have any thoughts related to it. In *Broadwith v Chief Constable of Thames Valley Police*,[137] the fact that the person wore a mask strengthened the court's acceptance that he could be reasonably believed to be a demonstrator. Nobody questioned the adequacy of such a conclusion. Therefore, there seems to be no legal controversy around the power of removal or its application. What was settled by the Divisional Court is only that guarantees surrounding stop and search powers are not applicable to the mask removal power, thus, for example, the constable requiring removal of the mask does not need to give their name and station, etc. Consequently, the person denying the removal is not exempted by the fact that the police officer did not identify themself.[138]

ii. Germany

Article 17a of the German Federal Assembly Law prohibits bringing so-called *Schutzwaffen* to public events[139] and to hide identity. *Schutzwaffen* or 'protective weapons' are protective covers, gas masks, helmets or similar devices capable of averting law enforcement activities of authorities.

Article 17a(2) also prohibits any makeup, design or appearance (*Aufmachung*) capable of, and, according to the circumstances, designed

[135] *R (on the application of Laporte) v Chief Constable of Gloucestershire* [2006] UKHL 55. See Ch 3, text accompanying nn 65–84.

[136] *Austin v Metropolitan Police Commissioner* [2005] EWHC 480 QBD.

[137] *Broadwith v Chief Constable of Thames Valley Police*, 2000 WL 553, [2000] *Criminal Law Review* 924.

[138] DPP v Avery [2001] EWHC Admin 748, [2002] 1 Cr App R 31.

[139] Assemblies under the open sky, processions, and other public events.

to prevent the identification of the participant or the would-be participant on her way to the assembly. The same applies to objects brought for the same use and with the same intent. Exemption *can* be granted if there is no reason to fear an endangerment of public security or order.[140]

Article 27 of the Assembly Law orders punishment of up to one year or a fine for violating article 17a, or, in a curious parallel, bringing weapons to a public event. It shows the legislative finds masks and helmets all in all just as dangerous or undesirable as arms. This connection supports the view shared by constitutional lawyers that both the uniform and the masking ban are the concretisations of the peacefulness requirement,[141] as if these bans were not limits, but are inherent to the substance of the right (*Grundrechtsausgestaltung*). I cannot subscribe to this view even if I accept that unpeaceful assemblies are out of the scope of constitutional protection. To claim, however, that non-wearing of masks and uniforms is evidently as necessary to maintain peace as not being violent, is just to spare authorities from providing evidence on an empirical question. Available data, including social psychology, certainly does not unequivocally suggest such a stance. Sometimes, there might be an increased readiness for violence for reasons of a bigger chance of not being caught, but deindividuation studies show that such a correlation is not necessary.[142] Clearly, the exempted categories, and the possibility to lift the ban in particular cases, show that the legislator itself knows that not every masked demonstration turns violent. Article 17a was first introduced in 1985 after several occasions of masked violence. Before that, the police were entitled to impose the condition of not wearing masks if it found it necessary to prevent endangerment of public order and security. Basically, the legislator decided to shift 'the burden of proof', and since 1985 the rule has been the ban, the immunity the exception. This would not be in itself problematic. However, the norm finally accepted only authorises, and does not oblige, the authority to lift the ban where there is no danger to public order and safety—an anyway too broad a concept. Such a discretion granted is unfounded.

These severe concerns are well registered by German legal scholarship. Some thus maintain that the ban is unconstitutional.[143] Others suggest an interpretation which is consistent with constitutional principles, which thus

[140] Also exempted are traditional assemblies which are exempted from advance notice requirement. See Ch 2.

[141] Eg Otto Depenheuer, 'Kommentierung zu Art 8' in Roman Herzog, Rupert Scholz, Matthias Herdegen and Hans H Klein (eds), *Maunz/Dürig Grundgesetz, Loseblatt-Kommentar*, 62nd edn (München, Beck, 2011) ann 144; Dietel, Gintzel and Kniesel, above n 119, 353.

[142] Eg Steven Reicher, Russell Spears and Tom Postmes, 'A Social Identity Model of Deindividuation Phenomena' in Wolfgang Stroebe and Miles Hewstone (eds), *European Review of Social Psychology*, Vol 6 (Chichester, Wiley, 1995) 161–98.

[143] Eg Wolfgang Hoffmann-Riem, 'Kommentar zu Art 8' in Erhard Denninger, Wolfgang Hoffmann-Riem, Hans-Peter Schneider, and Ekkehard Stein (eds), *Kommentar zum Grundgesetz für die Bundesrepublik (AK-GG)* (Neuwied, Hermann Luchterhand Verlag, 2001) ann 27.

considerably narrows the scope of the ban. For instance, there should not be discretion in lifting the ban in case there is no reason to fear unpeaceful activities (and not simply danger to public order and safety). Also, for exercising freedom of art, and of non-verbal expression, an exception should be carved out.[144] Hoffmann-Riem explains that participants must be able to bring protective objects if they only want to protect themselves from militant counterdemonstrators.[145]

Courts also interpret the bans restrictively, though they do not go as far as Hoffmann-Riem. *Brokdorf* is relevant as there the GFCC reinforced the general principle that administrative discretion is always limited by fundamental rights,[146] thus theoretically the wearing of masks and bringing 'protective weapons' is allowed in every case where there is no risk to public order. For instance, the GFCC found that wearing animal masks in a protest entitled 'Patenting of life' in front of the European Patent Office in Munich cannot be subjected to the condition that 'protesters wearing masks identify themselves at the request of the police' as there was no showing of direct danger to public order or safety.[147]

What counts as a protective weapon, or similar device capable of being used as such, appears reasonably limited, for example, a gumshield being more capable of preventing an accident than averting an attack was found to be outside the ban.[148] A Hannover court, in line with earlier decisions, found that there must be a proven intent to not be identified *by law enforcement* authorities, hiding faces from *counterdemonstrators or the political opponents* photographing the protestors does not fall under the ban on masks.[149]

In a similar vein, it has been found that wearing sports gloves, reinforced by glass sand in the knuckles, are thought capable of being used as a protective weapon, but specific intent to use them that way is needed for it to fall under the ban.[150] Thus, intent to evade law enforcement is necessary in both wearing masks and having protective weapons (or, at least, objects capable of being used as such), otherwise there is no criminal responsibility. This does not mean, inversely, that law enforcement must be lawful, as even unlawful law enforcement must not be averted by protective weapons.

144 Dietel, Gintzel and Kniesel, above n 119, 354–57.

145 Hoffmann-Riem, above n 143, ann 25.

146 BVerfGE 69, 315, 345 (1985), *Brokdorf*.

147 BVerfG, 1 BvR 943/02, 25 October 2007.

148 LG Cottbus, 22 December 2006, 24 jug Qs 61/06.

149 LG Hannover, 20 January 2009, 62c 69/08. (Left-wing protestor hiding her face from photographing right-wing onlookers), reference found in Tronje Döhmer's online Leitsatzkommentar at www.leitsatzkommentar.de/VersammlungsG.htm. In effect an identical ruling was brought about earlier by AG Rotenburg (Wümme), 12 July 2005, 7 Cs 523 Js 23546/04 (9/05).

150 OLG Dresden, 17 June 2008, 1 Ss 401/08.

Such use can only be exempted on the basis of general criminal norms of self-defence.[151]

iii. France

In recent years in France the hiding of faces in public has brought government hostility to the surface. In the last years two bans, both relevant to assemblies, have been adopted. The first was a 2009 Decree on the illegal covering of the face in public demonstrations and the second has been the (in)famous burqa ban.

The 2009 Decree[152] was adopted in the aftermath of the April NATO summit protests where ultra leftist groups in the tradition of Black Block destroyed banks and industrial sites in Strasbourg. The Decree inserted in the Criminal Code a fifth class (most serious) contravention. Article R 645-14 prohibits voluntarily hiding one's face in order not to be identified in, or in the immediate proximity of, a demonstration on the public route in circumstances giving rise to fear of attacks to public order. Paragraph 3 allows for exemptions in case of assemblies conforming to local usage and when the covering of the face is justified by a legitimate reason. The first one—conforming to local usage—probably refers to religious processions, as the same formulation is applied in the 1935 Decree Law (and, since 2012, in article L 211-1 of the Code of Internal Security) exempting such processions from the notification requirement.

The Conseil d'État rejected a challenge to this contravention,[153] as the applicant has not proven a grave and manifestly illegal violation of a fundamental liberty, as it is required in the *référé-liberté* procedure. The Decree was strongly criticised, even by police, as being a grotesque and inapplicable measure.[154] The main police union considers they would be obliged to go into the middle of a demonstrating crowd, basically a provocation, enhancing the chances of clashes.[155]

It was for some time unclear whether the provision ought to be understood as imposing a ban in every case, or only in circumstances giving rise to a risk of public order, and this latter element refers to the cases where someone needs to be identified, that is opening the possibility for

[151] OLG Hamm, 22 October 1997, 2 Ss 735/97.

[152] Decree no 2009-724, 19 June 2009 (relatif à l'incrimination de dissimulation illicite du visage à l'occasion de manifestations sur la voie publique).

[153] CÉ, 28 July 2009, no 329991, CÉ, 28 July 2009, no 329992.

[154] Antonin Sabot, 'Décret anti-cagoule: une measure inapplicable?' *Le Monde*, Mis à jour le 22.04.09, www.lemonde.fr/societe/article/2009/04/22/decret-anti-cagoule-une-mesure-inapplicable_1184187_3224.html. 'Le décret "anti-cagoule" officiellement publié' *Le Monde*, 20 June 2009, www.lemonde.fr/societe/article/2009/06/20/le-decret-anti-cagoule-officiellement-publie_1209177_3224.html.

[155] Audrey Vassalli, 'Insécurité—Fous pas ta cagoule!' www.lepetitjournal.com/homepage/a-la-une/39844-sarkozy-estrosi-nice-sritnquance-insritagoule-bande-gagny.html.

identification. This interpretation would mean that on assemblies conforming to local usage a mask can be worn even if the circumstances give rise to fear to public order.

The provision went again to the Conseil d'Etat in 2011, in a challenge of excess of power, initiated by several national level general and specialised unions such as that of high schools and attorneys. The Conseil d'Etat found the regulation both constitutional and to conform to the ECHR, emphasising the precise definition of the scope of the ban, the existence of such ban in other countries, and judicial supervision as a safeguard. Most importantly, the Conseil d'Etat explained that the provision does not target masked demonstrators as long as their masking does not aim at preventing identification by police forces in a context where their conduct constitutes a threat to public order that their identification could prevent.[156] This is quite a narrow reading of the text, but of course, it does not explain when exactly a threat to public order exists. The process of explaining to police that actually the mask is not being worn for avoiding identification is also hard to imagine. Theoretically, however, after this decision of the Conseil d'Etat, one can always argue that there is no threat to public order in the actual circumstances, thus, masks can be worn without hindrance. What that exactly means, will be tested in practice. As mentioned, police appear quite reluctant to enforce the law strictly in any case.

The other ban, which clearly has been prominent in and outside France, was enacted as law in 2010.[157] Article 1 states that 'nobody shall, in public, wear a garment destined to conceal the face'. Article 3 sanctions a fine for the violation of second class misdemeanours, that is wearing the burqa 'in the public space' is considered less serious than hiding a face at a demonstration—in my view, certainly rightly so. Among the possible sanctions is a citizenship training (*stage de citoyenneté*)[158] where the delinquent gets familiarised with republican values of tolerance, and of respect of dignity of the human person,[159] a sanction introduced in 2004. Public space (*espace public*) includes 'streets, places open to the public, or affected by a public service'.[160] The garment is exempted if 'prescribed or authorised by law or regulation, or if it is justified by health or professional reasons, or if it is worn in the context of sports training, or artistic or traditional feasts or such demonstrations'.[161] The same law also criminalises 'forcing another person or persons by threat, violence, or duress, abuse of authority or

[156] CÉ, 23 February 2011, no 329477.

[157] Law no 2010-1192 of 11 October 2010 (loi interdisant la dissimulation du visage dans l'espace public).

[158] Art 131.16, 8° Penal Code, referred to in art 3 of the 'burqa law'.

[159] Art R 131-35 of the second part of the Penal Code, inserted by Decree no 2004-1021 of 27 September 2004.

[160] Art 2 of the law no 2010-1192 of 11 October 2010.

[161] Art 2 II ibid.

power, to conceal the face, for reason of their sex'. This is a proper crime, with serious punishment,[162] raising no constitutional concerns.

The Conseil Constitutionnel examined the law in preliminary review proceedings and found it constitutional, though it made a constitutional reservation in interpretation. Notably, it would be unconstitutional if the ban on concealing the face would restrict exercise of freedom of religion 'in places of worship open to the public'. The Conseil Constitutionnel thereby carved out an exception, but otherwise found the legislator realised a not manifestly disproportionate reconciliation of public order on the one, and constitutionally protected rights on the other hand.[163] By adopting the general ban, the legislator has only 'generalised and completed' rules so far reserved for individual situations of protecting public order, and the Conseil Constitutionnel seems to accept the argument that 'women concealing their face—*voluntarily* or not—are placed in a situation of exclusion and inferiority manifestly incompatible with constitutional principles of liberty and equality' (emphasis added).[164]

The burqa ban has been discussed worldwide in both journalistic and scholarly writings, and earned quite some critique in terms of freedom of religion.[165] It can also be strongly criticised from the point of view of freedom of assembly, as such a ban also deprives burqa-wearing women from their right to assembly. In one case, there were arrests in a demonstration against the burqa ban, the demonstration was dispersed, and at least one person in niqab was interrogated by police, however, not on the basis of the dissimulation provision, but for lack of prior notice.[166]

For these cases I would argue that the ban on masks in demonstrations is *lex specialis*, and thus carves out an exception from the burqa ban in cases where it is worn in a demonstration for legitimate reasons, for example, to protest against the burqa ban itself, or against religious discrimination, or even for any reason unrelated to the burqa, because the individual cannot be made to choose between exercising her freedom of assembly or freedom of religion. As the Conseil Constitutionnel begins to accept that wearing a burqa in public is per se a threat to public order, the Conseil d'Etat's above interpretation on protest masks does not help; so one would have to rely on the exceptions, most easily that of legitimate reason. It only adds to the confusion that the Conseil d'Etat had earlier also given a (strictly

[162] Art 225-4-10 Penal Code.

[163] Decision no 2010-613 DC, 7 October 2010, considérant 5.

[164] Ibid, considérant 4.

[165] In English see, eg Britton D Davis, 'Lifting the Veil: France's New Crusade' (2011) 34 *Boston College International and Comparative Law Review* 117.

[166] 'Niqab: arrestations lors d'une manifestation interdite devant Notre-Dame' *Lemonde.Fr with AFP* 11 April 2011, www.lemonde.fr/societe/article/2011/04/11/la-loi-sur-le-voile-integral-est-entree-en-vigueur_1505688_3224.html#xtor=EPR-32280229-[NL_Titresdujour]-20110411-[zonea]&ens_id=1502515n.

confidential) advisory opinion on 'the general ban of the integral veil' in which it expressed serious doubts about compatibility with constitution and convention.[167] However, the Conseil d'Etat's principled opposition to a full ban does not imply a resistance to the Conseil Constitutionnel's deferential decision.

iv. United States

In the United States, there is a strong tradition of valuing anonymous speech, which goes back to the experiences of the colonial or even English period. As the Supreme Court noted:[168]

> Anonymous pamphlets, leaflets, brochures and even books have played an important role in the progress of mankind. Persecuted groups and sects from time to time throughout history have been able to criticize oppressive practices and laws either anonymously or not at all.

On this basis, the Supreme Court has struck down laws requiring the divulgence of membership lists of the National Association for the Advancement of Colored People (NAACP),[169] or the law mandating that on every handbill names and addresses of the sponsors be displayed,[170] or another one requiring identification for door-to-door canvassing.[171] However, this line of jurisprudence is not necessarily applicable to wearing masks at a demonstration. The US Supreme Court has never decided on exactly this issue, just issued denials of *certiorari*. As there appear to be some arguments—discussed in relation to other jurisdictions such as enhanced dangerousness, or intention of adverting law enforcement—for distinguishing anonymous speech from anonymous (especially crowd) protest, the US Supreme Court's opinion would be useful. Also, we know in *Brandenburg v Ohio* that a meeting in hoods was found constitutionally protected, though the main thrust of the decision was quite unrelated to this issue.[172]

There have been attempts to ban masks on demonstrations in the US as well. A Georgia Anti-Mask Act was found constitutional by the State Supreme Court, but it never went to the federal level. As the Georgia Supreme Court is of the view that the Georgian Constitution protects

[167] See only the press reports on it: 'Le Conseil d'Etat contesterait une interdiction totale du voile' *Lemonde.Fr with AFP and Reuters*, 14 May 2010, Cécilia Gabizon, 'Burqa: l'interdiction générale écartée par le Conseil d'État' *Le Figaro*, 26 March 2010.

[168] *Talley v California*, 362 US 60, 64 (1960).

[169] *NAACP v Alabama ex rel Patterson*, 357 US 449 (1958).

[170] *Talley v California,* 362 US 60 (1960), and *McIntyre v Ohio Elections Comission*, 514 US 334 (1995).

[171] *Watchtower Bible and Tract Society of New York, Inc v Village of Stratton*, 536 US 150 (2002).

[172] *Brandenburg v Ohio*, 395 US 444 (1969). See Ch 3, text accompanying nn 32–38.

speech more broadly than the federal Constitution,[173] it is worth looking closer at their arguments *allowing for the ban on masks*. The Anti-Mask Act[174] was adopted in 1951 in reaction to several occasions of lynching and other violent 'vigilante' events mostly carried out by the Ku Klux Klan. The current application of the law was also related to a KKK member, who went to streets wearing KKK regalia, including the hood with a mask concealing the face. The applicable test was *O'Brien*, and the Georgia Supreme Court found that the statute, regulating conduct including both speech and non-speech elements, furthered substantial government interest unrelated to speech, no more burdensome than necessary, for the following reasons. Concealing the face is 'an effective means of committing crimes of violence and intimidation', as it hinders law enforcement, and 'calms the criminal's inward cowardly fear'.[175] In an impressive passage, the court adds:[176] 'A nameless, faceless figure strikes terror in the human heart. But, remove the mask, and the nightmarish form is reduced to its true dimensions. The face betrays not only identity, but also human frailty'.

The ban was to prevent not only threat, intimidation or violence, and apprehension of criminals, but also 'restore confidence in law enforcement by removing any possible illusion of government complicity with masked vigilantes'.[177]

This latter can be quite an important, but not obvious concern not only in the United States before the civil rights movement, but also in every society where police regularly mistreat discernible social groups. These are rightly said to constitute substantial, or even compelling, government interests, quite independently of whether—as the Georgian court claims—it also counts as the affirmative constitutional duty of the state.

As to claims of content discrimination and overbreadth, the court replied by a narrow construction of the (in my view, clearly content-neutral) statute to cases where the mask worn is perceived intimidating or threatening by a reasonable person, though I think the concurring opinion is right in also requiring actual intent.[178] This is a kind of reasoning clearly similar to *Virginia v Black*, the 2003 US Supreme Court cross burning case, but in the Georgia case without the problems Justice Souter raised stemming from a ban on particular symbols. To wear a mask as intimidation is in my view different from cross burning as intimidation because a mask is a significant aid in evading law enforcement. Thus, I disagree with dissenting Justice Smith

[173] *State v Miller*, 260 Ga 669, 671 (1990): 'The 1983 Constitution of Georgia provides even broader protection' (than the First Amendment).

[174] The 'Anti-Mask Act,' OCGA § 16-11-38.

[175] Ibid, by quoting M Abram and A Miller, 'How to Stop Violence! Intimidation! In Your Community', 15 August 1949.

[176] 260 Ga 669, 671–72.

[177] Ibid, 672.

[178] Ibid, 677, Hunt J, concurring.

who believes the statute is content-based and *Brandenburg* should apply.[179] Even so, however, the dissenting justice might be right that in the particular case, circumstances indicate that the KKK member wore the mask out of protest against the anti-mask statute, not for intimidation, thus his conviction should not stand.

More striking is the decision of the Second Circuit from 2004 dealing with the New York State's Anti-Mask Act. This statute was enacted in 1845 in response to attacks on police by disguised farmers; and goes as follows:[180]

> A person is guilty of loitering when he:
>
> Being masked or in any manner disguised by unusual or unnatural attire or facial alteration, loiters, remains or congregates in a public place with other persons so masked or disguised, or knowingly permits or aids persons so masked or disguised to congregate in a public place; except that such conduct is not unlawful when it occurs in connection with a masquerade party or like entertainment

The district court found the provision unconstitutional,[181] but the Second Circuit[182] reversed the decision. The US Supreme Court denied *certiorari.*[183]

At issue has been a KKK related organisation, the Church of the American Knights of the Ku Klux Klan, which was denied a permit to demonstrate in front of a courthouse in masks. Circuit Judge Cabranes found that the 'mask does not communicate any message that the robe and hood do not. The expressive force of the mask is, therefore, redundant'. With this, the Court dispensed with any apparent need to examine free speech doctrines, be they of anonymous speech or symbolic conduct, and spelled out flatly that mask wearing does not fall under the First Amendment. As a critic notes, the precedent referred to—a case which held that the operator of a place of prostitution could not rely on the First Amendment against the closure of his business simply because the premises were also used as a bookstore[184]—is clearly inapplicable as the burden on wearing masks is certainly not an incidental burden on expressive activity, as it was in the prostitution/bookstore parallel. The reasoning is all the more surprising as in this case some Knights actually experienced violence in a previous, non-masked

[179] Ibid, 677 ff, Presiding Justice Smith, dissenting.

[180] New York Penal Law § 240.35(4), as cited by *Church of American Knights of the Ku Klux Klan v Kerik*, 356 F 3d 197, 201, CA 2 (NY) (2004).

[181] *Church of American Knights of Ku Klux Klan v Kerik,* 232 F Supp 2d 205 (SDNY 19 Nov 2002).

[182] *Church of American Knights of the Ku Klux Klan v Kerik*, 356 F 3d 197 CA 2 (NY) (2004).

[183] *Church of the American Knights of the Ku Klux Klan v Kelly*, 543 US 1020 (2004).

[184] Arcara v Cloud Books, Inc, 478 US 697, 706 (1986), as cited by NN, 'Constitutional Law—Free Speech—Second Circuit Upholds New York's Anti-Mask Statute against Challenge by Klan-Related Group—*Church of the American Knights of the Ku Klux Klan v Kerik*, 356 F 3d 197 (2d Cir 2004)' (2004) 117 Harvard Law Review 2777, 2781.

gathering at the same place,[185] and this circumstance cries, if not for the application, then at least the discussion of anonymous speech precedents mentioned above. Strangely, the Supreme Court did not find it necessary or useful to review this decision. Basically the same argumentation in a 1992 Virginia case was also not reviewed by the US Supreme Court.[186]

All in all, from the 6 federal and 18 state cases ever decided related to wearing masks in public,[187] no clear pattern emerges. It appears more or less certain that overbreadth and vagueness are a concern in this area as well,[188] especially post-Second World War cases, when the current speech doctrine was gradually taking hold. However, parallel to this, lower courts sometimes stick to a rigid speech-conduct doctrine—of a kind never approved by the Supreme Court itself—which even leads to non-application of the rather permissive *O'Brien* test. Again, other courts would find that the American Knights of the KKK wore the mask for expressive reasons—among them, to preserve anonymity for fear of retaliation—and thus strict scrutiny (not simply *O'Brien*) applies. I think such a view is correct, especially if there is indication that the 'Knights' experienced threats, violence, etc in the past for reasons of their views.[189] However, to put the burden of proof on the speaker in this regard appears to me to be completely[190] dubious.

The lesson is that masks can be worn both out of fear of being intimidated, as well as with the purpose of intimidating others. As intimidation can be banned without reference to masks, therefore, in my view, there is no need for statutes specifically targeting masks in a demonstration.

III. ONE MAN'S NOISE IS ANOTHER'S MUSIC

Public assemblies make noise. Part of the noise is essential to the activity itself, to convey some message normally requires some sound, most naturally the sound of speaking. In addition, assemblies are typically accompanied by music, chants, clapping, shouting slogans, etc. Even at small or

185 Ibid, 2778.

186 *Hernandez v Superintendent, Fredericksburg-Rappahannock Joint Security Center* (1992, ED Va) 800 F Supp 1344, cert denied by *Hernandez v Superintendent, Fredericksburg Rappahanock Joint Security Center*, 510 US 1119 (1994).

187 Thomas R Trenkner, 'Validity and Construction of State Statute or Ordinance Prohibiting Picketing, Parading, Demonstrating, or Appearing in Public while Masked or Disguised' 2 *American Law Reports Annotated, Fourth Series* 1241 (originally published 1980, weekly update from 12 March 2011).

188 Eg *Ghafari v Municipal Court for San Francisco Judicial District* (1978, 1st Dist) 87 Cal App 3d 255, 150 Cal Rptr 813, 2 ALR4th 1230, *Knights of Ku Klux Klan v Martin Luther King Jr Worshippers* (1990, MD Tenn) 735 F Supp 745, *Robinson v State* (1980, Fla) 393 So 2d 1076.

189 *American Knights of Ku Klux Klan v City of Goshen, Indiana*, 50 F Supp 2d 835 (ND Ind 1999).

190 *People v Aboaf*, 721 NYS 2d 725 (City Crim Ct 2001).

middle-sized events sound amplification might be needed to reach audience and passers-by. Thereby, assemblies can cause quite an auditional nuisance. One man's noise, however, is another's music, to paraphrase Justice Harlan.[191] Sound level regulations are part of general law in every country, and rightly so. Equally obvious is that sound is integral to the exercise of the right to assembly. In the following, I will discuss those few cases where courts had to face a choice between tranquillity and protest.

Two famous decisions of the US Supreme Court, both shaping general free speech doctrine, have to be discussed first in relation to this. *Kovacs v Cooper*[192] is a 1949 case, involving a city ordinance prohibiting the use of sound amplifiers attached to vehicles. Kovacs was emitting music and statements related to a labour dispute from a soundtruck on a street.[193] He was found to be violating the ordinance for employing a sound amplifier emitting 'loud or raucous noise' 'on or upon the public streets, alleys or thoroughfares'. A strongly divided Supreme Court affirmed the conviction. A prior restraint case, where the Chief of Police had total discretion in granting advance permission for dissemination of 'news and matters of public concern and athletic activities'[194] was quickly distinguished, for the ordinance in this case involved neither prior restraint, nor discretionary powers, and 'loud and raucous'—though certainly not exact—can be interpreted reasonably clearly. More indicative is perhaps how the court distinguishes another case where an ordinance prohibiting hand-billers or pamphleteers summoning the homeowners to their doors was found unconstitutional. As the lead opinion in *Kovacs* stated:[195]

> The Court never intimated that the visitor could insert a foot in the door and insist on a hearing ... The unwilling listener is not like the passer-by who may be offered a pamphlet in the street but cannot be made to take it ... In his home or on the street, he is practically helpless to escape this interference with his privacy by loudspeakers except through the protection of the municipality.

The harshness of this equalisation of the street to the home is striking, just as the unusually speculative intimation that actually Kovacs used the sound truck because this way he could save money:[196]

> [T]hat more people may be more easily and cheaply reached by sound trucks, *perhaps borrowed without cost from some zealous supporter*, is not enough to call forth constitutional protection for what those charged with public welfare reasonably think is a nuisance when easy means of publicity are open. (Emphasis added)

[191] 'One man's vulgarity is another's lyric'. *Cohen v California*, 403 US 15, 25 (1971), majority opinion by Harlan J in the 'Fuck the draft!' case.

[192] *Kovacs v Cooper*, 336 US 77 (1949).

[193] The message itself was not reported in the litigation.

[194] *Saia v New York*, 334 US 558 (1948).

[195] 336 US 77, 86 ff.

[196] Ibid, 88 ff.

It is very hard not to see a strong elitist–conservative stance in this reasoning.

The strong separate dissenting opinions of Justices Murphy, Black and Rutledge (and even the concurring opinion of Justice Jackson, but from the opposite angle) fault the court for disregarding that as interpreted by state courts, Kovacs was convicted for using sound amplification as such—not for emitting loud and raucous noise by sound truck, as the text of the ordinance would suggest. The lead opinion cursorily states that 'We cannot believe that rights of free speech compel a municipality to allow such mechanical voice amplification on any of its streets'[197] while elsewhere it appears only to decide on the use of emitting loud and raucous sounds by amplification on public streets. In the meantime, the two concurring opinions necessary for the majority find a flat ban on sound amplification in streets and parks constitutional.[198] Apart, or maybe inherent, to this cacophony, it remains equally doubtful what test—if any—the court is applying. Maybe the beginnings of the TMPs (time, manner, and place restriction) thinking can be found in references to 'hours and place',[199] even if the quote is taken from *Saia v New York*,[200] a case decided under a whole different philosophy in my view.

The other central precedent relating to noise and protest is *Ward v Rock against Racism (RAR)*[201] from 1989 relying on the new test currently applicable to TMP restrictions in general. The dispute was about a New York City Central Park regulation which made it mandatory for performers in the bandshell to use city-provided sound amplification, administered by the city's technician who would thus also control volume levels and sound mix in order to avoid volume problems. The court found the regulation constitutional relying on *Clark v Community for Creative Non-Violence*[202] according to the majority, and modifying it according to the dissent. In any case, the regulation was deemed content-neutral as it was justified without reference to the content of the speech, certainly a correct statement. As such, the content-neutral test should be applied which only requires a substantial (as opposed to compelling) government interest, which in the present case is double: to protect citizens from unwelcome noise, and to provide sufficient sound amplification for those who wish to listen to the

[197] Ibid, 87.

[198] Black J even argues that the lead opinion affirmed the conviction on grounds on which Kovacs was neither charged nor tried, thereby the Supreme Court itself violated due process: 336 US 77, 99. Rutledge J notes that 'in effect, Kovacs stands convicted, but of what it is impossible to tell, because the majority upholding the conviction do not agree upon what constituted the crime', 336 US 77, 105.

[199] 336 US 77, 89 citing *Saia v New York*.

[200] *Saia v New York*, 334 US 558 (1948).

[201] *Ward v Rock against Racism*, 491 US 781 (1989).

[202] *Clark v Community for Creative Non-Violence*, 468 US 288 (1984), see also Ch 6, text accompanying n 16 and this chapter, below nn 233–39.

music, that is the audience on the concert ground.[203] Note the somewhat strange argument—especially from a court not normally favouring positive rights—that one and the same regulation is at once a restriction on speech and a promotion of listeners' speech interests. Still, the court found the restriction was narrowly tailored to serve a substantial government interest, especially because it also did not have 'a substantial deleterious effect on the ability of bandshell performers to achieve the quality of sound they desired'.[204] Finally, the guidelines also left open 'ample alternative channels of communication', thus it met the third step of the content-neutral restrictions test. In this regard, the court emphasises that the regulation did not restrict speech at any particular time or place. The fact that the regulation might reduce the number in the audience as people far away would not hear the concert, was found irrelevant because the organisation Rock Against Racism (RAR) did not show that 'remaining avenues of communication [were] inadequate'.[205]

Justice Marshall, dissenting, considered that the regulation failed the narrow tailoring requirement, and it was an impermissible prior restraint.[206] As the majority deferred to governmental determination as to volume levels, I subscribe to the view that it is not narrow tailoring. Instead of total control over volume level and sound mix, it would have been equally effective, but less intrusive, to ban excessive noise itself.[207] For the majority, it was enough to ascertain that the city technician tried to compromise and fulfil the wishes of the performers, including the need to reach the audience on the concert ground. The dissent points out in reply that then why not simply set a maximum permissible decibel level, and what is the need for the city equipment and technician at all? The majority contents itself that the guidelines exclude taking into consideration what content of speech is to be delivered. In reply, one could say, it is one thing to proclaim an obligation, and another to institute mechanisms which by themselves ensure the realisation of that obligation (such as regulating maximum decibel level). Especially problematic here is the lack of judicial supervision—the Supreme Court renounced it.

The difference between the approach of the majority and the dissent shows exactly the weakness of the content neutrality test, but also the more hidden esoteric of general tests: the majority claims the applicable test is not one of least intrusive means, while the dissent thinks in any case, narrow

[203] 491 US 781, 791 ff.

[204] Ibid, 801.

[205] Ibid, 802.

[206] For reasons of the discretion granted in the guidelines. The majority thinks there is no impermissible prior restraint because the regulation does not authorise suppression of speech in advance of actual expression, and practice has limited the discretion to a significant degree. At 491 US 781, 795, incl fn 5.

[207] 491 US 781, 807, Marshall J, dissenting.

tailoring was not fulfilled. The prongs of narrow tailoring and least intrusive means are in effect merged.[208]

Germany is the other jurisdiction where the issue of noise and freedom of assembly figures prominently. Significantly, general noise regulations are, as a rule, not applicable to those assemblies where sound amplification is necessary for conveying the message,[209] the idea being that the means of exercising a basic right is protected by the right.[210] There is no indication that the test applicable to such means is different from the one applicable in general to the basic right.

However, sound amplification is protected only during the demonstration, and not for its preparation or invitation. These latter ones, I believe, must be covered at least by general freedom of action under article 2 II of the Basic Law, although with weaker (more permissive) justificatory grounds. Also, on the opposite side, sound amplification will often be protected by freedom of art, a right not subject to statutory limits, only to inherent constitutional ones. Whether a particular use of sound amplification is related to an ongoing demonstration, or not, or whether it is part of an art performance, will be ultimately determined by the authorities, subject to judicial review.[211]

As general noise regulations do not apply, the use of loud speakers and similar devices on a demonstration can only be restricted when criteria in assembly laws for imposing conditions or ban are met. These, even if not anymore unitary on the entire federal territory, are still subject to unitary constitutional control. In effect, only those conditions are permissible which are suitable, necessary and proportionate in case of foreseeable likely direct endangering of public safety, this latter one meaning protection of central legal goods such as life, limb, property, liberty, honour, etc. Thus, certainly it is clear that noise endangering health can be constitutionally restricted. Such protection extends to the police, too. For instance, when accompanying a demonstration in order to protect it from counter-demonstrators, police cannot be exposed to too much noise.[212]

Among lower courts, there is disagreement about the interests sufficient to justify restrictions on sound levels.

The High Administrative Court (OVG) Lüneburg decided in 2010, in relation to a music event by the extreme right-wing party (NPD), that noise

[208] A commentator thinks the narrow tailoring was in effect abolished: Carney R Shegerian, 'A Sign of the Times: The United States Supreme Court Effectively Abolishes the Narrowly Tailored Requirement for Time, Place and Manner Restrictions' (1992) 25 *Loyola of Los Angeles Law Review* 453.

[209] Dietel, Gintzel and Kniesel, above n 119, 265.

[210] Ibid, by referring to BVerwGE 7, 125, 131, BVerwG, DRiZ 1969, 158, etc.

[211] In general, see Wilhelm Kanther, 'Zur "Infrastruktur" von Versammlungen: vom Imbissstand bis zum Toilettenwagen' (2001) *Neue Zeitschrift fur Verwaltungsrecht* 1239.

[212] Eg OVG Lüneburg, 10 November 2010, 11 LA 298/10.

levels can be restricted even if they do not endanger health. I am doubtful about the constitutionality of its reasoning, which nonetheless points to a very typical view about freedom of assembly: the Lüneburg court found that noise endangering public safety can be restricted (this much of the argument is clearly right in application of the federal assembly law logic), *and* public safety includes the whole of the legal system, including thus, for example, federal emissions protection law. In my view this understanding of public safety goes against *Brokdorf* where it was interpreted only to mean 'central legal goods', not any legal norm. Secondly, in effect the Lüneburg court makes exercise of assembly, a basic right, dependent on other—lower level—statutory norms, and, in substance, on lower-ranking, though legitimate interests other than basic rights. More consistent is then the US approach confessing that modal restrictions on assembly are judged by a less stringent constitutional standard.

Fortunately, the view of OVG Lüneburg is not the homogeneous view of all German courts. The High Administrative Court (OVG) of Berlin-Brandenburg, for example, has undertaken a more thorough review related to an anti-Iraq War demonstration. First, it differentiates between inner- and outer-communication, referring to communication between participants and between participants and audience or would-be audience.[213] Both of these types are covered by the right to assembly, and to use loudspeakers to reach participants and would-be audience belongs to the self-determination of the organiser of an assembly.[214] In addition, OVG Berlin-Brandenburg also makes clear that police or local authorities cannot legitimately fix the permissible volume level so low that passers-by can only perceive that some (unintelligible) speeches are going on at the assembly. Instead, the volume level needs to be allowed to be high enough for passers-by to also hear the content of the speech, as a function of assembly is to turn public attention to an issue. Thirdly, and consequently, the Berlin court discards the proposition that any sort of legal norm is sufficient to justify restrictions on sound level. The interests of traffic participants, passers-by and residents which the law aims to protect, have to have relevance for basic rights. A specifically emphasised basic right aspect is the negative right to opinion of passers-by, in effect a generalised and theorised captive audience concern, which would protect against coercing another to participate in an assembly or listen to a speech to which one does not want to. In my reading, the threshold for coercion is not set too low: you cannot exclude hearing what the other wants to say, you can just go away, and be left in peace after you have once heard the message. Thus, how loud a particular assembly can become must be decided considering the circumstances of the case at hand. It appears in

[213] Note that this distinction reproduces the French concern about differences of *manifestation and réunion*.

[214] OVG Berlin-Brandenburg, 18 November 2008, 1 B 2/07.

any case that the Berlin court would dispute the (later enacted) standard applied by OVG Lüneburg, and requires a thorough examination or balancing of *constitutional* interests on every side. Clearly, the test is balancing and not categorical, as always in German constitutional law, but it is the normal basic rights standard, not a lowered standard.[215]

Finally, apart from the United States and Germany, the ECtHR has touched the issue. Though it was not overly occupied by the human rights problems of noisy demonstrations, it pronounced in *Galstyan v Armenia* that a certain amount of noise is unavoidable at a demonstration. Thus Armenia violated article 11 ECHR by condemning to three days administrative detention someone for 'making loud noise' at a demonstration, without, for example, any allegation that the noise would have included obscenity or incitement to violence.[216] The decision is clearly incapable of providing a more detailed view of the Court on this question, because the particular circumstances have shown unequivocally abuse on behalf of the Armenian authorities.

IV. MODES AND MEANS OF PROTEST AS AESTHETIC HARM

Similarly to noise, assemblies might also create visual nuisance, or indeed might well not be in harmony with majority views on beauty or cleanliness of surroundings. There are aesthetic or sanitary regulations dealing especially with leafleting, handbilling, displaying billboards, and similar activities regularly accompanying demonstrations, or being necessary to inform about an upcoming demonstration. Leaflets and handbills are transient media of the protestors, a means of expression. Of similar function is the practice of signage, be it on public or private property; and US case law treats it analogously. Still, signage relates only indirectly to freedom of assembly, most importantly as invitation to a demonstration. In its semi-permanent nature signage shares a function with billboards and information desks or installations.

If these (in particular any of the above) are not available for the organisers of a demonstration, it also certainly influences the exercise of the right to assembly. In contrast, the more these means are publicly available, the more the means of demonstration to show grievances or other concerns becomes an option for the most deprived, not only the wealthier relatively or subjectively deprived. The possibility, or not, of posting to billboards, of attaching signage to the façade of one's own home or to the (public) utility pole or

[215] For the sake of clarity, it should also be added that US courts might not apply strict scrutiny to these situations because these are horizontal relations, and US courts do not tend to see rights clashes and conflicts as much as German courts do.

[216] *Galstyan v Armenia*, Application no 26986/03, Judgment of 15 November 2007, § 116.

telegraph post, or of installing temporary information desks on the street might prove crucial in enabling an assembly to come about at all.

Material objects put, or left behind, on streets and parks are different from noise discussed above (and odours) in that the eye can be averted while the ear (and nose) cannot.[217] On the other hand, the 'litter' or visual clutter left behind is damage which stays there unlike the noise which fades away.

A. United States

In the United States, litigation to aesthetic regulation has revolved to a large extent around (commercial) billboard regulations. In the first decades of the twentieth century such regulations were perceived as an attack on property rights, and mostly discouraged by courts. Aesthetics alone was explicitly judged insufficient for restricting property rights.[218] Later, more or less parallel to the demise of *Lochner*,[219] property rights of the *neighbours* have also come to the forefront. Finally, in the seminal *Berman v Parker* (1954) decision the Supreme Court allowed even taking of property for aesthetic reasons.[220] In a famous passage, the Court described how wide the deference to police power is in this regard:[221]

> The concept of the public welfare is broad and inclusive. The values it represents are spiritual as well as physical, aesthetic as well as monetary. It is within the power of the legislature to determine that the community should be beautiful as well as healthy, spacious as well as clean, well-balanced as well as carefully patrolled.

The *Berman* rationale has been cited many times to allow for billboard regulations, and by 1984 the Supreme Court declared it 'well-settled that the state may legitimately exercise its police powers to advance esthetic values'.[222]

It was only in the middle of the 1960s that the First Amendment became to be seen as involved. Signs on our surroundings have become seen not only as the legitimate object of police power, but increasingly as expression and communication. Meanwhile, in accordance with their overwhelming use, billboards are considered more within commercial speech, a low (or

[217] This proposition is questioned in relation to highway billboards especially in the United States, but that is less relevant for assemblies, as they are the commercial billboards par excellence.

[218] See, eg Darrel C Menthe, 'Aesthetic Regulation and the Development of First Amendment Jurisprudence' (2010) 19 *Boston University Public Interest Law Journal* 225, 238, similarly David Burnett, Note: 'Judging the Aesthetics of Billboards' (2007) 23 *Journal of Law and Policy* 171, 193 ff.

[219] *Lochner v New York*, 198 US 45 (1905), see Menthe, ibid; and Burnett, ibid.

[220] *Berman v Parker*, 348 US 26 (1954).

[221] Ibid, 33, opinion of the court by Douglas J (internal citations omitted).

[222] *Members of City Council v Taxpayers for Vincent*, 466 US 789, 805 (1984).

at least somewhat lower) value speech category in US law developed by around 1980.[223] On this basis, *a contrario*, in 1981 it was decided that non-commercial speech cannot be disadvantaged as opposed to commercial speech. In *Metromedia Inc v City of San Diego*[224] the court invalidated a billboard regulation in part for the reason that it allowed onsite commercial billboards, but not non-commercial billboards.

Secondly, the regulatory technique of allowing a few exceptions[225] for non-commercial signs was found clearly unconstitutional as it favoured some content for public debate while excluded others. *Metromedia* on its own is an easy case, less easy is to figure what follows from it for the topic of this work. Certainly the holding disallows favouring commercial over non-commercial and some sorts of non-commercial over other sorts of non-commercial speech. Thus, whenever a city allows for billboards as exceptions, it cannot do it in a way which would harm persons most relevant here, that is organisers of protests, demonstrations, or other sorts of ('non-commercial') assemblies. However, when a city absolutely, unconditionally bans all billboards, it would probably be constitutional on the basis of *Metromedia*. The court starts out with the assumption that 'billboards by their very nature, wherever located and however constructed, can be perceived as an 'esthetic harm'.[226] Thus, *Metromedia* would allow aesthetics alone to justify suppressing (all kinds of) billboards as a means of expression.

Parallel to these developments, aesthetic regulation has always been exposed to challenges of vagueness and overbreadth.[227] Early on, *Schneider v State*,[228] in 1939, spelled out that a blanket ban on handbilling was

[223] The commercial speech jurisprudence of the Supreme Court is somewhat fluid. A specific commercial speech test was first announced in *Central Hudson Gas and Electric Corp v Public Service Commission*, 447 US 557, 566 (1980), and stated the following steps: (1) The First Amendment protects commercial speech only if that speech concerns lawful activity and is not misleading. A restriction on otherwise protected commercial speech is valid only if it (2) seeks to implement a substantial governmental interest, (3) directly advances that interest, and (4) reaches no further than necessary to accomplish the given objective. This test was restated in *Metromedia Inc v City of San Diego*, 453 US 490, 507 (1981), but later cases might have actually strengthened the test. See *44 Liquormart Inc v Rhode Island*, 517 US 484 (1996), and then *US v United Foods*, 533 US 405 (2001), and *Lorillard Tobacco v Reilly*, 533 US 525 (2001), not clarifying exactly what test should apply.

[224] *Metromedia Inc v City of San Diego*, 453 US 490 (1981).

[225] 'A fixed sign may be used to identify any piece of property and its owner. Any piece of property may carry or display religious symbols, commemorative plaques of recognized historical societies and organisations, signs carrying news items or telling the time or temperature, signs erected in discharge of any governmental function, or temporary political campaign signs'. Ibid, 514.

[226] Ibid, 510.

[227] See, in general, Randall J Cude, 'Beauty and the Well-Drawn Ordinance: Avoiding Vagueness and Overbreadth Challenges to Municipal Aesthetic Regulations' (1998) 6 *Journal of Law and Policy* 853.

[228] *Schneider v State*, 308 US 147 (1939).

unconstitutional, as those who actually littered should be sanctioned and not those who expressed their views via handbills. Later on, unbridled discretion of the mayor in issuing newsrack permits resulted in unconstitutionality in 1988, as newsracks were considered being included under dissemination of newspapers (thus, ideas).[229] Basically, the prior nature and the discretion required strict scrutiny notwithstanding that 'manner' regulation is normally subject to less strict standards.[230] For example, in 1984 in the case of *Members of City Council of City of Los Angeles v Taxpayers for Vincent*[231] the court upheld a ban on posting signs on public property (slogan of a political candidate on utility poles). The decisive argument in the judgment applying a merged *O'Brien* content neutrality standard seems to be that the ban on signs on public property—unlike the ban on handbilling in *Schneider v State*—leaves open ample alternative modes of communication. That means that a municipality cannot shut down all means of expression, thus *Metromedia* also needs to be read in this light. Nonetheless, in which case there are 'no ample alternative means' and what the standard is for comparing 'alternatives' appear increasingly opaque, just as the question of the relationship between the substantial interest pursued and the means applied. The following two seminal, but heavily criticised, cases helped to clarify the doctrine applicable to 'content-neutrally regulated symbolic speech'.

Heffron v ISKCON,[232] in 1981, was about a 12-day state fair where solicitation of donation, and sale and distribution of literature were only allowed from rented booths. The International Society of Krishna Consciousness, Inc (ISKCON) asserted that the ban would prevent them from practicing Sankirtan, a ritual of going to the streets and distributing or selling literature and soliciting donations, claiming infringement of their speech rights (but not accommodation under free exercise). The majority found the rule constitutional, while Justices Brennan and Blackmun wrote in partial dissents that the ban on distribution of literature violated free speech for being not narrowly tailored to substantial interests of crowd control or fraud prevention.[233] The test applied by the court itself sounded the same, but the majority has not taken into account at all that simply distributing leaflets surely does not hinder the flow of people any more

[229] *City of Lakewood v Plain Dealer Publishing Co*, 486 US 750 (1988).

[230] Therefore, newsracks possibly can be banned altogether. See, *Globe Newspaper Co v Beacon Hill Architectural Commission*, 100 F 3d 175 (1st Cir 1996), as cited by Cude, 'Beauty', above n 227, 883, fn 114.

[231] *Members of City Council of City of Los Angeles v Taxpayers for Vincent*, 466 US 789, 812 (1984).

[232] *Heffron v International Society for Krishna Consciousness*, 452 US 640 (1981).

[233] Brennan J thought solicitation and sale could be restricted to fixed places in order to prevent fraudulent activites, while Blackmun J found the exchanging moves involved in solicitation and sales raise special crowd control concerns, 452 US 640, 657 (Brennan J), 452 US 640, 665 (Blackmun J).

than other allowed activities, such as people being stopped by a speech or other performance. Thus, the narrow tailoring is certainly not as narrow as understood normally in fundamental rights doctrine.

An even more problematic decision related to sleeping in a park as a way of political protest came in 1984. In *Clark v Community for Creative Non-Violence*[234] (CCNV) an NGO, highlighting the plight of the homeless, staged a protest in areas of central Washington DC such as the Mall and Lafayette Park, both under the management of the National Park Service. The use of the parks can be regulated by such means as conform to the fundamental purpose of the parks, which is[235]

> to conserve the scenery and the natural and historic objects and the wild life therein ... in such manner and by such means as will leave them unimpaired for the enjoyment of future generations.

According to park regulations, camping was not allowed except in designated areas, none of which were in Lafayette Park or the Mall. Camping included sleeping, making preparations to sleep, storing personal belongings, making fires, etc but also the reasonable appearance of camping, independent of the intent of the participants. CCNV was permitted to install 20 tents in Lafayette Park and 40 tents in the Mall, two symbolic tent cities, and to stage a 24-hour protest, but protestors were not allowed to sleep in the tents. Protestors claimed sleeping was an inherent part of the expression, and thus should be allowed. An extremely divided Court of Appeals—the bench included Judges Ginsburg and Scalia, on different sides—ruled in favour of the protestors. The US Supreme Court reversed the decision. Justice White 'assumed' that the sleeping would be expressive conduct, and relied on *O'Brien*, *Taxpayers for Vincent*, and public forum cases, and after all applied a mixture of these tests, as is regular in these cases. The regulation was certainly 'content-neutral', the majority not finding it objectionable that the sleeping ban was actually introduced after the same NGO staged protests elsewhere in national parks. The substantial interest furthered—according to the majority—is 'maintaining the parks in the heart of our Capital in an attractive and intact condition',[236] clearly an 'aesthetic interest'. The regulation was found narrowly tailored to the further attractive and intact condition of the parks, dismissing argument of protestors that if a 24-hour vigil is allowed, then the ban on sleeping only incrementally furthers said interest. Justice White replied that the First Amendment does not require the Park Service to allow the 24-hour vigil in tents accommodating 150 people in the first place, let alone sleeping. Also, he dismisses the wish of sleeping for being largely only 'facilitative'

[234] *Clark v Community for Creative Non-Violence*, 468 US 288 (1984).
[235] 39 Stat 535, as amended, 16 USC § 1, as cited by *Clark at* 468 US 288, 290.
[236] 468 US 288, 296.

to the demonstration as the organisers wrote in the permit application that without hot meals and sleeping spaces homeless people would not be likely to show up. Referring to *Heffron* he maintained that the validity of such regulations is not to be judged 'solely by reference to the demonstration at hand',[237] in other words the sleeping ban is necessary because otherwise several other groups would also want to sleep in core areas, and that would present 'difficult problems for the Park Service'.[238] This appears to be an argument against dissenting Justice Marshall who emphasises that the First Amendment cannot be abridged in order to avert what he calls 'imposter' uses,[239] in this case sleeping not as expression, but just simply sleeping. Justice Marshall thinks such uses need be prevented by means other than abridging political protest at central sites of American history. That this does not persuade the majority is a consequence of the loosened test applied by Justice White:[240]

> If the Government has a legitimate interest in ensuring that the National Parks are adequately protected, which we think it has, and if the parks would be more exposed to harm without the sleeping prohibition than with it, the ban is safe from invalidation under the First Amendment as a reasonable regulation of the manner in which a demonstration may be carried out.

This basically reduces the test applicable to manner regulation to a rational basis test, a highly deferential standard. Already in 1987 Geoffrey Stone criticised these standards for being too deferential,[241] and the critique since then has only intensified. Still, the test remains the same, and, as explained above, in *Ward v RAR* Justice Kennedy made explicit that 'narrowly tailored' does not mean 'least intrusive' in the TMP doctrine.[242]

Clark and *Ward* were cited in the decision affirming the ban on *marching at all* in New York City against the nearing Iraq War in 2003. The protest thus turned stationary, not being able to march past the UN building, among others, for unsubstantiated fear of a terrorist attack.[243] *Clark*, though not exactly applicable, was also cursorily discussed and affirmed by the Supreme Court in the 2011 funeral protest case.[244]

[237] 468 US 288, 297.

[238] Ibid.

[239] 468 US 288, 306, dissenting opinion of Marshall J in which Brennan J joins.

[240] Ibid, 297. (Majority opinion).

[241] Geoffrey R Stone, 'Content-neutral Regulations' (1987) 54 *University of Chicago Law Review* 46, 79.

[242] *Ward v Rock against Racism*, 491 US 781, 798–99 (1989).

[243] *United for Peace and Justice v City of New York*, 243 F Supp 2d 19, 25 (SDNY 2003). For an excellent analysis, see Nick Suplina, 'Crowd Control: The Troubling Mix of First Amendment Law, Political Demonstrations, and Terrorism' (2005) 73 *George Washington Law Review* 395.

[244] *Snyder v Phelps*, 131 S Ct 1207, 1217 (2011).

Finally, to add to the aesthetic puzzle, a 1994 case needs to be referred to which applied the content-neutral test and found a violation, a rare occurrence. In *Ladue v Gilleo*,[245] the US Supreme Court declared a city ordinance banning residential signs (on *private* property) unconstitutional by finding that no ample alternative substitutes were available, and intimating that the use *of an entire medium* was foreclosed.[246] Residential signs are distinct as they provide information about the speaker's identity, 'an important component of many attempts to persuade',[247] as they are cheap and convenient, and as they are particularly apt to address the neighbours, an audience 'that could not be reached nearly as well by other means'.[248] The court also stresses that 'individual liberty in the home' mandates a special treatment.

Ladue thus merges several rationales, and it is not quite clear which one would be self-standing. Seen in the light of the other TMP decisions, I would think most important here was the distinctiveness of the home,[249] a concern not normally present in relation to freedom of assembly, only as a limit. Still, the court emphasises that the case law strongly dismisses foreclosure of an entire medium,[250] mentioning early cases on distribution of pamphlets and handbills.

Therefore, *Ladue* reinforces that activities more relevant for my purposes, that is handbilling, distribution of literature, etc on the street, are each a

[245] Margaret Gilleo, a Ladue resident placed on her front lawn in December 1990 a 24 by 36 inch sign printed with the words, 'Say No to War in the Persian Gulf, Call Congress Now'. The sign was removed by someone and, the police, when asked to help, advised Ms Gilleo that such signs violated a city ordinance. *Ladue v Gilleo*, 512 US 43 (1994).

[246] O'Connor J concurs by contending the ordinance's list of exceptions renders it content-based, but agrees that even if it were content-neutral, it would be still unconstitutional.

[247] Aristotle, *Rhetoric*, Book 1, ch 2, in M Adler (ed), *Great Books of the Western World, Encyclopedia Britannica*, 2nd edn (1990) Vol 8, 595, as cited by 512 US 56.

[248] 512 US 57.

[249] This seems to be the view of another commentator, Jason R Burt, 'Speech Interests Inherent in the Location of Billboards and Signs: A Method for Unweaving the Tangled *Web of Metromedia, Inc v City of San Diego*' (2006) *Brigham Young University Law Review* 473, 499 *et seq*.

[250] 'Our prior decisions have voiced particular concern with laws that foreclose an entire medium of expression. Thus, we have held invalid ordinances that completely banned the distribution of pamphlets within the municipality, *Lovell v City of Griffin*, 303 US 444, 451–52, 58 S Ct 666, 669, 82 L Ed 949 (1938); handbills on the public streets, *Jamison v Texas*, 318 US 413, 416, 63 S Ct 669, 672, 87 L Ed 869 (1943); the door-to-door distribution of literature, *Martin v City of Struthers*, 319 US 141, 145–49, 63 S Ct 862, 864–66, 87 L Ed 1313 (1943); *Schneider v State (Town of Irvington)*, 308 US 147, 164–65, 60 S Ct 146, 152, 84 L Ed 155 (1939), and live entertainment, *Schad v Mount Ephraim*, 452 US 61, 75–76, 101 S Ct 2176, 2186, 68 L Ed 2d 671 (1981). See also *Frisby v Schultz*, 487 US 474, 486, 108 S Ct 2495, 2503, 101 L Ed 2d 420 (1988) (picketing focused upon individual residence is "fundamentally different from more generally directed means of communication that may not be completely banned in residential areas"). Although prohibitions foreclosing entire media may be completely free of content or viewpoint discrimination, the danger they pose to the freedom of speech is readily apparent—by eliminating a common means of speaking, such measures can suppress too much speech'. *Ladue v Gilleo*, 512 US 55.

separate *medium* and thus cannot be fully banned even by content-neutral regulations. However, *Ladue* does not affect the loose approach as to what counts as *alternative channel* or *means* of communication, as settled in the previously discussed decisions.

To sum up, aesthetic regulations in the United States can often limit freedom of expression and assembly in ways which do not seem justified not only to me, but to American commentators. Vagueness and overbreadth sometimes can be serious limits against references to aesthetics, just as content-based restrictions will not regularly survive constitutional scrutiny. However, if an ordinance is framed and applied in a content-neutral fashion, but for special cases including foreclosure of an entire medium, it has a good chance of survival in an ever loosening review by the Supreme Court.

B. Germany

In Germany the relation of expression and aesthetic regulation arose in the 1970s in the issue of littering.

Concerning handbill littering a decision of the Federal Administrative Court is of importance.[251] The Berlin law on city cleaning required an official preliminary certificate for the distribution of handbills (precisely: *Werbemateriel*, ie advertising material). The Court (and all the lower courts) found the *application* of the law by police reached over to constitutionally protected expression especially that no exception was granted to handbills with political content. The Court emphasises that not only the opinion itself, but also the means and forms of its expression, are protected by article 5 of the Basic Law. The law clearly interferes with article 5, and it is not justified by any grounds listed in article 5 II. The aim of the law is solely the prevention of pollution of the streets by castaway paper. The concern in effect is an aesthetic one; the law does not protect, for example, health. Promotion of street cleanliness is not a value as important as freedom of expression and thus it cannot justify restrictions on expression. What is more, the *prior* permit is required only to better prepare the authorities on how to clean the streets *afterwards*, a fact which belies that the restriction meets compelling needs.

The GFCC issued a decision similar to that in relation to handbill distribution in 1991.[252] An association founded by members of the Scientology Church protested against 'inhuman treatment' of psychiatric and drug patients by distributing handbills in Hamburg pedestrian streets. The district authority prohibited the distribution by arguing that the members

[251] BVerwG, 7 June 1978, 7 C 45/74 (Berlin), *Strassenbenutzung für politische Werbung*.
[252] BVerfG, 1 BvR 1377/91, 18 October 1991.

have pursued economic activity, which requires a specific prior permission and payment. The OVG (Higher Administrative Court) found the requirement served to ensure a safe and smooth flow of traffic, and thus, though it interfered with freedom of opinion, as a general law in the sense of article 5 II (GG), it was justified. The GFCC found the value of safe and smooth flow of traffic was generally not sufficient to counterbalance a *prior* restraint on freedom of opinion in the form of a permit. Especially unwarranted appears the claim with regard to pedestrian zones and other streets with low traffic, as it is possible to evade the distributor. In a typical turn, however, the court finds safe and smooth flow of *pedestrian* traffic a legitimate aim, but still one which cannot be proportionally pursued by way of a prior permission on the exercise of freedom of expression.[253] Thus, it can be more or less safely concluded that handbill distribution in Germany cannot be made dependent on prior approval, except maybe where it causes real safety or health hazards (eg on a very busy traffic line, or on a highway, etc). Certainly, again, the applicable constitutional standard is the general proportionality.

The GFCC reviewed the question of constitutionality of *fees* within imposition of conditions on assemblies in 2007.[254] It stated that such a fee can only be exacted if conditions of imposing condition on assembly are met; that is public safety or order is directly endangered and cannot be averted by milder means. This implies that general street cleaning regulations are only applicable to the extent the constitutional conditions of freedom of assembly are upheld, proportionality requirements apply. Also, the GFCC confirmed individual responsibility in the sense that the organiser cannot be held liable for deeds outside his or her circle of action, thus, in principle cannot be made to pay for the litter and other damages caused by participants. This now seems to be accepted for the situation where authorities would impose the fee as part of a condition on the assembly.[255]

Earlier case law of ordinary courts, for example two decisions[256] of the Federal Administrative Court from 1989, differ, however, from the view of the GFCC in relation to imposition of compensation for cleaning the streets after or during the assembly by city services. The Administrative High Court notably treated street cleaning regulations as generally applicable laws which do not interfere with freedom of assembly, as their regulatory scope is different. Thus, it is not settled yet whether cleaning fees or compensation imposed *not as part of a condition* should also fulfil criteria of direct danger to public order or safety, and individual responsibility. I argue

[253] The rest of the opinion deals with rule of law issues not relevant for my purposes.

[254] BVerfG, 1 BvR 943/02, 25 October 2007.

[255] Eg VGH Mannheim, 21 January 2009, 1 S 1678/07.

[256] BVerwG, 6 September 1988, 1 C 71/86 (Münster), BVerwG, 6 September 1988, 1 C 15/86 (Mannheim).

it should, because although the GFCC refers to article 15 of the Federal Assembly Law on conditions on assemblies, the interpretation of that very article is rooted in article 8 of the GG.[257]

A further issue arose in Germany in relation to information desks. In a case which went to the GFCC, four persons installed an information stand on a street in order to distribute political message.[258] They had not applied for a special use permit, and thus were fined. The GFCC has not taken the case, reasoning sparsely that the regulation is a justified interference with freedom of expression as long as the fee is not prohibitive, and the discretion not unlimited. The right to freedom of assembly is not even affected—to install information desks is not covered by the right—thus it can be regulated by general laws other than the law on assembly.

C. United Kingdom

In the United Kingdom, the same section 5 of the POA 1986 that was applicable in *Percy v DPP* to 'flag desecration',[259] was also applied to placards and posters. To recall: the section criminalises causing harassment, distress, or alarm by threatening, abusive, insulting behaviour, words, or signs. Conviction for holding a sign saying 'Stop immorality', 'Stop Homosexuality' and 'Stop Lesbianism' was upheld in *Hammond v DPP*[260] as discussed above.[261] The case of *Norwood v DPP*[262] was about a BNP (British Nationalist Party) politician displaying a poster from his own window stating 'Islam out of Britain' and 'Protect the British people' next to a photo of the 9/11 twin towers in flame, and a crescent and star surrounded by a prohibition sign. His conviction was upheld on the basis that the display was not an intemperate criticism of the tenets of Islam, but an 'insulting attack' on its followers.[263] However, these cases do not appear to turn on the modes and means employed, neither on directly perceived aesthetic harms, but on the substantial message.

[257] Interestingly, a comment on fee paying and freedom of assembly highlighting the difference between constitutional and administrative ultimate courts does not explicitly express a similar stance. Holger Greve and Fabian Quast, 'Gebührenerhebung versus Versammlungsfreiheit' (2009) *Neue Zeitschrift fur Verwaltungsrecht* 500.

[258] BVerfG, 1 BvR 306/76. 22 December 1976.

[259] See above, text accompanying nn 101–04.

[260] *Hammond v DPP* [2004] EWHC 69 (Admin).

[261] See Ch 5, text accompanying nn 105–06.

[262] *Norwood v DPP* [2003] EWHC 1564 (Admin).

[263] Ch 5, text accompanying nn 107–08.

D. European Court of Human Rights

The ECtHR, similarly to the UK courts, has so far not developed a doctrine of content-neutrality in the sense of a lesser standard applicable to modal restrictions, and it has not dealt with such claims raised by governments in any significant decision reflected in the literature. Two decisions on means of protest exemplify this, as there is no discussion on whether the specific means by which the expression is pursued requires the application of lower standards. An (otherwise important) leaflet decision is *Incal v Turkey* where a politician of a later dissolved Turkish Kurdish party was jailed for a leaflet protesting against 'state terror' towards the Kurdish people and, partly, Turkish people or proletarians. The Turkish Government was unsurprisingly unsuccessful in making the European Commission on Human Rights and the ECtHR believe that to portray a group as suffering discrimination is incitement to violence.[264]

However, the *Norwood* case, discussed above in relation to the United Kingdom, was declared inadmissible by the ECtHR, finding article 17 ECHR applicable, as[265]

> the words and images on the poster amounted to a public expression of attack on all Muslims in the United Kingdom. Such a general, vehement attack against a religious group, linking the group as a whole with a grave act of terrorism, is incompatible with the values proclaimed and guaranteed by the Convention, notably tolerance, social peace and non-discrimination.

This is a very clear content(even viewpoint)-discrimination, earlier only applicable with regard to denial of facts, largely as a form of racial hate speech,[266] as was discussed above in relation to dignity.[267] A speculation that the extension comes in a case related not to verbal, spoken expression, but to a largely symbolic one because of a tendency to grant lesser protection to that seems ungrounded, at least so far.

[264] According to the Turkish Government: 'Through its aggressive and provocative language the leaflet in question had been likely to incite citizens of "Kurdish" origin to believe that they suffered from discrimination and that, as victims of a "special war", they were justified in acting in self-defence against the authorities by setting up "neighbourhood committees"'. *Incal v Turkey*, Application no 22678/93, Judgment of 9 June 1998, 29 EHRR 449, § 44.

[265] *Norwood v UK*, Application no 23131/03, Decision on admissibility, 16 November 2004.

[266] Ian Leigh, 'Damned if they Do, Damned if they Don't: The European Court of Human Rights and the Protection of Religion from Attack' (2011) 17 *Res Publica* 55, 63.

[267] Ch 5, text accompanying nn 116–27.

8

Restrictions on the Place

PLACE, SIMILARLY TO time and manner, has also entertained the imagination of protesters, legislators and courts. The fundamental cause of this particular attentiveness is simply the fact that places are full or filled with meaning, and thus act just like a theatrical setting which colours, enriches or reinforces a message, even to the extent of changing the meaning of the place itself. If you manage to change the meaning of a place, you have changed the identity of your people: it is the power of redefining, maybe the one true power one (or more, out of compromise) might ever have. No wonder it is so attractive.

In some cases the place has a commemorative meaning, as it reminds us of a specific historical event, either because historically it happened there, or because subsequently it became an official memorial site. Such protest-free sites have been widely designated around Europe especially in remembrance of the Holocaust, and against neo-Nazi demonstrations. In other (though sometimes overlapping) cases, the place has meaning because the object of protest, or the target of the request made by demonstrators lies there, such as governmental buildings, prisons, courts, residency of a public person, or even abortion clinics. Special cases have arisen in relation to cemeteries, and in the United States the term 'funeral protest' was even coined.

As a flipside, there are not only protest-free zones, but also protest-zones which designate the place for protest in an exclusive way, the most vivid memories of such being probably the speech pens in New York City before the Iraq War or the 'caging' of protestors in national conventions of the main US parties, but even next to diplomatic events of the global world.

Restrictions related to special places (or spaces even) are widespread in most of the examined jurisdictions and can be classified in several ways. As all activity covered by freedom of assembly takes up some public space, the whole book could be restructured along the criterion on restrictions on space. Reasons for preventing the use of specific (or less specific) places by assemblies are also extremely divergent across the jurisdictions. In the following text I will be concentrating on a more or less simple intuitive structure, putting together first residence, cemetery, hospital and other more private-oriented places such as airports and malls, then places relating to the state in its public power function, and then, thirdly, memorial sites as sites designated for assemblies, just not the ones banned, and, finally, the speech pen or cage phenomenon.

I. PRIVATE PUBLIC PLACES

A. Cemeteries

Protest in cemeteries shows in an extreme way the many conflicting values that can be involved in the context of freedom of assembly. A cemetery is normally a quiet, private place dedicated to the remembrance of close friends and relatives in a certain atmosphere of sadness and restraint contemplating the tragedy of life and death. A funeral is an event designed to make death acceptable and normal, so one can go about their everyday life. Protest, to the contrary is a public, loud, agitated event, which does not aim at normalising, but at changing and eliminating the painful. In the cemetery the central feeling is grief, in a protest it is grievance.

Still, a cemetery might become politicised in several ways which then opens up an occasion for the exercise of freedom of assembly. Commemoration, official or social, also often takes place in cemeteries, which otherwise function as natural places for exercising rights of privacy and, importantly, religion. Two European cases straightforwardly show this potential of the ritual around the dead, while the American case is a more atypical exploitation of the same potential.

The ECtHR dealt with cemetery protest in *Öllinger v Austria*,[1] and found a compromised solution. In the case, Austrian authorities banned a protest demonstration against Comradeship IV, an organisation mainly of former SS-members commemorating the death of SS soldiers in the Second World War on All Saints' Day at the Salzburg Municipal Cemetery. The Court rejected that article 9 ECHR rights of cemetery-goers would prevail over the article 11 ECHR rights of Öllinger, a Green MP protesting against the crimes of the SS. Though the Government tried to argue, the ECtHR rejected that the dignity and quiet required in a cemetery absolutely prevented Öllinger from protesting, especially since he and his fellow protestors had organised a silent event, without chanting or banners. The ECtHR noted that there was no previous violence (only heated discussion at other such occasions), neither would have been the protest noisy or in other ways directed against cemetery-goers' beliefs. *A contrario* then, freedom of religion is possible to be involved in cemetery protest cases, and also being quiet and as we have seen, possibly not using banners, might be a permissible limit on such assemblies.

The German Constitutional Court (GFCC) also handed down a ruling recently in the context of assembly and cemeteries. This time, the victims of the 1945 Dresden allied bombings were commemorated by the city

[1] *Öllinger v Austria*, 46 EHRR 38, Application no 76900/01, Judgment of 29 June 2006. See Ch 3, text accompanying nn 202–07.

of Dresden and a civil society organisation in a cemetery, and counter-protestors showing banners were fined for violating the dignity of the place. The GFCC found that the counter-protest was protected by freedom of assembly. The court pointed out that, in general, the cemetery is a place which is destined only for specific, limited purposes, and is in general not to be considered a public place open for general communication. However, in this specific case, the cemetery was voluntarily opened up for communication by the city, thus it was rightly used by protestors as a place for communicating their views on the commemoration. The court emphasises that the protestors reacted to the communicative event created or allowed by the city, and that their protest was silent.[2] It is unlikely, therefore, that protest on a different topic, let alone assemblies in cemeteries in general (ie which are not specifically opened up by the state for other communicative events) could not be rather easily restricted.

Partly similar concerns, and similar answers, have arisen in *Snyder v Phelps*,[3] decided in 2011 by the US Supreme Court. Phelps was the founder of Westboro Baptist Church which had picketed funerals in the previous 20 years, protesting against various issues, such as the American tolerance of homosexuality, or the Catholic Church's paedophile scandals. Basically, the congregation appears to believe that God is killing Americans as a punishment for their sins. By 2008, the Church, consisting of around 75 members, mostly relatives, managed to irritate the American public so much that the federal government and 41 states had adopted laws restricting funeral protests.[4] Snyder was the father of the late Matthew Snyder, a soldier killed in Iraq. Westboro conducted a picketing on the day of Matthew Snyder's funeral. The picketing started 30 minutes before the funeral, and was on a public plot adjacent to a public street about a 1,000ft from the church in which the funeral was to be held. When Snyder drove to the funeral, he saw the top of the picketers' banners, but did not become aware about the content of their message until later when he saw a news broadcast on the Westboro protest. Snyder claimed that the Westboro protest amounted to intentional infliction of emotional distress and intrusion upon seclusion and amounted to a civil conspiracy. The Supreme Court assumed without deciding[5] the tortious nature of Westboro's speech, but nonetheless found that the First Amendment shielded Phelps from tort liability. The most important concerns were the following. The location of the protest was public land adjacent to a public street, a par excellence traditional public forum,

[2] BVerfG, 1 BvR 980/13, 20 June 2014.

[3] *Snyder v Phelps*, 131 S Ct 1207 (2011).

[4] Christina E Wells, 'Privacy and Funeral Protest' (2008) 87 *North Carolina Law Review* 151, 159.

[5] 131 S Ct 1207, 1214, fn 2.

the sort of place on which speech enjoys highest constitutional protection.[6] Also, speech on public matters, as the court found Phelps' to be, is again at the core of the First Amendment. Dispositive in deciding if a speech is of private or of public concern is 'content, form, and context as revealed by the whole record'.[7] As the content was clearly of public concern, it did not matter whether—as Snyder tried to argue—the context, that is the funeral of his son, was private. Even so, the majority opinion by Chief Justice Roberts goes on to quote *Clark v CCNV*, as stating that such speech of public concern, in a traditional public forum, can be subject to reasonable time, manner and place regulation, that is content-neutral regulation. However, as Phelps' picket was out of sight of those in the church, it was not interfering with the funeral itself. Thus, any objections to the protest were clearly content-, even viewpoint-based, and as such, impermissible.[8] The captive audience claim also did not stand because of the distance of the protest from the funeral.[9] The decision is not as simple as it appears. Justice Breyer added a concurring opinion emphasising the narrow holding of the court, and Justice Alito was the only one to dissent. Justice Alito based his dissent in a broader context: he also included more personally assaultive language by Westboro stated in a press release and online post before and after the picketing itself, and claimed these also reinforced the equally personally attacking nature of the banners at the picket itself. Actionable speech should not be immunised just because it is interspersed with protected speech.[10] The majority counters that these pre- and post-picketing communications were outside the issue in the case as Snyder did not rely on them.

These two perspectives vividly demonstrate how hard choices are necessarily made by lawyers when interpreting what actually is meant by 'an expression'. Justice Alito undoubtedly has a point when he emphasises that unprotected speech of private matter does not get protected just because it is infused with matters of public concern. Also, I tend to agree with him on the point that, actually in the case, Matthew Snyder's death was used to create public (including media) attention for Westboro Baptist Church. Death and especially the ritual around it are symbolic moments easily exploitable for expressing political views, or promoting one's interests, as we have just seen on both sides of the *Öllinger* case. On my part, however, I would still allow for the protest to go ahead as it did, without interfering with the funeral. Nonetheless, the tortious press release and post-picket online communication should remain actionable independent of the protest, though

[6] 'Such space occupies a special position in terms of First Amendment protection', 131 S Ct 1207, 1218, citing *United States v Grace*, 461 US 171, 180 (1983).

[7] 131 S Ct 1207, 1216, internal citations omitted.

[8] Ibid, 1219.

[9] Ibid, 1220.

[10] Ibid, 1227, dissenting opinion of Alito J.

I doubt the torts would pass constitutional muster, unless a new jurisprudence emerges.[11] True, the Snyders were clearly private persons, and they should have been able to remain so, hence I take *Hustler v Falwell*[12] as being clearly inapplicable. I think such an approach would not mean that civility (as opposed to intrusion-based privacy interests), so characteristically and importantly rejected in classic American jurisprudence, would override free speech rights.[13] However, the possible torts at hand were not defamatory: not false statements of facts, but offensive or outrageous. Thus, jurisprudence allowing for speech restrictions for reasons of negligent false defamatory statements of private persons, such as *Gertz v Robert Welch,*[14] does not apply here either. Outrage or feelings of rage or hurt are probably unavoidably categories of speech content which cannot be a basis for restriction for the classic reasons.[15]

Snyder v Phelps has been the only case that the Supreme Court decided specifically in relation to funeral protests. Lower courts seem to agree that (unlike surrounding public streets) the cemetery itself is a non-public forum, and for the protection of mourners, buffer zones might be constitutional if the funeral protest would closely coincide in time with a funeral.[16] 'Unreasonable' and 'interfering' sounds and images might be constitutionally prohibited according to some courts, but a blanket ban is unconstitutional for overbreadth and lack of narrow tailoring.[17] Also, a *floating* buffer zone within 300ft of any funeral procession was found unconstitutionally overbroad in one case.[18] The Supreme Court denied *certiorari* in a case where the Eighth Circuit found that criminalising protest activities 'in front of or about' funeral locations would likely turn out 'not narrowly tailored' or 'facially overbroad' on closer inspection.[19] Thus, in summary, it seems that in the US intermediate scrutiny applies to funeral protest restrictions if the regulation is

[11] On the difficulty, but necessity of sooner or later creating an applicable constitutional rule separating public and private in such cases, see Jeffrey Shulman, 'Epic Considerations: The Speech that the Supreme Court Would Not Hear in *Snyder v Phelps*' (2011) *Cardozo Law Review* 35.

[12] *Hustler Magazine, Inc v Falwell*, 485 US 46 (1988).

[13] The fear and its implications are very aptly shown (and supported) by Wells, 'Privacy', above n 4.

[14] *Gertz v Robert Welch, Inc*, 418 US 323 (1974).

[15] For more discussion, see Eugene Volokh, 'Freedom of Speech and the Intentional Infliction of Emotional Distress Tort' (2010) *Cardozo Law Review* 300.

[16] *Phelps-Roper v Heineman*, 720 F Supp 2d 1090 (D Neb 2010), as cited by Fern L Kletter, 'Actions by or Against Individuals or Groups Protesting or Picketing at Funerals' (2008) 40 *American Law Reports Annotated, Sixth Series* 375, § 6.5.

[17] *McQueary v Stumbo*, 453 F Supp 2d 975 (ED Ky 2006) as cited by Rodney A Smolla, *Smolla and Nimmer on Freedom of Speech*, vol 1, § 5:11.50 [online update March 2011].

[18] *Phelps-Roper v Taft*, 523 F Supp 2d 612 (ND Ohio 2007), judgment affirmed in part on other grounds, 539 F 3d 356 (6th Cir 2008) as cited by Kletter, 'Actions by or Against Individuals', above n 16, § 8.

[19] *Phelps-Roper v Nixon*, 545 F 3d 685 (8th Cir 2008), cert denied, 129 S Ct 2865, 174 L Ed 2d 578 (2009), as cited by Kletter, 'Actions by or Against Individuals', above n 16, § 7.

content-neutral, but courts tend to exert a rigorous version of the scrutiny, especially in relation to overbroad statutes. It is not clarified exactly how big a buffer zone is constitutional. The logic of the decisions is not simply spatial, but rather visual and aural: funeral-goers can be constitutionally protected against even simply 'unreasonable' images and sounds because of their privacy interest in non-intrusion. The problem is that 'unreasonable' sounds like a content-based criterion, at least in relation to images. Here again the general approach is that the eyes can be averted, while the ear cannot. This approach has a general validity, though there might be cases where extreme visual nuisance might create a captive audience, especially in closed places where one cannot avoid going there.

B. Clinics

Abortion clinics have been a similar target of protest outraging parts of the American public, and had resulted in intense legislation and litigation, but the height of the litigation preceded the funeral protest issue. Therefore, some similarities will be easily recognisable in this—to a large extent—earlier jurisprudence. One difference is, however, that abortion clinic protests have clearly taken place in traditional or quintessential public forums, while funeral protests would sometimes occur on the territory of the cemetery itself. The jurisprudence for abortion clinic protests appears quite settled. The court in *Madsen v Women's Health Center*[20] struck down a 300ft no approach zone around the clinic and residences of doctors performing abortions, a ban on displaying 'images observable' from the clinic, and a 36ft buffer zone on private property to the north and west of the clinic. Meanwhile the court upheld the injunction as to the 36ft buffer zone around clinic entrances and driveways, and the limited noise regulation as these passed a heightened[21] content-neutral test and did not burden more speech than necessary to accomplish the 'significant governmental interests in protecting a pregnant woman's freedom to seek lawful medical or counseling services, public safety and order, free flow of traffic, property rights,

[20] *Madsen v Women's Health Center*, 512 US 753 (1994).

[21] There has been disagreement among the justices about the applicable standard. Rehnquist CJ, writing for the majority, claims injunctions are more dangerous to liberty than statutes as they can be selectively issued, thus a somewhat more stringent test is applicable, where no more speech than necessary can be burdened to further a significant governmental interest. Scalia J, dissenting, finds the injunction both not content-neutral and a prior restraint, and thus would apply strict scrutiny, while Stevens J thinks injunctions pose a lesser risk to free speech than statutes as the former are issued as a consequence, or punishment for prior unlawful action. For an analysis, see Tiffany Keast, 'Injunction Junction. Enjoining Free Speech after *Madsen, Schenck*, and *Hill*' (2004) 12 *American University Journal of Gender, Social Policy and the Law* 273, 293 ff.

and residential privacy'.[22] *Schenck v Pro-Choice Network*, a second major decision on the abortion protest controversy similarly upheld a fixed buffer zone regulation (15ft from clinic doorways, driveways, and driveway entrances), but struck down so-called floating buffer zones requiring protestors to stay 15ft from people and vehicles entering and leaving clinics.[23] In *Hill v Colorado*,[24] in a somewhat different fashion, the court upheld an 8ft floating buffer zone, defined as knowingly approaching another person within 8ft, unless such other person consented,[25]

> for the purpose of passing a leaflet or handbill to, displaying a sign to, or engaging in oral protest, education, or counseling with such other person in the public way or sidewalk area within a radius of one hundred feet from any entrance door to a health care facility.

The court, in a much criticised opinion, upheld the floating buffer zone, again finding the regulation content-neutral, thus applying a *Ward*-type[26] loosened test. Critics and dissenters would argue that oral protest, education or counselling are categories of speech, and as such, are content-based. What is more, as *pro-choice* activists would likely get consent for such activities (supporting the right to abortion) next to abortion clinics, the regulation is even viewpoint-based. In any case, referring to the loose *Ward* test, the majority remains unwilling to look into evidence hinting that the purpose of the regulation was indeed discriminatory against one type of speaker, and was not simply motivated by privacy and health interests of hospital-goers. That the Supreme Court does not investigate legislative motive in free speech (and all the more so in speech-plus like scenarios) cases, is an unfortunate heritage of *O'Brien*, a self-limitation of the court not present in free exercise, establishment or equal protection cases.[27] Both Justices Scalia and Kennedy, in separate dissents, argued that already on its face (banning protest-type attitudes only, not, eg gratification) the regulation was content-based.[28] The majority per Justice Stevens emphasised that it is only the place that is regulated, and it in effect is only 'a minor place restriction on an extremely broad category of communications with unwilling

[22] *Madsen v Women's Health Center*, 512 US 753, 767 ff (1994).

[23] *Schenck v Pro-Choice Network of Western New York*, 519 US 357 (1997).

[24] *Hill v Colorado*, 503 US 703 (2000).

[25] Ibid, 707.

[26] *Ward v Rock against Racism*, 491 US 781 (1989). See Ch 7, text accompanying nn 203–10.

[27] See *United States v O'Brien*, 391 US 367, 383 ff; *Washington v Davis*, 426 US 229, 242 (1976); and *Church of Lukumi Babalu Aye, Inc v Hialeah*, 508 US 520, 534 (1993) as cited by Jamin B Raskin and Clark L Leblanc, 'Disfavored Speech about Favored Rights: *Hill v Colorado*, the Vanishing Public Forum and the Need for an Objective Speech Discrimination Test' (2001) 51 *American University Law Review* 179, 218, fns 255–58.

[28] See Scalia J dissenting at 503 US 742 ff and Kennedy J dissenting at 503 US 766 ff, or Raskin and Leblanc, ibid, 212 ff.

listeners'.[29] I find this labelling quite unsatisfactory as where else can one find targets for anti-abortion speech for the purposes of face-to-face communication other than around abortion clinics? Clearly, here place is part of the communication. In addition, it is not in accordance with general First Amendment standards to impose the obligation of getting consent for a speaker. Normally, nobody has a right not to be talked to. Communication, on the other hand, is a dynamic interactive process where actually you can change your mind about whether you are willing to listen or not. Part of the communication is to persuade someone to listen to what you say. I find the consent provision wholly vague and ignorant or disregarding of how everyday talk actually happens.

That health interests might justify restrictions on speech has been settled already in *Madsen*, but the very mediated connection between speech and rising stress levels and thereby increased health 'risks' is even more distant in *Hill* as it was not based on previous unlawful action. Also, if feelings normally do not justify restrictions on political speech—as both *Hustler* and *Snyder v Phelps* apparently affirm—then what indeed lies behind the reference to health needs to be thoroughly checked. That would require a strict scrutiny—an enquiry blocked by the Supreme Court in these cases by claiming content-neutrality. Thus, these cases demonstrate perfectly the way the categorisations as 'content-neutral' and 'place restriction' effectively prevent any meaningful discussion of countervailing values or interests in the abortion protest context. If abortion protests happen not 'in place', then content-neutrality arguments would have far less importance. Therefore, the abortion clinics controversy shows, in a palpable way, how originally speech-protective doctrines can be twisted to deny the right to assembly and protest, upholding regulations which would certainly fail the normal speech tests for at least overbreadth or vagueness, if not simply for illegitimate purpose of integrity of feelings. All this happening, when there is clearly a possibility under classic speech doctrines to prevent or punish physical obstruction, violence, coercion, threats or stalking which certainly have occurred in much of the abortion protest events. If one compares the funeral and the abortion protest jurisprudence, the different outcomes are striking. It remains to be seen how the funeral protests jurisprudence might evolve in the Supreme Court, but so far there is clearly a difference which can only be explained by a special sensitivity shown towards women seeking abortions and their doctors. It has to be seen that in the abortion clinics setting real persons are the target, while in the funeral protests cases a death is used as the opportunity to spread an ideological message, and thus, health risks cannot be involved per default.

[29] 503 US 703, 723.

C. Residence

Finally, the residential picketing issue is also partly an abortion related issue in the United States, but the case law originates in a civil rights protest around a mayor's home who did not support the busing of schoolchildren. The Supreme Court in *Carey v Brown,* struck down a ban on picketing around residences and dwellings because there was a content-based exception for labour picketing.[30] This decision has also spelled out very clearly that 'public streets and sidewalks in residential neighborhoods', were public places.[31] The less straightforward 1988 case of *Frisby v Schultz,*[32] arose out of a controversy where anti-abortion advocates picketed the home of a doctor performing abortions. In reaction, an ordinance was enacted banning residential picketing. The ban was judged content-neutral, narrowly construed by the Supreme Court (ie against the broad construction of lower courts, a rare move) to only ban focused picketing in front of one residence or dwelling, and not banning marching into residential neighbourhoods, or protesting, demonstrating there at large. The significant governmental interest in 'residential privacy' was described by the court in really elevated language, partly stemming from earlier case law, such as the following:[33]

> The State's interest in protecting the well-being, tranquility, and privacy of the home is certainly of the highest order in a free and civilized society. Our prior decisions have often remarked on the unique nature of the home, 'the last citadel of the tired, the weary, and the sick', and have recognized that 'Preserving the sanctity of the home, the one retreat to which men and women can repair to escape from the tribulations of their daily pursuits, is surely an important value'. One important aspect of residential privacy is protection of the unwilling listener. Although in many locations, we expect individuals simply to avoid speech they do not want to hear, the home is different. 'That we are often "captives" outside the sanctuary of the home and subject to objectionable speech ... does not mean we must be captives everywhere'. Instead, a special benefit of the privacy all citizens enjoy within their own walls, which the State may legislate to protect, is an ability to avoid intrusions.

Later, the court adds that[34] 'The resident is figuratively, and perhaps literally, trapped within the home, and because of the unique and subtle impact of such picketing is left with no ready means of avoiding the unwanted speech'.

Thus, even though the street in front of a 'home' is a public forum, the resident in his or her home can become a *captive audience* as a result of the

[30] *Carey v Brown*, 447 US 455 (1980).

[31] Ibid, 460–61.

[32] *Frisby v Schultz*, 487 US 474 (1988).

[33] Ibid, 484 ff (internal citations omitted). Interesting critique of this approach has come lately in scholarly literature in relation to domestic workers, see, eg Terri Nilliasca, 'Some Women's Work: Domestic Work, Class, Race, Heteropatriarchy, and the Limits of Legal Reform' (2011) 16 *Michigan Journal of Race and Law* 377.

[34] 487 US 474, 487.

ongoing focused picketing in front of the house. Six years after *Frisby*, in *Madsen*, the court upheld a 300ft buffer zone around residences of staff of abortion clinics, as mentioned above. What emerges clearly in relation to residential protest in the United States is that general protest is protected, but focused picketing can be regulated in a content-neutral way if narrowly tailored to a significant governmental interest such as tranquillity of the home, and—in a somewhat strained meaning—prevention of a captive audience. It is worth recalling how German courts struggled with the notion of coercion and the differences between psychological and physical pressure,[35] but also how the famous *Skokie* controversy appears to conclude that the fact that Skokie residents could just leave their home for the duration of the Nazi march means they are not a captive audience.[36]

At the ECtHR, the closest decision is *Patyi and others v Hungary*,[37] where creditors losing their money as a result of insolvency of a company were not allowed to demonstrate in front of the residence of the Prime Minister in several instances, which were claimed at the ECtHR in one proceeding. The police banned a series of demonstrations on different days, sometimes presenting reasons bordering on the ridiculous. The police claimed the 5m wide pavement was not enough to hold the 20 protestors for 20 minutes without disturbing (vehicular) traffic; and no alternative route for the buses was available. In one case, disturbance to traffic was heightened because on All Saints Day a lot of people would go to cemeteries, thus the road had to bear intensified traffic, while later the winter weather prompting intensified travelling to ski resorts around Budapest allegedly necessitated the demonstration being cancelled. Police also claimed that the traffic disturbance rationale was applicable to Christmas Eve—when buses stopped running around 4pm. The Court of course has not taken these statements at face value,[38] and found violation, applying the type of scrutiny generally applicable in ECHR jurisprudence (some sort of proportionality review).

D. Malls and Airports

Demonstrations in malls have been the other issue where both the US Supreme Court and the ECtHR have stated their view. In *Marsh v*

[35] Ch 4, text accompanying nn 2–19.

[36] Ch 3, text accompanying nn 172–80.

[37] *Patyi and Others v Hungary*, Application no 5529/05, 7 October 2008.

[38] To their credit, it has to be added that the Hungarian police believed they could not possibly rely on any other ground as the law on assembly only allowed for prior ban if the assembly would 'seriously jeopardise the undisturbed functioning of democratic institutions and courts or road traffic could not be redirected onto other routes'. For a discussion on the Hungarian situation, see Péter Sólyom, 'The Constitutional Principles of Freedom of Assembly in Hungary' (2008) *Fundamentum* 5, 36.

Alabama,[39] the issue phrased carefully by Justice Black was 'whether a State ... can impose criminal punishment on a person who undertakes to distribute religious literature on the premises of a company-owned town contrary to the wishes of the town's management'.[40] He found that the state lacked that authority, and the First Amendment rights of Jehovah's Witnesses prevailed over the state's interest in protecting property rights. Justice Black believes that whether the title of land belongs to government or to a private person is not decisive, as 'the more the owner opens up his property for use by the public in general, the more his rights become circumscribed'[41] by the rights of those who use it. As in the case the company town was basically a functional equivalent of a municipality, the First Amendment was found to apply. *Marsh v Alabama*, however, is not the end of the story, and though it was never overruled, basically it appears to be in decline or only surviving in exceptionally narrow situations. First, however, in *Logan Valley*[42] *Marsh* was applied in an extensive way to labour picketing inside a shopping mall directed against one of the stores, thus equating a simple shopping centre with a company town. A few years later, in the contrary case of *Lloyd v Tanner*,[43] similar protection was denied to anti-war leafleting, the court reasoning that the leafleting was unrelated to the shopping centre or to any tenant of it, and thus could have been performed as effectively outside the premises of the centre as inside. A final blow to a broad interpretation to *Marsh* seems to be *Hudgens v National Labor Relations Board*[44] from 1980 where the—extremely divided—court clarified that it does not see a private shopping mall as a place where the First Amendment applies. The Supreme Court also held,[45] however, that state constitutions could grant more extended speech rights than the federal Bill of Rights. Indeed, several state courts have interpreted their own constitutions as granting rights of expression and protest in places which are privately owned, but which are open to the public to the benefit of the owner. On my part, together with very many authors, I see reason for such an extension, especially since 'truly' public spaces are rapidly declining,[46] while governments still need to be controlled and criticised. I also agree with Justice Black's idea about the voluntary 'publicisation' of property for gain, which—quasi in exchange—extends the reach of constitutional

[39] *Marsh v Alabama*, 326 US 501 (1946).

[40] Ibid, 502.

[41] Ibid, 506.

[42] *Amalgamated Food Employees Union Local 590 v Logan Valley Plaza, Inc*, 391 US 308 (1968), 88 S Ct 1601, 20 L Ed 2d 603.

[43] *Lloyd Corp v Tanner*, 407 US 551 (1972), 92 S Ct 2219, 33 L Ed 2d 131.

[44] *Hudgens v National Labor Relations Board*, 424 US 507 (1980).

[45] *PruneYard Shopping Center v Robins*, 447 US 74 (1980).

[46] See, eg Josh Mulligan, 'Finding a Forum in the Simulated City: Mega Malls, Gated Towns, and the Promise of Pruneyard' (2004) 13 *Cornell Journal of Law and Public Policy* 533.

protection. Still, it is clear that all this is apparently irreconcilable with the idea of a strict line between public and private, quite fundamental in constitutional law. This problem is registered by state courts which then examine these cases first in terms of state action, a complicated doctrine outside the reach of this project.[47] Important to note is, however, that even if a court finds state action in a given situation, it does not mean that the applicable standard to the speech restriction will be the same as it would be for state-owned public places.[48]

As to the European Court of Human Rights, *Appleby v UK*[49] is the parallel case. Here the owners of a private shopping centre, that also functioned as the town centre, denied a group permission to collect signatures against a local plan to build on a part of the only remaining park area in the vicinity of the town centre. The Court first of all denied that some sort of quasi-public forum requirement would flow from the ECHR. It also stated that it did not have much relevance that the town centre had originally been built by a government owned company, and only later sold to the current private owner. Based on a comparative analysis where the Court considered cases from the United States and Canada, it concluded that there is no emerging consensus that would bestow 'automatic' access rights to private property. Nonetheless, the Court was cautious not to exclude all possibility of access rights for the future. In case the bar on access to property would have the effect of preventing any effective exercise of expressive rights, or would destroy the essence of the right, a positive obligation of the state might arise.[50] The Court refers to *Marsh v Alabama* to demonstrate an example where—if it happened in Europe—a positive obligation to grant access rights to private property would be imposed by the ECHR.[51] However, in the present case, demonstrators had the option to go to the old town centre (frequented by far fewer people), or employ alternative means of communication such as door-to-door canvassing etc.[52] The decisive consideration here is basically the same as in US time, manner, place (TMP), and content-neutrality doctrines: whether or not there are alternatives to the one restricted. The *Appleby* decision could be reframed in 'US legalese' as saying that the property right of the owner is a significant government

[47] For paradigmatic judicial occurrences, see *Shelley v Kraemer*, 334 US 1 (1948). Classic criticism of the doctrine can be found, eg in Gary Peller and Mark Tushnet, 'State Action and a New Birth of Freedom' (2004) 92 *Georgia Law Journal* 779, 789. A recent approving reconstruction is provided in Lillian BeVier and John Harrison, 'The State Action Principle and its Critics' (2010) 96 *Virginia Law Review* 1767.

[48] See *Union of Needletrades*, 65 Cal Rptr 2d, 852–53; *Green Party*, 752 A 2d, 325–26, as cited by Mulligan, 'Finding a Forum in the Simulated City', above n 46, 559, fn 214.

[49] *Appleby and Others v United Kingdom*, Application no 44306/98, Judgment of 6 May 2003.

[50] Ibid, § 46.

[51] Ibid, § 47.

[52] Ibid, § 48.

interest, the restriction on place is minor, thus narrowly tailored to the significant interest, and the restriction left open alternative channels of communication. Judge Maruste, dissenting, criticised the fact that the forum was not considered public or quasi-public and especially that it went from the public hand to the private, and that the applicants were discriminatorily denied a permit which was granted to various other groups, including—significantly—to the local government for statutory consultation purposes. Thus, Judge Maruste's judgment could be reframed in US language to the effect that the discretion granted to the private owner resulted in content-discrimination. Judge Maruste does not claim that freedom of expression should always prevail over property, but makes this important point:[53]

> It cannot be the case that through privatisation the public authorities can divest themselves of all responsibility to protect rights and freedoms other than property rights. They still bear responsibility for deciding how the forum created by them is to be used and for ensuring that public interests and individuals' rights are respected.

This feature of previous public forum could have made the *Appleby* case an occasion for further analysis of positive obligations or how to resolve the tension between privatisation of public spaces and classic vertical effect of human rights. I doubt whether the kind of essence doctrine hinted in the judgment would be a principled reply, as that would discriminate between private owners according to the contingent features of the given vicinity: whether there are other available channels and places for protest is not dependent on the owner of a single shopping mall, except in the case of a company town unlikely in Europe. Critics of the decision advocate reasonable access rights, what the national legislator would be required by positive obligation to secure.[54] The ECtHR has all in all chosen a solution similar to the US Supreme Court: the ECHR does not require the state to grant access rights to private land, except for narrowly understood company town situations where there are no alternative places, but it also did not proclaim an absolute property right which would prevent Member States from legislatively granting such access.

The German Federal Constitutional Court (GFCC), the one that could be expected to develop a fully-fledged theory on the constitutional evaluation of privatisation of public spaces, has yet only partially done so. Recently it handed down a decision[55] proclaiming that there is a right to assembly on

[53] Ibid, 17, partly dissenting opinion of Maruste J.

[54] For more details, see David Mead, 'Strasbourg Succumbs to the Temptation "To Make a God of the Right to Property": Peaceful Protest on Private Land and the Ramifications of *Appleby v UK*' (2004) *Journal of Civil Liberties* 98, Jacob Rowbottom, 'Property and Participation: A Right of Access for Expressive Activities' (2005) *European Human Rights Law Revue* 186.

[55] BVerfGE 128, 226 (2011), *Fraport*.

Frankfurt Airport, owned by Fraport AG, a joint-stock company. According to the court, the airport is bound directly by basic rights, basically because the state has a 52 per cent share in the company. Earlier interpretations already clarified that businesses owned (solely) by the state are directly bound by basic rights.[56] The current decision adds to that that undertakings with mixed (private and public) ownership are also directly bound by basic rights if the state has a 'controlling influence' in the enterprise. Controlling influence is certainly there if more than half of the shares are publicly owned. The court declined to discuss the applicability of basic rights below the level of 50 per cent public share.[57] In the present case, the 52 per cent public share, and the controlling influence theory thus enabled the court to straightforwardly proclaim the prevalence of the subjective right to expression and assembly, without the need to balance it against a countering property right of the airport, under the certainly correct, but here in application a bit strained, theory that the state does not have fundamental rights. The court goes as far as to intimate that those private shareholders who do not like their company being bound by the Constitution, should sell their shares or influence the management to get rid of the controlling state influence.[58] Despite all its apparent radicality, this part of the decision is reasonably moderate, even minimalist, as after all it does not address—even explicitly excludes[59]—the far more challenging issue of protest rights on (fully, or largely) privately owned public places. Certainly basic rights can have application in such situations in the form of indirect binding force, or in the form of protective duty of the state, the parallel German doctrines to state action and positive obligations which are, on their own, outside this discussion. How far this application would go in reality is explicitly undecided by the GFCC.

A comparable case at the US Supreme Court was decided in exactly the opposite way. In a much criticised opinion, the majority of the US Supreme Court bluntly declared the (entirely!) publicly owned airports of New York and New Jersey being a non-public forum where only a reasonableness standard applies to restrictions on some expressive activities. In *International Society for Krishna Conscieousness v Lee*[60] the court faced a Port Authority ban on solicitation and on sale or distribution of literature in the entire area (including publicly accessible parts) of the major New York–New Jersey airports. The divided court managed to issue a majority opinion on the constitutionality of a ban on solicitation, and a plurality opinion on the unconstitutionality of the sale or distribution of literature

[56] BVerwGE 113, 208, as cited by the GFCC in *Fraport*, § 50.
[57] *Fraport*, § 53.
[58] Ibid, § 53.
[59] Ibid, § 56. 56.
[60] *ISKCON v Lee*, 505 US 672 (1992).

(basically leafleting). Most importantly the majority agreed that the freely accessible terminal areas are a non-public forum, and thus only a reasonableness test applies, and solicitation is reasonably banned for disturbance to the proper running of the airport, and of the people minding their own business (somehow the court seems to take it that air travellers have less time and are busier than ground travellers).[61] Justice Kennedy concurred in the result as to the solicitation while maintaining the airport as a public forum. Justice O'Connor, concurring, thinks that airport terminals are non-public fora, but the leafleting ban fails even the loosest reasonableness test. Thus, all in all, solicitation can be banned, while leafleting cannot, but it is unclear why, and what tests are applicable. Though the particular case was clearly 'speech plus', the fact that the majority considers a publicly owned airport a non-public forum also extends the easy regulability (ie simple reasonableness review) to any sort of assembly. Certainly this is a very surprising result from the US Supreme Court—especially if compared with the GFCC—and the fault again lies with undue respect paid to 'tradition' in the forum analysis, this time going as far as to pronounce that clearly airports are not public fora as they are new phenomena.[62] Note, however, that this argument, though lacking any normative explicative power, might actually leave place for later flexible application—though how late remains a question as the decision is from 1992, and still today it has not been overruled. The archaic property logic still appears to haunt the public forum doctrine in the United States.

In the United Kingdom, a planned eight-day long camping demonstration near Heathrow Airport was enjoined for reasons that the camping would likely be accompanied by direct action protests.[63] The court rejected that a simple direct action would automatically realise harassment, especially since the would-be protestors had not committed harassment in the past.[64] However, there were calls for mass direct actions,[65] clearly aimed at slowing down airport operation. These were found to have 'serious and damaging consequences' on the operator and users of the airport, especially as the resulting disruption would increase the risk of a *terrorist* attack against the users of the airport. The decision to grant the injunction clearly turns on the disruptive aim of the planned assemblies, thus the facts are very different from the facts of the airport cases discussed in relation to the United States or Germany. The disruption might seriously hinder, not only the lawful business of hundreds

[61] Ibid, 684.

[62] '[G]iven the lateness with which the modern air terminal has made its appearance, it hardly qualifies for the description of having 'immemorially . . . time out of mind' been held in the public trust and used for purposes of expressive activity'. 505 US 680, majority opinion per Rehnquist CJ.

[63] *Heathrow Airports Ltd and Bullock v Garman and Others* [2007] EWHC 1957 (QB).

[64] Ibid, [99].

[65] Ibid, [8]–[9].

of thousands at Heathrow, but also authorities in preventing, averting or containing the effects of a potential terrorist act, an argument which takes its bite from the expected mass feature of the protests, widely publicised in the UK press. Note this is different from the argument sometimes found in US discourse where the protestors themselves are to be protected from terrorist attacks.[66]

With this in all jurisdictions discussed (apart from the UK airport case) one faces a similar situation: while courts tend to see that privatisation of public places results in a receding possibility for the exercise of assembly right, and thus, they typically would not prevent any 'democratic majority' to grant access rights to privately owned open places, courts are at this moment unwilling to create a fundamental right of access on their own. In my view this is an acceptable approach from a court in general, and I only see inconsistency in US jurisprudence in this regard. If in one segment, abortion protests, the US Supreme Court is willing to loosen First Amendment protection on traditionally speech-friendly parts of public property, that is on streets and sidewalks, for quite mediated privacy interests, then in the other segment (shopping malls, airports, etc) it should be willing to strengthen First Amendment protection on private or quasi-private (government-owned, but 'managerial') property where no privacy interests are at stake.

II. GOVERNMENTAL BUILDINGS: MANAGERIAL OR AUTHORITARIAN PROTECTION?

Protest around governmental[67] buildings (eg parliaments, courts, prisons) is often restricted. Sometimes such restriction might be justified by interests in running the government, perhaps a subcategory of what Robert Post influentially meant by the 'managerial function'.[68] Managerial function would first imply that access needs to be secured as government has to run properly, and government work, be it legislative debates, court hearings and deliberations or executive decision-making, should not be threatened by mob violence or even only disruptive noise. There would be no problem with such restrictions if they really served the undisturbed work of government by preventing extortious or otherwise clearly incapacitating 'speech', substituting rule of law for the rule of street. Nonetheless, government is

[66] Eg Nick Suplina, 'Crowd Control: The Troubling Mix of First Amendment Law, Political Demonstrations, and Terrorism' (2005) 73 *George Washington Law Review* 395.

[67] Government in this chapter, just as generally in the book, is meant to cover all three branches of power, ie not only the executive and administration.

[68] It is certainly only a subcategory, Post's claim and theme are more general. See Robert Post, 'Between Governance and Management: The History and Theory of the Public Forum' (1987) 34 *University of California at Los Angeles Law Review* 1713.

the last institution in a democracy to be shielded from public criticism, and any prohibitive scheme runs the risk of degenerating into an authoritarian means which isolates the mighty machinery from public scrutiny. Thus, protest restrictions around government buildings would be the best field to analyse the Janus-faced nature of the right to freedom of assembly of being the most important, but at the same time the most dangerous, right.

Two countries, Germany and the United Kingdom, have instituted famous protest restrictions around government buildings, but the stories behind them are strikingly different. The United Kingdom is the easier case as the highly criticised authorisation scheme for demonstrations in the vicinity of Parliament was repealed in September 2011.[69] Thus, the most notorious UK place restriction belongs to the past, and only existed for six years. Stationary protest meetings can again be held on the streets around Westminster without prior restraint, and processions are subject to the normal regime under the Public Order Act 1986. However, the offence of trespass on a designated site, introduced in the Serious Organised Crime and Police Act 2005 (SOCPA), remains in force.[70] Sites on Crown land, and on the private land of the Queen and her heirs can be designated without any further provision in the law, while any other (ie even private) sites can be designated if the Secretary of State finds it appropriate in the interests of *national security*.[71] The site is thus to be designated not by law, but by the Secretary of State in an Order. Indeed there have been several dozens of such sites designated so far, including nuclear sites (power stations, but also research sites), all sorts of RAF bases, and a wide range of royal, governmental, and parliamentary sites, thus including basically all important government and Parliament buildings in London.[72] Being designated prevents access to the inside of the site, but it does not preclude holding protest events outside, in front of, the site. Therefore, these provisions do not on their own directly hinder protests on adjacent public streets, but create an arrestable offence for those who do not do anything else other than put a foot on the designated area, and have the threat of imprisonment for up to 51 weeks and

[69] Section 141 of the Police Reform and Social Responsibility Act 2011. The original provisions, ss 132–38 of the Serious Organised Crime and Police Act required authorisation for demonstrations in the vicinity of Parliament which could be granted subject to conditions of place, time, period and noise levels if it served the purpose of preventing '(a) hindrance to any person wishing to enter or leave the Palace of Westminster, (b) hindrance to the proper operation of Parliament, (c) serious public disorder, (d) serious damage to property, (e) disruption to the life of the community, (f) a security risk in any part of the designated area, (g) risk to the safety of members of the public (including any taking part in the demonstration)'. For a detailed analysis and critique of the original provisions and related case law, see, eg David Mead, *The New Law of Peaceful Protest. Rights and Regulations in the Human Rights Act Era* (Oxford, Hart Publishing, 2010) 148–62.

[70] Sections 125–31 SOCPA.

[71] Section 128 SOCPA.

[72] A list as of 2007 can be found in the schedules to the Serious Organised Crime and Police Act 2005 (Designated Sites Under s 128) Order 2007 (SI 2007/930), available at www.legislation.gov.uk/uksi/2007/930/made.

a level 5 fine, a quite severe punishment for an activity not harming anyone. It is a defence if the person proves that 'he did not know, and had no reasonable cause to suspect', that the site was a designated site. However, the provision might fall into disuse and is criticised for several reasons.[73] First, there is no tangible harm required, simple entrance is enough. If there was some tangible harm, then other offences would come into play, which then makes the offence of trespass on a designated site appear superfluous. Recall, for example, that aggravated trespass is committed if the trespasser disrupts or obstructs some activity. The argument from national security, basically prevention of terrorist acts, is not convincing either, as there are ample powers under terrorism legislation to stop someone suspected with being a terrorist. Finally, it is also pointed out rightly in the literature that the mode of designation in Order by the Minister, that is not by Act of Parliament, might raise rule of law concerns, but at the same time opens up the possibility for courts to strike it down for incompatibility with the ECHR under the Human Rights Act 1998 (HRA).[74] Time will show how police and courts will apply, if at all, and interpret the designated site provisions. There is certainly a way to interpret them only to secure access to and safety of employees of the designated site, which would raise no serious questions of the right to protest or assembly.

In Germany, so called *Bannmeilen* (banned zones) were instituted in 1920 around buildings of representative bodies, to prevent incidents similar to the Weimar Reichstag bloodbath in which 42 protestors and 20 policemen were killed in a chaotic and mismanaged effort to prevent protestors from entering Parliament and preventing deliberation on a controversial law on works councils. Hitler's first day as a Reichskanzler saw the law abolished, and later the Ermächtigungsgesetz was adopted among shouts from SA and SS troops 'We want the law—or blood and thunder!'.[75] The Bonn Republic reintroduced such a law,[76] but that became obsolete with the government relocating to Berlin. Article 16 of the Federal Assembly Law banned open sky assemblies in so-called 'pacified districts' or 'pacified ban zones' (*befriedete Bezirke or befriedete Bannkreise*) around legislative organs of the federation and the Länder, and of the GFCC. A 1999 Federal Law[77] introduced pacified districts around the Bundestag and Bundesrat in Berlin, and around the GFCC in Karlsruhe, the zones being significantly

[73] See Mead, *The New Law of Peaceful Protest*, above n 69, 144–45.

[74] Ibid.

[75] Alfred Dietel, Kurt Gintzel and Michael Kniesel, *Versammlungsgesetz*, 15th edn (Köln, Carl Heymanns, 2008), 337 with reference to Alan Bullock, *Hitler: A Study in Tyranny* (London, Harper & Row, 1990) 251 and William L Shirer, *Aufstieg und Fall des Dritten Reiches* (Köln/Berlin, Kiepenheuer & Witsch, 1961) 195. The same sentence and references (with different page numbers) can be found in Sasha Werner, 'Das neue Bannmeilengesetz der "Berliner Republik"' (2000) *Neue Zeitschrift fur Verwaltungsrecht* 369, 370, fn 17.

[76] See Law on Banned Zones (Bannmeilengesetz) 6 August 1955 (BGBl I S 504).

[77] Law on reregulating the protection of constitutional organs of the Federation, 11 August 1999 (BGBl I S 1818).

smaller than the previous ones in Bonn.[78] In 2008, basically for reasons of transparency and federalism reform,[79] the 1999 law and the relevant norms of the Federal Assembly Law were incorporated in a single new Law on Pacified Districts.[80]

According to the old–new scheme, it is prohibited to demonstrate in these zones, unless authorised by the Minister for Internal Affairs jointly with the President of the respective organ. An authorisation could be given when no interference with the activities of the respective bodies, their organs or boards, including parliamentary fractions, is to be expected nor would the free entrance to the buildings be blocked. As a rule, on days when the Bundestag and Bundesrat are not in session, the authorisation is to be granted.

The violation of the ban was decriminalised, but remains an administrative offence (fine up to €20,000).[81] Thus, there is currently a regime of preventive ban subject to the possibility of authorisation[82] (*präventives Verbot mit Erlaubnisvorbehalt*), a reverse of what normally would be the case with fundamental rights, though with limited discretion on the authorities, or, a claim right to authorisation if conditions are fulfilled.[83]

Strong counter-arguments arise regarding the necessity of *Bannmeilen* regulation, since, under general law, police (or other authority) are entitled to impose conditions on the time, manner, and place of an assembly, and can even declare a no-go zone (*Platzverweisung*) if public safety or even the looser German concept, public order is seriously endangered.[84]

Commentators also argue that historically the *Bannmeile* served purposes either quite irreconcilable with a democratic rule of law state or was a reaction to very specific crises of it. In the Middle Ages, *Bannmeilen* served to protect friends and keep outside (of the castle, or of the city) foes,[85] while during the Weimar era, the law on *Bannmeilen*—in itself a constitutional amendment—was adopted as a reaction to a series of emergencies.[86] The mentioned Reichstag bloodbath, or the Kapp-Lüttwitz putsch attempt, the Federal Government and the Federal President being moved from Berlin to

[78] Michael Kniesel, 'Versammlungs- und Demonstrationsfreiheit—Entwicklung des Versammlungsrechts seit 1996' (2000) *Neue Juristische Wochenschrift* 2857, 2866.

[79] See the reasoning in the Bill introduced to the Bundestag, Drucksache 16/9741, dipbt.bundestag.de/dip21/btd/16/097/1609741.pdf.

[80] Law on Pacified Districts for Constitutional Organs of the Federation, BGBl I 2008, 2366.

[81] Ibid, s 4.

[82] For the translation (referenced by SAvL), see the forum discussion on dict.leo.org/forum/viewUnsolvedquery.php?idThread=148684&idForum=1&lp=ende&lang=de.

[83] Werner, 'Das neue Bannmeilengesetz', above n 75, 369.

[84] Hans-Peter Schneider, 'Frieden statt Bann—Über eine Reform, die nichts kostet, aber auch wenig wert ist' (2000) *Neue Juristische Wochenschrift* 263, 264.

[85] Ibid, 265.

[86] Werner, 'Das neue Bannmeilengesetz', above n 75, 370.

Stuttgart all provide very specific evidence of serious violence and serious physical threats against constitutional institutions.

Thus, the question arises to what extent the Weimar-analogy holds true. The 1920 Bannmeilengestz failed to prevent the take-over of a new culture of total violence, and was swiftly swept away by history. On the other hand, the FRG under the Basic Law has never faced such open and serious challenges of its legitimacy as the Weimar republic had. Some certainly would think the high legitimacy of post-Second World War German constitutional institutions might be supported by measures similar to the *Bannmeilen* regulation. Even if so, as Werner points out, the Weimar precedent only aimed at preventing physical intrusion and threats of physical violence, not in some more vague sense the promotion or protection of the representative function of Parliament this way, as hinted in the explanation of the Bill.[87] Quite to the contrary, assemblies and protests actually ought to be free to influence, even to pressure, though not to extort, political decision-making in the logic of the *Brokdorf* decision[88] of the GFCC.

Another serious question is the relation of the *Bannmeilen* scheme to the general notification regime. Someone wishing to demonstrate within the *Bannmeilen*, needs both to notify the police (or authority competent for assemblies), and to request authorisation by the Minister and the President of the respective organ. As article 8 I GG grants freedom of assembly without notice or permit, it is highly problematic (disproportionate) to impose both, even if one accepts that notice is constitutional under article 8 II.

Furthermore, spontaneous demonstrations are clearly disadvantaged by the scheme, and recommendations to dispense with the *Bannmeilen* regulation exactly with regard to spontaneous (unorganised) demonstrations will be unlikely to be followed in legal practice.[89] One of the promoters of the 1999 law, an MP for the Social Democratic Party, simply takes for granted that spontaneous demonstrations are excluded from the pacified districts.[90] Even he acknowledges, however, that police have some margin of appreciation as they are bound by the 'principle of opportunity' instead of 'the principle of legality' in deciding whether to intervene. If the 'wrong' to be done by the assembly (*Unrechtsgehalt*) is insignificant, and a police intervention would risk escalation rather than achieving formal integrity of law, then the principle of opportunity requires that the assembly can be allowed.[91] Note again, however, the language: it is very far from saying that the police are accountable for securing the exercise of a fundamental right, or only intervening when absolutely necessary. Clearly, such an interpretation

[87] Ibid.

[88] BVerfGE 69, 315 (1985), *Brokdorf*.

[89] See Werner, 'Das neue Bannmeilengesetz', above n 75, 373.

[90] Dieter Wiefelspütz, 'Das Gesetz über befriedete Bezirke für Verfassungsorgane des Bundes—ein Gesetz, das seinen Zweck erfüllt' (2000) *Neue Juristische Wochenschrift* 1016, 1017.

[91] Ibid, 1018.

would render the scheme close to meaningless, or at least redundant, as then the general test for bans would apply.

While the existence of the scheme is thus highly problematic, its jurisprudence is ambivalent, courts strictly limiting its scope of application, but within that scope not exercising rigorous review. Generally, the authorisation has to be granted not only at session-free times, but also when the target of the protest is not Parliament or the GFCC,[92] or even when the protest is not aiming at the issue currently deliberated by the respective body.[93] In my view an interpretation that conforms to the Constitution would require a case-by-case risk analysis of whether any planned demonstration would with high probability significantly hinder or extortiously influence the deliberation inside the buildings even if the topics are the same. In general commentators also require a close examination of same facts,[94] but I have not found any clear stance taken on such particular issues, even if the commentator recommends abolition of the scheme.

Courts generally stay within the reverse logic of the law, thus in effect apply a rationality type of loose review. Recently, even freedom of art—recall, the usual suspect for overriding legal incapacitations on freedom of assembly, for example, with regard to flag desecration—was found limited to performances *outside* the pacified district around the Reichstag,[95] in a judgment based on warnings of enhanced danger of terrorist (!) acts against Germany. The decision of the Administrative Court of Berlin, as it often happens with terrorism, does not discuss in any substantive way the existence of such a threat, and whether the ban (in the form of condition imposed as to the place) is proportionate to the aim pursued, but applies a kind of 'no alternative channel' argumentation, finding that it would not be a major issue for the performance to be displayed a few hundred meters away from the western ramp of the Reichstag.

Apart from English and German law, the ECtHR had to deal with a place restriction around a Parliament. Two decisions were handed down relating to a blanket ban imposed, in effect for months, by police around the Hungarian Parliament. Nonetheless, as domestic courts found that the order declaring a 'security operational zone' was illegal, the Strasbourg Court has declared that the order did not have any basis in law and thus there was no need to discuss whether the interference was necessary in a democratic society.[96]

[92] OVG Münster, NVwZ-RR 1994, 391; VG Hamburg, NVwZ 1985, 678 as cited by Werner, 'Das neue Bannmeilengesetz', above n 75, 371.

[93] OVG Münster, ibid, as cited by Werner, 'Das neue Bannmeilengesetz', above n 75, 371.

[94] Werner, for example, claims that the authorisation cannot be denied if there is 'a complete lack of details about the endangerment of the purpose of the protection' ('Hinweise auf eine Gefährdung des Schutzzweckes völlig fehlen'), Werner, 'Das neue Bannmeilengesetz', above n 75, 372. A 'complete lack of details' sounds like recommending a very weak rationality test, indeed where the state has not provided any reason for the restriction.

[95] VG Berlin, 20 May 2011, VG 1 L 174.11.

[96] See *Szerdahelyi v Hungary* Application no 30385/07, 17 January 2012, and *Patyi v Hungary (No 2)*, Application no 35127/08, 17 January 2012.

In the United States, unsurprisingly, there are nowadays no federal laws designating no-protest areas around governmental buildings. This does not mean, however, that it is constitutionally always impermissible to restrict protest around such buildings. Protest around courts, on capitol grounds, prisons, and military bases evoked a significant, though not necessarily doctrinally consistent, Supreme Court jurisprudence.

In relation to capitol grounds, or grounds where state representative bodies have their seats, the jurisprudence is clear: the grounds are traditionally places of assemblies, and as such, there is no cause for special restriction. Peaceful assembly on the sidewalks is clearly protected by the First Amendment.[97] Dicta from a decision on an anti-noise ordinance related to demonstrations around schools seems to imply that even noisy demonstrations must be allowed on such grounds normally open to the public.[98]

As to courts, the jurisprudence seems settled that courts need a higher level of isolation and quiet than legislative bodies, but the contours are unclear. In *Cox v Lousiana II*, a ban on picketing 'near' a courthouse with the intent to obstruct justice and impede access was found constitutionally permissible.[99] The Supreme Court, though quite divided, appears unified in the understanding that 2,000 people protesting 101ft away from the courthouse against what they considered an illegal arrest, hoping to persuade the court to dismiss the charges, is an attempt to influence the judicial process, and is not constitutionally protected expression, but conduct regulable for reasons of integrity of law and order. The Supreme Court supported the need for no outside influence or pressure on the courts or any judicial officer because 'mob law is the very antithesis of due process'. One could add that protestors' singing and clapping could be heard inside the building[100]—which necessarily influences the work inside. A compromise solution—with regard to courts only, because of the special need to protect judicial integrity and due process—would be to disallow not only physically obstructive or clearly threatening, but also noisy (audible from the inside

[97] *Edwards v South Carolina*, 372 US 229 (1963), (breach of the peace statute found unconstitutional, see above Ch 3 text accompanying nn 150–52); *Jeannette Rankin Brigade v Chief of the Capitol Police*, 342 F Supp 575 (DDC), aff'd mem, 409 US 972, 93 S Ct 311, 34 L Ed 2d 236 (1972) (a complete ban on assemblies on capitol grounds found to violate the First and Fifth Amendments).

[98] Cf this quote from *Grayned v City of Rockford*, 408 US 104, 120 (1972): 'We recognize that the ordinance prohibits some picketing that is neither violent nor physically obstructive. Noisy demonstrations that disrupt or are incompatible with normal school activities are obviously within the ordinance's reach. Such expressive conduct may be constitutionally protected at other places or other times, *cf Edwards v South Carolina*, 372 US 229 (1963)'.

[99] Though application in the present case was reversed for reasons that officials told protestors they were rightfully protesting on the street. *Cox v Louisiana*, 379 US 559 (1965).

[100] See the facts in Clark J's partially dissenting and partially concurring judgment: 'The record is replete with evidence that the demonstrators with their singing, cheering, clapping and waving of banners drew the attention of the whole courthouse square as well as the occupants and officials of the court building itself'. Ibid, 586.

of the building) protests, but still keep with the principle of the 'eye can be averted', and thus allow assemblies for or against some judicial outcome to go on at a distance not interfering with ingress and egress. However, the court's argumentation in *Cox* rather implies that restrictions on protests around courts could go further than that, especially that the distance might be bigger than the one that guarantees no noise penetrating inside the building, but no exact criteria are set.

In other cases related to protest around courts, the Supreme Court did not address the question of the limits of protests threatening or influencing judicial action any further, but did make clear a few other principles related to protest around courts. In 1968, it held in *Cameron v Johnson* that picketing in front of a courthouse against racial discrimination in voter registration could be constitutionally banned as the law did not serve to stifle protest, but to ensure unfettered access to municipal buildings to all citizens.[101] The law prohibited

> picketing ... in such a manner as to obstruct or unreasonably interfere with free ingress or egress to and from any county ... courthouses.[102]

Before the enactment of the statute, protests were allowed to go on with the exception of a barricaded march route, while after the statute entered into force, some pickets were dispersed, some were tolerated, some protestors were arrested, but no charges brought against them, thus no criminal conviction ensued. The facial challenge at the Supreme Court failed, and I think rightly so with regard to the text of the statute. It is less obvious, however, that it was not applied in bad faith to some of the protestors, but the US Supreme Court did not engage in a close examination of this for procedural reasons (injunctive relief). All in all, the provision was the sort which—if correctly applied—properly delineates rights of assembly on the one hand, and proper functioning of government (even though it was a courthouse, the activity in question was voter registration, but the logic could equally apply to judicial activity proper) on the other hand. That such a managerial concern is clearly present, is also shown in *US v Grace*,[103] where the US Supreme Court annulled a federal ban on 'displaying any flag, banner, or device designed or adapted to bring into public notice any party, organisation, or movement'[104] on the premises of the US Supreme Court which included public sidewalks around the building. As a public sidewalk is considered to be a 'public forum', and the sidewalks in question were 'indistinguishable from any other sidewalks in Washington DC', the court thus applied the rules for a public forum, and dispensed with any claim of private

[101] *Cameron v Johnson*, 390 US 611 (1968).
[102] Mississippi Anti-Picketing Law as cited by 390 US 611.
[103] *United States v Grace*, 461 US 171 (1983).
[104] Title 40 USC, § 13k.

property of government. The purpose of the Act[105] was the 'protection of the building and grounds and of the persons and property therein, as well as the maintenance of proper order and decorum', which is a legitimate purpose. Nonetheless, the court went on to find that the nexus between pursuing this interest and a total ban on displaying any signs on the public sidewalks around the court was *insufficient.* There was no showing that protestors 'in any way obstructed the sidewalks or access to the building, threatened injury to any person or property, or in any way interfered with the orderly administration of the building or other parts of the grounds'.[106] I take it that this list—obstruction of access, injury to person or property, interference with the administration of the building—supplies those dangers which can be constitutionally averted by restrictions on protest. Note that the US Supreme Court in *Grace* does not repeat *Cox II* concerns about influencing the judicial process, though clearly it does not repudiate any of them either. Thus, doctrinally, *Cox II* remains the closest explanation in that regard.

Apart from (publicly open) capitol grounds and courts, the US Supreme Court has ruled on protest restriction with regard to jailhouse grounds and military bases. The 1966 case of *Adderley v Florida*[107] found a trespass conviction for entering the premises of a county jail for protesting segregation in prisons constitutional. Justice Black, not inconsistently with his general hostility towards 'speech plus', considered the law a general one regulating conduct, which was applied to the protestors without discrimination. *Edwards v South Carolina*,[108] was distinguished, inter alia, because there the protest was on South Carolina state capitol grounds, not on jailhouse grounds, and 'traditionally, state capitol grounds are open to the public. Jails, built for security purposes, are not'.[109]

In a similar vein, the US Supreme Court found a ban on political partisan speeches and prior approval of distribution of literature within the confines of a military base in *Greer v Spock*[110] constitutional. Regulations granted free civilian access to some unrestricted areas of the military base, but still the court has not found the content-based regulation on partisan speech and the discretionary prior restraint on distribution of literature impermissible. The military's function appears to be the decisive factor in the majority opinion, and this factor counselled against granting constitutional free speech and assembly rights on the premises of the fort. *Greer* thus rejected that the military base would be a public forum, irrespective of the fact that it was opened up for civilian access, where people sometimes for

105 Title 40 USC, § 13k.
106 Ibid, 182.
107 *Adderley v Florida*, 385 US 39 (1966).
108 *Edwards v South Carolina*, 372 US 229 (1963).
109 385 US 39, 41.
110 *Greer v Spock*, 424 US 828 (1976).

some purposes would assemble and discuss some issues. What matters are not the particular circumstances of the particular military base, but that in general, traditionally, or in abstract, military installations are not meant for First Amendment activity.[111] Without really giving any justification, *Greer* firmly established—or revived as Robert Post shows—the basic divisions of places for First Amendment activity: 'non-public' forums are outside any protection except against 'irrational, invidious, or arbitrary'[112] government action. A military base is a non-public forum, where there is simply no constitutional right to speech or assembly.

III. MEMORIAL SITES: IDENTITY FIGHT OVER COLLECTIVE MEMORY

Memorial sites are places of common remembrance, places with regularly held commemorative assemblies, and, thus, places where other types of assemblies, questioning the commemorated meaning of the site, might need to be restricted by the state.

There has not been much legislation, litigation and jurisprudence related to protest on or near memorial sites, except in Germany. This does not mean that such protests do not happen elsewhere. In the United States, for instance, the same Westboro Baptist Church which regularly pickets funerals in order to spread what they call 'God's hate toward homosexuals', also organises anti-Jewish events, including protesting at the Holocaust Memorial in Washington DC and other cities, but no constitutional concerns have arisen.[113]

In accordance with general free speech law, there is no way in the United States—apparently even no serious political will, unlike in the case of the funeral protests—to prevent such protests. Other groups occasionally protest at Holocaust memorials, but only one police report could be found about an arrest for disturbing a public assembly—a commemoration of Holocaust in Boston.[114] Apparently no litigation followed in either of the cases.

In the United Kingdom, apart from the quite different bans on demonstrations around Stonehenge[115] and the general possibility of issuing

[111] See the classic discussion by Robert Post, 'Between Governance and Management: The History and Theory of the Public Forum' (1987) 34 *University of California at Los Angeles Law Review* 1713, 1739–45.

[112] 424 US 828, 840.

[113] See, eg www.dallasobserver.com/slideshow/summer-vacation-of-hate-with-the-westboro-baptist-church-30319832/.

[114] Martin Solomon, 'Boston: Anti-Semite Arrested at Holocaust Memorial Day Event. Arrest Report Revealed' www.solomonia.com/blog/archive/2010/04/boston-anti-semite-arrested-at-holocaust/index.shtml, April 14, 2010 and here apparently the arrest report: www.solomonia.com/blog/images/2010/04/bob%20bowes%20arrest.pdf.

[115] See Ch 2, text accompanying n 122.

banning orders discussed above,[116] there is no specific protection provided to memorials. When activist Peter Tatchell, an invited guest in the UK Parliament at the 2005 Holocaust Memorial Day, started to shout after the ceremony in protest at the planned quota on asylum, he was arrested although he was released after two hours.[117] Further details could not be verified.

In France, in a strange but rights friendly inconsistency with the mushrooming *lois mémorielles* and fight against 'negationnism', there are no special laws restricting protest around or on memorial sites, or else there probably would have been some litigation or public discussion on their usefulness. Arguably, however, any imaginable need for such laws is eliminated by the otherwise very many restrictions on expression causing public order issues etc discussed throughout this book.

A specific ban on assemblies around memorial sites was introduced in Germany in 2005. A second paragraph was added to article 15 of the Federal Assembly Law, the article authorising conditions and bans of assemblies directly endangering public safety and order. The newly added paragraph II states that 'in particular' an assembly can be banned or made subject to conditions if the assembly or procession takes place at a location which as a memorial site of 'outstanding historical and supra-regional significance' commemorates the victims of National Socialist violence and tyranny, which treated them in a way violating human dignity.

The ban, or conditions, may only be imposed if at the time of the imposition particular circumstances make it likely that the dignity of the victims would be infringed.[118] The law designates a site around the Holocaust Memorial in Berlin as such a place, and leaves to the Länder to designate such other sites within their borders. Originally, the law was introduced to prevent the NPD, the Nationalist Party, from marching through the Brandenburg Gate on the sixtieth anniversary of the end of the Second World War. At the end, however, the adopted law did not limit protest around the Brandenburg Gate, but only around the Holocaust Memorial.

The law was criticised for many other reasons as well. Scholars pointed out that if read properly, the law limits the recourse to public order beyond the restrictions read in it by the GFCC,[119] such as the explicitly granted possibility to re-schedule neo-Nazi demonstrations from the Holocaust Memorial Day to another day,[120] or other permissible 'manner' restrictions

[116] See Ch 2 on prior restraints, text accompanying nn 116–31.

[117] See, 'Tatchell arrested in Holocaust Memorial Day asylum protest at Michael Howard's asylum quota to block refugees' London, 27 January 2005, his own website: petertatchell.net/a2/print_versions/419.htm.

[118] Art 15 II Federal Assembly Law.

[119] Wolfgang Leist, 'Die Änderung des Versammlungsrechts: ein Eigentor?' (2005) *Neue Zeitschrift fur Verwaltungsrecht* 500, 501.

[120] See Ch 6, text accompanying nn 1–11.

of aggressive and provocative, intimidating conduct leading to a 'climate of violence', whatever that might mean.[121] Maybe most significantly, the law leaves out a large number of favoured neo-Nazi sites which are not memorial sites, but festive or military sites of the National Socialist regime, or smaller memorial sites (including less well-known former concentration camps designated as memorial sites) lacking a supra-regional significance.[122]

On its own, the new provision was found constitutional shortly after its adoption by the GFCC in a short Chamber decision rejecting a request for injunctive relief ('*einstweilige Anordnung*' to suspend the restrictive condition).[123] The youth organisation of NPD planned a march entitled '60 years of Liberation Lie—End the guilt cult!' from Alexanderplatz to the Brandenburg Gate, passing next to the Holocaust Memorial. Police imposed a shortened route, which would end before reaching the Holocaust Memorial and would also not get to the Brandenburg Gate.

The court found that such a shortening of the route was permissible because the march obviously would fulfil the criteria of article 15 II of the Assembly Law. Most importantly, the authorities could correctly assume that the human dignity of Jewish persons would be violated by such a march along the Holocaust Memorial on the anniversary of the capitulation of Germany. The march—as it can be inferred from its motto—would portray millions of Jewish victims as the 'object' of a cult,[124] which in accordance with the usual Kantian approach is a violation of human dignity. In this case, unlike (years later) in relation to the Rudolf Hess memorial march, the court thus found the dignity rationale explicitly applicable and fulfilled. Thus the rationale is not public order, nor a manner-type ban on provocation, but simply human dignity as a constitutional limit. Consequently, it appears to me that the legislator could (but is constitutionally not required to) equally introduce legislation to the effect of banning such marches anywhere else, as the described objectification is realised independently of the time and place of the expression.

As to the portion of the rerouting away from the Brandenburg Gate, the court has accepted that the Senate of Berlin (the government of the Land Berlin) has primacy in using the place for a commemorative event, called 'Day for Democracy', even if the request was submitted *after* the NPD youth organisation had notified the march. Not because it is initiated by the government which does not have a basic rights claim, but because the programme was of general interest, and it was an assembly worthy of basic right protection because of the 'public' who wished to participate in it.

[121] BVerfGE 111, 147 (2004) *Stoppt den Synagogenbau!* or *Inhaltsbezogenes Versammlungsverbot.*

[122] Claudia Haupt, 'The Scope of Democratic Public Discourse: Defending Democracy, Tolerating Intolerance, and the Problem of Neo-Nazi Demonstrations in Germany' (2008) 20 *Florida Journal of International Law* 169, 193.

[123] BVerfG, 1 BvR 961/05, 6 May 2005.

[124] Ibid, § 21.

Practical concordance thus requires the 'rights of the public' to be balanced with that of the NPD youth organisation. The special character of the date (anniversary of the surrender) and the place as being representative of the whole of the German Federal Republic and its polity, also weighs in favour of the Day for Democracy, overriding a strict, mechanical application of the principle of temporal priority of the requests. Otherwise such common interest events could always be pre-empted by special interest groups, reserving a certain place symbolising the whole of the political community and identity for years in advance.

The GFCC thus had no difficulty declaring that the otherwise constitutionally mandated state neutrality is unaffected by such an arrangement, that is by proclaiming which commemoration is the 'common' one, of general interest. One wonders how this scheme would fare in the opposite case if the NPD—a lawful party—was in government in Berlin, and the 'democratic' parties wanted to organise an assembly protesting against the official commemoration of the day of surrender in the spirit of the NPD. Obviously, that would be much more important to counterbalance, but this decision would actually sanction the priority of the NPD commemoration in such a case.

Thus, in my view, it would be more consistent and wise to stay with the luck-directed temporal principle as it does not elevate to the level of common value an event organised by government, and does not sacrifice the long-term consistent solution for saving face today. After all, the Brandenburg Gate is not even the site of the Parliament or any government building. As a complementary rule a time limit on the submission of advance notice could be introduced, for example, a maximum of three months before the planned date of the assembly. If the real reason for suppression of the NPD march in the present case was some sort of militant democracy consideration (a democratic state does not have to give media space for promoting an anti-democratic agenda), then that should have been clearly stated and discussed by both the ordinary courts and the GFCC. Also, under general doctrine, the court could just have said that the entire march could have even been banned for violation of human dignity, thus the lesser restriction is clearly constitutional. Violation of human dignity normally does not get balanced away in a practical concordance.

IV. DESIGNATED ZONES: SPEECH PENS, PROTEST CAGES

A final phenomenon of limits on assemblies virtually 'imprisons' protestors in one way or the other. Some techniques, such as preventive detention and kettling, raise the question of right to liberty and security as well, an issue touched upon earlier.[125] But detainment-like restrictions can also arise in

[125] Recall the German practice of preventive police detention to avert dangers found violating art 5 of the ECHR. *Schwabe and MG v Germany*, Application nos 8080/08 and 8577/08,

the form of specific place restriction: circumscribed 'free speech' zones, speech pens (actually cages) designated by authorities for demonstrations have increasingly appeared in practice in the United States.

The issue became salient at the 2004 Democratic National Convention where would be protestors were relegated more than a block away, in something with 'overhead netting, chain-link fence, razor wire and armed guards'[126] which *the judge* described as follows:[127]

> I at first thought, before taking a view (of the protest zone), that the characterization of the space being like a concentration camp was litigation hyperbole. Now I believe it's an understatement. One cannot conceive of other elements put in place to create a space that is more of an affront to the idea of expression than the designated demonstration zone.

Still, in the decision, he upheld the restriction,[128] as did other judges in similar cases, on content-neutrality grounds, especially if coupled with fear of terrorism.[129]

As it must be clear by now, content-neutrality doctrines basically mandate to uphold such restriction, and nobody (except for scholars) actually wonders when no protestors show up and take their place in the cage.[130]

Judgment of 1 December 2011, discussed above in Ch 2, text accompanying n 158, Ch 3, text accompanying nn 57 and 123, but also the *Austin* case from the United Kingdom, where police held inside cordons a few thousand persons, among them peaceful protestors and total bystanders innocently caught up. The ECtHR has upheld this latter case. *Austin and Others v UK*, Applications nos 39692/09, 40713/09 and 41008/09 [GC] Judgment of 15 March 2012, discussed above, Ch 3, text accompanying nn 85–88 and 124–29.

[126] David S Allen, 'Spatial Frameworks and the Management of Dissent: From Parks to Free Speech Zones' (2011) 16 *Commercial Law and Policy* 383.

[127] Woodlock J as quoted by Theo Emery, 'Judge Upholds "Free Speech Zone" but Permits March on Fleet Center', Associated Press, 22 July 2004, available at www.boston.com/news/politics/conventions/articles/2004 (last visited 29 September 2004) as cited by Allen, ibid, 384.

[128] *Coalition to Protest the Democratic National Convention v Boston*, 327 F Supp 2d 61, 78 (D Mass 2004).

[129] Suplina, 'Crowd Control', above n 66.

[130] Timothy Zick, *Speech Out of Doors, Preserving First Amendment Liberties in Public Places* (Cambridge, Cambridge University Press, 2009) 3.

Conclusion

I. SPECIFIC COMPARATIVE FINDINGS

A. Forms and Values of Assembly

ON THEIR FACE, the examined jurisdictions vary strongly in what sorts of gatherings they consider to be assembly, and how they go on to categorise them. Three dividing lines appear relevant, those between: (i) stationary or moving assemblies, (ii) indoor and outdoor assemblies, and (iii) deliberative and demonstrative assemblies. The jurisdictions' choice of which criterion to apply and which not appears haphazard.

All three dimensions are present in the definition of the French understanding of *réunion*, which is stationary, indoor, and deliberative (at least this is the starting point of the *Benjamin* argument, which broadens deliberation to the possibility of dialogue).

German constitutional law oscillates between (ii) and (iii) in that constitutional text only mentions in- and outdoor, while jurisprudence and scholarship also deal with demonstration. The Federal Law on Assemblies is titled law on assemblies and processions, implying a type (i) categorisation present as well. In fact, however, constitutional jurisprudence operates with the general test of proportionality, which homogenises protection given to all assemblies to a large extent.

The English understanding appears to comprise deliberation (iii) and stationary (i) in the concept of 'meeting', while moving and demonstrative are understood to go together.

The US Supreme Court and the ECtHR are entirely out of this discussion. While the ECtHR explicitly endorses all these mentioned varieties without much differentiation among them, the US Supreme Court is stuck with the content-based/content-neutral and public/non-public distinctions, in theory equally applicable to any 'expression'.

The generalising or homogenising tendency of the German jurisprudence is in sharp contrast especially with the American, where very different tests apply to speech and speech plus. This is all the more puzzling because both the US and the German courts maintain the division between content and form, one in the split between content-based and content-neutral restrictions, the other by splitting the scope of the applicable rights into modality and content or substance. The solution to the puzzle lies exactly in this difference. The US Supreme Court derives the applicable test partly from the nature of the restriction (content-neutrality) and partly from the place of the activity (public forum doctrine) and partly from the nature of the activity (speech or speech plus). Meanwhile the German court deals first with the scope of the rights, and thereafter applies a proportionality test of the restrictions by a unified theory on permissible limits, where, however, again the importance of the value *in the particular case* plays a decisive role, always weighed against competing (conflicting) values in the particular setting.

Both the German and the US approach diverge significantly from the fragmented English understanding on both free speech and public order law within which is located—at least traditionally—assembly, except for the curious right to passage.

The ECtHR, where it does not actually matter much if something is decided under article 10 or article 11 ECHR, may be true to its nature as an international court, because this way it can accommodate the certainly even more diverse concepts of Member States' domestic law than it is apparent in this book.

In France, conceptual confusion clearly relates to the very distinct nature of rights doctrines in French law (if there are any at all, and we should not instead speak of the doctrine of *loi*), and to the historical contingency where *réunion* was protected by proportionality standards for long, but *manifestation* was—much later—accorded constitutional protection or else it would not have had any.

Freedom of assembly's status as a fundamental *constitutional* right is not self-evident in every examined jurisdiction, with the United Kingdom and France still not having fully developed constitutional rights doctrines. Maybe more importantly, the issue of 'ranking' does not give a conclusive answer about the extent to which 'assembly' is protected. The French, after all, *manifest* all the time, and it would be hard to deny that there is quite a lively culture of assembly events in the United Kingdom as well. There might be in important regards lesser burdens on freedom of assembly in these countries than in others, even if the high status is not recognised at all. A good example is the lack of prior notification on stationary meetings in the United Kingdom. Lack of a higher constitutional status does not necessarily result in lesser assembly activity. However, it might very well influence—that is limit in a selective way—the sorts of assemblies which take place by relieving authorities and courts from exercising the rigorous or more transparent review a constitutional right at stake normally induces. This (dis)advantage of not dealing with a fundamental right becomes very apparent in some English decisions, and is less apparent in the extremely short French decisions (where brevity is often itself a sign of under-rationalisation of what is at stake).

While the notions of assembly and the status accorded to freedom of assembly show immense variations in the jurisdictions, the values or rationales behind freedom of assembly prove to be strikingly similar. All courts—though the English only through the mediation of the Human Rights Act 1998 and the ECtHR—find that assemblies are eminently related to expression, participation and democratic governance. They have all left behind historical views about assembly being unnecessary in a representative system, and embrace its mediating function between minority and majority, people and government, in more or less elaborate terms. In principle, the courts thus do understand the importance of freedom of assembly. This almost perfectly overlapping value consensus, however, cannot be overrated in light of the rest of the findings: it is possible to proclaim abstract values in the first phase of review in the strongest terms, and then to allow all kinds of far-reaching restrictions at the end of the review.

B. Prior Restraints

This is in fact what happens with regard to prior restraints. All the legal orders dealt with in this book claim that notice or permit is necessary for distribution of place, and balancing interests of others, which is a fairly reasonable motivation. But they also find notice or permit necessary so the police could prepare for securing the event itself, that is in a sense the notification is imposed for the benefit of the demonstrators as well. There might be much in this argument, however, from this it only follows that a voluntary notification be introduced, as suggested, for example, by Edwin Baker.[1] Therefore, a mandatory notice, or even permit regime, necessarily has to rely on arguments from public interest, rather than on paternalistic arguments. In consequence, the mandatory prior restraint on assemblies has to benefit someone else other than the demonstrators, for instance, rights of passers-by, the Millian 'corndealer', the target of the protest, other (counter-)demonstrators, and so on.

Nonetheless, the argument is valid that notice—unlike censorship—is not necessarily an occasion to suppress the assembly, but it might be an occasion for reconciling conflicting interests in using the public place on which many rights, not only that of assembly, and not necessarily that of only one particular assembly can be exercised. Thus, it appears reasonable that for such strictly practical, distributory purposes the notice requirement is acceptable.

Beyond that, it is doubtful that principled arguments really exist for the requirement of notice. Most emphatically, enhanced readiness for violence is not more often a companion of assemblies than of a lot of other conduct,

[1] Edwin Baker, *Human Liberty and Freedom of Speech* (Oxford, Oxford University Press 1992) 137.

and it is especially unlikely that people who wish to be violent would adhere to the notice requirement anyway. In such cases the notice requirement clearly functions as a pretext (an authorisation) for preliminary police measures, which are normally possible only by concrete suspicion or with judicial authorisation. To what extent the police can constitutionally employ compulsive measures for crime prevention or prevention of disorder is quite unclear. Any such measure necessarily involves a risk assessment, a prediction for something which—if the measure taken is effective—will not materialise. If that measure is a prior restriction, then the danger might not materialise because its entire context—the assembly itself—has not materialised, or just because it would not have materialised anyway. The seemingly most important concern behind the notice requirement is to prevent degeneration of the assembly into riot. This can happen, but more often than not it does not seem that advance notice or permit would be able to prevent it, or to prepare the police with how to handle it.

Another point is that, in terms of prevention of violence, police presence is not necessarily the best solution, as police might be the outgroup for the protesters, as often protest is against the state or at least the mainstream. The duty and/or practice to bargain with police before the assembly takes place might certainly help reducing the 'outgroupness' of police, but is theoretically problematic, and practically more likely anyway in cases where hostility is minimal (ie more mainstream protestor groups).

As to the general view of particular jurisdictions to prior restraint, there are significant variations. In US constitutional law, there is a very strong historical aversion towards prior restraints on the press, and press freedom cases can have some application to freedom of assembly. This, however, happens through the wide understanding of the concept of the press, and not through a wide understanding of the ban on prior restraint: if you leaflet, you have better chances to be able to hold your demonstration. Ordinances which condition the holding of a march, a demonstration or a meeting in general on a prior permit, are substantively acceptable.

On the other hand, the US Supreme Court has for a long time been cautious in decreasing the discretion inherent in permit ordinances to a considerable degree. This is not a negligible step from the point of view of fundamental rights: the court has regularly struck down ordinances for granting too much discretion, for example, interpreting the expression 'preventing riot' or 'religious cause' is in itself too much discretion, and in such cases, the protestor can go ahead with the protest even with the lack of a permit. However, the obligation for the state to provide an effective and speedy remedy is conspicuously missing from the US jurisprudence on freedom of assembly, including prior restraints.

Unlike in the United States, in Germany, prior restraint has not become a central issue in freedom of assembly, and perhaps neither that of free speech. This is somewhat peculiar regarding strong textual and historical aversion towards prior restraint. Prior restraints on assemblies in German law are not seen as inherently more problematic than any other restraint. Although the prior ban of neo-Nazi demonstrations gave rise to an important debate in Germany, it revolved around the interpretation of substantive values such as dignity and public order, and, finally, around the basis of post-War German constitutionalism itself. Thus, the issue of banning Nazi demonstrations was not conceptualised at all as a question of prior restraints.

A peculiarity of the German regime, of prior restraints on assembly, is clearly the constitutionalisation of the duty to cooperate with police, problematic for requiring private persons, as Kunig emphasised, to 'co-form state power'.[2]

Unlike the duty to cooperate, the other originally German doctrine of 'spontaneous assemblies' is rightly conquering the continent, but hopefully without the calculation whether there was pretension in a flash mob or not.

In the United Kingdom, bad memories of the Star Chamber do not seem to be as lively as in the United States in the argumentation of the courts. Still, this country maintains a quite liberal statutory advance notice system in comparison with the other countries (especially the United States). The United Kingdom is also—silently—the most liberal with regard to exemptions from the notice requirement, without much theoretical effort.

In France, there is an important theoretical distinction between preventive and repressive regimes of public liberties, with a clear preference of repression, in other words a subsequent restriction. This is an issue which is discussed and kept in mind, not only in relation to freedom of the press or art, but also with regard to freedom of assembly. The ever *manifesting* French show this particular sensitivity in scholarship, though not in positive law. Scholarship warning against a sliding into authorisation implies that prior notice is acceptable, but not the possibility of prior ban.

The ECtHR also employs in general free speech jurisprudence a presumption against the validity of prior restraints. Nonetheless, it accepts advance notice and even prior permit requirements widespread in the Member States without much ado, implying that the advance notice, or even permit, is not even an intervention in the scope of freedom of assembly. The explanation of the ECtHR is often especially apt to only justify a voluntary notification system. The ECtHR has to be credited for a sensible application of the spontaneous demonstration doctrine, though to introduce the concept of urgent, but still notifiable assemblies, as in German law, is suggested.

[2] Philip Kunig, 'Kommentar zu Art 8' in Ingo von Münch and Philip Kunig (eds), *Grundgesetz-Kommentar I*, 5th edn (München, Beck, 2000) ann 20.

C. Peacefulness, Prevention of Violence and Disorder

The requirement that assemblies be peaceful is not equally elaborated in the jurisdictions. German law and ECHR jurisprudence offer the most detailed interpretation of peacefulness as this question defines whether an activity falls within the protected scope or not. The German Constitutional Court in effect limits this exclusionary notion to the occurrence of concrete violent acts of a considerable intensity, while the ECtHR requires the state to show that the violence was, or was to be, pervasive. Neither the US, nor UK law is structured specifically around the question of scope, though of course these countries also disallow unpeaceful gatherings. US law is special in that there is no general ban on wearing guns at a demonstration, contrasting with Europe regarding gun wearing in general.

The examined jurisdictions show variation in the notion of disorder as well, that is on the question of what amounts at all to a state of affairs which needs to be prevented or eliminated even at the price of restricting freedom of assembly. Secondly, the jurisdictions also differ in the degree of probability of the occurrence of the state of affairs which justifies intervention. An important common principle is that of individual responsibility. At a minimum, no legal (civil or criminal, or even disciplinary) responsibility can arise unless one personally participated in or supported violent acts. A harder question is when an assembly can be dispersed or kettled for anticipation of disorder. Here the jurisdictions are not very consistent, and thus probably the judgement of police is taking over, and review might be limited. Germany and the United Kingdom increasingly make use of a kind of pre-emptive detention, often arresting masses of people from whom later only a tiny number will be convicted. The mass arrest emerges, therefore, as a prior measure intended to prevent the demonstration, or the participation of specific persons, perceived as 'trouble makers', without any specific data as to their intents, let alone a precise assessment of the imminence of violence.

It appears more or less settled that there is no right to heckle while there is a right to counter-demonstration in every examined jurisdiction. The United Kingdom is the only country where the issue of counter-demonstration is not clearly thematised, and might be hidden by the practice of general banning orders (by the way a clearly content-neutral mode of regulation).

The extent of the protection granted in case of potential clashes is much less settled. German law explicitly concedes that there might not be enough police available, and this justifies even prior ban. US courts, especially lower courts, might actually go as far as to accept the first part of the German view (not always possible to prevent violence), but that would not mean that the demonstration cannot constitutionally take place. This is the exact opposite of German thinking; perhaps because the figure of positive obligations is absent in US law, or because German law is more focused on preventing danger. In France, the few cases available spell out that a demonstration cannot be banned solely because of the risks inherent in a counter-demonstration, but previous violent clashes, where the source of the violence is unclarified, might justify even a prior ban, but certainly conditions. The ECtHR probably would not go beyond the German approach, but might find UK and French blanket- and quasi-blanket bans disproportionate.

D. Coercion, Direct Action and Disruption

Jurisprudence related to the question of coercion proved perhaps even more deferential than that related to disorder. In particular courts in the United Kingdom are not willing to provide protection even to minimal disruption. With regard to obstruction, protestors can go unpunished only if they show they somehow fit within the exceptions of the norm: a clash frozen halfway between a privilege and a right.

In the United States, the relatively consistent and generous jurisprudence towards sit-ins and coercive speech clearly broke down in the abortion protest cases, hardly masked by claims of content-neutrality. The Supreme Court allows restrictions on conduct way below obstruction, intimidation, or threat, in a quintessential forum (public street), in fact it allows bans on entering an area. What is more, injunctions are applied to persons who are not aware of it, who have come to the area for the first time, for the sole reason that they are acting 'in concert' with organisations cited in the injunction in case they express an anti-abortion view. A similar trend might be evolving with regard to 'animal rights' or environmental protests, facilitated by this jurisprudence.

The German compromise with regard to direct action appears quite clear, although it is anything but principled. After a long and complicated line of cases, the court seems settled that direct action without using any tools—chains, cars, etc—does not qualify as coercion. What is more, even actions which do might be so important for debate on public matters that a restriction cannot be justified. As to France, no detailed theorisation on the question was possible to find, their standard appears to be somewhat below the German one.

The ECtHR basically does not grant protection to coercive, disruptive, obstructive, or any direct action type of protests. This cautious stance might well be due to the fact that European states—certainly the ones examined here—are also not clear and consistent about where coercion starts and freedom of assembly ends, but provide a very fragmented picture.

E. Dignity

Dignity-type arguments arise especially in Germany and France, in relation to the Holocaust, Jews, people of colour, immigrants, and so on, in other words what is commonly called hate speech. Therefore, dignity in this part of human rights law acts like a buffer between different groups, it basically functions as protecting social identity, as a perimeter (and not, eg as an autonomy-enhancing argument). That is why in some jurisdictions, dignity appears to mingle with public order, also a dubious concept with at times identity, at times authoritarian, or again other times militant democracy overtones. German legal language here focuses on the individual, while in French law the focus on discrimination might signal a more collective identity-based approach.

Although English law is exempt from a specifically dignitarian argument, it embraces restrictions for similar scenarios often more than German or perhaps even French law. The ECtHR's somewhat chaotic hate speech jurisprudence increasingly rubberstamps national restrictions in pursuance of interests way below the German standard. The US Supreme Court has unsurprisingly proved most resistant to explicit or implicit dignity-like interests.

F. Time, Manner and Place

Content-neutrality is a more or less explicit principle of free expression law in every examined jurisdiction. When applied to freedom of assembly, however, content neutrality is often insufficient to protect the protestor. The reason for this is another principle which primarily affects the exercise of freedom of assembly. An idea deeply engrained in both the US and the German approach is to split 'expressive content' and modality of expression or conduct.

Accordingly, modality is the form of expression, in contrast to the substance or message of the expression. Modality includes, at the abstract level, the questions of when, how, and where an idea is expressed. In free speech law, there is a very legitimate reason to perceive modal limits as less harmful to liberty than substantive limits: substantive limits prevent the speaker from saying what they actually want to say, while modal limits only operate as an alteration of the time, place, or manner of saying whatever the speaker intends to say. Logically, for courts there is less an urge to apply the same rigorous standard of review to modal than to substantive limits. All the more so, as the choice of modalities of the speaker—time, manner, and place—might well conflict with the choice of modalities of other exercises of human rights, or other important interests. Everything happens within the modalities, after all. The legislator (and, by its authorisation, local administrators) might seem more equipped to distribute modalities than courts, and more legitimate even.

This above argumentation would indeed be flawless but for one decisive misrepresentation which weighs even heavier when applied to protests and demonstrations. Meaning is not only substance, it is modality, too. Any linguist would find the argument from content versus form/modality wholly unscientific and misrepresentative of how semantics actually works. Most of them would probably claim that what is called by me (and by courts) 'modal' or 'content-neutral' might convey more meaning than what is called substance or content. In interpersonal psychology and communication studies, non-verbal communication is certainly understood to convey at least as much if not more—and more accurate, reliable—meaning than verbal communication.[3]

Relegation of some aspects as modality or conduct is largely missing from the language of the ECtHR, and is also not present in the English or French legal discourse. However, while the fact that the ECtHR does not apply a looser test for restrictions on modalities so far is laudable, in France and the United Kingdom there are so many restrictions on protest anyway that these countries just do not need this doctrinal trick, they can instead rely on the heavy hammer of substantive restrictions, often not content-neutral at all, targeting only one type of modality of expression, or even discriminate substantively between viewpoints.

II. GENERAL EVALUATION AND SUGGESTIONS

Among the examined courts, the US Supreme Court certainly went furthest when voluntarily adopting an obligation *not to look at* the real issue when it comes to assemblies—by relying on content-neutrality as understood by scholars and judges, that is letter and argument. Overall, the results of this study strongly challenge the commonplace belief that US law protects free expression so much, and provides a much more fragmented and nuanced picture.

The German Constitutional Court makes constant effort to keep shadows of the past controlled without simply suppressing them, and at the same time preserving at least some firmness to the notion of human dignity. The *Hess Memorial March* decision—claiming Nazism is outside general categories of human thinking, thus its legal treatment also cannot

[3] Eg Mark L Knapp and Judith A Hall, *Nonverbal Communication in Human Interaction*, 7th edn (Wadsworth, Cengage Learning, Boston 2010); Paul Ekman and WV Friesen, 'The Repertoire of Nonverbal Behavior: Categories, Origins, Usage, and Coding' (1969) 1 *Semiotica* 49; Paul Ekman, 'Basic Emotions' in T Dalgleish and M Power (eds), *Handbook of Cognition and Emotion* (Sussex, John Wiley & Sons, 1999) 45.

be submitted to and scrutinised by rational categories—might be the closest to lawyerly honesty, naturally at the price of severe inconsistency with the carefully balanced architecture of basic rights jurisprudence. German law, however, is the most incoherent in another regard: the very elevated language about freedom of assembly in the scope phase and the very numerous and often openly viewpoint-discriminatory limits the GFCC allows on assemblies. The general feature of German law, that is the fact that human dignity is used to limit other rights, naturally also applies to freedom of assembly. Indeed, there is no one subcategory examined in this book, where German law does not allow for restriction, apart from speech pens.

UK law regarding assemblies still oscillates between public order protection and granting a fundamental right. Thus, courts often expect the protestor to disprove the legitimacy of a restriction, which in number likely exceeds all the other countries examined here. In many regards the liberty framework—coupled with an apparently functioning representative government (see, eg the withdrawal of prohibition around Parliament, abolition of ASBOs, or the quite sensible policing visible in the last riots)—proved to be quite liberal, especially with regard to prior restraint. Still, the lethal weapon of blanket bans is always at hand, just as the many, many seemingly unrelated provisions (eg harassment or anti-terrorism provisions) which get applied to protests and demonstrations as well.

French jurisprudence on assemblies proved far too lacking in transparency to base very certain conclusions on. Clearly it also strongly stays within the expression framework, though this has probably more textual reasons than conceptual ones. The understanding of a *droit législatif* and accompanying textualism still appears to animate much of the field, despite the—necessarily fragmented, perfunctory—efforts on the side of the Conseil Constitutionnel and Conseil d'État. The whole system is undergoing fundamental changes in the *référé liberté* and the priority preliminary ruling (QPC)[4] procedures, the fruits of which might be visible in years to come, probably shifting French fundamental rights law in the German direction. However, on a more practical basis, looking at the amount of demonstrations, protests, and importantly, strikes constantly taking place in France, coupled with a largely reasonable policing, it is very difficult to state that freedom of assembly is so much more limited in France than elsewhere. Formally maybe it is, but in fact assemblies are likely to be handled very generously in practice, at least by and large, and that is what makes unnecessary too much theorisation or the development of sophisticated judicial doctrines.

The ECtHR rubberstamps governmental claims about legitimate aim, but then exerts an increasingly strong review in the proportionality phase, both

[4] The QPC is a form of concrete review introduced in French law in 2008. See Otto Pfersmann, 'Concrete review as indirect constitutional complaint in French constitutional law: a comparative perspective' (2010) 6 *European Constitutional Law Review* 223.

in terms of procedural and substantive guarantees. Maybe not much more can be expected from an international organ which needs to preserve its integrity and acceptance on the part of Member States.

Freedom of assembly doctrine involves various tensions in itself as well, largely valid in each of the examined jurisdictions. The most general is clearly the high value accorded to it when the court tries to define the scope of the right, and the very wide-ranging limitations allowed in the second or third step of rights review—as if to hide a mystic secret: what is most important is at the same time the most dangerous and fearful. Another contradiction is between some of the values and the limits: for instance, that the German court claims the function of freedom of demonstration is being the main element of a political early warning system on the one hand, and the various, widely available prior restraints on assemblies on the other. A demonstration prohibited in advance, or a demonstrator put in jail, cannot in any way serve as a signal, as an early alarm that something is going wrong in the political process. Also, there is a tension in some aspects between the doctrine of minority protection (scope, rationale for freedom of assembly) and the application of the content neutrality and symbolic speech principles to demonstrations, as most of the times such restrictions affect disparately groups diverging from the mainstream in one way or the other.

The empirical 'assembly' was not often seen as an object of 'freedom of assembly' by courts. Freedom of speech and opinion was the first category courts would put assemblies in, disregarding the way meaning is generated in assemblies. Here and there, freedom of *art* was referred to as a potential—this time beneficial—surrogate of freedom of assembly. Leafleting protestors are also luckier, because they can come under the protection of freedom of the *press*.

Art and the press are at first sight a far shot from assemblies. I claim, however, that their appearance in some decisions on assemblies is not accidental. They testify to the narrow sense in which 'expression' is used by courts, because their sudden appearance reveals its imperfection. In fact, no court examined in this book made their understanding of 'expression' clear. We might have gained some vague sense about what is 'speech plus', and '*Art und Weise*', but it remains fully unexplored what is 'pure speech', or expression.

In my view, courts implicitly see reason and argument, especially in its written form, as the worthiest of legal protection. That explains both the twists and turns of the content-neutrality doctrines and the luck of protestors who come under the protection of the press. By valuing reason and argument, courts can remain safely embedded in the Enlightenment tradition, and keep away from the abyss of aesthetisation of politics.[5]

[5] See, eg Isaiah Berlin, *The Crooked Timber of Humanity. Chapters in the History of Ideas*, 2nd edn (Princeton, Princeton University Press, 2013).

There are, however, at least two serious problems with such a methodology to keep away the evil. Both problems relate to honesty, and thus the integrity of the judicial process, quite important concerns in an enlightened democracy.

First, such a narrow construction of expression is plainly wrong and false. In a commonsensical understanding, expression should be used in a broader sense. An adequate concept also encapsulates non-verbal, non-argumentative and other forms of expression, and necessarily also the 'form' in which the 'expression' is made. Translated to the issue of freedom of assembly, this means that *performances or other symbolic actions* are expressive, not only because of what they perform and what they symbolise, but also *because* or with regard to the element of performance or symbolism. In short, the content depends on the form or changes with the form, or content and form cannot be meaningfully separated. Furthermore, properly seen as expressive *activity,* expression also particularly encompasses the *process of creation* of expression: that is the creation of meaning, in the case of assembly, social or political meaning.

To clarify further these two senses of expressive, it is useful to extrapolate them to activities protected by other rights. Expressive activity, in the narrower sense, reaches its highest and most sophisticated form in scholarly writing: it is the reasoned argument or argumentative essay, the process of arriving at it is scientific research with accompanying methodology. At the other end of the expressive spectrum, which is encompassed by the use of expressive in the broader sense I propagate in the context of assembly, can be found artistic activity: every artistic activity is expressive, nonetheless it is also essentially, or maybe even primarily a process of creation.

The activity of assembling can be conceived as being in a sense situated between these two activities, scientific and artistic. Of course, assembly is most of the time neither science, nor art as it lacks *the quality* we expect from science and art. All three, that is science, art, and assembly, are however expressive in the wider (and commonsensical) sense of the word. Thus, in my view, it is not possible to grant protection to freedom of art without giving protection to the expressive 'modalities' of assemblies as well.

As to the second problem with avoiding aesthetisation by a narrow concept of expression: it also has to be clearly seen that the construction by courts of a separate category of facially content-neutral or modality restrictions, let alone highly infirm concepts such as public order, peace, and such like is not only a reductionist pseudo-rationalisation of street theatre, but *at the same time* a judicial rationalisation of highly or deeply emotionalised legislative (and majoritarian) politics. It results in avoidance of looking into the abyss—if and to the extent it is an abyss—of self-perception of the community, especially into the boundaries of who belongs in and who is out. Courts should not make themselves believe that by this they are not constructing identity. The apparently neutral categories of time, place, and manner, or concepts seemingly unrelated to expression such as public peace, public order or dignity are the backdoor through which otherwise (ie in freedom of *speech or opinion* law) allegedly surpassed or defeated fears come back and find their place in legal reasoning, on its own image an outstandingly rationalised process. It is not to mean that there is *necessarily* no abyss into which it is better not to look. After all, social psychology and sociology are not able to *completely* disprove Le Bon, Freud, Canetti or Moscovici. It is just if there be any hope for the 'abyss' ever to disappear or shrink at least, honesty, transparency, and certain courage ought to be constantly aspired to, otherwise there is no sense in not looking into it. Judges are always most vulnerable to the type of critique exacted throughout these pages, because they are the anointed protagonists at the centre-stage of that hopeful performance, institutionally vested with the independence of the scholar and the artist, coupled with the authority of the state.

This book took the stance that assembly is about expression in the broad sense. Thus, to apply the frame of expression in the narrow sense upon assembly is a misconstruction of the potential of freedom inherent in the exercise of this right.

A few potential criticisms of this use of concepts need to be addressed.

First, it is very important to keep in mind that associative aspects of assemblies—as Inazu rightly pointed out[6]—need to be protected. Nonetheless, in my view, this should be taken care of within freedom of association. The United States might be special in this regard as the First Amendment does not protect association in its text. This American-only textual lacuna does, however, not mandate a different use of concepts elsewhere and globally.

Secondly, and in contrast, some might argue that it is unfortunate to stay within the framework of expression, however broadened, and a more distinct label should be found to denote the specificities of assembly.

My reply to this is twofold. First, it is courts, and not me, who wrongly use the word 'expression'. Philosophy and other disciplines take it for granted that the aspects left out by the courts—that is action or conduct, time, manner, and place or modalities as opposed to 'content'—are or might be expressive. Secondly, therefore, courts' use of the label 'expressive' can be corrected without dispensing with the label: by adequately changing jurisprudence to include expressive in the broad sense.

[6] John D Inazu, *Liberty's Refuge. The Forgotten Freedom of Assembly* (New Haven, Yale University Press, 2012).

In addition, nothing in my argument prevents courts from actually granting enhanced protection to assemblies for maintaining the conditions for an active citizenry. Quite to the contrary: since assemblies are more important in this regard than 'pure speech', the almost absolute protection granted to political speech applies a fortiori to assemblies in the framework suggested here.

Finally, the broadening of the notion of expression or 'content' in the sense suggested here would mean the application of the same standards to the full range of expressive activities, but would still allow potentially more severe limits on assemblies, if a thorough examination finds them justified.

Index

www.ingramcontent.com/pod-product-compliance
Lightning Source LLC
LaVergne TN
LVHW052252200926
848481LV00002B/342

nucleus is introduced into an activated egg produces DNA.

(vi) Harris (1965) introduced erythrocytes taken from fowls into the human tumour cells. Though the erythrocytes of fowls contain nuclei they are normally nonfunctional. However, when they are introduced into the tumour cells they begin to start DNA and RNA synthesis.

A study of all these and many more experiments clearly proves that the cytoplasm has a definite role in controlling the activity of the nucleus. As protein synthesis is controlled by genes, differentiation can be brought about by modification of the process of protein synthesis. This can occur in three places viz —

(i) in the chromosomes

(ii) during transcription, and

(iii) during translation.

Differentiation Effected in the Genome

A. Change in the Quantum of DNA

The quantity of DNA can be increased or decreased and thereby differentiation can be brought about. The increase or decrease can be brought about by the following methods:

Chromation Diminution : Boveri (1889) first discovered this phenomenon in the nematode *Parascaris.* He found that the nucleus of the cell that is very near the animal pole always lets off chromosomal material into the cytoplasm at the time of the second cleavage. A similar spilling of chromosomal material occurs in more cells. At the 32 cell stage, only two cells have the full quota of chromatin material while all the rest undergo this phenomenon of chromatin diminution.